Reviews for *Courage Under Fire*

"The National Infantry Association proudly recommends adding this book to your leadership reading list …. Undaunted personal courage, the never quit attitude that enabled young soldiers to overcome miserable conditions, giving everything for their family—their team in combat, and charging into hell are the focus of Lieutenant Colonel (Ret) Ed Sherwood's new book, *Courage Under Fire: the 101st Airborne's Hidden Battle at Tam Ky.* Ed relives the close combat fighting of Delta Company, 1-501st from a junior officer perspective. He tells the unknown story of the decisive battle of *Operation Lamar Plain.* Through photos, eyewitness accounts, date-time-grid location accuracy, he reveals the heroics and valor of those wounded and killed. It is a memorable tribute to those that fought there …. We know that this is a book about infantrymen, for infantrymen, by an infantryman!"—COL (Ret) Robert E. Choppa, President of the National Infantry Association

"If I could choose one book about infantry fighting in Vietnam to recommend to others, Sherwood's *Courage Under Fire: the 101st Airborne's Hidden Battle at Tam Ky*, would be it."—CPT (Ret) David Gibson, former Charlie Company commander, 1st Battalion, 501st Infantry (Geronimo), 101st Airborne Division in 1969 at Tam Ky

"*Courage Under Fire* tells the untold story of the grunts of Delta Company, 1-501st infantry. In May 1969, as *Operation Lamar Plain* began at Tam Ky, the 1-501st was the tip of the spear of the 101st Airborne Division's powerful new airmobile capability. Ed Sherwood, a former Delta Company platoon leader, writes as one who knows the ethos of 'the brotherhood of the close fight.' He clearly captures the bravery and tenacity of the men who defeated a determined enemy. It is well time their story is told."—Dr John O'Brien, historian, US Army Center of Military, Fort Campbell, Kentucky

"A fine bit of hidden history about the 101st Airborne's Battle at Tam Ky. I recommend it highly!"—Joe Galloway, co-author with Hal Moore, *We Were Soldiers Once and Young*, and co-author with Marvin J. Wolf, *They Were Soldiers*

"With *Courage Under Fire*, Ed Sherwood fills in a long-missing chapter in the history of the Vietnam War: the 28 days of bloody fighting near Tam Ky in May 1969 that came in the immediate wake of 'Hamburger Hill.' The Nixon administration, fearful of adding fuel to the anti-war fires raging in the United States, managed to keep Tam Ky out of the headlines back home. But now, some 50 years later, Sherwood brings us a blow-by-blow account of this decisive and largely unknown battle."—Bill Hogan, editor, *MHQ: The Quarterly Journal of Military History*

"We are forever grateful *Courage Under Fire* captures what Dad and his fellow soldiers endured during the battle at Tam Ky. Because Dad was in Vietnam before we were born, the book is priceless in telling stories he and others kept quiet for so long. Dad was passionate about the book. As his close friendship developed with Ed Sherwood, the author and his former platoon leader, he began to open up. Like a storyteller, Dad shared his memories of the war he did not want forgotten after he was gone. We are glad he and Ed were so close during the three years before he died."—Jen, Jamie and Will, adult children of deceased, former SGT Jim Littleton, 3rd Platoon, Delta Company, 1-501st Infantry, 101st Airborne Division

"As one of LT Sherwood's guys in Vietnam at Tam Ky, without a doubt, this book gives me closure and a peace that I have been wrestling with for over 50 years."—John Meade, disabled veteran, rifleman, former member 3rd Platoon, Delta Company, 1-501st Infantry, 101st Airborne Division

"*Courage Under Fire* is a story that should have been told in 1969 but was not for a variety of political and military reasons. The brave soldiers of the 101st Airborne Division and other Vietnam veterans had a profound impact on my own military career that spanned from 1970–1996. The Vietnam War changed the way the American people look at war, media, and politics. The Vietnam War changed the military for the better. *Courage Under Fire* tells the story of the courage and bravery of the Vietnam soldier in a compelling fashion fit for audiences of all generations; As a retired Army Infantry officer, retired US history teacher, and a proudly still serving veteran, I highly recommend *Courage Under Fire*."—LTC (Ret) Dale Barnett, former National Commander, The American Legion 2015–16

"As a former 101st Airborne platoon leader in 1969 with the 2-502nd Infantry battalion in Vietnam and a 101st battalion commander of the 1/327th (1986–1988), I am impressed that *Courage Under Fire* is a true account of the sacrifices, values, and determination of the brave soldiers who fought with distinction at Tam Ky. Sherwood gives careful attention to battle details using historical combat records and personal soldier accounts. His book is highly readable and an appealing testament to the courage of all Vietnam combat veterans. It should be read by today's young officers and non-commissioned officers serving or those preparing to serve."—COL (Ret) John S. Haluski, US Army

"*Courage Under Fire* is the most solid book written thus far about a ground combat unit in the Vietnam War. Colonel Sherwood's research and documentation is the best I have seen concerning that era of our history. It is not a beach or airport novel. It is written for the serious reader who is seeking knowledge about how that war was fought at the platoon and squad level by the most dedicated of our soldiers. The men that fought on the ground against a determined enemy at Hill 376 are depicted as they really were, resolute and determined, not boastful or flashy. Sherwood has resisted telling the story with bravado and flair just to sell a book. Rather, he depicts the battle and the men in that unit with the gritty reality of the day, facing uncertainty with discipline and unity. For the Infantry veteran of Vietnam, Sherwood will bring back to you dozens of facts that you have forgotten or chosen to forget, from the weight of radio batteries to the length of helicopter rotor blades to the heat and the dust. He captures the details. If you are a genuine military historian, he provides you with actual coordinates and locations that can be precisely traced and followed, casualties by each day and much more. This is a book that should be well placed in our National Archives, The National Infantry Museum, and in the historical files of the 101st Airborne. A must read for aspiring ground combat leaders."—COL (Ret) Walter Chrietzberg led two platoons and commanded an infantry company during Vietnam in the 101st Airborne from 1969–1970. He later commanded three Special Mission Unites (SMUs) and the Special Warfare Training Group (ABN), Ft Bragg, North Carolina

"*Courage Under Fire* tells how grunts fought for each other in a time most Americans do not remember or want to forget. The sacrifices of our young soldiers must be told. Sherwood tells how they controlled fear and accomplished their missions. Through their eyewitness accounts, Delta Company soldiers bring this story alive. Being a wounded Vietnam grunt myself, I can verify Sherwood's details of the harsh conditions in which they lived, fought, and died. This is the perfect story to honor the Vietnam service of so many."—Command Sergeant Major (Ret) Robert G. Nichols, former CSM of 1st Brigade, 101st Airborne Division, 1990–1994; Executive Director, Fort Campbell Historical Foundation

COURAGE UNDER FIRE

COURAGE UNDER FIRE

The 101st Airborne's Hidden Battle at Tam Ky

ED SHERWOOD, LTC, US ARMY (RET.)

CASEMATE
Philadelphia & Oxford

Published in the United States of America and Great Britain in 2021 by
CASEMATE PUBLISHERS
1950 Lawrence Road, Havertown, PA 19083, US
and
The Old Music Hall, 106–108 Cowley Road, Oxford OX4 1JE, UK

Hardback Edition: ISBN 978-1-61200-964-3
Digital Edition: ISBN 978-1-61200-965-0

A CIP record for this book is available from the British Library

Printed and bound in the United States of America by Sheridan

Typeset by Versatile PreMedia Services (P) Ltd.

For a complete list of Casemate titles, please contact:

CASEMATE PUBLISHERS (US)
Telephone (610) 853-9131
Fax (610) 853-9146
Email: casemate@casematepublishers.com
www.casematepublishers.com

CASEMATE PUBLISHERS (UK)
Telephone (01865) 241249
Email: casemate-uk@casematepublishers.co.uk
www.casematepublishers.co.uk

The appearance of U.S. Department of Defense (DoD) visual information does not imply or constitute DoD endorsement.

In accordance with Department of Defense Instruction 5410.20 this book is a historical and education publication in which limited sales are not expected to recover the cost of developing and distributing the book.

In Memoriam

Edward L Sherwood III, 1983–2019, beloved son, brother, husband, and father. Former US Army Infantry Sergeant and Combat Veteran with the Georgia Army National Guard, Afghanistan, 2013, Soldier of the Cycle, C/1-19th Infantry, 198th Training Brigade, Fort Benning, GA April 2010

Dedication

This book is dedicated to the courageous men killed in action during combat operations 1 March to 13 August 1969 while serving with Delta Company, 1st Battalion, 501st Infantry (Geronimo) including their sister units and the families who suffered great loss of their loved ones.

May their sacrifice be long remembered and honored.

Rest, comrades, rest, and sleep!
The thoughts of men shall be
As sentries to keep
Your rest from danger free.
Your silent tents of green
We deck with fragrant flowers.
Yours has the suffering been,
The memory shall be ours.

From the 1882 poem *Decoration Day* by Henry Wadsworth Longfellow 1807–1882

Contents

Foreword

Richard K. Kolb, editor and contributing author of *Brutal Battles of Vietnam: America's Deadliest Days, 1965–1972*

1969 was the second deadliest year of the Vietnam War for Americans. In the first six months alone, 7,554 GIs sacrificed their lives there. For perspective, a total of 6,826 US service members lost their lives during the entire Afghanistan and Iraq wars combined. Despite the immense loss of life in 1969, ground action that year—with one major exception, the Battle of Hamburger Hill—has largely escaped the attention of popular historians. Indeed, at the time, the news media seemed to relegate the fighting to the back pages.

It is not surprising media and public attention waned. On 14 May 1969, President Richard Nixon, in a prime-time nationally televised address, proclaimed: "We have ruled out attempting to impose a purely military solution on the battlefield." For the first time, pursuit of military victory in Vietnam was no longer a US objective. At the time of his announcement, the 101st Airborne Division's Battle of Hamburger Hill was raging and a second major, but much lesser known, 101st engagement, *Operation Lamar Plain*, was just getting underway.

In *Courage Under Fire: The 101st Airborne's Hidden Battle at Tam Ky*, Ed Sherwood recounts the perseverance of one infantry company of the 1st Battalion, 501st Infantry (Geronimo) during *Operation Lamar Plain* at Tam Ky. In doing so, he provides long overdue recognition for his unit and all the infantrymen who fought there during the late spring and summer of 1969. Sherwood tells of these exploits from firsthand experience as a Delta Company platoon leader until he was wounded on 2 June. Yet, his account goes well beyond that date.

What prompted this book 50 years later? Veterans of Delta Company who fought in *Operation Lamar Plain* are passing off the scene and Sherwood wanted to tell their untold story for their families and others. A second motive is the inadequate portrayal of combat soldiers in Ken Burns' widely acclaimed Public Broadcasting Service (PBS) documentary series on Vietnam, *The Vietnam War*.

Sherwood knew that the men with whom he fought were not consumed by guilt and shame for having worn their country's uniform. He wanted to correct the record for his men and countless other Vietnam veterans who have not been accurately portrayed by Burns' series, news media, or Hollywood. As James Wright said in his book, *Enduring Vietnam: An American Generation and Its War*, "Popular criticism of the war had not yet expanded [in May 1969] to portray those serving in Vietnam as *perpetrators* of a cruel and heartless war. *That would change.*" It certainly did and has wrongly persisted in many circles.

There is a need for *Courage Under Fire* and similar books. The American public simply cannot comprehend the sense of duty that motivates young Americans to risk their lives in wartime. The men who fought in *Operation Lamar Plain*, especially those who died, were publicly unknown and unheralded at the time except by their families and those with whom they served—until now!

After the 50th anniversary of the ultimate sacrifice of Delta Company's soldiers and its sister units at Tam Ky, Ed Sherwood in *Courage Under Fire* has given them the recognition, respect, and remembrance they so richly deserve. His book fills a void sorely needing to be filled. Anyone interested in understanding the perils and courage of an infantryman in Vietnam during 1969 would do well to read it.

The Infantryman's Creed

"I am the Infantry.

I am my country's strength in war. Her deterrent in peace. I am the heart of the fight ... wherever, whenever. I carry America's faith and honor against her enemies.

I am the Queen of Battle. I am what my country expects me to be ... the best trained soldier in the world. In the race for victory I am swift, determined, and courageous, armed with a fierce will to win.

Never will I fail my country's trust. Always I fight on ... through the foe, to the objective, to triumph overall. If necessary, I will fight to my death.

By my steadfast courage, I have won more than 200 years of freedom. I yield not to weakness, to hunger, to cowardice, to fatigue, to superior odds, for I am mentally tough, physically strong, and morally straight.

I forsake not ... my country, my mission, my comrades, my sacred duty. I am relentless. I am always there, now, and forever.

I AM THE INFANTRY! FOLLOW ME!"

Written in 1955 by Lieutenant Colonel (LTC) Stephen H. White, former editor of *Infantry Magazine* and published in the magazine in 1956. Its present form was developed by LTC White, assisted by Colonel (COL) Francis Bradley and Specialist Howard Webber. The creed ends with the motto of the Infantry, "Follow Me!"

Preface

Courage Under Fire *is a true combat account of* Operation Lamar Plain, *a major Vietnam War battle near Tam Ky in 1969. The operation was never disclosed to the American people during the war for strategic political and military reasons. 1969 was a turning point in the long conflict. As US casualties and war protests accelerated, it was the first year that a majority of the nation's population turned against the war. This is how the first book to be written on* Operation Lamar Plain *came to be.*

It was late May 2015. I was sitting in a restaurant at lunch time with my adult son. He was a young sergeant soon to finish his Army enlistment including an Afghanistan combat tour in 2013. We were waiting for former Captain (CPT) Leland Roy to join us. Leland and I had not seen each other since the day he took command of our infantry company in Vietnam, 46 years ago.

Days prior, I learned that we have lived 15 minutes apart in the same suburban community south of Atlanta, Georgia, for well over 20 years. We have not met or talked since Vietnam and likely would not have recognized one other had our paths crossed without introductions. I called Leland inviting him to lunch and he quickly accepted. CPT Roy had come into Delta Company as the new commander where I was a young lieutenant platoon leader. He took command on 1 June 1969.

The very next day I was wounded. On 3 June he led his new company into a hard ten-day battle on Hill 376. Already well understrength due to earlier casualties, he was missing all three platoon leaders and had only one newly promoted staff sergeant. Other platoon positions were filled by young, junior-enlisted infantry soldiers serving their first term of Army enlistment and first combat duty.

Over the years, my thoughts sometimes drifted back to Vietnam. What had happened to our company and my platoon? Vietnam was an unpopular war. Few talked about it after going home. In time, I did what many Vietnam veterans had done. I let it go. The Army had moved on. In the early 1970s, attention turned to the Soviet Union threat in Europe, then in the 1980s, to threats in the Persian Gulf. My follow-on duty assignments looked forward, not backward.

In 1988, I left the Army with a permanent, service-connected pulmonary disability likely due to Agent Orange exposure in Vietnam. That closed an important chapter in my life. In May 2015, age 70 and nearing the end of my work career, I was both surprised and glad to learn of an upcoming Delta Company reunion in Bardstown, Kentucky. When I received a call about the reunion, it was then that I learned Leland and I were practically neighbors.

It was a riveting first meeting. In his customary low-key manner, Leland told me of the Hill 376 fight, the heavy casualties, the ten days of fighting, and the steadfast performance of his young soldiers. Time passed quickly. Rather than closure, my interest in finding out more about the battle increased. I especially wanted to learn more about the young soldiers who fought it.

Days later, Leland and I attended the reunion. Others were there whom I had not seen since 1969. I saw firsthand the respect these former soldiers had for their former commander. At a cookout, Roy sat quietly nearby. One by one, sometimes in small groups, the men came up and talked with him. To a man, they were thankful for his leadership and combat experience at Tam Ky. They knew, if it were not for him, many of them would have been killed in battle. They all had stories to tell and wondered why *Operation Lamar Plain* was never made known publicly.

In 2017, at a second reunion also at Bardstown, there were more old faces and more stories of bitter fighting from long ago. Some stories had never been shared even with family. Some still weighed heavy on hearts, troubling minds. There were thoughts of comrades killed in action. Men remembered with tears, some with humor, all with honor. That is when I decided to write their story. My first inclination was simply to record their stories for their families. Over time, the book took on a wider purpose.

Three Reasons Why I Wrote *Courage Under Fire*

First—To Leave a Legacy of the Faithful Service of Our Young Soldiers. The battle at Tam Ky is a largely unknown and untold story. I wrote *Courage Under Fire* so the battle accounts of the young soldiers who fought there will live beyond their deaths. As the age of Vietnam veterans edges into 70s and beyond, fewer are available to tell their stories. Their story is worthy to be passed down within families to other generations. A legacy of honor, a story to be remembered long after they are gone.

Second—To Encourage and Instruct Young Soldiers. My aim is that the story of "Never Quit" Delta Company might be especially instructive for young soldiers, junior sergeants, and junior officers now serving. They must never underestimate their vital role in frontline combat. It is they who win battles. May other young men and women not yet in the US military consider serving in the infantry or its supporting services. That would make my labors in writing this book all the more satisfying and worthwhile.

Third —It Is Past Time to Make Known the 101st Airborne's Hidden Battle at Tam Ky. The initial reasons for not disclosing the battle seem justified for strategic military and political reasons. However, *Operation Lamar Plain* is essentially omitted in official

US Army Vietnam War records. It is as if the fighting never occurred, even though it was one of the last large offensive operations of the 101st Airborne's excellent, seven-year record of Vietnam combat. It is a great story, a story that needs to be told.

Considerations in Writing

The challenges of writing have been many. Almost 50 years after our time in Vietnam, each person interviewed (and I talked with over 40 of our soldiers), first told me they had forgotten much of what happened. Some had forgotten on purpose. Many could not recall when or where events happened. Names and faces of fellow soldiers often known only by nicknames were lost in the past. Others had told the same war stories for decades, not always based on firsthand accounts. Some had memories so vividly imprinted on their minds, it seemed as if they happened yesterday. More than a few were content to let the past stay in the past. Many volunteered their stories only after learning my book's purpose.

The Turbulent US Culture in 1969. What makes the bravery and sacrifice of soldiers described in my book all the more remarkable is they grew up in "The Sixties," one of the most difficult and transitional times in recent US history. The decade was one of dramatic change in social norms and great civil unrest. The Vietnam War was a major catalyst for change both good and bad. In 1968, when many US soldiers were in training before going to Vietnam, Dr. Martin Luther King Jr was assassinated on 4 April. Racial tension was high. Senator Robert F. Kennedy was assassinated 6 June while running for president. During 26–29 August at the Democratic National Convention, there were violent riots by war protestors, radical leftist students from Students for a Democratic Society (SDS), Black Panthers and others. US forces and casualties in Vietnam were reaching an all-time peak. The turmoil of 1968 set the stage for events in 1969.

Back in the World. Despite the conflict in the US, during lulls in combat soldiers often thought and talked about home and "getting back to the world." For those isolated on Vietnam's battlefields, their world was changing fast and so were they. Throughout the book, I have included several inserts titled "Back in the World" to depict some of the major events that occurred in 1969 while young soldiers put their lives on the line in fierce combat on behalf of their increasingly divided nation.

Personal Interviews. I talked with nearly 40 Delta Company veterans who were eyewitnesses of the events of which I write. Many more are mentioned in the book. I also contacted a few veterans in sister units. Two people mentioned often in my account, LTC Raymond Singer, the 1st Battalion, 501st Infantry Regiment (1-501st) Battalion commander, and CPT Bobby Begley, the Delta Company commander before CPT Roy, died years ago after honorable Army careers. I used their original battle reports from Vietnam.

February 1969 Back in the World

1 Feb	Top hit *Crimson and Clover* by Tommy James & the Shondells
4 Feb	John Madden, age 32, becomes youngest NFL head coach of Oakland Raiders
5 Feb	First battery-powered smoke detector invented
8 Feb	*Saturday Evening Post* ends publication after 147 years
9 Feb	Boeing 747's maiden flight
13 Feb	Black student takeover of Duke University admin offices to protest campus concerns
17 Feb	Players boycott major league baseball spring training
21 Feb	Washington senators hire Ted Williams as manager
24 Feb	Supreme Court rules 7–2 for 13-year-old public school student right to protest war
25 Feb	Mariner 6, first Mars probe, is launched
27 Feb	Thousands of students protest Nixon visit to Rome

My initial intention was to limit my book to Delta Company alone. I later decided to include the combat activities of Alpha, Bravo, and Charlie Company as well as the Recon Platoon. Medics from our Headquarters Company's medical platoon are mentioned throughout. It seemed more appropriate to portray Delta Company operating within the 1-501st Battalion, a distinguished infantry battalion with a long and notable record from its beginning in World War II. Unfortunately, neither time nor resources permitted me to expand my interviews to soldiers in the other units. Hopefully, they will add to the story I tell.

Reliance on Battle Documents. I was fortunate to have access to the actual battle records of all the units who participated in *Operation Lamar Plain*. Though the official documents sometimes contained errors or were incomplete, they were an essential supplement to recall and confirm timing and location of events with personal, eyewitness accounts. Many battle records were located at the National Archives at College Park Maryland. Other official records were obtained from the US Army Center of Military History; Texas Tech University's Vietnam Center and Archive; various internet sites; and expert authors. My bibliography is extensive.

Identifying Inconsistencies, Errors, and Omissions. When battle records had inconsistencies, obvious errors, or omissions, I relied heavily on individual, eyewitness accounts. For example in Chapter 16, the 9 June 1969 climax of the book, the staff journal maintained in the battalion tactical operations center (TOC) is not consistent at many points with eyewitness accounts of Delta Company leaders and soldiers who did the fighting that day. The inconsistencies include several omissions of major events, wrong descriptions of combat actions, and assumptions of what was occurring. Several apparent errors relate to the sequence, timing, and location (by grid coordinate) of some combat events.

Reasons for Discrepancies in Battle Records. Explanations for inconsistencies in a staff journal are typically straightforward. During fast-paced combat operations there is a lot of activity in the battalion TOC and, of course, on the battlefield. For example, on 9 June, though the operations non-commissioned officer (NCO) was monitoring Delta Company's radio net, there was little time for the company commander and artillery forward observer (FO) to make reports. Their attention was completely devoted to directing the morning long fight. Entries in the journal were made by overhearing events on the radio. Sometimes events were missed, others may have been inaccurate or incomplete. Three other infantry companies were also involved besides Delta Company and the battalion TOC was simultaneously relaying and receiving reports and instructions from brigade headquarters. The word "hectic" does not come close to describing a battalion TOC during heavy, combat operations.

Resolving Discrepancies. Because of the importance of events on 9 June, I identified and examined every questionable entry in the battalion staff journal for that day. I then conducted multiple, separate interviews with eyewitness participants in the combat. I used the eyewitness accounts and the staff journal to develop a more complete and accurate initial, draft narrative of events. Eyewitnesses then reviewed my drafts for accuracy and completeness. This review-revision-review of draft narratives was repeated numerous times. Eyewitnesses included, but were not limited to: CPT Roy, the company commander; Specialist Fourth Class (SP4) Ed Medros, his radio-telephone operator; Lieutenant (LT) Paul Wharton, the artillery FO; Staff Sergeant (SSG) Sahrle, the company's senior non-commissioned officer; and my own best combat leader, Sergeant (SGT) Jim Littleton. My former platoon sergeant, SSG Gary Tepner, who also served as a battalion ops NCO while our company was fighting at Tam Ky, provided insight on the TOC's internal procedures. As the author, I am satisfied the chapter describes what actually happened.

Describing Combat Actions. This book is essentially a combat chronicle, a detailed written, factual account of events in the order they occurred. My matter-of-fact style may sometimes seem tedious, much like combat operations themselves. I deliberately avoid embellishing combat accounts. However, straightforward accounts of combat events are always set in the context of uncertainty, anxiety, and sometimes abject fear that characterizes all infantry combat. I wish I could have verbally conveyed those conditions along with the disorienting noise and rapid pace of battle. The deafening sounds of battle and limited visibility (usually due to terrain, bad weather, or vegetation in the daytime) added to the confusion of combat. Danger and death were constantly close at hand even in what appeared to be most routine combat operations.

Combat Units of the 101st Airborne Division. For those unfamiliar with the organization of US Army Infantry units for combat during the Vietnam War. I have provided a brief introduction in Appendix 3. This brief summary focuses on the 101st Airborne Division during Vietnam from division, brigade, battalion, company, platoon, squad, and fireteam down to the individual soldier. First time readers of Army combat operations may find it helpful to review the appendix. The glossary may also be helpful. Most of the battle action in *Courage Under Fire* takes place at the individual soldier through battalion level.

Locating Where and When Combat Occurred. I made a special effort to identify the time, date, and grid coordinates of unit positions and enemy engagements. This gives readers a sense of the time, distance, flow, and intensity of battle actions. Veterans, their families, or historians can also readily identify when and where combat actions occurred. Related maps are identified in the bibliography. Few readers have an accurate idea of the size of South Vietnam or the operational areas of combat forces. In Figure 1, South Vietnam easily fits among five eastern US states.[1]

The combat operations described in this book occur in what is called the I Corps Tactical Zone or Region, the most northern region of South Vietnam. That area falls almost entirely within the state of West Virginia in Figure 1. Figure 2 in the introduction shows the three areas in I Corps where our unit fought (Hue, the A Shau Valley, and Tam Ky). During the Vietnam War, I Corps had the most US casualties of the four military regions.

US Casualties. I have several reasons for giving special attention to casualties suffered by Delta Company and its sister companies. First, the book is dedicated to soldiers killed in action and their families. My intention is to accurately describe the tough battle conditions in which our soldiers lost their lives. Second, in 1969 the high number of US combat casualties was a top concern of the Nixon administration, national media, war protestors, and the American people. High casualties were a major factor in bringing US participation in the war to an end. Third, the high US casualties in the fighting at Tam Ky were a primary reason *Operation Lamar Plain* was never publicly disclosed during the Vietnam War. As a result, soldiers who fought there and the many who were killed or wounded never received recognition for their participation in one of the bloodiest and fiercest combat operations of the war.

Casualty Tables. Thirteen casualty tables summarize the number of 1-501st soldiers killed, wounded, or missing in action during various enemy engagements or time periods. Each is numbered and dated. The figures in the casualty tables are taken from official battle records or other government casualty records. At times, casualty totals in the various enemy encounters recorded in daily battle records may differ from the casualty tables. This is because casualty reporting as combat takes place may not be as accurate as later official accounting of casualties shown in the casualty tables.

Soldiers Killed in Action (KIA). Soldiers KIA are not mere numbers or statistics, they were courageous young men whose names and lives should be forever remembered

Figure 1: South Vietnam's size compared to the US

and honored. With this in mind, I have included the names and brief biographical detail of each of the 1-501st soldiers killed in action from 1 March to 13 August 1969 at the end of each chapter. I relied on the Coffelt Database (see bibliography) for confirmation of official information concerning KIA soldiers.

Soldiers Wounded in Action (WIA). Soldiers WIA are identified by name, rank, and date wounded. This was a particularly difficult undertaking. Information was not readily available for a large number of wounded soldiers. If I missed anyone (KIA or WIA) and that is likely, please forgive my unintentional omission. Hundreds of hours were dedicated to casualty research. The book's index can be used to find the names of soldiers who may have been casualties (KIA or WIA) included in battle accounts.

Allied and Enemy Casualties. Missing and outside the scope of my book is the high number of combat deaths suffered by our principal ally in the war, South Vietnam. Their casualties numbered well over 200,000 military deaths. Regrettably, over two million Vietnamese civilians in North and South Vietnam died in the war. Other readily available sources offer detailed information on these important topics.

Sensitivity to Family Members and Young Readers. I have purposely omitted grisly descriptions of injuries of those who died or were wounded in battle. This was done out of consideration for family members of the deceased who might read my book, though many combat wounds are not gruesome even if fatal. However, the death of a soldier is always a solemn matter. For similar reasons, I eliminated the use of profanity in the narratives so young boys and girls may read of the courage of their grandfathers, uncles, cousins, or other family members who fought in *Operation Lamar Plain.*

Awards. Awards for combat action are only sometimes mentioned in personal accounts. With frequent changes of commanders and the intensity of combat operations, awards were not always submitted for those deserving them. After most major actions, I have summarized combat awards by unit, date, and name of the soldiers. My source for awards is the 1-501st Battalion's *Operation Lamar Plain* after action report (AAR) cited in the bibliography. This list may not be complete, may contain errors, and may not include all the awards for each person listed. The book's index can be used to locate the names of specific soldiers who may have received an award.

Errors of Fact and Opinions Expressed. At times, I made judgments when there was conflicting and sometimes erroneous information in personal accounts or battle records. In such cases, I reviewed all available information, consulted with others who were there, and then wrote what I thought was the most convincing and accurate account. I regret if inadvertent mistakes have been made in transcription of interviews, casualty reports, names of soldiers, location descriptions, timing of combat events or platoon assignments. Identifying which platoon individual soldiers served in was sometimes difficult since some soldiers were moved between platoons because of casualties.

I am hopeful readers will find *Courage Under Fire: The 101st Airborne's Hidden Battle at Tam Ky* not only an interesting account, but one that gives readers a close up look at what infantry fighting in Vietnam was really like.

Acknowledgements

I am indebted to the former soldiers of Delta Company who assisted in this book's development. I wrote it for them and was rewarded with their stories, encouragement, insights, and in many instances their friendship—the latter an honor I hold dear.

Leland Roy, former captain and Delta Company commander, made an extensive and valuable contribution by his detailed and accurate memory of the combat on Hill 376. We spent countless enjoyable hours discussing battle records, events, and soldiers from long ago. He has my greatest respect, and I am privileged to call him friend.

Paul Wharton, our former artillery forward observer, made many detailed reviews of my endless draft manuscripts and kept me straight on artillery matters beyond the competence of infantry officers. He is the only artillery officer I have known who was awarded a Combat Infantryman's Badge.

Gary Tepner, my former platoon sergeant and now good friend, was first to alert me that the National Archives held our battalion's original daily staff journals. I would not have written this book without the detailed journals. He also provided me expert technical, infantry knowledge and constant encouragement.

Jim "Duster" Littleton also became a close personal friend a few years ago. He led a squad in my platoon and was my best combat leader at Tam Ky. He took over my platoon when I was wounded. Jim died 19 October 2018. In the two years before his death, Jim's personal accounts and feedback were major contributions. His humor always lifted my spirits. Jim once told me when the movie based on my book is made, he wanted Steve McQueen to play his part. When I reminded him McQueen died in 1980, he just looked at me and grinned as I took the bait hook, line, and sinker.

Rob Sitek provided my first copies of the 1st Battalion, 501st Infantry, Vietnam AAR from his personal files. Though I also later found the report in my research at the National Archives, having an early copy of this document heavily influenced my decision to write.

Ron Sahrle contributed his personal accounts as one of Delta Company's junior sergeants who became the most senior NCO and leader in critical fighting at Tam Ky.

George Dennis had a lead role organizing Delta Company reunions and keeping our company roster updated.

Bill "Scotty" Scott made frequent coordination among Delta Company veterans providing information, resolving issues, and staying in close touch with our veterans.

Stephen Klubock provided his official US Army photos as the sole combat photographer at Tam Ky. Sadly, he succumbed to illness as a result of Agent Orange in early 2020.

Dick Motta, my brother-in-law, provided helpful research. Others in my circle of friends and family, too many to name, provided much welcome support.

Major Andrew "Red" Powell, an armor officer, and my grandson, kept me abreast of current US Army developments and the suitability of my book for young enlisted and junior officer combat leaders. My only known failure as his grandfather was not persuading him to become an infantryman.

Richard Arnold and Ken Davis, who oversee *The Coffelt Database of Vietnam Casualties*, were of immeasurable support providing accurate details about the soldiers killed in action to whom my book is dedicated.

Rich Kolb was the publisher and editor-in-chief of *VFW Magazine* for 27 years. He is also the general editor and contributing author of the excellent 2017 book *Brutal Battles of Vietnam: America's Deadliest Days, 1965–1972*. Rich graciously wrote the foreword and personally provided me vital professional guidance from his accumulated store of wisdom. He too is a combat veteran and fellow soldier of the 101st Airborne Division in Vietnam. *Brutal Battles* is a must-have book.

Tom Sherwood, my brother and former *Washington Post* journalist and longtime political analyst at *NBC Channel 4* in Washington DC provided the sharpest and smartest editorial pen I have experienced firsthand. His initial edits on my preface and introductory chapter were golden. Tom did good for a former Navy sailor, Yeoman Third Class.

The 101st Airborne's continuing support of its combat veterans from prior wars is well-known. I benefited much from the historical expertise of Dr. John O'Brien, Captain Daniel Herbster, and Command Sergeant Major Robert Nichols (US Army Retired).

Of special help to me as first-time author were Ruth Sheppard, Publisher, and Isobel Fulton, Managing Editor of Casemate Publishers who maneuvered me and *Courage Under Fire* through the wickets from proposal to print.

Almost finally, my dear wife Jackie, was my biggest fan and "editor at my elbow" always ready to read whatever I set in front of her. She patiently put up with me cloistering in my study for long stints of research and writing over the last three years. She and my daughters had long "pestered" me to write my Vietnam experience. Not until I decided to tell Delta Company's story did that seem a truly worthwhile undertaking.

Finally, and most importantly, my faith in God is the most important underpinning of this book and my life. Why I was spared in Vietnam when others were not, remains a mystery. What I do know, God used my combat and Army experience to shape my life of faith. My commitment as a soldier taught me much about what it means "to fight the good fight of faith as a good soldier of the Lord Jesus Christ" (1 Timothy 6:12 and 2 Timothy 2:3). For that I am eternally grateful.

A Hard Day at Tam Ky

21 May 1969 is a brutal day for Delta Company. It is our first, heavy combat at Tam Ky. An estimated 100 disciplined North Vietnamese Army (NVA) soldiers wait quietly and patiently in concealed, fortified bunkers, holding their fire. Their bunkers are expertly positioned and camouflaged in heavy brush, unseen from air or ground. Approaching troopers of the 101st Airborne are unaware of their presence.

The overgrown, football field-sized bunker complex rises several feet above the surrounding long-abandoned dry rice paddies. Like an emerald island, the enemy fortification looks serene and beautiful against a sea of brown dirt under a brilliant blue sky. Late in the morning, an already hot, broiling tropical sun climbs higher overhead. Our 2nd Platoon of 30 combat-experienced troopers cautiously crosses the open 50 m of sun-hardened ground. Once safely across, the platoon enters part way into the thick brush and stops pending further orders.

Jungle fatigues already soaked and dark with sweat, the soldiers welcome a short break. A sharp-eyed young soldier in the lead squad sees what may be an old bunker immediately to his front. In the past five days, dozens of such bunkers have been found without incident. Given permission by his platoon leader to clear the bunker, the soldier approaches in a low crouch, hand grenade in his right hand, M-16 rifle in his left.

Five meters from the bunker, an enemy AK-47 fires two sudden bursts of five 7.62 mm rounds. The soldier is hit, violently slammed to the ground by the sledgehammer blows of several rounds. Bleeding and in pain, he somehow holds on to his grenade and rifle. Lying on his back, cradling his rifle in one arm, he pulls the pin and throws the grenade into the small open firing port of the bunker. The ear-shattering violent explosion startles everyone. In the deathly quiet that follows, eyes and ears of friend and foe are now anxiously alert. Both know their enemy is at hand.

Hearing the enemy rifle fire and explosion, platoon sergeant, Sergeant First Class (SFC) Pedro Rios, instinctively knows his young soldier is in trouble. Rios immediately moves toward the soldier's position, approaching in a low crouch. An enemy sniper positioned in a tree above the bunker sees Rios, shoots, and instantly kills him. The wounded soldier Rios sought to help returns fire and kills the sniper. Again, all is silent.

SFC Rios, age 40, is Delta Company's most experienced senior sergeant. With 20 years of Army service, he is both father figure and mentor to his platoon's young soldiers. All are in their first or second year in the Army. Rios is loved and respected by his men. Their crusty sergeant cared for them as sons. They knew, if need be, he would give his all on their behalf. Today, he did. Rios is also father of three young children. His wife expects his return home in three short months. Sadly and unexpectedly, he will come home sooner to be mourned and buried by his grieving family.

This is Delta Company's introduction to a fierce day of combat at Tam Ky. A long, seemingly endless day with high casualties. Today is only a prelude of things to come. No one yet knows a longer, more grueling ten-day battle on Hill 376 is just days away. The soldiers of "Never Quit" Delta Company will live up to their name. They will fight understrength along with their sister companies with increased casualties and loss of leaders, under harsh battlefield conditions. On "the Hill," after many setbacks, a new "Never Quit" commander will lead them to victory.

Into the Fray

"Courage above all things is the first quality of a warrior."—Carl Von Clausewitz

An Untold Story About Infantrymen

Courage Under Fire is the untold story of Delta Company, 1st Battalion, 501st Infantry Regiment at Tam Ky during *Operation Lamar Plain*. It is a true tale of infantry soldiers in combat who live up to their "Never Quit" motto. An infantry company of young soldiers, many not long out of high school, with the US Army's hardest job—fighting as infantrymen on an unfamiliar battlefield far from home. In their late teens and early twenties, they are a mix of draftees and volunteers. Except for their current company commander, CPT Bobby Begley and SFC Rios, all are first-termers on their initial Army enlistment. Most arrived in Vietnam with less than a year of training and service.

Battle weary after 26 days of continuous combat at Tam Ky without a break, much reduced in numbers by casualties, they do more than hang on. They fight a decisive battle on Hill 376 against a tough and determined enemy under a new company commander, CPT Leland Roy. They are courageous young infantrymen in an unpopular war. Men who will carry memories of combat at Tam Ky the rest of their lives. Some good, some bad, many troubling. Some withheld even from family. They will forever remember those who didn't make it—honored fellow soldiers known only to these men, their families, and friends who loved them.

Battlefield conditions facing these young soldiers surprise many. Replacements are few as casualties multiply, including loss of junior officers and experienced enlisted leaders. They fight as frontline soldiers bearing the brunt of high-level political decisions adversely affecting their circumstances. Without wavering, they faithfully do their duty despite danger and death. It is a story of tough combat and tougher men, courageous soldiers upholding the US Army's Infantry's long, honorable lineage. Men worthy of the infantry's memorable battle cry, "Follow Me."

Background

The year 1969 is a turning point in the Vietnam War. The number of US military in Vietnam hits an all-time high of 549,500. US casualties in 1968 were the highest yet, 16,899 killed in action. Casualty rates in early 1969 begin to surpass 1968. Total war dead is now over 31,000 with more than 200,000 wounded. The American public is tiring of the seemingly endless war and its heavy casualties.

In late 1968, President Nixon is elected on his campaign promise to end the war. US national media and war protests are increasing strident demands to stop the war. Five days after Nixon is sworn in as president, he sends negotiators to Paris to begin direct peace talks with North Vietnam. Fast-climbing US casualties are a top concern for the new administration, more so for families sending soldiers to war.

In May 1969, sensitivity to staggering US casualties gets much worse. The 101st Airborne Division, the storied "Screaming Eagles" of World War II, fights two major battles. Each begins less than a week apart separated by 100 miles. This is the renowned 101st Airborne Division, known by an older generation for its valor in Normandy on D-Day and later in the Battle of the Bulge at Bastogne, Belgium. It is the same 101st introduced in 2001 to a new generation by the popular HBO World War II series *Band of Brothers*.

Today, few know the seven-year history of the 101st in Vietnam. The Screaming Eagles suffer nearly 20,000 casualties killed and wounded, twice their 9,328 WWII casualties. They fight in Vietnam from 1965 to 1972, a period much longer than their valiant one-year service in WWII (from 6 June 1944 to 8 May 1945). Their Vietnam service exceeds the entire six years of WWII (1939–1945). In Vietnam, 19 101st soldiers receive the Medal of Honor, most posthumously.

The 1st Brigade of the 101st is the first of the division's units to deploy to Vietnam, arriving in July 1965, and is one of the US Army's first combat brigades to join the war. The rest of the division, including the 2nd and 3rd Brigades, arrive in Vietnam in December 1967 in the largest and longest airlift to date directly from the US to a combat zone. Despite its early arrival in Vietnam, the 101st is the last combat division to leave Vietnam in 1972.

In just over 30 days during May and June 1969, the 101st suffers its highest casualties in the Vietnam War, the direct result of two major operations. One becomes well known and famous, the other is undisclosed and hidden for strategic political and military reasons. The first, *Operation Apache Snow* fought by the 3rd Brigade, is better known as the "Battle of Hamburger Hill." The second, *Operation Lamar Plain*, fought by the 1st Brigade, is hardly known at all and is now mostly forgotten.

Hamburger Hill—A Familiar First Battle

The term "battle" is used here in a general sense. The Battle of Hamburger Hill is not the official name for the combat on Dong Ap Bia. The official US Army name

Casualty Table 1: Two Intense 101st Battles

Operation	KIA	WIA	MIA	Total	Remarks
Apache Snow* 3rd Brigade, 101st (Hamburger Hill) 10 May–7 June 1969	78	536	7	621	*Source: The 101st Operational Report for Period Ending 31 July 1969 dated 9 December 1969. See bibliography.*
Lamar Plain** 1st Brigade, 101st (Tam Ky) 15 May–13 August 1969	120	404	1	525	*Source: Coffelt Database and Official US Army Casualty Records. A detailed accounting of Lamar Plain's casualties is found in Chapter 20.*
Total	198	940	8	1,146	

*Most casualties occurred in the first 12 days of *Apache Snow*, 10–21 May 1969
**Most casualties occurred in the first 28 days of *Lamar Plain*, 15 May–12 June 1969

is *Operation Apache Snow*. Similarly, the later reference to *Operation Lamar Plain* as a "second battle" is not made in a technical sense. As a matter of official policy, the US Army in Vietnam preferred to use the term "operation" instead of "battle." However, "battle" is widely and informally used in and out of the Army and it is used in that sense here.

"Hamburger Hill" was the central battle of *Operation Apache Snow*. It was fought primarily on Dong Ap Bia, the mountain the Vietnamese call "The Crouching Beast." On military maps it's simply Hill 937, the number designating its height in meters. *Operation Apache Snow* is unfortunately first known by its negative press accounts. The 1980 film *Hamburger Hill* and later the 18-hour 2017 documentary *The Vietnam War* by Ken Burns and Lynn Novick add to the battle's notoriety.

The personal courage of the young soldiers who fought the battle was initially downplayed or overlooked. It is unfortunate that Vietnam War movies too often portray infantry soldiers who fought in the jungles, coastal plains, and mountains as victims or pawns in the lost cause of an ill-advised war. That inaccurate description is a grave disservice to the hundreds of thousands of soldiers who answered their nation's call and faithfully fought in combat in which tens of thousands died.

The 3rd Brigade, 101st Airborne Division (supported by the Marines' 3rd Division and several battalions from the Army of South Vietnam) bravely fights the 11-day Battle of Hamburger Hill. Most of its US casualties occur from 10–21 May 1969, though *Operation Apache Snow* continues for 28 days until 7 June. The battle is the 3rd Brigade's "most intense and brutal conflict" since its December 1967 arrival in Vietnam.[3]

With the battle raging, on 14 May newly elected President Nixon makes his first, national, television address announcing his new war policy and its key tenet: "We have ruled out attempting to impose a purely military solution on the battlefield."[4] Unfortunately, the battle underway on Hill 937 seems to openly contradict Nixon's just proclaimed, but not yet implemented, policy. In the battle, the NVA's 29th Regiment is decimated with 630 enemy soldiers killed. An unknown, much larger number are wounded. US casualties are high. But much less than the enemy: 78 killed, 536 wounded, and 7 missing, a total of 621 casualties. Major General Melvin Zais, 101st commander, aptly calls the battle a "tremendous gallant victory" and by military measures, he is right.

But outside Vietnam, and particularly in Washington DC, the general's words fall on deaf ears. Media reports filed in Saigon and amplified in the US national media call the battle a "meat grinder." Emphasis on the high US casualties further underscore "the failure" of successive frontal attacks on the enemy's mountain stronghold. Some major media outlets conclude the battle was not worth the cost in US lives. The obvious, tough political question is hard to answer: "If the US no longer seeks a purely military solution, why are we fighting big battles with such high casualties?"

Other accounts fault the 101st for abandoning the mountain fortress just days after capturing it at such a high cost. Colonel Joseph Conmy, the 3rd Brigade commander, is accurately quoted, but his words, "the mountain has no strategic value" are misconstrued and taken out of context. Ignored by the press and those against the war is the truth that the mountain was targeted only because the enemy was located there. Once the enemy was destroyed, there was no reason to keep battle-worn soldiers on the desolate, decimated mountain top.

Despite the military victory, media accounts of battle casualties create an uproar among President Nixon's political adversaries in Congress and anti-war protestors. Just as the fighting ends, on 20 May, US Senator Edward Kennedy hotly denounces the battle on the US Senate floor. He calls the repeated frontal assaults and high casualties "senseless and irresponsible." His words unleash a firestorm of protests and political fallout on the home front against Nixon's conduct of the war.

In response, President Nixon accelerates his plans drawn up in March 1969 to withdraw US troops from Vietnam. On 28 March 1969, after a National Security Council review of Secretary of Defense Melvin Laird's visit to Vietnam and his trip report, President Nixon decides to begin comprehensive redeployment planning.[5]

General Creighton Abrams, the astute and competent Commander of Military Assistance Command Vietnam (MACV) has been under constant pressure to reduce large US offensive operations and their high casualties. Hamburger Hill becomes the impetus to accelerate implementation of Nixon's new strategic "Vietnamization" policy to turn the war over to the South Vietnamese government, permitting early withdrawal of US combat troops. In support, MACV initiates a new policy of highlighting South Vietnam's military forces and downplaying the role of US forces. There is just one complicating problem—a second major battle by the 101st is already underway.

A Troublesome Second Battle

The second 101st battle begins 15 May and is fought by the 101st Airborne's 1st Brigade at Tam Ky, some 100 miles south of Hamburger Hill. Despite the battle's lackluster name, *Operation Lamar Plain* resembles *Operation Apache Snow* in two ways: bitter fighting and high US casualties. Both are hard fought by 101st soldiers against well-trained, well-equipped, and disciplined enemy forces. Most of *Lamar Plain*'s casualties (85%) occur in the first 28 days of fighting from 15 May to 12 June though the operation doesn't officially end for 60 more days on 13 August. Casualties for the two operations shown in Casualty Table 1 underscore the problem faced by MACV, the Joint Chiefs of Staff, Secretary of Defense, and the President.

Operation Lamar Plain's high casualties occur while shock waves from Hamburger Hill's losses are still reverberating in Washington DC and the nation. The timing couldn't be worse for the Nixon administration. News of a second major battle so soon after Hamburger Hill with a high death toll could be politically disastrous. Like the 1968 Test Offensive the previous year, the announcement of over a thousand US casualties in a matter of weeks could result in an immediate, significant loss of popular support for the war, louder demands to stop the war, and undermining President Nixon's goal to achieve peace with honor.

To prevent damage to on-going strategic military initiatives and Nixon's war plans, General Abrams manages to keep *Lamar Plain* and its high US casualties undisclosed to the media and thus to the US Congress and the American public. The intent is both clear and understandable—avoid escalating the growing outcry against Nixon's conduct of the war and buy more time to implement Nixon's new strategic policies of Vietnamization and US troop withdrawals. General Abrams and his staff at MACV are successful in keeping *Operation Lamar Plain* off the front pages and out of TV coverage. As a result, 1st Brigade's battle and its high casualties at Tam Ky are largely unknown even today over 50 years after the war's end. Also unknown is the bravery and sacrifice of the young soldiers who fought there.

For those interested in a full account of why and how the battle at Tam Ky was hidden see Appendix 1. However, readers should note that *Courage Under Fire* is not about the MACV decision to keep *Lamar Plain* hidden. Operational reports of the battle are no longer classified and are readily available. Nor is this book about Nixon's new policy of Vietnamization or his decision announced 8 June 1969 to begin troop withdrawals. These important matters are mere backdrops to 1st Brigade's heavy combat at Tam Ky. The story here is about the young soldiers who fought at Tam Ky and their courage in combat.

Why It Was Fought

Lamar Plain begins out of military necessity. In early May 1969, just south of the 101st Airborne Division in the I Corps Region, the enemy is increasing attacks in the American Division's area of responsibility (AOR). North Vietnamese Army and Viet Cong (VC) forces are overrunning South Vietnamese units. They also threaten LZ Professional, a US Army firebase, and Tam Ky, the capital of Quang Tin Province. With one of the largest divisional AORs in Vietnam and with limited mobility, the American Division is unable to immediately stem the enemy advance and declares a "tactical emergency." MACV orders the 101st to send an airmobile brigade to destroy the enemy forces.

The 1st Brigade led by COL Richard Bresnahan answers the call. Since their arrival in 1965, the brigade has earned the reputation as MACV's "fire brigade." As the saying goes, "If you want it done, call the 101." The emergency requires swift, decisive action. The brigade's new operational area is just southwest of the coastal city of Tam Ky.

The 1st Brigade deploys to Tam Ky with two airborne infantry battalions, the 1-501st "Geronimo" and the 1-502nd "First Strike." Each has six companies (four rifle companies, one combat support company, and a headquarters company). A third battalion, the American Division's 1-46th Infantry "the Professionals," is also attached to the brigade. All will fight bravely and take heavy casualties at Tam Ky. (For more information on how the 101st Airborne was organized for combat in 1969 at Tam Ky, see Appendix 3.)

Other vital elements of the 101st Airborne deploying with or supporting 1st Brigade include air cavalry, assault helicopters, artillery, medical, engineers, signal, maintenance, and supply units. Counting augmentation from the American Division, all total the 1st Brigade's formidable combat force is well over 3,000 soldiers, a large offensive operation by any measure.

Veterans of *Lamar Plain* will later call their operation "The Battle of Tam Ky." Some simply refer to it as "Tam Ky." It could be called "The Forgotten Battle of Tam Ky" though veterans who fought there remember it well. They paid for the privilege to call it what they will and it is their story to tell.

The Story of Delta Company

The brave young men of Delta Company fight alongside their sister companies of the 1st Battalion, 501st Infantry Regiment (Geronimo). The battalion's history dates back to 1942 and its activation at Toccoa, Georgia and its follow-on training at Fort Benning during the early years of World War II. The 501st is the US Army's first airborne unit with a memorable tradition of fighting at Normandy on D-Day (June 1944) and in the Battle of the Bulge (December 1944) to stop the last German offensive.

The name "Geronimo" was attached to the 501st Infantry Regiment early. During initial parachute training, just after having watched the 1939 movie *Geronimo*, two soldiers got into an argument about who was scared to jump. One of the soldiers said he would prove that he wasn't scared by yelling the Apache battle cry "Geronimo" as he jumped. He did and the cry "Geronimo" became a favorite among 501st soldiers. The 501st finally adopted Geronimo as their nickname and it remains so, reportedly with the permission of Geronimo family descendants. Today the 501st regimental crest features an Apache Thunderbird symbol of power and strength.

Delta Company is front and center in *Courage Under Fire*. Their fighting spirit in battle matches their company's motto "Never Quit!" Delta's sister units in the 1-501st Battalion: Alpha, Bravo, Charlie, and Headquarters Company (along with Echo Company's battalion reconnaissance platoon) are frequently mentioned. At Tam Ky, they all fight faithfully and honorably in close support of one another while political considerations, war protests, and diplomatic peace initiatives in Paris overshadow their courageous fighting and sacrifice.

Delta Company's story is told in three parts following this introductory chapter. Figure 2 shows the three operational areas in which they fight (Hue, the A Shau Valley, and Tam Ky).[6]

Part 1: Combat Operations Before Tam Ky (Chapters 1 and 2) covers 1 March to 15 May 1969, combat operations at or near Hue and near the A Shau Valley. At Hue, Delta Company warily expects a repeat of the previous hard fighting during Tet 1968. Next, in the A Shau, they anxiously anticipate the heavy combat experienced there by others, departing just as the fighting begins at Dong Ap Bia to their north. To their surprise, engagement with the enemy and casualties in Hue and the A Shau are limited.

Part 2: Initial Combat Operations at Tam Ky (Chapters 3–9) covers 15 May through 2 June 1969. Delta Company makes a surprise move to Tam Ky as part of 1st Brigade's mission to locate and destroy a large, well-trained, and disciplined enemy. Initial combat operations include uncertain, difficult days on unfamiliar terrain in scorching heat, heavy rains, and high humidity. Delta Company and the Geronimo Battalion fights its first, brutal day-long fight, suffering heavy casualties with harder times ahead.

Part 3: The Decisive Battle at Tam Ky (Chapters 10–20) tells of the 1-501st Battalion's ten-day struggle on Hill 376 (3 to 12 June 1969). Delta Company's combat-weary, young soldiers endure more hard fighting despite losing their junior officers and senior enlisted leaders. They are led by an inspiring new company commander who embodies their "Never Quit" resolve. Despite heavy losses and setbacks, they finally break the back of enemy resistance at Tam Ky.

The epilogue looks back at *Operation Lamar Plain* from the perspective of veterans who fought at Tam Ky and considers the often asked, haunting question, "Was our sacrifice and effort worth while given the high cost of lives lost?"

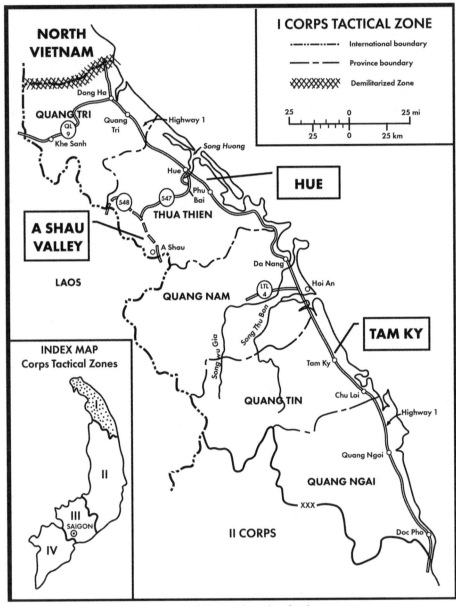

Figure 2: I Corps, where they fought

PART I

Combat Operations Before Tam Ky

1 March–15 May 1969

"Nothing can make a complete soldier except battle experience."—Ernie Pyle[7]

CHAPTER I

Hue and Beyond

1 March–11 April

The Tet Offensive

In February 1969, Delta Company is conducting combat operations in the southeast outskirts of the city of Hue, the third largest city in South Vietnam. The former capital of Vietnam with its imposing Citadel along the Perfume River is preparing for its annual celebration of Tet, the Vietnamese New Year which begins 23 February. A year earlier, during Tet, Hue was the scene of one of the most fierce and longest battles in the Vietnam War. For details see Mark Bowden's *Hue 1968: A Turning Point of the American War in Vietnam.*[8]

Fought in 1968 from 30 January to 3 March, the several-week battle in Hue caused more US and South Vietnamese Army casualties than any battle to date. The 3rd Marine Division and the US Army's 1st Cavalry Division were the main US combatants in the battle. The 101st Division's 2nd Brigade and three battalions (1-501st, 1-502nd, and 2-502nd) were attached to the 1st Air Cavalry and participated in the fight.[9] Over 5,000 civilians were executed in the Hue area by the Viet Cong. Casualty Table 2 shows just how intense the fighting was.

MACV, the senior US military headquarters in South Vietnam, estimated that 5,133 enemy soldiers were killed at Hue. Another 2,980 were killed in fighting outside of Hue in other parts of South Vietnam. The enemy's bloody Tet Offensive resulted in a US and South Vietnam military victory. However, it soon became a political and propaganda victory for the NVA and National Liberation Front (NLF) or Viet Cong.

Casualty Table 2: 1968 Tet Offensive, Hue			
US Casualties	KIA	WIA	Total
US Marines	142	1,100	1,242
US 1st Cavalry Division	63	453	516
US 101st Airborne Division	6	56	62
South Vietnamese Army	333	1,773	2,106
Total	544	3,382	3,926

The enemy's Tet attack came just months after General William Westmoreland, the senior US commander in Vietnam, had stated in a November 1967 speech at the National Press Club in Washington DC, "We have reached an important point where the end [of the war)] begins to come into view."[10] The scope and intensity of the enemy's Tet Offensive and heavy US casualties surprised everyone including General Westmoreland, the South Vietnam government and army, the US administration in Washington, and especially the American people.

The enemy's offensive was "the worst intelligence failure of the war."[11] The result in the US was an unrelenting barrage of protests against President Johnson's conduct of the war. On 29 February 1968, the US Secretary of Defense, Robert McNamara, resigned. He had been the principal US architect of the Vietnam War, having served as defense secretary for seven years. He had decided the war was not winnable and had announced his intention to resign months earlier. The Tet Offensive was a final blow to his unsuccessful tenure in managing the war.

McNamara was not the only high-level official to go. On 22 March, President Johnson announced General Westmoreland would be replaced as top commander in Vietnam. Soon afterwards, on 31 March, Johnson announced his decision not to seek reelection for the presidency. Perhaps more important than Tet's severe political consequences at the top of the US government, the enemy's Tet Offensive was a major turning point in which the American people's support for the war took a downward turn. As these events occurred in 1968, soldiers who will be fighting in 1969 are just entering the US Army to receive their initial training before being sent to Vietnam.

Tet 1969: One Year Later

As Tet approaches in late February 1969, what happened one year ago in Hue is on the mind of every 101st soldier. No one now in Delta Company was in Vietnam last year when the Battle of Hue occurred. But we are all aware that the Tet 1968 offensive was a bloody surprise attack that caught US and South Vietnamese units off guard. There's uneasiness about the onset of Tet, but so far there's no signs the NVA or Viet Cong will repeat last year's offensive.

Delta Company is conducting patrols and cordon and search operations. The latter involves setting up blocking forces around a series of villages which are part of "Eight Click Ville" (a string of villages 8 km long), while a unit goes in to search for enemy activity. The biggest danger is encountering booby traps. The enemy Delta Company now faces at Hue is local force Viet Cong irregular forces. Usually operating in two or three person teams, they are few in number, not well equipped, or well trained, but still a tough and resourceful enemy. Last year, they were effective in serving as local guides for North Vietnamese forces new to the Hue area.

Our platoons in Delta Company have been rotating security on a small bridge that spans entry into a small US military port managed by the US Coast Guard.

At the end of the bridge is a big, above-ground sandbag bunker. Ten feet high and about 20 ft square, the top had a parapet where we located our machine gun and M-79s. We also slept there. No one wanted to go inside the bunkers. They were too hot and rat infested. We ate our C-Rations from cans while the Coast Guard grilled steaks close enough for the smell to waft its way to our bunkers.

On 23 February 1969, the eve of the lunar new year and the beginning of Tet, LT Black's 2nd Platoon is taking their turn guarding the bridge. Our company is on full alert. As Black lies sleepless in the dark on top of one of the bunkers, he can hear the sounds of music coming from the streets on the outskirts of Hue just blocks away, He can also hear the sound of rats scurrying about inside the bunker. Having been in country just a month (like me and our other platoon leader, LT Rich Boyd), this is the first time he experiences the fear of an impending enemy attack. And for good reason. His platoon is isolated far from our company and is in an exposed position. Despite the watchful eyes of his soldiers, the bunker is an easy target, sitting just off the roadway. Sometime during the night, he falls asleep.

As Tet begins, battle accounts in other parts of South Vietnam report large enemy units are active elsewhere. Attacks are being made all over South Vietnam, but not at Hue. On 23 February, beginning in the early hours, the enemy attacks over 125 major targets and 400 lesser ones, mostly by indirect fire and sappers. Two enemy divisions mount ground assaults against Saigon.[12] That information is not being passed down to us at company level. Frankly, as Tet starts, we are surprised we are not getting reports of enemy activity around Hue, much less in other parts of South Vietnam. We know only what we can see with our own eyes and we haven't seen much enemy activity.

The common experience of US ground forces in Vietnam is that enemy units usually initiate large engagements only when it's to their advantage. Otherwise they are good at keeping their distance. Delta Company's contact with Viet Cong in the first months of 1969 remains sporadic. There are no pitched firefights in our area of operations near Hue. The VC limit their operation to hit-and-run tactics and booby traps to harass, wound, or kill soldiers. North Vietnamese Army units are nowhere to be seen in or close to Hue.

Our Infantry Mission

The US Army's infantry mission in combat is simply: "Find, close with, and destroy the enemy." Accomplishing this mission in our current area of operations has been difficult. Since the beginning of 1969, we have done a lot of looking, but not much finding. We have constantly conducted combat patrols and ambushes in the vicinity of Hue with only limited, periodic, minor engagements. No one is complaining, but it is surprising not to have more enemy contact. After all, we are infantry soldiers.

CPT Bobby Begley is our commanding officer. All three of our infantry platoons are led by airborne-ranger 2nd Lieutenants on our first combat tour and first time leading soldiers in combat. Lieutenant Rich Boyd has 1st Platoon, Ron Black, 2nd Platoon, and I have 3rd Platoon. We will all soon be 1st Lieutenants. Our soldiers don't care about our rank. What they care about is whether we will do something dumb to get them killed. Our infantry platoons average 24–30 soldiers divided into three squads of 8–10 men. In addition, each platoon normally has a platoon leader, platoon sergeant, two radio-telephone operators, and a medic. These positions and numbers will later drop significantly due to casualties.

Our operations in the coastal plains outside of Hue are mostly independent platoon operations. Enemy contact being light, our platoons prefer to operate alone. Small unit combat patrolling is a demanding mission, but it's an opportunity for our platoons to build teamwork and hone our infantry skills. I love the independent operations. Part of the reason for that is my platoon sergeant. He does a great job breaking me in as a new platoon leader during my "training wheels" stage.

My Grizzled, Old Platoon Sergeant

The past year, during the infantry officer basic course and my first assignment with the Ranger Training Command, both at Fort Benning, Georgia, I often heard the refrain, "Don't worry about that lieutenant, when you get to your unit in Vietnam you will have a grizzled, old platoon sergeant with about 15 years in the Army, likely be on his second combat tour. He will teach you what you need to know."

When I joined Delta Company in January 1969 at Firebase Birmingham, 12 km southwest of Hue, the same helicopter that brought me in took my platoon sergeant, SSG Gary Tepner, out for his two-week R&R with his wife in Hawaii. We exchanged brief greetings on the helipad and then he was gone. I was not so much surprised by his leaving as I was by his young age. Twenty-three, the same as me. Lesson number one in Vietnam—the real world is often different from the Army school house.

Though young and with little more time in the Army than me, Tepner is a proven combat veteran who I was also surprised to learn is the second-most senior non-commissioned officer in our company. This is my introduction to the hard fact that in 1969 most of the senior NCO positions in an infantry company are filled by newly promoted junior NCOs with little time in the Army. All of the platoon sergeant and squad leader positions in Delta Company (except one) are filled by young, junior-grade sergeants. The higher grade NCOs who would normally bring years of experience and expertise to our platoons are missing.

In 1965, when the 101st first deployed to Vietnam and as late as 1967, infantry units had their full complement of experienced infantry sergeants at squad and platoon level. Most were on their second, third, or even fourth terms of enlistment. Now in 1969, there are multiple reasons they are missing from our units: the rapid expansion of the Army's combat mission in Vietnam; the shortage of airborne qualified NCOs; continuing casualties; physical profiles due to injuries; assignment to rear jobs; lower re-enlistment rates; the aging NCO corps; NCOs leaving the Army to avoid going back to Vietnam, and retirements from active duty. This makes the outstanding performance of junior NCOs in combat all the more remarkable, commendable, and memorable.

With my platoon sergeant on R&R, I am pretty much on my own my first night with my platoon at Fire Support Base Birmingham. At about 2200H, my platoon's sector on the firebase perimeter receives enemy automatic weapons fire and we respond with all of our platoon weapons. An 8" howitzer battery right behind my platoon informs me they are preparing to direct fire right over my platoon. I am more concerned about that than the enemy fire. Thankfully, the artillery isn't fired as the enemy soon ends their harassing attack typical of small, understrength enemy units.

The next morning, I lead my first combat patrol to locate the enemy firing position and do a sweep around part of the base. SGT Jim Littleton acts as my platoon sergeant. I am aware he is keeping an eye on me, trying to pick up clues about my readiness to lead a platoon in combat. Littleton, I will soon learn, is my best combat leader after Tepner. All goes without incident, but I am happy to get my feet wet on day one.

When SSG Tepner returns, I am especially pleased to learn of his combat experience, knowledge, and leadership skills. Quiet-spoken and calm under fire, he has the respect of our platoon members. Tepner doesn't finish his Vietnam tour until August so I think we are set to work together for quite a while. Like almost all soldiers in Delta Company, Tepner is on his first term of enlistment and first combat tour. His leadership ability was recognized before he came to Vietnam.

After Advanced Individual Training (AIT) in infantry skills, Tepner completed the Primary Non-Commissioned Officer Course (PNCOC) at Fort Benning. Graduates of that course automatically become junior NCOs in the rank of sergeant. By some, they are derisively called, "instant NCOs" or "shake and bakes." I only mention those terms to say how much I dislike them. These soldiers were not only well above average, but they accepted the increased responsibility to fill the gaps in our infantry squads and platoons. With few exceptions, they performed admirably in combat.

Following PNCOC, Tepner and 16 of his classmates were assigned to an AIT Company at Fort Polk to gain on-the-job experience. At the end of their temporary assignments, the Army allowed one graduate per unit to be promoted from sergeant to staff sergeant. Tepner was the top performer in his company and was soon promoted and sent to Vietnam.

I didn't know it at the time, but Tepner's hometown, San Diego, California, is a large Navy and Marine community. His family did not have much when he was a young boy. His mother and father and their four children lived in a 400 sq ft duplex. Later, his father, Fred Tepner, established a career at Naval Air Station North Island, San Diego. In WWII, Fred repaired F4U-Corsairs then repaired UH-1 helicopters and F-4 Phantoms shot up or damaged in the Vietnam War. Tepner's father instilled a good work ethic in him from an early age.

At age 14, Tepner started a printing business in his garage. Later, he worked for a printing business in San Diego and was promoted to foreman before he was drafted at age 21. He has been on active duty since 26 September 1967, six months longer than me. He attended basic training at Fort Lewis, Washington, and advanced individual training (AIT) at Fort Polk. Tepner, married at 19, was also influenced by his father-in-law, retired Marine Sergeant Major Garland Respess. He joined the Marines in 1922 and fought four years in the Pacific as a gunnery sergeant at Guadalcanal, Bougainville, and Tarawa, retiring in 1952 after 30 years. Military service and support of the military is a long-standing Tepner family tradition. As a new platoon leader, I could not have done better or been more fortunate to have Tepner as my platoon sergeant. After many years of getting to know Vietnam veterans, I learned a large number of them came from families of WWII and Korean War veterans. They served in the military with honor, ready to uphold the family legacy of service to their nation set by their fathers, grandfathers, and uncles.

Light Casualties Are Not So Light

Delta Company casualties have been light as we have had little enemy contact. None in February. In March, Delta Company has three casualties. All were in our 1st Platoon. On 29 March, while conducting a night ambush, 1st Platoon was moving into an assigned ambush position in its area of operations. SGT John Clark was scouting the ambush location at dusk along with Specialist 4th Class (SP4) Ted Blass and Private First Class (PFC) Gilbert Taylor. This is standard procedure prior to the entire platoon moving in and setting up. Clark was out front checking the position when he noticed movement near a large anthill several feet high. Just as he turned to tell Blass and Taylor to go back, they were hit by a heavy volume of fire from across a nearby canal.

SGT Clark was killed instantly. Blass and Taylor were both wounded, but managed to crawl back to their platoon. LT Boyd recognized by the sound that the firing was coming from US weapons. After several tense radio calls back and forth with CPT Begley, it was learned that a US Marine ambush patrol, either out of position or firing across a friendly unit boundary, had engaged our platoon in a grievous error.

SGT Clark was an excellent soldier. He will be remembered by those with whom he served as saving the lives of his entire platoon. There is no telling how many 1st Platoon members may have been killed or severely wounded had he not been so alert. His own family, however, still takes the full brunt of his unfortunate death.

It is hard enough to take casualties from enemy action. Taking them from friendly US forces is as bad as it gets. Infantry soldiers know firsthand the many dangers of friendly fire. The battlefield often has friendly US units working close together with many dangerous US weapons all designed to kill. The long list includes indirect fire from mortars and artillery; bombs, napalm, and cannon fire from close-support jet aircraft; rocket and mini-gun fire of attack helicopters; and soldiers using rifles, machine guns, claymore mines, and hand grenades.

These weapons are frequently employed under conditions in which the location of other US ground forces is not precisely known. It is the nature of combat that miscalculation, poor judgment, incomplete information, lack of coordination, or a dozen other reasons may cause things to go wrong. The enemy is not the only danger on a battlefield. That is why effective training, and more training, is needed prior to combat and even in combat. No endeavor depends on continuous improvement of preparation, procedures, and practices like infantry operations.

"Friendly fire" is an innocuous, euphemistic term. There is nothing friendly about being killed by your own side in combat. It happens more than one might think and in every war. There are no accurate statistics of friendly fire incidents for the Vietnam War. In this long war, the number of friendly fire casualties is likely in the thousands with incidents occurring in all US forces, the Army, Navy, Marines, Air Force, and Coast Guard. On 24 March the Army, and especially the infantry, with the most men in the ground war, has the highest number by far of friendly fire casualties.

Notification of Next of Kin

For bereaved families like that of SGT Clark's who lose a son, husband, or brother, grief will soon become their constant reminder and lifelong companion of their terrible loss. By 1969, next of kin are notified quickly. Not by telegram as in the early days of the war, but by a two-man, uniformed team that arrives at the home of parents or a wife in a military sedan. Their sudden, unannounced arrival is an unwelcome, silent harbinger of the bad news they bring.

The next-of-kin notification team are themselves soldiers from the nearest military base or a nearby recruiting station. They approach their task with great dread, but don't refuse the duty. They understand that someone must do it in honor and recognition of those who sacrificed their lives in the service to their country. The families who suffer the terrible loss deserve the courtesy of a personal notification and the team is responsible for doing it. They will be the first to see the deep sorrow and anguish of those who will likely be receiving the worst news of their life.

The notification is given verbatim, word for word to the next of kin, "As a representative of the President of the United States, it is with great regret …." The rest of the statement is often not heard. Their mind shuts off the horror of what they have long feared. Overwhelming cries of deep anguish or anger often expressed in moans or loud shouts of disbelief arise from deep within the soul. Some faint. Some absorb the blow with quiet sobbing. Their lives now changed forever. For families, there is no such thing as "light casualties"!

My own family knows this full well. In the last months of World War II, my 26-year-old uncle, LT Peyton Turner, a navigator on a B-24 Liberator heavy bomber, was killed. He was the beloved son of his father and the revered older brother of his two sisters, one of which was my mother, the other a dear aunt. They were sad to see their brother Peyton join the Army Air Corps. They had lost their mother to illness before the war. They did not want to even think Peyton could be killed.

Peyton had completed his required number of combat missions and was due to come home soon. He volunteered to fly one last mission with a crew short of a navigator. In just three months on 8 May 1945, the war against Germany would end. On 16 February 1945, Peyton's bomber was knocked out of the sky on his squadron's last bombing mission against a German fighter aerodrome near Regensburg, Germany.

As their bomber formation turned coming out of their bomb run, a bomb hung up in another bomber fell and hit Peyton's bomber flying below. All but two of his seven-man crew died in the fiery crash. When the next-of-kin notification was made to Peyton's father, he had a heart attack and died soon after. Generations later, that fateful day is still vividly remembered with much sorrow. My grandfather was another casualty of the war, all due to a friendly fire incident.

Combat Operations Southeast of Hue

Since 1 March, Delta Company has been participating with our battalion (the 1-501st) under the leadership of LTC John Rogers in *Operation Massachusetts Striker*. This large spring offensive by 2nd Brigade, 101st Airborne Division, led by COL John Hoefling, includes four infantry battalions: the 1-501st, 1-502nd, 2-501st, and 2-327th. They have 16 infantry rifle companies and another four combat support companies with reconnaissance and mortar platoons. The brigade's mission is to conduct airmobile operations in the southern end of the A Shau Valley to locate and destroy enemy forces, caches (weapons and supplies), and lines of communications.

In Delta Company, the name, size, and mission of the brigade-level operation are not known to us at platoon level. CPT Begley typically gives us our daily mission in simple terms: go from Point A to Point B or set up an ambush at Point C. Beyond that, we usually don't receive much information on the friendly or enemy situation. In most cases, we are not aware of the missions or locations of our sister companies in the battalion. It would be good to know more and have an idea of the bigger picture of our battalion operations.

We don't yet know of our upcoming move to the A Shau. The likely reason is the move has been delayed. The brigade's mission is dependent on creating a chain of

March Back in the World

1 Mar	Top hit *Everyday People* by Sly and the Family Stone
1 Mar	Micky Mantle retires from baseball with the NY Yankees
3–9 Mar	Apollo launches, orbits moon, safely returns
7 Mar	Kissinger forwards Secret CIA study of Student Unrest to President Nixon
10 Mar	James Earl Ray pleads guilty to Dr. Martin Luther King's murder, later retracts his plea
13 Mar	*The Love Bug released* (#2 film in '69)
20 Mar	Chicago 7 tried for inciting '68 Democratic Convention riots, not convicted
22 Mar	Protestors smash and pour blood on Dow Chemical offices in Washington DC
25 Mar	John Lennon and Yoko Ono's 14-day anti-war "bed in," record *Give Peace a Chance*
28 Mar	President Eisenhower dies, WWII top general, 34th president born in 1890

five new fire support bases (FSBs) in the southern A Shau Valley. That construction is underway but well behind schedule due to monsoon rains in the high mountains 40 miles southwest of Hue near the Laotian border.

While the bases are being constructed, the 1-501st finishes its mission near Hue and is attached temporarily to the 1st Brigade. Our new area of operations is a smaller mountainous region 25 km (15 mi) directly south of Hue. Perhaps not knowing about the move to the A Shau is for the best. We need to concentrate on the task at hand.

Seen so far only at a distance, the mountains south of Hue remind me of those in north Georgia at the southern end of the Blue Ridge chain. They are modest in size, rugged, green, and wet. It is an operating environment far different from the coastal plains. We will have to adapt our tactics and operating techniques. Movement in the mountains will be difficult, enemy concealment much easier. All three of our platoon leaders were introduced to mountain operations during three weeks in Ranger School conducting combat patrols in the North Georgia mountains. We are certainly not experts in mountain warfare, but at least the terrain is similar.

Our battalion S-3 operations officer, Major (MAJ) Warren MacDiarmid, tells CPT Begley there's a large NVA force in a 10 km (6 mi) square area in the mountainous area where we are headed. That's an attention getter. I think, kidding myself, maybe the only thing worse than not knowing the enemy situation is knowing.

We soon learn our company will conduct reconnaissance in force (RIF) patrols only on the northern edge of the area. Perhaps we will have a "trip wire" role, giving an alert in case the large enemy force moves toward Hue. Other companies in our battalion have similar RIF missions in other sectors.

The term "reconnaissance in force" replaced the earlier one "search and destroy." By 1969 the latter was officially ended as being politically inappropriate. It conjured up negative visions of civilian hooches (small huts often with thatch sides, dirt floor, and straw roofs) being burned by soldiers with cigarette lighters and all kinds of other unpleasant images seized on by war protestors.

Infantry doctrine of the day says a RIF mission is an "attack to discover the enemy's position and strength."[13] By definition, the primary aim is reconnaissance. If enemy weaknesses are discovered, they may be exploited for tactical success. That is not exactly what we are doing. We are actively looking to attack the enemy wherever we find him.

The term RIF mission is still an appropriate term because we never know where we will find the enemy. It bears mentioning again, the usual practice of the NVA is to evade US forces unless it is to their advantage to engage. When they do engage, it is typically at very close range and under conditions favorable to them.

Our First Combat Assault into the Mountains

On 5 April, Delta Company makes a combat assault by helicopter at the base of a heavily forested mountain range south of Hue. Our entire company is lifted to the landing zone (LZ) in one flight by 15 HU-1 (nicknamed Huey) helicopters. The Huey (now designated the UH-1 for utility helicopter) is the workhorse helicopter of our airmobile division. Each aircraft can easily carry six combat-loaded soldiers. Eight can be squeezed in if need be. At a cruising speed of up to 125 mph, they can get us where we want to go in a hurry,

The flight of Hueys drops us in an open grassy area at the foot of the mountain range forming the northern boundary of the enemy's reported location. We land unopposed at the LZ and soon begin a two-hour climb up the mountain, avoiding existing trails and making our own. The going is slow, vegetation is thick, and the angle of our ascent is steep. Most in our company have never operated in jungle mountain terrain. We are moving up in a single file stretching out easily 200 m. For a rifle company we are moving quietly. No one is talking.

The steep slopes are covered with "wait a minute" vines that slow our progress. We have to be careful not to develop large gaps in our file. We are fully loaded with heavy rucksacks weighing 70–90 lbs. Some carry more. Breaking contact with the man in front of you can cause problems. Squads and platoons can become separated. That is not a good idea in enemy territory. The temperature and humidity are high. Our jungle fatigues are quickly saturated with sweat. Monsoon rains forecast for late afternoon will be welcome, at least at first. Operating in heavy rain gets old fast.

My 3rd Platoon leads the climb with 1st and 2nd Platoons following. CPT Begley, his artillery FO, two radio-telephone operators (RTO), and company medic follow immediately behind 3rd Platoon. SGT Jim Littleton, age 21, my most experienced squad leader, is the lead squad in our platoon. SP4 James Parvin is our point man as we move up the mountain. I am following right behind Littleton's squad with my RTO. SSG Gary Tepner, my 23-year-old platoon sergeant, follows with our last squad,

Parvin is five meters out in front of Littleton's squad by himself. Littleton and another soldier stay close enough to keep him in sight and provide him cover. The point man is the most exposed soldier in our formation. His main job is to keep us from walking into an enemy ambush. His skills in detecting the presence of the enemy are critical. Point men are among the unit's best and most experienced soldiers. Typically, they volunteer for the assignment to protect their fellow soldiers and themselves. No one wants a rookie out front.

Littleton is from Wilhite, a small rural community northwest of Monroe, Louisiana. He grew up in the swamps and forests of Louisiana hunting and fishing and says he didn't know his family was poor until he went to college. With a smile, he once told me he had been elected senior class president of his small rural high school by the girls in his class. I never knew if that was true. He has a great sense of humor, but is all business on combat operations.

Littleton's father, William P. Littleton, had been an infantryman with the 2nd Infantry Division during World War II in Europe. He was captured in battle and spent nine months in a German prisoner of war camp until his release at the end of the war. Littleton remembers his dad telling stories of how he witnessed firsthand the bravery and toughness of airborne soldiers in combat.

Littleton was drafted when he dropped out of college to work. Upon completing basic and advanced infantry training at Fort Polk, Louisiana, Littleton volunteered to be a paratrooper. He joined Delta Company on 14 July 1968 as a PFC straight from airborne training at Fort Benning, Georgia. He has been in 3rd Platoon eight months, first as a rifleman then an M-60 machine gunner. He was promoted to sergeant a couple of months ago. I have learned to trust his combat instincts and skills.

A Brief Enemy Encounter

After a strenuous climb to the top of the mountain, we are hot, thirsty, and soaked in sweat. We could use a short break, but security comes first. Littleton's squad has come upon a well-travelled mountain trail running both directions along the ridgeline. With his left arm, palm raised, he signals for the platoon to halt. He next drops and flattens his palm toward the ground, motioning us to get down. An index finger to his lips signals us to remain silent.

The hand signals are passed backwards to our following platoons. There is no need to talk. Everyone intuitively knows what to do. I point a finger motioning Littleton to take his squad to the left. SGT John Horan's squad is signaled to go right. Our company waits quietly taking a knee, but remaining alert while we check out the trail.

Minutes later, Littleton returns and whispers, "We hear someone on the trail about 50 m down. Maybe three or four people. Sounds like they're not moving. We heard talking and singing." "Singing?" I ask. "Yes, singing," Littleton says with a slight smile. I tell Littleton to lead me and several men from his squad back down the trail. Littleton chooses his M-60 machine-gun team, PFCs Andrew Ramos and Gerena Nieves, and his M-79 grenadier, SP4 Ralph Franklin. He positions the rest of his squad in firing positions to cover our movement down the trail, ready to reinforce us if needed.

SGT Horan's squad moves a short distance up the trail. They are set up to block the trail if an enemy force should come from that direction. Our third squad led by SGT Larry Hoffa remains in place in the middle astride the trail. My RTO informs CPT Begley's RTO, "We have an enemy position identified not more than 50 m away, 3-6 (our platoon's call sign) will soon engage it."

Littleton leads as we move slowly and quietly back down the trail. We stop about 30 ft from the Vietnamese voices. We can't see them nor can they see us because of the thick bushes between us. We assume they are enemy because we're in a "free fire zone." There are no restrictions on our use of firepower. Carefully and silently taking prone positions side by side behind the bushes, we listen with hearts pounding as we try to remain calm.

One enemy soldier is singing softly. Two are conversing with one another. Their voices aren't loud, but apparently they think they're alone and safe. They don't know death is lurking nearby. From what we can tell, it is a small team of at least three enemy soldiers. We don't know if others may be near. There is only one way to find out.

At Littleton's signal, we open fire through the bushes. Our machine gun and three M-16 rifles on full automatic open fire at the same time, creating an abrupt, thunderous hailstorm of bullets. Franklin fires an M-79 grenade over the top of the bushes. We are too close for the round to detonate.

The sound of the firing and explosions reverberates through the mountains shattering a peaceful quiet. There is no return fire. Our firing continues for ten seconds. Then we stop. Littleton and I each throw a grenade. Those of us with M-16s reload new magazines. The sudden quiet is eerie. The only sound is ringing in our ears. The smell of gunfire hangs heavy in the mountain air. Slowly, we move cautiously around both sides of the bushes ready to open fire again. Two NVA soldiers lie dead in a small clearing at a trail junction.

Littleton silently motions to the machine-gun team and grenadier to move across the clearing for security. Each takes a side of the trail. They quickly discover the abandoned equipment of two fleeing enemy soldiers. One has run down one side of the ridge, one down the other. They dropped AK-47 rifles and other equipment as they ran. No blood trails are seen. They got away, no doubt terrified by our surprise attack.

While our machine-gun team and grenadier cover us, Littleton and I search the two bodies. The soldier I search is lying face down. He is wearing the dark green uniform of an NVA soldier. His helmet lies close by. Perhaps he is the team leader. I take hold of his shoulder and turn him over. He has several bullet and fragment wounds in his chest and arms. His face is youthful and clean-shaven without any wounds. He appears to be in his early twenties.

Searching his shirt, I find a small, black plastic wallet in his left chest pocket. Opening it, I see a black and white photo of an attractive, young Vietnamese woman. She is smiling widely. A girlfriend? A young wife? She likely will never know what happened to her soldier. I have the photo of my own wife of six months in my left shirt pocket. I put his wallet back in the same pocket. He is not carrying papers or maps. Littleton finds a large amount of Vietnamese piasters on the soldier he searches. The four soldiers were probably a supply team waiting on supplies from the valley below. A path branches off the main trail at the clearing leading down the mountain. The sound of our weapons warns those below not to make deliveries today. We leave the two NVA bodies in the clearing so they can be easily found. The NVA are good at recovering their dead.

We move back up the trail with four captured AK-47 rifles. CPT Begley and his command group are now up on the trail. I make a situation report (SITREP) to Begley giving Littleton full credit for his initiative and leadership. He and his squad likely prevented us from being ambushed. Later, SGT Littleton will receive a well-deserved Bronze Star for Valor for his actions. I'm proud of the performance of all my guys today, especially that we took no casualties.

CPT Begley decides we will stay in our current location for the night. It is late afternoon. Our attention turns to setting up our defensive position. The two escaped enemy soldiers will likely report our position. We anticipate we'll be attacked soon. If the NVA come up the ridgeline trail, 3rd Platoon will be hit first. Our 1st and 2nd platoons have taken up positions on each side of the trail behind us. We all know the enemy could approach from any direction.

End of the Day

As night falls, we are dug in. Trip flares and claymore anti-personnel mines are out. Sectors of fire for each position have been checked. Our platoon's machine gun is positioned by the trail able to fire right or left. All ears and eyes are alert in the deep darkness of the triple canopy jungle. Each jungle sound gets our immediate attention. Knowing a large enemy force is nearby, anticipation of an attack keeps our adrenaline flowing. We wait and watch, peering into the black night.

My mind is unsettled as I imagine the enemy moving up the trail toward our position. My sense of dread is unlike any I have yet experienced. Likely, I'm not the only one battling fear. Though no one talks about it in the midst of combat, fear's ever present shadow falls on us all. A soldier's survival instinct is strong in combat, strong enough to overcome his fears. Soldiers will often act to save their fellow soldiers even if it requires putting themselves in danger.

The best way to make it through danger in combat is to rely on our training and one another. For extra measure, I pray the proverbial foxhole prayer, "Lord help us get through the night." As has often been said, there are no atheists in foxholes. I am embarrassed to say it is one of the few prayers I remember praying in Vietnam. Several hours into the night, fatigue from the long climb and enemy encounter finally sets in. Everyone but those on watch falls sound asleep.

Nothing happens. On waking to the morning light, I don't remember to thank God for getting through the night. Over the next week, we have no further enemy contact. While continuing our RIF mission, often in pouring rain, our 1st and 2nd Platoons discover a major enemy cache of food and weapons. Shortly afterwards, our mission ends. We walk out of the mountains tired and wet to a pickup zone (PZ) in an open, grassy valley. The sun is shining, there is a rainbow in the late morning sky.

We set up in our pick-up positions and bask in the warming sun as we await the helicopters. We are still alert, but more relaxed than we have been in days. Prior to pick up, LTC John Rogers, our battalion commander, swoops in and drops off several waterproof bags filled with ice and cold beer, welcomed with smiles and loud shouts of "Cold beer!" This is not exactly the time or place to lounge around with a beer. We consume them quickly. I'm not a beer drinker, but it's the best beer I've ever had. At the battalion tactical operations center, plans are already complete for our next mission—the A Shau Valley.

***

Casualties and Awards

During March 1969, in addition to Delta Company's casualties, already mentioned, Alpha Company has four soldiers WIA on 3 March: SGT Roger Long, SGT William Bray, SP4 Dean Neilson, PFC Michael Fredricks. Bravo Company has one soldier WIA on 21 March, PFC Kenank Kidd. Charlie Company has one soldier WIA, SP4 Jack Cumminsky. Headquarters Company and Echo Company (Recon Platoon) have no casualties.

Casualty Table 3: 1-501st Hue, 1–31 March 1969

Casualties	HHC	A Co	B Co	C Co	D Co	E Co	Total
KIA	0	0	0	0	1	0	1
WIA	0	4	1	1	2	0	8
Total	0	4	1	1	3	0	9

1-501st Soldiers Killed in Action, March 1969

Delta Company—1
29 March: SGT John J. Clark, age 20, born 25 July 1948 from Manchester, TN

1-501st Soldier Awards, March 1969 (other awards may have been made that were not mentioned in after action reports)

Bronze Star—2
Alpha Company: SGT Frederic Davis
Delta Company: SGT James Littleton
Purple Heart—awards were made to all soldiers KIA or WIA

CHAPTER 2

The A Shau Valley

12 April–15 May

The Valley of Death

The A Shau has a bad reputation with US forces. Soldiers have dubbed it "the Valley of Death." Typically, swarming with enemy activity, the valley is a natural conduit for North Vietnamese Army (NVA) soldiers and supplies coming into South Vietnam. During nine years of US fighting in the valley, 15 Medals of Honor were awarded for combat action there.[14]

Having been defeated decisively during Tet in the coastal lowland areas in 1968, the NVA withdrew west into the Laotian mountains for protection, resupply, and reconstitution. From their logistics bases in Laos, they have built extensive fortifications in the A Shau and use it to move troops and supplies from North Vietnam to support operations throughout the northern provinces of South Vietnam. The southern end juts menacingly into the three provinces of Thua Tien, Quang Nam and Quang Tin. The latter province's capital is Tam Ky.

The valley's strategic importance is due to its size, location, terrain, weather, and heavy use by the enemy. The A Shau lies 70 km (42 mi) southwest of Hue in the

---

April Back in the World

1 Apr	Top hit *Dizzy* by Tommy Roe
3 Apr	*Goodbye Columbus* released (#10 '69)
4 Apr	Anniversary of 1968 assassination of Dr. Martin Luther King in Memphis TN
4 Apr	First artificial heart implant by Doctors Cooley and Liotta
5–6 Apr	Major anti-war protests in New York, San Francisco, Los Angeles, Washington DC, and others
8 Apr	Montreal Expos first game as only non-US major league team baseball team

9 Apr	300 white leftist SDS students protest ROTC at Harvard president's home
17 Apr	Palestinian Sirhan of Jordan guilty of Robert Kennedy's 1968 assassination
19 Apr	100 armed black students take over Cornell University building
22 Apr	First human eye transplant attempt fails
28 Apr	French President Charles de Gaulle resigns

same Thua Tien Province as Hue. The 40 km (25 mile) long valley is 1.5 km (1 mile) wide and bounded by two high mountain ridges on each side varying from 900 to 1,800 m (3,000 to 5,900 ft). The valley runs from the northwest to the southeast just east of the Laotian border.

The A Shau is usually cloaked with low-hanging clouds with rainfall of biblical proportions. Use of aircraft in and over the valley is often limited, making it difficult for US forces to sustain combat operations there. Two connecting highways run the length of the valley forming a main enemy supply route from North Vietnam through Laos to South Vietnam. Highway 548 is in the northern half of the valley and is connected to Highway 614 in the southern half. Together the roads are known as "The Yellow Brick Road," and are a major part of the "Ho Chi Minh Trail." A third road, Route 547, runs east to Hue. (The Ho Chi Minh Trail was named by US Forces, but was not intended to honor Ho Chi Minh, the longtime North Vietnam leader. It was much more than a trail. The strategic network of multiple roads and trails in a 30-mile wide corridor stretched some 600 miles from North Vietnam through Laos and Cambodia to South Vietnam. All total, there was 3,500 miles of roadways used effectively by the North throughout the war.)

2nd Brigade's A Shau Mission

In early April 1969, 2nd Brigade continues its *Operation Massachusetts Striker* mission begun 1 March, "to conduct airmobile operations on the southern end of the A Shau Valley to locate and destroy enemy forces, caches, and lines of communications." Execution of the mission has been held up for weeks due to the delayed construction of firebases slowed by monsoon rains. Four infantry battalions (1-501st, 2-501st, 1-502nd and 2-327th) are being inserted on staggered dates into the area of operations. They will conduct reconnaissance in force (RIF) operations from five newly constructed fire support bases (FSB): Fury, Whip, Thor, Pike, and Lash. All are located just east of the southern end of the A Shau Valley in a crescent-shaped line from north to south. See Figure 3.

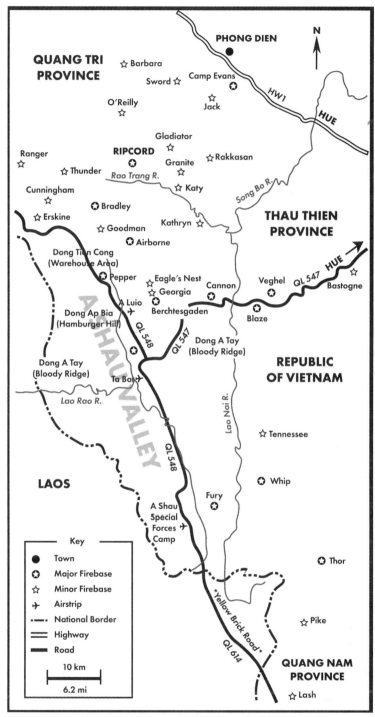

Figure 3: 1–501st firebases, southern end of the A Shau Valley

Current enemy intelligence, known at battalion and higher headquarters, says the NVA's 559th Transportation Battalion is moving supplies through the southern A Shau and then east in support of the NVA's 4th and 5th Regiments. The 815th Battalion of the 9th NVA Regiment provides security for the supply routes. The NVA's 4th Engineer Battalion is working along the supply routes to improve roads. The Katu Montagnards, indigent people in the A Shau Valley area, are growing, harvesting, and distributing crops to support NVA units. Whether these units remain in our area of operation or have been pulled out is an open question.

To clear thick jungles for the five firebases, a 10,000 lb. bomb, facetiously nicknamed "daisy cutter," is dropped on each mountain location to blow down trees. Next, construction teams from the 101st Division's 325th Engineer Battalion are flown into each location. They are reinforced by Navy Seabees with heavy bulldozers. Yes, the US Navy is working deep in the mountain jungles of South Vietnam. They clear the forest debris and flatten the mountain tops or ridges where the bases are built. The engineers construct the artillery firing positions, helipads, bunkers, and other fortifications. Each FSB is big enough for an artillery battery or two, a couple of helipads, and defensive fortifications for an infantry company.

Fire Support Base Pike

On 12 April, the 1-501st Battalion gets a new commander, LTC Raymond Singer. It is a tough time to take over the battalion. The battalion's TOC moves from Camp Eagle to FSB Thor (YC666835) signaling the start of the 1-501st and Delta Company operations near the A Shau. On the same day, the 1-501st is returned to OPCON of 2nd Brigade. The eventual plan is to move the 1-501st TOC to FSB Pike (YC667747) when construction is complete. In the interim, the TOC remains at Thor during the night (where security is tighter) and operates from Pike during the day. The move to occupy Pike 24 hours a day is finally made on 19 April.

The TOC serves as the battalion's command post (CP) under the direction of the S-3 operations officer, MAJ Warren MacDiarmid. The TOC oversees battalion operations and controls the radio net for the battalion commander. Battalion commanders in the 101st typically operate from a helicopter away from the TOC to control the ground maneuver of the battalion's companies. There are of course exceptions to this standard operating procedure.

FSB Pike is located just under 7 km (4 mi) east of the Laotian border and 12 km (7 mi) east of Highway 614. Pike sits atop a steep mountain ridge in dense triple-canopy jungle. The terrain is much more rugged than the mountains south of Hue. The A Shau mountains are higher, the valleys deeper, the slopes steeper, and the jungles thicker. The area is alive with poisonous snakes, spiders, leeches, huge snake-like worms, malaria-bearing mosquitos, and insects like foot-long centipedes. Monkeys abound and tigers are known to dwell there. In his book, *A Shau Valor*,

Thomas Yarborough, says, the A Shau is "home to over 100 different types of venomous snakes ... Over 97% of the snakes in the A Shau are deadly poisonous; the other three percent will eat you."

On 12 April, all four 1-501st companies are transported by air to FSB Pike. Bravo Company, led by CPT John Pape, remains on the not-yet-finished base to pull security, Alpha, Charlie, and Delta Company along with the battalion's Recon Platoon begin RIF missions around Pike while combat engineers from the 325th Engineer Battalion hurry to complete its construction. Later, Bravo and Delta Company will alternate providing security for Pike. One company remains on the base while the other conducts RIF operations. Alpha Company, commanded by CPT Patrick McGuire, and Charlie Company, commanded by CPT David Gibson, will move to FSB Thor and take turns pulling security and RIF missions there.

Conducting RIF Operations Near FSB Pike

From 12 to 27 April, Delta Company conducts RIF operations to the west, southwest, and south of FSB Pike. We encounter limited enemy contact. Delays in constructing and occupying FSB Pike and the other firebases gave the enemy ample time to withdraw their forces from the areas near the bases. Small enemy teams are left behind to keep tabs on our movement and to harass our operations. They will try to kill US soldiers every chance they get.

At 0841H on 13 April while providing security on FSB Pike, Bravo Company receives 20–30 rounds of AK-47 fire. Then another burst at 1015H. Two soldiers are WIA. At 1107H another long burst kills SP4 Ralph McMurtry. Enemy fire continues to be received throughout the day. At 1215H, sniper fire wounds another soldier. At 1627H, five enemy 60 mm mortar rounds land just outside Pike's perimeter. Wounded today are: 1LT Lester Dixon, who is slightly wounded and remains in the field. He will be wounded again later on Hill 376. SP4 Bernard Simmons and PFC Jerome Martin are wounded and evacuated. Then on 14 April, Bravo Company's PFC Charles Crosby is killed as the enemy continues to contest the building of FSB Pike.

On 15 April at 0705H, southeast of FSB Pike at YC673742, a small enemy force engages Charlie Company with small arms. The enemy has the advantage of knowing the terrain and fighting from concealed, covered bunkers. An intense firefight continues until 0805H. It's the battalion's heaviest combat action near Pike. Charlie Company casualties are two KIA and 16 WIA. Killed in action are SGT Albert Creamer and PFC John McDonald.

Wounded are 1LT Hollis Lucas Jr; SGT Donald West; SP4s David Cutright, Henry Furguson, Melvin Johnson, Danny McCoy, Freddie McLendon, Eugene Mossbrucker, Norman Prather, Cecil Wells, and PFCs James Coats (later WIA again on 18 May), Joseph Lehner, Jerry Scott, James Sgroi, and Arthur Whitmore. SP4 Fletcher Nowlin, HHC medic supporting Charlie Company is awarded the

Silver Star for valor in treating the wounded under heavy fire. He survives unharmed, but is later fatally wounded at Tam Ky.

At 1245H the same day, Delta Company operating to the west of FB Pike at YC659743 finds a large, camouflaged cache of weapons, ammunition, and supplies. There is evidence the enemy weapons cache was brought in on elephants. Finding and destroying enemy stockpiles is a vital part of our mission. If we deny the enemy use of these stored weapons, he can't use them against us or anyone else.

The huge find includes: 1,914 60 mm mortar rounds, 172 81 mm mortar rounds, 103 75 mm recoilless rifle rounds, 20 30 mm rounds, 100 land mines, 1 RPD light machine gun, 1 SKS rifle, 1,400 9 mm pistol rounds, 450 12.7 mm heavy machine gun rounds, and 2,160 AK rounds. Our engineer team destroys the cache with several 40 lb. cratering charges. For guys who like to blow things up, the explosion is awe-inspiring. It's a good day!

As Delta Company continues to conduct RIF operations, one of its more unusual finds is two coffins hollowed out from large tree trunks. One has a body in it. Trung, our Kit Carson Scout (KCS), tells Begley the manner of burial is reserved for senior commanders. Kit Carson Scouts are Vietnamese who often were former Viet Cong soldiers. Trung is a particularly gifted soldier who has served loyally with Delta Company for many months and has saved lives of Delta Company soldiers. All our companies, including Delta, continue to discover enemy bunkers; hooches set up as living, eating, and sleeping quarters; small weapon and ammunition caches; and foodstuffs including live animals like pigs and goats. We find a lot of enemy supplies, but few enemy.

Enemy harassing fires continue to inflict casualties using mortars and small arms against Pike and the other firebases for much of the time we occupy them. Helicopters routinely receive fire coming in and out of FSB Pike.

On 18 April at 1021H, Bravo Company is given the mission to secure a CH-47 Chinook downed by enemy fire at YC680720, several kilometers southeast of Pike. They will also recover the five bodies of the flight crew and return to Pike. At 1215H, Alpha Company engages an enemy unit at YC681736 and has one soldier killed, SP4 Lloyd Jones. Two are wounded: PFC Hoyt Pierce and PFC Charles Wilder, a medic.

On 20 April at 1350H, Alpha Company receives a burst of AK-47 small arms fire and an enemy grenade thrown into its perimeter. SGT Gerard Mosely is wounded by shrapnel.

Another Friendly Fire Incident

On 22 April, our company is conducting a reconnaissance in force mission near FSB Pike. The heavy vegetation in triple-canopy jungle in the mountainous terrain makes navigation difficult. CPT Begley has directed LT Black's 2nd Platoon to follow a route up a ridge line to our front.

Once on the ridge line, Begley tells our artillery FO to fire artillery in front of our 2nd Platoon. Black has his compass out ready to shoot an azimuth to the sound of the artillery 105 mm round when it explodes. By knowing the grid coordinate of the round, the direction to the explosion, and the estimated distance to the explosion, Black can calculate the location of his platoon. Unfortunately, LT Black doesn't know his platoon has been put on the artillery's gun-target line. The gun-target line is the line drawn between the location of the guns and the target. Three rounds are to be fired.

Black is on one knee ready to shoot an azimuth to the sound. His RTO Nick Garcia is kneeling by his side. They hear the first round arching high overhead and its explosion well to the platoon's front. As Black determines the compass direction to the round, the shrill scream of the second round pierces the jungle canopy. In a split second everyone realizes it is incoming! There is no time to react except to dive for cover.

Those who survive will never forget the moment of terror as they hear the high-pitched scream of the incoming round moving at supersonic speed followed instantly by the thunderous blast shattering tree limbs and scattering hot metal shrapnel everywhere. SP4 Nickolas Garcia is killed instantly. SP4 Lawrence Troyan, a medic, is wounded by shrapnel in his chest and upper leg. LT Black attends to him, examining and treating his wounds. PFC Roger Georgette suffers a concussion from the exploding round. He is bleeding from his ears. Both wounds are serious and require a medevac.

Those in the platoon not injured by shrapnel are dazed by the errant round. It is a mystery why more were not killed. It just wasn't their time to die. The firing of artillery in front of a moving infantry unit in enemy territory is standard practice. Another purpose is to take out enemy snipers or ambushes. Typically, if a friendly unit is on the gun-target line, artillery is fired a safe distance well ahead of friendly troops and then walked back toward the unit under close observation.

What likely happened is one of two mistakes. First the artillery gunner may have miscounted the number of powder bags used to propel the round the right distance. Second, the gun crew firing the round may have made what is called a "hundred mil error." The gun barrel was not set at the proper angle of fire. A hundred mil error in elevation, up or down, can cause the artillery round to fall short or long. Rather than hitting several hundred meters to the front of 2nd Platoon, the round hit the trees above the platoon with devastating effect.

On arrival in Vietnam as I prepared to join the 101st, I met CPT Steve Tanner, a friend from college, who had just finished his combat tour with the 101st as an artillery officer. He said he had only one piece of advice for me as an infantry officer that I should always heed, "Stay off the gun-target line!" That is excellent advice for any infantry leader.

Pulling Security on FSB Pike

On 28 April, Delta Company completes its RIF mission near FSB Pike and moves on to the base to provide security. On FSB Pike, CPT Begley rotates each of our three infantry platoons on combat patrols a short distance from Pike. The platoon with the patrol mission sends one to two squads out. The other two platoons stay on Pike for perimeter security. We are subjected to intermittent enemy hit-and-run harassing attacks using small arms and mortars. One or two enemy soldiers, usually from several hundred meters distance, fire a quick burst from their AK-47 rifles or 60 mm mortars and disappear without being seen. Helicopters coming into Pike are frequently targeted by enemy small arms fire.

Despite the light enemy contact, every night we expect a more substantial enemy attack. A small enemy sapper team could penetrate our perimeter during darkness with satchel charges and wreak havoc. Sapper teams are highly trained demolition teams specializing in slipping undetected through the outer defenses of a US or ARVN base with a satchel of high explosives to blow up key facilities such as a command post, fire direction center, ammunition, and storage areas. They may or may not be suicide teams. Both the NVA and VC are experts at using this tactic. We are not equipped with night vision devices. That technology is not yet available in our infantry companies. Our security watches use only their eyes and ears. After dark, we are told to randomly toss grenades down the dark, steep banks of the firebase every 30 minutes or so. The intent is to disrupt enemy sapper teams that may try to get up the steep sides of our position with explosive satchel charges. We are not sure the periodic throwing of grenades is effective.

One of my soldiers asks the question, "What if the enemy uses our exploding grenades to cover noise they make infiltrating our positions?" I smile in appreciation of his insight. There is a lot of common sense wisdom in foot soldiers. Their lives depend on it. His follow-up question is also a good one. "Why don't we have lots of barbed wire on the slopes of the firebase?" The firebase is so new that wire obstacles have not yet been laid. I'm not sure it has even been brought in. If it hasn't, that should be a higher priority. It is worth checking out.

Sporadic Enemy Contact Continues in the 1-501st Area of Operations

Over the next week we have "sporadic contact" with the enemy. It is a common military term that sounds innocuous, but isn't. Brief, intermittent, enemy contact may occur unexpectedly at any moment, but is deadly just the same. That is why soldiers in the field must continually anticipate enemy contact at any moment. Their guard must always be up.

Sporadic contact adds significantly to the stress of combat especially when operating in unfamiliar, difficult, mountainous terrain during fast-paced operations. On the upside, the week passes rapidly with few casualties as our battalion continues searching for the enemy. In the following paragraphs, I briefly summarize our battalion operations giving a quick review of a typical week in the A Shau.

29 April. With Delta Company securing Pike, the other elements of the battalion conduct a heliborne combat assault into a suspected enemy area using three LZs. All three LZs are hot, drawing enemy fire. Participating are Alpha, Bravo, and Charlie companies, our battalion's Recon Platoon, and the 2-501st Recon Platoon. Two helicopters are hit landing soldiers, but remain operational. There are no friendly casualties during the landing. The assault's purpose is to open FSB Shield (YC749645) as a temporary new base of operations for conducting RIF operations to find and destroy enemy units, supplies, and equipment.

30 April. During morning operations both Bravo and Charlie Companies find and destroy a number of recently used, but now deserted hooches, bunkers, tunnels, and gun positions. At 1455H, as COL John Hoefling, 2nd Brigade commander, flies in to commend his soldiers on their efforts, his helicopter is hit twice, without casualties, and is still operational. Back at FSB Pike, at 1852H as dusk falls, Delta Company and the 1-501st TOC receive a pounding with near 60 enemy 60 mm mortar rounds. Thankfully, there are no casualties.

1 May. Operations continue at and near FSB Shield. At 1250H, the base receives a burst of AK-47 fire. No one is hit. At 1459H, an inbound CH-47 receives some 40 rounds of AK-47 fire. No damage or casualties result. At 1350H, an artillery LOH-6 Cayuse pilot spots an abandoned enemy bulldozer about 600 m south of Shield.

2 May. At 0602H, Delta Company still on Pike receives a long burst of AK-47 fire. At 1050H, near Shield, Bravo Company finds and destroys another area (YC791663) with hooches and bunkers. This one has several live pigs, a favorite enemy food supply. No refrigeration needed. Another indication that the camp has been recently occupied. Documents are found in one of the bunkers. At 1127H, a Huey (HU-1D) logistics helicopter (log bird for short) coming into Shield is fired on by several bursts of AK-47 fire.

3 May. At 0820H, the Recon Platoon discovers another bulldozer at YC755638. At 0955H, a Huey log bird is shot down by enemy small arms fire at YC732658. Both crewmembers are wounded and soon picked up by another helicopter. At 1515H, Charlie Company has a brief engagement with a small enemy force. Two soldiers are wounded. SP4 Jerry Scott by gunfire and PFC William Sassano by a punji stake, a sharpened bamboo stake placed in a camouflaged pit. Punji stakes were frequently used inexpensive booby traps. Each sharpened stake tip was usually coated with human or animal feces to cause infection.

4 May. At 1347H, FSB Shield is closed and combat operations near FSB Shield are completed. There's light enemy contact with no enemy casualties. Remaining enemy bunkers and hooches are destroyed. The two abandoned enemy bulldozers used to improve nearby supply routes are blown up. Bravo Company returns to FSB Pike to continue RIF operations nearby. Alpha and Charlie Company and Recon return to FSB Thor. The 2-501 Recon Platoon returns to its battalion.

5 May. At 1015H, Alpha Company has two soldiers WIA by sniper fire from YC723668: SP4 Terry Lucarelli and PFC Harold Smith.

6 May. At 1126H, Charlie Company conducts a combat assault to an LZ at YC639762. At 1224H, Bravo follows into an LZ at YC645751 about a kilometer from Charlie Company. Both companies find large caches of enemy supplies, weapons, and equipment.

Loss of an Experienced Squad Leader

On 6 May at 1105H, my first casualty in 3rd Platoon since I took over as platoon leader in January this year occurs unexpectedly at Pike. The north side of Pike is the only side that doesn't have almost impenetrable slopes. To the north of the firebase is a series of trails running along the top of the ridge and down each side into the heavily forested jungle valleys. The mountain slopes there are steep and the vegetation so thick that movement off the trails is extremely difficult.

SGT Larry Hoffa, who also joined 3rd Platoon in January from Fort Benning's PNCOC, is leading his squad on a combat patrol to the north of Pike. SP4 James Parvin, an experienced soldier, is out front as point man. Returning to the firebase, they are about 300 m out, moving alongside the single narrow trail on the ridge line that frequent patrols are forced to use going out and coming in.

All is going well. Soon they will be back inside the wire and safe. That is when Parvin notices freshly dug small holes in the trail. He turns around and reports what he has observed to Hoffa. No sooner has he spoken when Hoffa hears a distinct loud pop, like a muted explosion to his rear. PFC John Meade had just stepped on an anti-personnel mine. Apparently the detonator in the small mine exploded and the main explosive charge was defective. Still, the force of the explosion was enough to knock Meade down, even though he's 6' 3", 215 lbs., and carrying another 30 lbs. of weapons and gear. Meade falls into the vegetation on the side of the trail.

Just as he is recovering, Meade sees Hoffa a short distance up the trail coming toward him to find out what happened. Parvin and Hoffa do not yet know that most of the squad have unknowingly passed right through a newly emplaced minefield, or at least one the enemy had not yet completed. The empty holes Parvin saw likely meant more mines were to be laid. The squad's return likely interrupted the enemy's effort.

When Hoffa goes back down the trail to find out what happened to Meade, he reenters the minefield and steps on a buried mine. It is not defective. The explosion

THE A SHAU VALLEY • 29

blows off the front part of his right boot, his toes and half of his foot. Surprisingly, he is not knocked off his feet and remains alert though in extreme pain. Blind by dirt from the explosion in his right eye, he hops on his good foot to the side of the trail and throws himself into the brush. He sees the force of the explosion has blown some of the loose sandy soil off the other mines. Though wounded, he directs the rest of his squad through the minefield to safety.

One of Hoffa's squad members tries to encourage him with the words, "Sergeant, you're going home. You've got a million dollar wound!" It doesn't make Hoffa feel any better. He looks at his mangled foot and feels sick. Without an RTO that day, Hoffa is carrying the squad's PRC-25 radio. He calls on the radio to let me know he has been wounded not far outside our firebase perimeter. I inform my platoon sergeant, SSG Gary Tepner and we both hurry to the squad's location. When we arrive Hoffa is sitting up cradling his injured foot in severe pain.

Our company medic has come out with us. After examining Hoffa's wound, he gives him a shot of morphine and then begins to clean and bandage his wound, attempting to save his severely damaged foot. Surprisingly, no one else is hurt. Meade has a sore foot, but otherwise he is okay. But his narrow escape is enough to make him think he won't make it out of Vietnam alive. True enough there are a lot of different ways to die here.

Soon a medevac helicopter comes on scene and hovers just above us, dropping a "jungle penetrator" hoist through the trees. Hoffa is lifted out with some difficulty. Halfway up the hoist gets stuck on a tree limb and he has to get it unstuck to allow his lift to continue. Once safely in the helicopter, he asks for a cigarette. The onboard medic at first refuses, pointing to nearby oxygen tanks, but then relents. It seems medics always have a soft spot in their hearts for wounded infantry guys—and they are all champs to us.

Tepner and I then begin to examine the trail. We see the evidence of other mines scattered along the trail. We also see the one Chinese hand grenade with a tripwire not yet strung across the trail that Hoffa had mentioned. The mine which wounded Hoffa and almost wounded Meade is just over 2" in diameter and about 2" in height, no bigger than the size of a small tuna fish can. In military slang it is called a "toe-popper." Quite an understatement looking at Hoffa's wound. Similar to our US-made M-14 Anti-Personal Mine, both mines are designed to wound, not kill. The enemy mine did its job.

Tepner sends a team to the engineers for Bangalore torpedoes. (Bangalore torpedoes were invented in Bengaluru India in 1922 by a famous sapper unit called the Madras Engineer Group. The explosive device was instrumental in breaching beach obstacles on D-Day 6 June 1944.) The 3 ft long tube-shaped explosive charges can be connected end to end, extending their length and reach. They are perfect for destroying obstacles and mines. Together Tepner and I spend the next hour clearing 11 mines from the trail. In hindsight, we should have given the task to our engineers. In any case, our hard-to-find enemy will likely install more mines nearby soon. For sure, we will call on the engineers next time.

Getting off the trails is extremely difficult in the mountains. It is the only recourse to avoid mines. Patrols won't move as fast and won't go as far. They also won't see as much or provide as much security. Every decision in combat, even at small unit level, has advantages and disadvantages. The tradeoff is between security, safety, and mission needs. Decisions must often be made quickly with the lives of soldiers always in the balance.

Loss of My Platoon Sergeant

I hate to lose Hoffa. He is a good soldier and an experienced leader. But soon I will also lose my right-hand man, my platoon sergeant. All three of our infantry platoons have outstanding platoon sergeants. SSG Ronald Sahrle (age 21), 1st Platoon; SFC Pedro Rios (age 40), 2nd Platoon; and SSG Gary Tepner (age 23), 3rd Platoon. They are likely as good, we think better, than any group of platoon sergeants in our battalion. SSG Sahrle in 1st Platoon is our newest platoon sergeant. He was promoted just eight weeks ago and moved from 2nd Platoon where he has a solid reputation as a squad leader. He will prove to be one of the top combat leaders in our company.

Still, I wouldn't trade Tepner for anyone, I know him the best. He has been my platoon sergeant and right-hand man since January. I credit him with helping me successfully transition in as a new platoon leader. Before I came into the platoon as an individual replacement, Tepner had already served several months as the senior squad leader in 2nd Platoon and later as acting platoon leader of 3rd Platoon. With the exception of Rios, Tepner is the Delta Company's senior NCO in the field. He is the best combat leader in my platoon and one of the best in our company.

While in 2nd Platoon, back in October 1968, Tepner helped SFC Rios get acquainted with 2nd Platoon and Delta Company when Rios was first assigned. At 40 years old and by rank our most senior platoon sergeant, Rios is in top, rugged, physical condition and proficient as an expert infantryman. He is the best combat leader in our company. Before long, he is easily the most beloved leader in our company.

Rios is called "Dad" by his men. Though older than anyone in the field with Delta Company, the title is mostly out of respect for him as a leader. He looks out for his young soldiers much like a father for his sons. Thousands of years ago Sun Tzu, in the oldest military treatise in the world dating from the 5th century BCE, said, "Regard your soldiers as your sons and they will follow you to the deepest valleys, look on them as your beloved sons and they will stand by you unto death."

SFC Rios, age 40, born 16 March 1929, from Ponce, Puerto Rico, is the most experienced NCO in Delta Company. His men would follow him anywhere. His love for his men is returned by all. When SP4 Michael "Big Mike" Tomaszewski wanted to go to the 101st Airborne's Long Range Reconnaissance Patrol (LRRP) Company, Rios told him, "You go there and you're likely to get killed. You need to stay here where I can look out for you." Rios is tough on his men when someone gets out of line, but is always teaching them what he's learned over nearly two decades as an infantryman. In May, Rios has only a few months left on his combat tour. Afterwards, he plans to go home to his family in Puerto Rico and retire from active duty.

Rios will be hard to replace. So would Tepner. Just recently at Pike, Tepner demonstrated his expertise in directing mortar fire on an enemy position. Having seen the enemy's green tracers fire upon one of our helicopters coming into Pike, Tepner quickly placed effective mortar fire on the enemy position several hundred meters from the base's perimeter. His former military occupation specialty (MOS) is 11C—Indirect Fire Infantryman. In short, he is well qualified with mortars clearly adding to his versatility and value as a platoon sergeant.

Soon after directing the mortar fire, Tepner goes to the battalion TOC on Pike to report the enemy action. He arrives just as the battalion is needing sergeants to fill positions in the TOC now co-located with us at Pike. Tepner is a top prospect. MAJ Hans Reich, the battalion executive officer, peppers him with questions about his experience. Next, Tepner is tested on his multi-tasking ability to handle situation reports, maps, and radio communications. Unfortunately for Delta Company and 3rd Platoon, he passes with high marks.

CPT Begley and I are soon notified Tepner is being pulled out of Delta Company to join the S-3 shop. We don't get a vote. Neither of us likes losing Tepner, but we support the decision. Tepner has put nine months in the field and served well. He is a great addition to battalion ops. We both think it is a good move for Tepner, our company, and battalion.

Our platoon will miss him. It's a good time to apply an important leadership principle passed to me by SFC Bob Dews, my step-father and long-time infantry soldier: "Make sure your men who work hard and do well are rewarded. Help them move up and be happy when they do!" I had nothing to do with Tepner moving up, but I am happy for him. It is good advice from an infantryman who fought in WWII and the Korean War and served a tour in Vietnam. He wore his Combat Infantryman Badge (CIB) with star with great pride. It was his most treasured award. The star on the badge above the rifle and in between the wreaths indicated a second award of the CIB. My step-father attempted to qualify for a third award during his Vietnam tour, but he wasn't eligible because of the nature of his assignment.

The loss of Tepner and Hoffa will be difficult in the short term, but fortunately I have two good squad leaders left. SGT Jim Littleton, now my best and most experienced combat leader, and SGT John Horan. Both good soldiers on their first term of service in the Army. Littleton will double up as my platoon sergeant until one is assigned. That never happens.

Tepner will serve well in the battalion TOC. However, later at Tam Ky he will hear firsthand over the battalion's radio net of the casualties Delta Company is taking. He will have deep regret that he is no longer with "his guys." He too will be sorely missed by them, but his assignment as a battalion operations NCO is now an important one. He will not return to Delta Company. After serving in Vietnam, Tepner returned to San Diego and his former job at the printing business. Within several years he had become a junior partner, then owner, growing the business into the largest printer in San Diego. He credits his military experience as the basis for his later leadership and success in business. See Appendix 9.

Summing Up the Last Few Months

Delta Company has spent most of our time over the last months since 1 March, conducting combat patrols, ambushes, and RIF missions. Our last stand down was in February and then only for three days. However, being continuously in the field has had many benefits. First, discipline, morale, and camaraderie in our company and within our platoons are excellent. George Washington said, "Discipline is the soul of an army. It makes small numbers formidable, procures success to the weak, and esteem to all."[15]

Use of drugs and racial tensions which often exist in rear areas are not a problem for us since we are always in the field. No one in our company tolerates use of drugs in the field. Being mentally sharp and constantly alert is paramount. The danger isn't only from our enemy. We are armed to the teeth. All of us are carrying and using loaded weapons. Racial tension in our company is lessened by several realities. Combat skills and experience are the measure of an infantry soldier, not the color of his skin. We know firsthand we all bleed red and our lives depend on our taking care of each other. There is common agreement on that up and down our leadership chain and within our units.

Another indication Delta Company is a disciplined unit is that we have had no incidents of mistreatment of civilians, detainees, or enemy soldiers whether the latter are dead or alive. Our soldiers also haven't shown any open antagonism toward our officers and NCO leaders. At least not beyond what might be an appropriate concern about an individual or incident. Incompetent leaders don't last long in infantry units. They tend to make their presence known pretty quickly by doing something dumb or not having adequate infantry skills. They are a danger to themselves and others. Commanders usually get them out of the field quickly.

Political discontent or siding with the growing war protest movement among our soldiers is surprisingly not evident. Anti-war demonstrations and political opposition to the war were already well underway and increasing in 1968 before most of the soldiers in Delta Company arrived in Vietnam. This doesn't mean that all of our soldiers agree with the war or want to be in Vietnam. Many clearly would prefer not to be here, but it is an indication of their sense of duty that they're here and doing a good job as soldiers.

Operating continuously in the field for months, we have practiced and honed our combat skills and techniques. Our soldiers, squads, and platoons have operated in rice patties, mountain jungles, and everything in between. Our squads and platoons have been building the trust and teamwork critical to our combat effectiveness. For the present, we have overcome many of the problems caused by the individual replacement system used in Vietnam.

One of the main problems with the Army's individual replacement system is leaders and men come in and go out as single soldiers in Vietnam units. New replacements aren't trusted at first. They must prove themselves. Not by heroics, but by showing veteran soldiers they won't get anyone killed because of their inexperience or ignorance. Individual enlisted replacements often take weeks to be trusted. Officers may take longer. Time is not always available for soldiers to get to know new soldiers or leaders. Soldiers and leaders must often fight with whoever is assigned for good or bad. We have not had much turnover due to end of tour rotations or casualties, so there hasn't been much disruption in our teamwork.

There is also mutual respect among our three platoons. Each has a solid reputation in the company. We have gained a lot of experience working independently away from the company. If we have a weakness (or at least an unpracticed skill), it's working together as a company under fire by a large enemy force. That capability isn't apparent because we haven't yet experienced a tactical situation that requires it. At least, not yet.

Perhaps that's why in the last months, our three platoon leaders have seldom met together with CPT Begley to be briefed on a mission, exchange information, hear about the enemy situation, or conduct an after action review when a mission is completed. We all would prefer more communication and Begley's interaction with our soldiers. In Begley's favor, our company has been effective on combat operations and we can take pride in what we have accomplished.

Absence of Heavy Enemy Contact

We expect, but haven't seen, significant enemy contact. As mentioned earlier, our senior leaders know the delay in the construction of our firebases caused the late arrival of our forces. During the time lag, the enemy apparently withdrew the bulk of their forces from our area of operations. Their "stay-behind teams" are small, but effective in bravely harassing our units with small arms and mortars. Except for the men we lost, the A Shau did not live up to its bitter reputation.

Later, it will be clear why. The enemy had decided to concentrate its forces for battle elsewhere in the A Shau. The location is a mountain 60 km (36 mi) to the northwest of FSB Pike. Its name, Dong Ap Bia. 101st soldiers who fight there will give it another name, "Hamburger Hill." On 15 May as we leave Pike, we are not aware the 3rd Brigade of the 101st, Marine, and ARVN units have already been fighting there for five days. In that battle, the A Shau will uphold its reputation as the Valley of Death.

Our New Mission

At 0100H on 15 May 1969, our battalion S-3, MAJ Warren MacDiarmid, receives orders from 2nd Brigade's headquarters. The 1-501st is to "prepare for extraction from FSB Pike for possible deployment outside of the 101st area of operations." At 0335H, the brigade provides additional information: "Responsibility for FSB Pike will pass to 2-327th Infantry at 0900H 15 May. Extraction of the 1-501st will begin at 0800H 15 May. Be prepared to deploy to Tam Ky, Quang Tin Province for an indefinite period under OPCON to 1st Brigade which will be OPCON to the Americal Division on order. Mission unknown."

At 0530H on 15 May, CPT Begley is awakened by a message from MacDiarmid telling him what battalion likely had known perhaps for 24 hours or more, though they may not have known the date or time. Delta Company and the rest of our battalion is being pulled off FSB Pike and Thor early this morning for another mission. Begley passes the message to each of our platoons. Get ready to move by 0730H. After weeks of duty in or around Pike, most of us in Delta Company are ready to do something else. We should be careful what we wish for. We are headed to some place unknown to us called Tam Ky.

Back in Washington DC

On 14 May, the day before we undertake our new mission, four months after he takes office, President Nixon makes his first major address to the nation on what he terms "our most difficult and urgent problem—the Vietnam War." He says:

> We can have honest debate about whether we should have entered the war in Vietnam. We can have honest debate about how the war has been conducted. But, the urgent question today is what to do now that we are there.

Then he makes a starting announcement: "We have ruled out attempting to impose a purely military solution on the battlefield." Realizing the great sacrifice of America's military in combat, he adds:

> I am proud of our men who have carried the terrible burden of this war with dignity and courage, despite the division and opposition to the war in the United States. History will record that never have America's fighting men fought more bravely for more unselfish goals than our men in Vietnam. It is our responsibility to see that they have not fought in vain.[16]

As President Nixon makes this address to the nation, the Hamburger Hill battle has been raging for five days. The fighting at Tam Ky is already underway with the 1st Brigade, 101st Airborne Division preparing to join the fight. Whatever opinion a person might have about President Nixon, his characterization of America's fighting men is on the mark.

The Initial Move to Phu Bai

At 0800H on 15 May, the 1-501st begins its extraction via three Boeing CH-47 Chinook helicopters. Each one can easily carry a platoon. They will shuttle our entire battalion, one company at a time, the 40 miles to the US Air Force airstrip at Phu Bai. The airfield is 7 miles southeast of Hue. Alpha Company is picked up at 0831H. Bravo Company at 0927H. Delta Company is extracted at 1010H. Charlie and Echo Company's recon and mortar platoons are extracted from FSB Thor at 0950H. Our entire battalion closes on Phu Bai by 1100H. Our battalion has never been moved with such urgency or so quickly. We still don't know why.

On landing at Phu Bai, we see the airstrip is a beehive of activity. Our infantry battalion of nearly 500 soldiers is gathered there. An additional 200 soldiers support preparation for our new mission. Our battalion has six companies, a Headquarters Company, Echo Company(with reconnaissance and mortar platoons), and four infantry companies (Alpha, Bravo, Charlie, and Delta). While in Vietnam, we've not ever seen so many soldiers in one place. We are reminded Delta Company is only one among many. Our sister battalion, the 1-502nd, is also moving to Tam Ky with us and is being marshalled at Camp Eagle.

There to meet us on the tarmac is the soon outgoing 101st Division commander, Major General (MG) Melvin Zais and also the 1st Brigade commander COL Richard Bresnahan. MG Melvin Zais will soon relinquish command of the 101st to MG John Wright on 28 May 1969. COL Bresnahan will turn over 1st Brigade to COL Frank Dietrich on 28 July 1969. Bresnahan will later retire as a Major General. Our new battalion commander, LTC Raymond Singer, is also present. It is the first time I've seen him. This greeting by our senior commanders is very unusual. So is the extensive resupply and refitting that we are about to undergo. It is clear we are being sent on a high priority, difficult mission. So far, that is all we know and we are anxious to know more.

Dozens of stations are set up to provide direct exchange of any weapon or piece of equipment carried, worn, or used by our soldiers. No questions are asked if we need anything. Everything is readily available. Rifles, ammunition magazines and bandoleers, machine guns, grenade launchers, rucksacks, LBEs (load-bearing equipment), helmets, uniforms, ponchos and poncho liners, canteens, radios, all-important radio batteries, strobe lights, first-aid dressings, anti-malaria pills, food rations, fuel tabs and personal care toiletries.

Ammunition and other weapons are available in abundance. We are to take whatever we need, want, or can carry. Large CONEX containers are full of every kind of ordnance. There is 5.56 mm ball and tracer ammunition and magazines for M-16 rifles; 7.62 mm ball for snipers, and boxes of belted 7.62 mm with tracer for machine gunners; M-79 40 mm grenades for grenadiers; two kinds of hand grenades (the 16 oz M-61 and the lighter 14 oz M-67, the latter being about the size of a baseball, easier to throw, and just as deadly); smoke grenades of various colors; bayonets, handheld red and green star cluster flares, trip wire flares, and claymore anti-personnel mines. On top of all that, each platoon member except the machine gunners and radio-telephone operators are asked to carry a 15 lb. 81 mm round for our newly attached mortar crew. The crew will have to do all they can to carry the heavy M29 mortar tube and its base plate.

There are also stations for water and rations. Twelve water trailers (nicknamed "water buffaloes") each holding 400 gallons are set up every 100 or so meters. Every soldier can fill his multiple canteens full. Infantry soldiers usually carry five to six quarts of water (about 10 to 12 lbs.) in either one or two quart plastic canteens. On the hot black asphalt in the noon day sun it is blistering hot and many do a quick face wash, soaking their neck towel with water to cool down.

Soldier meal rations are available in the tens of thousands. Each individual combat meal weighs another 2.7 lbs. Soldiers pick up rations for three days, another 24 lbs. Most soldiers forego the full weight of nine C-Ration meals and substitute some meals for the lighter LRRP rations pronounced "Lurp." The new freeze-dried rations are much lighter, but require 1.5 pints of water to eat. Hot water works best, but in combat there's little opportunity to heat water or even use heat tablets. The odor of burning heat tablets can be carried a long way by the wind. The smell is a dead giveaway of a unit's position. LRRP rations also don't include cigarettes. Smoking in the field near the enemy is prohibited. The smell of burning tobacco can travel a long way.

LRRP rations also have the notorious 2 oz. Hershey's Tropical Chocolate Bar. A lot of soldiers won't eat what they call "lifer bars" (the derisive word "lifer" is used by first-termer soldiers to describe those who are in the Army for the long term). They are my favorite snack. I'm always glad to trade for them. The hard chocolate bars won't melt even in Vietnam's high temperatures (up to 120 degrees). It is probably not a good idea to look at the label for ingredients. There is no truth to the rumor that soldiers carry the indestructible chocolate bars in their shirt pocket over their heart to stop AK-47 rounds.

No army is better equipped than the US Army, but a young infantry soldier's load is heavy. With extra water and ammunition, most of the soldiers in our platoon will be carrying upwards of 70–100 lbs. M-60 machine gunners and RTO's have the heaviest loads. Radio operators carry the AN-PRC-25 radio. The radio, handset, shoulder harness, and antenna pack weigh 25 lbs. Each battery, generally good for a day with normal use, weighs near 2 lbs. Most RTOs carried 3–4 extra batteries and may have a buddy or two carrying one, just in case. For RTOs, it is a point of pride never to be out of communication because of a dead battery. Our lives depend on good communications.

The M-60 machine gun is our platoon's most important weapon. It's nicknamed "the pig" because of its 23 lb. weight (without ammunition). Each 100-round belt of 7.62 mm ammunition weighs 6.6 lbs. Gunners usually carry four belts. Assistant machine gunners carry another four to six belts. In our platoon, some riflemen carry extra belts. The gun has a cyclic rate of fire of 500–650 rounds per minute and maximum effective range (using the attached bipod for stability) of 800 m on area targets, 600 m against point targets. We never leave home without it.

Infantry soldiers must live and fight with what they carry on their back. We are supposed to carry everything we will need for three days. Resupply is usually made at three-day intervals, but it's often held up due to weather, terrain, or the enemy situation. Of course, we load up with an extra day or two of supplies. In heavy contact, water and ammunition will always be in short supply.

On enemy contact, our heavy rucksacks (backpacks to civilians) are immediately dropped using a quick release latch. When under fire, extra weight is deadly. Agility, quickness, and speed is a must. Just as important, when a soldier hugs the ground under fire, he wants to make himself the smallest target possible. He doesn't want his ruck sticking up giving away his position. Despite the weight, with the right pace and frequent breaks on combat missions, infantry soldiers can typically carry a heavy rucksack all day in hot and humid weather. It is not surprising there are no overweight infantry soldiers in our unit. It's the best fitness program in the world—if you don't mind getting shot at from time to time.

As part of our send-off for the upcoming operation, our First Sergeant Paul Purcell has brought out a much welcome hot meal out of standard army issue mobile mess hall "marmite cans." (Purcell is a good first sergeant, but he can no longer join us in the field due to health problems.) The insulated mermite cans are made of aluminum and painted olive drab. Some say that's how the food tastes. Complaints about Army chow are legendary, but there are none today. We've not had a hot meal in weeks. Each mermite can holds 4.5 gallons of hot or cold food. It takes 6–8 mermite cans to serve a full meal to an infantry company and we completely empty every container.

The hot meal, cold beer, cokes, and ice cream are a rare treat for infantry soldiers. We don't know it, but it will be another four weeks before our next hot meal. Knowing we are being sent on a tough mission, one of our guys loudly jokes "Enjoy it fellows, they're feeding us our last meal!" For some, that will be true.

***

Casualties and Awards

During the past month, total casualties in the 1-501st are on the whole much less than we expected given the A Shau's notorious reputation. The lack of heavy enemy contact is the primary reason. Our entire battalion has 6 soldiers killed and 33 wounded. In our Headquarters Company no one has been KIA, 3 were WIA (all medics); Alpha Company has 1 KIA, 5 WIA; Bravo 2 KIA, 4 WIA; Charlie 2 KIA, 17 WIA; and Echo (Recon) no KIAs, 1 WIA. Delta Company has 1 KIA and 3 WIA (3 by friendly fire, 1 by enemy mine). Two soldiers, SP5 Robert Lyons, a medic supporting Bravo Company and SP4 Delmar Dennis, from the Recon Platoon, were KIA just prior to the 1-501st arriving in the A Shau.

Most of our wounded will recover, but they will carry the physical scars of their wounds for life, a constant reminder they escaped death in the A Shau. Soldiers who were very seriously wounded may also carry emotional scars. Those who lost their lives will be a stark reminder to all that death came calling. Those who make it home alive will long remember the men who died, faithful soldiers who gave their lives in the Valley of Death.

Casualty Table 4: 1-501st, 5 April–15 May 1969

Casualties	HHC	A Co	B Co	C Co	D Co	E Co	Total
KIA	1	1	2	2	1	1	8
WIA	3	5	4	17	3	1	33
Total	4	6	6	19	4	2	41

1-501st Soldiers Killed in Action, 6 April–15 May 1969

Delta Company—1
22 April: SP4 Nickolas Garcia, age 21, born 18 November 1947, from Five Points, CA
Alpha Company—1
18 April: SP4 Lloyd Jones, age 27, born 29 August 1941 from Mystic, IA
Bravo Company—2
13 April: SP4 Ralph McMurtry, age 24, born 1 July 1944 from Gallatin, TN
14 April: PFC Charles Crosby, age 19, born 21 September 1949 from Orlando, FL
Charlie Company—2
15 April: SGT Albert Creamer, age 24, born 9 July 1944 from West Pelzer, SC
15 April: PFC John McDonald, age 22, born 31 October 1946 from Hahira, GA
Echo Company (Recon)—1 (KIA prior to move to A Shau)
9 April: SP4 Delmar Dennis, age 20, 28 December 1948 from Salem, SC

Headquarters Company—1 (KIA prior to move to A Shau)
6 April: SP5 Robert Lyons (B Co medic), age 25, 10 August 1943 from Wichita, KS

1-501st Soldier Awards, 5 April–15 May 1969 (other awards may have been made that were not mentioned in after action reports)

Silver Star—1
Headquarters Company: 15 April, SP4 Fletcher Nowlin
Bronze Star—19
Delta Company: 5 April, SGT James Littleton, SP4 Ralph Franklin (prior to move to A Shau)
Alpha Company: 18 April, SGT Frederic Davis, SP4 Jeffrey Cahen, SP4 Lawrence Waite; 3 May, 1LT James Judkins, SGT Daniel Calabro, PFC Martin Beckham
Charlie Company: 7 April, 1 LT Donald Gourley, SSG Kenneth Buesing, SP4 George Drape; 15 April, 1LT Daniel O'Neill, SSG Walter Jensen, SGT Wallace Kruesi, SGT David Ratliff, SP4 Danny McCoy, SP4 Jerry Scott
Recon Platoon: 10 April, 1LT Valentine Zapert, SGT Charles Lewis
Army Commendation Medal—1
Alpha Company: 3 May, SP4 Stephen Spaulding
Purple Heart—41 awards to all those KIA or WIA

PART 2

Initial Combat Operations at Tam Ky

15 May–2 June 1969

"Their world can never be known to you, but if you could see them just once, just for an instant, you would know no matter how hard people work back home, they are not keeping pace with these infantrymen."—Ernie Pyle[17]

Arrival and First Combat Assault

15–16 May

15 May: The Move to Tam Ky

Transport and Arrival

Fed and fully combat loaded, at 1440H Delta Company and its sister companies board Air Force C-130 troop transports for their short 45-minute flight. Tam Ky is located 109 miles to the south of Phu Bai. Each infantry company requires two aircraft. It is one of the war's fastest, largest, and furthest daytime redeployments of a brigade within a combat zone. By 1821H on 15 May, our entire battalion has closed on the Tam Ky airstrip (BT309187) ready for combat. The 1-502nd will arrive early tomorrow.

The C-130 flights fly our battalion to Tam Ky without incident. In all, 69 C-130 sorties (individual aircraft flights) are needed to move the brigade. In addition, CH-47 Chinook helicopters are also used. The 1-501st Battalion S-3 section which now includes SSG Tepner, moves by CH-47. Not far from landing at Tam Ky, they take fire from an enemy 12.7 mm anti-aircraft heavy machine gun. A round passes through the cargo area leaving a 2" hole coming in and going out. Fortunately, no one is hit.

Our Battalion's Initial Field Strength at Tam Ky

The size or strength of an infantry battalion like the 1st Battalion, 501st Infantry varies significantly depending on which of three strength levels are being considered: authorized strength, assigned strength, or field (fighting) strength. In this late stage of the war there is a huge discrepancy between authorized strength and fighting strength.

The authorized strength for each of our four infantry companies is 6 officers and 164 enlisted. Echo Company's authorized strength is 4 officers and 96 enlisted. The battalion's authorized strength (not counting HHC) is 756. We are going into combat with 55% of our authorized strength. With expected casualties and even

Field Strength Table 1: 1-501st Initial Field Strength, Tam Ky, 15 May 1969

Unit	A Co	B Co	C Co	D Co	E Co	Total
Officers	5	4	4	4	2	19
Enlisted	88	93	80	99	39	399
Total	93	97	84	103	41	418

fewer replacements, our battalion will soon fall well below half of our authorized strength. Our sister battalions, the 1-502nd and the 1-46th, the latter attached from the Americal Division, are similarly undermanned. In addition to the three infantry battalions assigned to 1st Brigade, there's also supporting artillery, helicopter, and supply units. They will operate from support bases in our area of operations.

Our battalion's initial fighting strength at Tam Ky is 19 officers and 399 enlisted (according to the 1-501st *Operation Lamar Plain* after action report.) Field Strength Table 1 shows our field strength by company. Our Headquarters and Headquarters Company (HHC) includes another 14 officers and more than 100 enlisted. Echo Company incudes the Recon and Mortar Platoons.

The 1-501st after action report also shows the assigned strength of the five companies (Alpha–Echo) at the beginning of the operation is 601 soldiers. That includes those who are sick or injured, soldiers in rear jobs, on leave, and replacements not yet in the field. The field strength in the chart is based on numbers actually flown to Tam Ky for battle. The field strength of officers does not include the artillery forward observer lieutenant attached to each company from the supporting artillery battalion.

Information about our mission has been sketchy. After 1st Brigade is placed under the operational control (OPCON) of the Americal Division, we are finally told what's happening and why we have been rushed to Tam Ky. The Americal Division has declared a "tactical emergency." The 2nd NVA division is attempting to capture Tam Ky, the capital of Quang Tin Province. They are threatening to overrun LZ Professional and other US bases. They have already hit ARVN units hard. We are there to stop them. Other than that, not much information is yet available on our specific battalion or company's mission.

At Tam Ky Airfield

The small asphalt strip at Tam Ky is a strange sight, much different from Phu Bai. Our battalion of 400-plus combat-ready, heavy-laden soldiers is tightly packed in an encampment along both sides of the airfield. They are all doing what soldiers do before combat. Cleaning rifles, checking equipment, sleeping, a few reading a paperback novel carried in their rucksack. Some are talking in small groups. Others write letters home knowing it could be their last.

May Back in the World

1 May	Top hit *Aquarius/Let the Sunshine In* by The Fifth Dimension
1 May	Mr. Fred Rogers receives first PBS grant for *Mister Roger's Neighborhood*
9 May	100,000 in Wash DC protest Kent State shootings and Cambodia incursion
11 May	Mother's Day is an anxious day for hundreds of thousands with sons in Vietnam
15 May	Governor Reagan quells riots at Berkley UC by 3,000 white students
15 May	Abe Fortas is first Supreme Court Justice to resign for improprieties
15 May	Earliest confirmed HIV death, 18-year-old teenager
18–26 May	Apollo 10 launches, orbits moon 31x, rehearses moon landing, safely returns
20 May	150,000 rally on Wall Street in support of Vietnam War
21 May	Silver Springs MD draft office demolished by war protesters
25 May	*Midnight Cowboy* released (#3 '69)
28 May	University of Tennessee, 500 students protest war at Billy Graham Crusade
30 May	Memorial Day antiwar groups take 24 hours to read names of 35,000 war dead
30 May	Families from every state grieve Vietnam War dead from the US's longest war

Our soldiers are holding their most personal thoughts to themselves. No one is openly talking about their fears about the mission ahead. The tight bond within the company is a source of confidence. We are all in this together. There is lots of joking and good-natured teasing. A few dismiss their fears with bold talk. At some level, all of us are fearful both before and in combat. Some more than others. The unspoken expectation is soldiers will overcome their fear and do their duty. That is a good working definition of courage under fire.

My pre-battle anxiety is somewhat allayed because I'm confident we have a solid company. Our movement report shows we are 99 strong with about 30 soldiers in each of our three platoons. Our weapons platoon with machine guns and mortars are put in our three platoons. Only one 81 mm mortar crew is retained at company headquarters. Other mortarmen are serving as riflemen in the platoons. Most of our soldiers have been in the field for months, some for many months. We have had few replacements. We are an experienced unit. Our guys are physically and mentally tough. They know their weapons and small unit tactics.

In my mind and perhaps the mind of others, there is one area of uncertainty that remains. Our company has not been in any extended firefights with a large, well-trained, and well-equipped NVA unit. That is likely to happen and happen soon. It will be a tougher test than anything we've faced since I joined the company in January. It's not a thought to dwell on.

First Night at Tam Ky

The sun has set. We are getting ready for our first night at Tam Ky. It's been a very long day. In the last ten hours, we've moved from the A Shau to Phu Bai to Tam Ky. As dark closes over the airfield, we settle in for the night. Confined to the grassy area along the airstrip, we are not in a tactical setup. Alpha Company is providing our perimeter security so Delta and the other companies are able to get some needed sleep.

All of us are ready for a good rest not knowing what tomorrow will bring. At 2345H, we are well asleep when five 60 mm mortar rounds fall close by just outside our perimeter. There are no casualties. Most of our guys don't even stir. Those that wake up are soon back asleep. It's only the local Viet Cong welcome wagon saying hello and welcome to Tam Ky. Our arrival hasn't gone unnoticed.

16 May: Our First Combat Assault

Combat Operations Begin

The next day, we awake at first light expecting to be on the move soon. We are not. There is a delay while an aerial reconnaissance of our area of operations is made. At mid-morning, CPT Begley tells us we will make a battalion combat assault by helicopter later today. The pickup zone (PZ) is our current location at Tam Ky Airfield. Bravo Company and the Recon Platoon are going in first. Charlie and Delta will follow in order. Alpha Company will remain at the airstrip for security. We don't get any specifics on the enemy situation.

Alpha Company of the 101st Assault Helicopter Battalion will carry us to the battlefield with their UH-1D Huey Iroquois helicopters. Using 15 helicopters, they will continue to shuttle units from the PZ to the LZ until all three of our companies and the Recon Platoon are on the ground. Map 1 gives an overview of the battalion's initial heliborne combat assault and the first five days of combat operations at Tam Ky described in this and the following chapter. The battalion's plan, not known to us at platoon level, is for our three companies to be inserted well north (about 6 km or 3.6 mi) north of the firebase, LZ Professional. The companies will fan

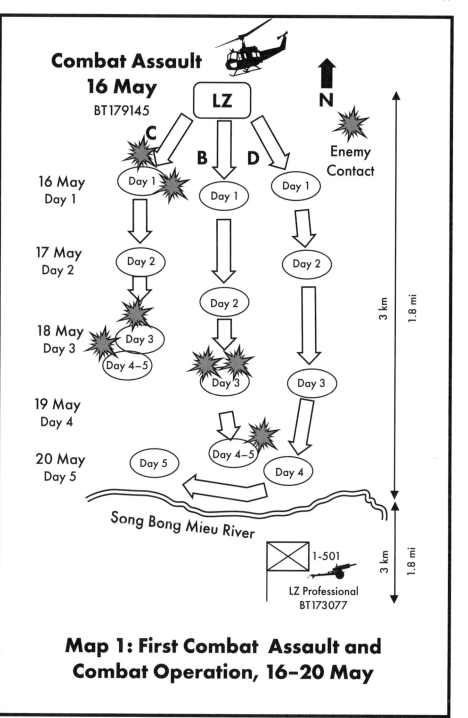

Map 1: First Combat Assault and Combat Operation, 16–20 May

out upon landing and move south toward LZ Professional (BT173077) on three parallel routes conducting reconnaissance in force (RIF) missions expecting to find and engage NVA forces of a yet unknown size.

The battalion LZ at BT179145 is 15 km (9 mi) southwest of Tam Ky. Temperatures are expected to climb to 120 degrees by mid-afternoon with humidity above 90%. The area around the airstrip where we're encamped is already approaching 100 degrees. Eggs could be cooked on the black asphalt runway. We haven't yet acclimated to the hotter climate. The mountainous A Shau Valley area was much cooler.

The terrain at the LZ is relatively flat and open with scrub brush and wild wheat-like grass surrounded by tree-covered hills. It's a large, former rural village, now uninhabited and in ruins from years of war. The LZ will be prepped with artillery before our arrival. We are told to expect a hot LZ, immediate enemy contact on landing. At 1455H artillery preparation of the battalion's LZ begins. As artillery fires fall, Bravo Company is picked up at the Tam Ky airstrip in three lifts offive UH-1 Huey's each. Bravo's first lift touches down at the LZ on time at 1511H just as the artillery ceases. The LZ is green. No enemy contact on landing. Bravo Company begins moving south to its objective.

An Air Cav team from Bravo Troop, 2-17th Cav, provides close air support as the artillery prep ends. The team's two AH-1G HueyCobras have a mix of aerial rockets, 7.62 mm miniguns, and a 40 mm rapid-fire grenade launcher. The team also has two LOH-Cayuse helicopters with mini-guns. They will scout targets for the team. By 1535H all of Bravo Company and the Recon Platoon have landed without taking enemy fire.

At 1600H, as one of the AH-1G Cobra gunships extends its reconnaissance 8 km to the south of the LZ, it receives 15–20 rounds of small arms fire from BT159069. The helicopter takes two hits and returns fire. A second Cobra gunship receives 50 rounds of small arms automatic weapons fire at 1615H from BT148067. It also takes two hits. Both aircraft remain on station covering our landing.

There is a temporary halt in the lift of Charlie Company while the two Cobras attack the enemy positions which fired on them. Charlie Company's lift is soon resumed and completed at 1640H. Once on the ground, Charlie Company begins moving southwest. There is no enemy contact on the ground so far.

Delta Company's Combat Assault

A combat assault by helicopter is a unique, fast-paced, often dangerous experience. Adrenaline is on full flow. Everything is rapidly accomplished by standard operating procedure (SOP) in four simple steps: pickup, load, air movement, then off load. Delta Company is first positioned on the airstrip prepared for pick up. We load by platoons. Each platoon is divided into loads of five or six soldiers. A seventh soldier will be fitted into loads as needed. Five helicopters are used to move a 30-man platoon. For rapid loading, we sit along the runway half of each load on one side, half on the other side. The five Hueys in each lift lands in between each pre-positioned load.

At 1650H, Delta Company's 2nd Platoon is the first lift to be picked up. That makes sense. LT Black has SFC Rios as platoon sergeant and he is our most experienced infantry leader. CPT Begley and his FO, two RTOs, and medic go on the first lift with 2nd Platoon. If we have enemy contact as expected, Begley will have the immediate capability to call in artillery or attack helicopters. At 1702H, the 1st Platoon, our second lift, is picked up with LT Boyd and SSG Sahrle leading them.

The lift of 3rd Platoon is at 1710H. As 3rd Platoon sits along the airstrip, we can see the returning helicopters about a quarter mile away turning and descending as they line up with the runway on their approach. They come in fast, nose high as they flare and slow for landing. The Hueys hover briefly before sitting down on the asphalt pavement.

From the tip of one Huey's rotor to the next is no more than 75 ft. Rotor blade and engine noise is deafening. Rotor wash is strong enough to blow a soldier's almost 3 lb. steel helmet off his head. Some soldiers use their helmet's chin strap only when jumping on or off a helicopter.

Loading takes less than a minute. As each helicopter lands, 3rd Platoon's pre-positioned loads stand up and move quickly in a crouch to the helicopter loading from both sides. The throbbing noise of the five Hueys landing is so loud talking is difficult. There's no need to talk. Everyone knows what to do. The large cargo doors allow two soldiers to get in each door at the same time. Once the first soldiers are in, they extend their hands and pull the others on board. I position myself and my RTO in the third Huey of our five-ship lift. My three squad leaders are in the first, third and fifth helicopters. When we land, I want to be in the middle of my platoon with my squad leaders close by.

There's a pilot and co-pilot up front. The Hueys have a door gunner on each side just at the rear of the open cargo door. Each gunner has a M-60 machine gun on a swivel mount. The two pilots and gunners all wear flight helmets with dark visors. They can talk to one another through their headsets which are part of their helmets.

The senior pilot is in the left seat. He is facing forward calmly controlling the aircraft and holding it steady as we load. He is busy monitoring his flight instruments for signs of trouble; scanning the area outside of the helicopter alert for danger or anything that might affect his helicopter's liftoff and flight. He is also listening for the flight leader's signal they're ready for liftoff.

The co-pilot in the right seat looking back at us as scramble aboard with our equipment and weapons. He gives a quick smile and wave. The lower half of his face shows he is not much older than the young soldiers piling into the open cargo space. Both pilot and co-pilot are brave souls. They've already carried soldiers of Bravo and Charlie Companies to the battle. They are not only taking us to battle, but they will also keep us supplied, fly out our wounded and dead, and pick us up when we are done. They are constantly in danger to enemy fire as they fly or land. Along with medics and artillerymen, they are the best friends of infantry soldiers.

As we finish loading, I give a thumbs up to the co-pilot signaling we are in. He returns it. We are ready to go. The pilot prepares to lift off. The engine revs, the blades are louder as they rotate faster, vibration shakes the chopper's light aluminum frame. The pilot is awaiting the flight leader's command. He's ready to lift off as soon as he hears "let's go" and sees the helicopter to his front take off. On cue, like a flock of huge birds, the five helicopters rise to flight. Each one pauses only a second or two to allow space between their helicopter and the one in front. Nose down, we make a short run down the airstrip and climb fast to our flight altitude of 300 ft. We fall into our flight's staggered trail formation flying southwest from Tam Ky. We are on the way.

The move to the LZ will take just five minutes. The small team of soldiers on our Huey lean back on their rucks, feet toward the open doors on each side ready to jump. I'm in the middle leaning against the rear bulkhead so I can exit from either door. I look at the faces of my soldiers. Two seem lost in their thoughts, another has his head bowed and eyes closed, perhaps silently praying. I smile and give a thumbs up to another. I admire these young soldiers. There is no whining or complaining. Whether volunteers or draftees, you can't tell them apart. They're all committed to getting our job done despite the imminent danger. Like Ernie Pyle said, no one is harder at work than an infantryman going into battle.

The cool, rushing wind blows through our jungle fatigues, a welcome relief from the hot, humid climate below. The momentary comfort is appreciated. Ahead, I can see the smoke from the artillery preparatory fires hanging over the LZ. As we approach, the Hueys drop to tree-top level to avoid enemy fire. The alert door gunners pull the bolt of their guns to the rear ready to fire.

In a minute or so, we will be on the ground. All eyes are looking out now, every ear listening for incoming small arms fire or worse. Worse are white trails of incoming rocket propelled grenades (RPGs) or the bright green tracers from tripod-mounted, anti-aircraft, 12.7 mm (.51 cal) heavy machine guns. We've all heard about the heavy machine guns.

I lean over to look out the right door to see the size and shape of the LZ. I also want to see where we are landing, the compass heading of our landing, and which way our platoon will move once we exit the chopper to link up with our company. There is a large grass fire covering several acres burning on other parts of the LZ sparked by artillery prep fires. We will land away and upwind from the fires. One of our sister companies had several soldiers suffer smoke inhalation serious enough to require medevac.

There is nothing like coming in low and fast into an unknown battlefield thinking you'll be shot at as you land or soon after. (This is why for many infantry veterans, the sound of a Huey chopper later in life immediately recalls tense moments that happened long ago.) We haven't been updated on Bravo and Charlie's previous insertions. To our surprise and relief, the enemy has decided not to engage us on the LZ.

At 1725H, the last flight of Delta Company is on the LZ. We jump off the Hueys, quickly spreading out, moving crouched low some 10 m away from the helicopter's blades. My squad leaders and I exit on the right side, the direction we will be moving. We kneel and take up hasty security positions. Once clear of the aircraft, I give the copilot a quick salute, thanking his crew for their good work. He acknowledges my signal.

The flight of Hueys takes off. Their time on the ground is less than a minute. We move into the tree line where our company is assembling its platoons preparing to move out to our first day's objective. There's only two hours or so of daylight left. We need to get on the move fast.

Moving to Our Objectives

It is late afternoon. All three companies have departed the LZ (BT179145) and are fanning out as they move south on separate axes of advance. See Map 1. Each company's objective is about 1.5 km or just short of a mile from the LZ. However, "straight line map distances" don't accurately indicate the actual distance units must move, the difficulty of the move, or the time it may take to make the move.

Due to the staggered arrival at the LZ, the units are not abreast of one another. Bravo and Recon who landed first are in the center and well out front of the other two companies by 500 or more meters as they move to their objectives at BT173132 and BT174132. Charlie Company is on the right flank to the northwest of Bravo Company and moving southwest to its objective at BT165137. Delta Company is on the left flank moving southeast to BT183131. Coming in last to the LZ, we are almost an hour behind Bravo Company. We are all moving cautiously at a slow walk in unknown territory, expecting enemy contact at any moment. The late afternoon sun is much hotter than expected.

The company objectives are chosen to guide the direction of our movement as we conduct our RIF missions looking for the enemy. The area through which we are moving has a number of heavily wooded hills several hundred feet high and up to 2 km in length, running from north to south. They tend to channel our movement. The area in between the hills is generally flat, but overgrown and like the LZ, appears abandoned. There are no visible intact huts and very few ruins. Were it not indicated on our maps, we would not know the area was once a large, thriving village. There are no signs of life, people or animals.

Ideal locations for enemy ambushes are everywhere. As the companies move south, we are increasing our separation from one another. On reaching our three objectives, we will be about 1,000 m (.6 mi) apart. The increased separation allows us to cover more ground and improves our likelihood of enemy contact.

First Enemy Contact

At 1745H, as Charlie Company moves up and along a 300 ft wooded hill just short of their objective, they are fired upon by several AK-47s from BT168139. They return fire with two M-60 machine guns, an M-79, and several M-16 rifles. As Charlie Company maneuvers their 2nd Platoon to flank the enemy position, they see three enemy soldiers flee to the south over the crest of the hill. Charlie Company requests aerial rocket artillery (ARA) from the Cobra Team's two attack helicopters still overflying our area of operations. After the engagement, Charlie's 2nd Platoon moves to the location where the enemy was engaged. They find one bloody shirt, no bodies.

At 1945H, Delta Company reports seeing six enemy soldiers at BT186146 on a wooded slope several hundred meters on our left flank to the east. As the enemy is engaged with artillery, they flee northeast. No enemy casualties are identified. It is getting late. The sun is setting and our movement must cease soon. We are in unknown territory. Moving at night is too risky.

End of Day One in the Field

At 2015H, Bravo Company and the Recon Platoon, having moved 1400 m, reaches their objective and establishes their night defensive position (NDP) at BT174132. Charlie Company is also at its objective after a move of 1200 m and has its NDP at BT165137. Soon afterwards, due to the loss of light, Delta Company, having moved 1100 m, stops 600 m short of its objective (BT183131) on easily defended terrain and sets up its NDP at BT183137. As a point of clarification, NDPs are often different from the day's initial objective. We had the furthest to go to our objective and were the last in to the LZ. There have been no further incidents and no casualties in our battalion today from enemy activity.

It has been another very long day. We are finally in the field at Tam Ky and glad to be away from Tam Ky Airfield. Our first day has been uneventful in terms of enemy contact. We got into the LZ without having to fight our way in. Our first tactical move was successful and unopposed. We and our sister companies have had our first enemy sightings even if they were small teams. They weren't seeking a fight with us, apparently just making their presence known.

The enemy knows we are here. The landing of nearly 50 helicopters over several hours at the LZ wasn't exactly a stealthy arrival. We are on our enemy's home turf and they know the neighborhood and we don't. That is not the only advantage the enemy has. Our units will be on the move. The enemy may simply keep tabs on us and avoid us until we are on terrain of their choosing.

With today's light contact, it is tempting to think this may be like the A Shau where we expected to have heavy contact but didn't. So far, we've had only general reports about large NVA forces in the area, nothing specific. We've had reports like that before. But this is no time to be complacent. It is better to keep our guard up and be ready for heavy contact. Things could change very quickly.

Safely in our NDP, we've set up our perimeter making the best defensive use of the terrain. There are trees and shrubs and some changes of elevation in the ground that permit good fighting positions. Our company perimeter is generally circular about 140 m (460 ft) around and near 40–50 m (130–164 ft) in diameter. We could fit neatly into one half of a football field. Each platoon has a sector to cover (or defend) that is about 50 m long. The company command post (CP) is in the middle. When we are set up no one can tell we are there. That is unless one of the enemy teams we saw today watched us move into our NDP. That is very likely.

After our positions are in and weapons checked, it's time to break out the C-Rations. There are no fires, lights, loud talking or other noises. A can of applesauce or fruit cocktail is high on the menu. Anything with liquid. We will soon be ready for sleep. Our platoon, like our other two platoons, is in three-man positions. One person in each position remains awake on two-hour watches before waking the next guy. The handoffs will continue until daylight. Each position usually draws straws or does rock-paper-scissors to see who is on watch first. Two-hour watches are common through the dark hours of the night. With longer watches, soldiers tend to doze off.

Sitting in a hole dug in the damp earth staring out into the dark looking and listening for enemy movement takes discipline. You can't lean back and rest your head or lean forward and rest your elbows for even a minute without falling asleep. Every now and then your eyes will play tricks on you. Did I see something move? Was it just my imagination? What was that sound? The guessing game goes on all night.

Infantry soldiers go to sleep in their clothes with boots on and weapons close by, realizing nighttime is a good time for an enemy attack. Sleep may be uneasy. If you are on the next watch, you'll be awakened in two hours no matter how much or little sleep you have had. Making it through the two hours on watch is tough. After a strenuous day, all soldiers fight falling asleep on watch. Time goes by slowly and slows down further if you keep checking your watch.

Sleep comes easy after a stressful day. For most infantry soldiers there is not much thought about the difficulties they will face tomorrow. The old saying, "Today is the tomorrow you worried about yesterday" applies well to infantry soldiers. Just getting through each day and taking one day at a time is what works best for most soldiers in combat. One of the few Bible verses I know seems appropriate: "Don't worry about tomorrow, for tomorrow will care for itself. Each day has enough trouble for its own" (Matthew 6:34). Right. We will see what tomorrow brings tomorrow.

(This doesn't mean planning is unimportant for leaders, but even combat leaders have to get through today before they can execute tomorrow's plans.)

The night is uneventful for Delta and our two companies in the field. Alpha Company, still back at the Tam Ky airstrip, receives twenty 60 mm mortar rounds. Fortunately, without casualties. The rounds are believed to be fired from a position populated with civilians, only 300 m from the airstrip. A reminder the enemy is always closer than you think.

**

Casualties and Awards

1-501st Soldiers Killed in Action, 16 May 1969—none

1-501st Soldier Awards, 16 May 1969—none (other awards may have been made that were not mentioned in after action reports)

CHAPTER 4

Finding the Enemy

17–20 May

17 May: A Light Day

An Unexpected Discovery

Waking up on a battlefield is not exactly like waking up in your bedroom back home. As first light dawns, you know sleep time is over. Your eyes open after being aroused from a deep, but short sleep. You quickly realize you are not dreaming. You are an infantryman on a battlefield in Vietnam. Just as suddenly, you realize nothing happened during the night. You are awakening to the beginning of another day, one less day to the end of your Vietnam tour.

At 0645H the battalion TOC, which has been busy through the night, passes a message from brigade to all companies: "Be alert to a strong possibility of increased enemy activity during 16–20 May with a subsequent phase [of activity] during 21–30 May." The intelligence comes all the way from the Joint Chiefs of Staff in Washington DC. This is highly unusual. Sources for the information are not referenced. At any rate, the information is not further communicated to Delta's platoons. Perhaps the intel is too general in nature. Another reason may be that we are already on high alert. No one needs to tell us to anticipate heavy enemy contact.

Delta Company, our other two companies, and the Recon Platoon will continue RIF missions today. Yesterday evening, new objectives were radioed to each unit except Alpha Company which is still on the Tam Ky Airfield security mission. Today's movement continues generally southward toward LZ Professional on three separate axes of advance. Bravo Company and Recon Platoon are to move to BT175117; Charlie Company to BT165126, and Delta to BT183127. The distance to the new objectives is about 1 km (little more than a half mile). See Map 1.

At 0710H before beginning today's move, Delta Company requests a medevac for a heat casualty identified yesterday evening after we moved into our NDP. It was too late to medevac him in the dark and the soldier hoped he would improve during the night. Though he is conscious, he is still too weak and wouldn't make it very far with the tropical sun beating down.

At 0745H, Bravo Company is already moving. They've come upon 20 children ages 6–12 huddled in a dilapidated hut at BT172137. They are detained and questioned by Bravo's Kit Carson Scout. Two women soon appear and they are also detained. Apparently the women were taking the children out of harm's way when they saw or heard soldiers approaching. They put the children in the hut and hid nearby until they thought it safe to come out. After being questioned, they are released and cautioned about the danger of going south in the direction our companies are moving. They head north.

Discovering children in large numbers is unexpected and somewhat disconcerting. No one wants innocent civilians, especially children, to be injured or killed. Clearly, our area of operations is still inhabited. Our rules of engagement during daylight conditions are clear, we don't fire on unarmed civilians. We have a responsibility to protect them.

Finding civilians in our immediate area of operations has raised caution flags. We are obviously not in a free fire zone. It is also likely that civilian hooches would have trenches or bunkers for their protection. Sorting out civilians and combatants is part of the difficulty on a battlefield where enemy soldiers may use civilian hooches, trenches, or bunkers to their advantage. Viet Cong fighters (male and female) supporting the NVA of course may appear as non-combatants during the day and soldiers at night.

Multiple Bunkers Seen from the Air

At 0830H, an Air Cav Team with two AH-1 HueyCobras and a LOH-6 Cayuse scout helicopter from B/2-17th Cavalry comes on station. They begin scouting the area to the front of our companies for enemy signs. At 0835, they see the open entrance of a tunnel at BT159135 with a U-shaped firing position at its front. No weapon is seen. The location is just 400 m to the west of Charlie Company's objective for today. They don't fire on the position.

At 0855H, the Cav Team discovers a hooch surrounded by fighting positions at BT170144 just off a heavily used trail running northeast to southwest. This position is now well to our north, just 400 m southwest of our LZ yesterday. Coming down to a low hover, they believe the area is occupied and request clearance to open fire on the position. (Typically, the Cav Team must be fired upon first or clearly identify enemy combatants.)

While awaiting clearance to fire (later denied), the Cav Team spots a dozen or so hooches at BT165116. The area is a kilometer south of Charlie Company's objective for today. Each hut has a trench leading to a concealed bunker. The hooches are each about 10 × 15 ft. The bunker appears to be 5 × 6 ft, but is likely larger underground. Each hooch seems to be in use. Clothes (not uniforms) are drying on a clothesline. Again, clearance to fire is withheld pending seeing uniformed enemy or being fired upon.

At 0928H, the Cav Team spots an enemy 12.7 mm (.51 cal) heavy machine-gun position (without a weapon or gun mount), and a connecting tunnel to a bunker. Nearby trails indicate heavy, frequent, and recent use of the position. It's not attacked, but marked for further observation.

Plans for Tomorrow

At 1000H, the battalion TOC receives brigade's plans for tomorrow (18 May). On the third day of the operation, the 1st Brigade commander directs the 1-501st to spread out more as they move south. This will increase the distance between companies with the intent of increasing the likelihood of enemy contact.

Bravo Company will remain on its current axis of advance and move to BT173113 (Hill 187). Charlie Company will be sent another kilometer to the west to BT164121. Delta Company will move a kilometer further to the east to BT183116. There is a risk to the new strategy. If any company engages a large enemy force, it will take longer to bring the companies together. High temperatures and humidity will limit the speed of movement. All combat, by its very nature, always involves taking risks. Alpha remains at Tam Ky Airfield.

At 1015H, the Cav Team spots a 12 × 12 ft bunker at BT178117 made of logs and dirt. It is not clear this is an enemy bunker. So far today, no enemy soldiers or weapons have been spotted or engaged by the Cav Team. Every time aviators fly up close to a bunker to check out suspected enemy positions, they risk their lives. Flying skills, courage, patience, and good judgment are required. Their decisions may be costly to themselves and others. Bravo Company will likely be passing near the bunker in a day or so.

At platoon level we are not getting reports of the frequent sightings of suspected enemy positions all over our area of operations. But, moving on the ground, we have seen enough to conclude we are operating in an area unlike any we've seen before. There are bunkers everywhere. Having the Cav Team overhead is reassuring. They can quickly engage verified enemy targets and their presence makes it difficult for enemy soldiers to move about during daylight.

More Heat Casualties

As the noon sun climbs high into the bright blue sky, our three companies and Recon Platoon continue their RIF missions. In the strength-sapping tropical oven and humidity, heat casualties begin to mount. We are new to Tam Ky's hot climate, frequently well over 95° in late May with humidity above 90%. In our first days we are moving exposed to the sun's merciless heat.

In the A Shau we mostly conducted operations under a triple canopy in much cooler temperatures. No one is complaining about the heat, at least not out loud.

Soldiers are allowed to gripe about conditions, but infantrymen are expected to tough it out no matter the weather. That's probably part of the problem. No one wants to admit the heat is getting to them.

At 1225H, Bravo Company requests medevac for two heat casualties. One is unconscious. At 1300H, Charlie Company has a heat casualty. By 1326H, Bravo has three more (two from Recon moving with Bravo). All need medevac. The serious casualty is taken direct to 27th Surgical Hospital in Chu Lai. Others are first taken to Tam Ky Airfield for medical evaluation. If their condition requires it, they are flown to Tam Ky North for further evaluation and given saline IVs, plenty of water, and a day or two of rest.

Soldiers are quickly returned to the field as soon as their condition permits. All of our soldiers know to stay hydrated. The problem is we haven't come across any water to refill our canteens. We will need water resupply every day in this heat. By 1400H, medevacs have picked up all heat casualties.

At 1417H, current locations for each unit are reported. Bravo and Recon are at BT175131. They've only moved some 500 m south from their NDP due to heat casualties and checking out suspected enemy bunkers. Charlie Company is at BT173138. They've spent most of the day moving east out of an area so thick with vegetation it was slowing their movement. They are now 700 m directly north of Bravo Company. Delta Company is at BT186133, a kilometer east of Bravo Company.

At 1435H, a Bravo Troop, 2nd Squadron, 17th Cavalry LOH flying over BT190079 spots a platoon-sized enemy unit and takes small arms fire shattering the helicopter's plexiglass canopy. Fragments of glass wound an onboard observer. An accompanying helicopter calls in artillery on the enemy location.

At 1510H, Alpha Company has a serious heat exhaustion case who must be flown directly to the 27th Surgical Hospital at Chu Lai. At 1540H, Bravo Company has two more heat injuries requiring use of a basket to extract the casualties. At 1645H, two more heat casualties are evacuated from Bravo Company.

At 1805H, unit locations are updated again. Bravo Company and Recon are at BT175117. They reached their objective for today having moved due south some 1400 m during a brutally hot afternoon. Perhaps too far, too fast in the heat. When infantry units are assigned objectives, they push to accomplish the mission. It is in an infantryman's DNA. Charlie Company has also moved a long distance in the heat, 1800 m to their objective at BT164126. They are still almost a kilometer northwest of Bravo Company. Delta is at BT183130. We've covered only 300 m in the afternoon and CPT Begley is calling a temporary halt in the heat. We were slowed down moving through terrain with pretty thick undergrowth. Morale is lifted by our stop. We have no further heat casualties.

At company, platoon, and certainly down at squad levels, we don't know the rationale behind the objectives we are told to reach. Our job is simply to get there and find the enemy as we move. That has been true for infantry in every war, including this one. Still, there is a temptation to think those up the chain of command are just sticking pins in a map. They aren't moving on the ground with us. An old saying comes to mind, "Nothing is impossible for the man who does not have to do it himself."

End of Day Two

Despite the nine heat casualties in our battalion today, there have been no casualties due to enemy contact. Perhaps the enemy is allowing the heat to soften us up before engaging us? Don't think that will work. We will get acclimatized soon enough. At 1915H, NDPs are occupied and reported. Bravo and Recon remain at BT175117 (Hill 187) and Charlie Company is at BT165126, all at their day's objective. Delta is now at BT183127, having moved an additional 300 m in the last hour. Alpha remains at the airfield in Tam Ky.

Everyone has moved into their night positions soaking wet with sweat. We will get a chance to dry out some before sleeping. The heat casualties aren't a matter of lack of leadership at the company level. Units are doing their best moving during the hottest part of the day. Water is being drank, but our supply is limited. The high tropical heat and humidity in Tam Ky's coastal region is the issue. It is physically draining even if soldiers stay somewhat hydrated. We will need a water source or resupply soon. The five to six quarts of water each soldier carries are not enough in these conditions with the combat loads we are humping.

In reflecting on the day's activity, the frequent sightings of bunkers and firing positions makes it clear we are in a combat zone with active enemy elements. We've been in the field two days and have yet to encounter an enemy force of any size. They are obviously here. Too many US aircraft have been fired on by both small arms and heavy machine guns. The heavy guns are a clear sign that larger NVA units are operating nearby. Anticipation is growing. It is likely only a matter of time before they let us find them. As we know, that likely will be at a time and place of their choosing. We have another night without incident.

18 May: Enemy Contact Increases

Today's Objectives

Company objectives given yesterday remain valid today. Bravo Company and Recon will move just a few hundred meters south to the high ground on Hill 187 at BT174114. Both have advanced much further south than Charlie and Delta Companies. It is tactically preferable, all things being equal (and they usually are not) for the three companies to advance on one front. This makes it more difficult for the enemy to engage one company at a time. We can also better cover each other's flanks. Bravo needs to slow down or Charlie and Delta need to catch up. Alpha remains at Tam Ky Airfield.

Charlie is to move 500 m south to BT164121. They will still be almost a kilometer to the northwest of Bravo Company. Delta Company is moving south approximately one kilometer to BT185116 along an elongated tree-covered hill. Delta Company will come abreast of Bravo Company one kilometer to the east and will also be on high ground.

Bravo Takes Heavy Casualties

At 0710H, Bravo Company receives 6–7 rounds of 60 mm fire. All rounds fall close, but outside Bravo's perimeter. At 0740H they are on the move to Hill 187. At 0830H, as Bravo Company approaches Hill 187, seven 60 mm mortar rounds are fired from an enemy position estimated to be in the vicinity of BT176117. One soldier is wounded by shell fragments. The rounds are too close for comfort. Artillery is called in on the position. No return mortar fire is received.

At 0835H, the 1-501st TOC closes operations at the Tam Ky Airfield and at 1100H moves to LZ Professional (BT173077) which becomes our battalion's forward operating base. For the time being, Alpha Company will remain at the airfield. Movement and activity of units is monitored as the TOC relocates.

At 0930H, Bravo Company receives three more incoming 60 mm mortar rounds without casualties. Again, artillery fire is called in on the suspected position. Again, no further 60 mm fire is received. Even so, it seems the enemy has Bravo Company under close observation. At 1050H, soon after Bravo's lead platoon arrives on Hill 187, five more 60 mm rounds land nearby. There are still no casualties.

Unknown to Bravo Company, the enemy has been in the area long enough to have established multiple mortar firing positions, with each firing position having predetermined target lists. Key terrain features like Hill 187 are likely high on such a list. By 1120H, artillery, attack helicopters and an air strike are used in sequence to fire on and destroy suspected enemy mortar positions. As is often the case, results are not known.

At 1225H, as Bravo continues to set up and dig in on Hill 187, three heavier enemy 82 mm mortar rounds slam into Bravo Company, wounding eight soldiers. Bravo Company's FO calls in artillery on the suspected mortar position causing a large secondary explosion. No further enemy mortar fire is received. There's a sigh of relief that the 82 mm mortar position appears to have been knocked out.

Two hours later at 1640H, three more 82 mm rounds fall on Bravo Company. The company command post takes a direct hit. The Bravo Company Commander CPT John Pape is severely wounded. He soon dies despite a medic's valiant effort to save him. CPT Pape's RTO, SP4 Lincoln Bundy is also killed by the same mortar round along with two medics, SP5 Hans Mills and SP4 Russell Jett. Several more Bravo Company soldiers are wounded.

At 1645H, CPT Begley reports he may know the location of the 82 mm mortar firing on Bravo Company and is moving our company to take it out. At 1656H, LTC Singer is enroute to Bravo's location in his command helicopter. He is bringing in two additional medics to aid in treatment of the wounded. Singer will remove CPT Pape and SP4 Bundy. He confirms medevacs are on the way to pick up the wounded.

At 1705H Bravo continues to be mortared. By 1720H, during a brief halt in the enemy shelling, all KIAs and WIAs are evacuated. More rounds are received at 1723H, another soldier is WIA. No further incoming rounds are received. Total casualties for Bravo Company today are 4 KIA and 12 WIA plus two Recon soldiers WIA and a medic from Headquarters Company. The medic, SP4 Daniel Thurston, will have his wound cleaned and bandaged by Gary Winkler, his close buddy and fellow Recon medic. Then, he will quickly return to the field.

Bravo Company's wounded include: SSGs Joe Little and Lee Pinkerton; SGT Dorsey Brewer; SP4s Robert Dawson, Jay Erb, Wayne Hastings, Randy Wright, David Yamamura, and PFCs Ellis Autman, Neil Forman, Lewis Kirkbride, and Eugene Simon. Along with these casualties, Bravo Company has five more heat casualties.

At 1730H, CPT John Gay, the battalion's S-3 air officer responsible for coordination of air support, is told by LTC Singer he is the new Bravo commander. Gay already had figured he was next in line and has his gear ready to go. At 1801H, Singer flies Gay into Bravo Company. It's a tough time to take command, but Bravo needs him now, not tomorrow.

Charlie Company Is Ambushed

At 0730H, while Bravo Company is being mortared, CPT Dave Gibson's Charlie Company moves toward its objective. Gibson sends SFC Isaac Hayward's 1st Platoon around the backside of the hill where they are headed. The rest of Charlie Company waits on a needed resupply. Just as the helicopter drops off ammunition, rations, and water, heavy firing breaks out on the top of the hill.

Hayward's platoon surprised an enemy platoon by coming up on their rear as they waited to ambush Charlie Company. Enemy fire is intense. PFC Rudy Rossi fires two rounds from his 90 mm recoilless rifle before being killed. PFC John Vollerhausen is also killed. PFC James Coats is wounded, CPL Paul Ganun, the platoon medic, is killed trying to aid the fallen soldiers.

Gibson sends LT Dan O'Neill's 3rd Platoon to reinforce Hayward. Gibson and LT Gourley's 2nd Platoon are attacked at the bottom of the hill before they can move. They kill five NVA with machine gun, rifle fire, and hand grenades. That done, they move the supplies to the top of the hill. They rejoin 1st and 3rd Platoons who have killed another eight NVA.

Charlie Company digs in on the hill preparing for further enemy action. Near dusk, they are hit by mortars. As the barrage ends, a gong sounds below the hill signaling an enemy attack. Charlie Company repels the first of three enemy ground attacks. The exchange of fire is deafening. Two more attacks occur at night, the last around 2200H. All are repelled. One enemy soldier breaks through their perimeter and is killed. The number of enemy casualties is unknown as the NVA remove their dead and wounded under cover of darkness. Gibson thinks the attack may have been a company-sized enemy force.

LTC Singer has an Alpha Company platoon on standby at Tam Ky Airfield to reinforce Charlie Company, but bad weather prevents its arrival. CPT Gibson requests a USAF "Spooky" gunship. Once on station the C-130 is of immediate assistance. The enemy once again attempts to mortar Charlie Company's position. As the mortar's distinct sound is heard as it fires its first round. before the round hits the C-130's mini-guns rain a torrent of 20 mm cannon fire directly on the mortar's firing position. No more mortars are fired at Charlie Company that night. The C-130 remains on station until it is replaced by another gunship. Charlie Company has a needed peaceful night.

End of Day Three

At 1900H in the last minutes of daylight, CPT Begley is moving Delta Company closer to Bravo Company's location before darkness closes in. After making a long southward move of over 1.5 km, we are able to come abreast of their position, but still a kilometer to their east. Surprisingly, we've not had enemy contact, shelling, or casualties today. As we moved, Begley and our three platoon leaders have been following today's battle action on our radios. We know we will soon join the fray.

Battalion casualties today are seven KIA and 16 WIA. This includes the casualties mentioned earlier in this chapter. Five other soldiers are heat casualties. Three of the seven KIAs are medics from Headquarters Company. Two were supporting Bravo Company: Medic SP5 Hans Mills and Medic SP4 Russell Jett. The other medic was supporting Charlie Company: Medic CPL Paul Ganun. All valiant young men.

No one working in support of the infantry has more respect than our medics. When an infantry soldier is wounded, if he can speak, his first words are the call "Medic!" There is no hesitation by medics in answering the call. They instinctively and without instruction move toward the wounded. Usually others have to hold them back, telling them to wait until it can be made safer for them. Sometimes that can't be done and they move to the wounded at great risk to their own lives.

At 2007H, the night defensive position for Bravo Company and Recon Platoon is Hill 187 at BT174114. Charlie Company made it to their objective and are at

BT164121, but are still a kilometer northwest of Bravo Company. Delta Company is at BT185116, a kilometer due east of Bravo Company. With permission from battalion, we moved an additional 400 m south of our day's objective and are now as far south as Bravo Company.

It takes a while to settle down tonight. At 2010H, a USAF AC-47 Spooky gunship is circling Charlie Company's position and dropping flares for the next two hours. Tomorrow is likely to be a different day for Delta Company. There is no doubt now the enemy is willing to engage us. Both Bravo and Charlie Company have been bloodied. Our turn is likely coming soon.

19 May: Heavy Contact Expected

Yesterday was a tough day for Bravo Company. The effectiveness of enemy mortar fire has everyone's attention. We all expect to receive more of the same today. Death raining down from the skies is unsettling. The enemy knows it is to their advantage to engage us with indirect fire weapons from a distance. However, Charlie Company's long afternoon firefight tells us NVA units will stand and fight, especially if they fight from concealed bunkers with overhead protection.

The further south our battalion moves, the more enemy resistance stiffens. Today Bravo Company and Recon Platoon will move southeast a short 500 m to BT178107. This will put Bravo Company just 200 m north of the Song Bong Mieu River. Recon's final position will be on the south end of Hill 187 at BT172109, 400 m north of the river and just several hundred meters to the west of Bravo Company. Our companies will have to cross the river if we are to continue moving south to LZ Professional.

Morning Operations

Charlie Company doesn't move today. It remains in the vicinity of its NDP last night (BT164122) conducting search operations of the enemy bunkers where yesterday's firefight occurred. After searching the abandoned enemy position, CPT Gibson confirms his company may have been fighting an NVA company. This is the largest enemy force engaged so far. They are fortunate their casualties weren't significantly higher.

At 0755H, before moving out, CPT Gay, Bravo Company commander, has his men do a crater analysis of the 82 mm mortar rounds that fell on the company yesterday. An analysis can usually determine the direction from which the rounds were fired and if they were fired from a single mortar or multiple mortars and firing positions. The mortar rounds came from the northeast, apparently from one 82 mm mortar. The craters show the rounds came in at a fairly steep angle, likely the mortars were no more than 1,000 m away.

At 0800H, log birds begin to resupply each company. Charlie Company has first priority due to its long engagement yesterday afternoon. They are in bad need of ammunition and water. At 0807H, a Forward Air Controller (FAC) and Artillery Forward Observer (FO) come on station to support air strikes in support of Charlie Company.

At 0910H, before beginning its move to the southwest, Delta Company finds an abandoned enemy 82 mm mortar firing pit at BT185116 which shows signs of recent use. Begley thinks this is the mortar firing position that fired on Bravo Company on Hill 187 yesterday. The range to Hill 187 is only 900 m, easy firing distance for the enemy mortar. The firing pit is several feet deep, about 8 ft in diameter with a camouflaged, dirt parapet around the position. It is a well-constructed, textbook mortar firing position. The NVA mortar crews know their business.

At 0937H, prior to Charlie Company's air strikes, the TOC asks each company to confirm their location. Bravo Company and the Recon Platoon are at BT174114 still in their NDP location. So is Charlie Company at BT164121. Charlie is still approximately one kilometer northwest of Bravo Company's location. Delta Company has already moved south one kilometer and is at BT177108, now just a few hundred meters east of Bravo Company.

During the afternoon, all 1-501st units in the field are conducting searches of bunkers and hooches near their current positions. Surprisingly, most of the day has gone by without any units having enemy contact including being fired upon by mortars. Earlier around mid-morning, Alpha Company moved from the Tam Ky Airfield to Tam Ky North to secure 1st Brigade's command post at BT280228. Alpha Company is now under the operational control of 1st Brigade.

End of Day Four

At 1845H, Bravo Company reports finding a tunnel complex at BT173100. The tunnel measures 25 × 5 m with a roof reinforced by what appears to be granite. An NVA medic is captured when he emerges from the tunnel with hands up. The tunnel holds assorted personal and medical equipment and a US claymore mine. The captured medic says his unit had 50 soldiers, but ten were killed late last night (18 May) by our (Spooky) gunship. This may be the unit that ambushed Charlie Company.

Whether true or not, the captured medic adds his unit has moved to the southwest and crossed the nearby river to bury its dead. He continues to give information saying three other NVA soldiers with AK-47s live with him in the tunnel. The prisoner will be extracted in the morning. He is tied up and guarded during the night after gladly accepting an offer of food and water.

At 2015H, NDP locations are reported. Bravo Company is at BT173107. Delta Company is close by on the east at BT177108. Recon is at BT172109 and Charlie Company is still at BT164122. While digging in positions for the night, Charlie

Company finds a month-old dead NVA body. The body is too decayed to tell if it had shrapnel or gunshot wounds. Field strength reports are also given as of 2000H.

There are no casualties today, but the battalion's field strength has declined 30 soldiers in three days due to enemy and heat casualties. Twenty-three of the casualties were yesterday, 18 May. Charlie Company received a few replacements to make up for the three soldiers they had wounded.

Charlie Company Attacked Again

At 2215H, Charlie Company is hit again with a night ground attack with heavy enemy fire from a number of AK-47s, likely at least one RPD machine gun, and RPGs. All are firing from 50–75 m outside Charlie Company's perimeter. Charlie Company soldiers return fire with their own heavy volume of fire glad to be fighting from dug-in positions. CPT Gibson immediately requests a Spooky gunship.

The enemy firing stops. For 20 minutes there is a lull in the firing. The enemy is likely withdrawing, knowing what is coming next. They resume their attack using only mortars as the enemy ground force pulls back. Charlie Company fires its own 81 mm mortar in return. Only one Charlie Company soldier gets a minor shoulder wound, but doesn't need medevac.

At 2250H, the Spooky comes on station and after coordination with Charlie Company's FO, begins to saturate the suspected enemy positions and likely withdrawal routes with its much feared firepower remaining on station until 2325H. A flare ship then comes on station for the next hour.

Finally, things settle down. The day began with expectations that all companies would be in heavy enemy contact. That shoe didn't drop. Today, only Charlie Company has any significant contact and that is believed to be with a largest enemy force yet engaged. The rest of the night is quiet for all 1-501st companies.

20 May: Heavy Contact Expected Again

Later Today in the Nation's Capital

In Washington DC, Senator Ted Kennedy goes to the US Senate floor to denounce the 11-day Hamburger Hill battle which ended today. He says in part:

> I am compelled to speak on this question today for I believe that the level of our military activity in Vietnam runs opposite to our stated intentions and goals in Paris. But more importantly, I feel it is both senseless and irresponsible to continue to send our young men to their deaths to capture hills and positions that have no relation to ending this conflict.
>
> President Nixon has told us, without question, that we seek no military victory, that we seek only peace. How then can we justify sending our boys against a hill a dozen times or more, until soldiers themselves question the madness of the action?[18]

Senator Kennedy, the US Congress, the national media, and the American people know nothing about the on-going fighting at Tam Ky 100 miles to the south of Hamburger Hill. Neither will they learn about it. It will be a well-kept secret, not revealed until Vietnam combat records from 1969 are released well after the war is over. In the meanwhile, the casualties of *Operation Lamar Plain* continue to climb.

Bravo Company's Busy Day

So far, no 1-501st company has had more difficulty at Tam Ky than Bravo Company. Despite heavy casualties, the loss of their commander, few replacements, and being significantly understrength, they are still an effective combat force. Today is CPT Gay's second day in command after CPT Pape was killed on 18 May. Bravo will have a series of welcome successes today that lifts their morale.

At 0710H, just as Bravo Company begins to move east along the north bank of the Song Bong Mieu River, they spot an NVA 12.7 mm heavy machine-gun position at BT174104 and request an immediate air strike. They keep the gun under observation until 0833H when an attack helicopter team from B/2-17th Air Cavalry with two AH-1 HueyCobras attack the position. The helicopters fire their 2.75 mm aerial rockets, 7.62 mm mini guns, and 40 mm grenades from their rapid fire grenade launcher.

The enemy gun puts up a heavy volume of fire driving off the attack helicopters who are unsuccessful in knocking it out. At 0940H, a second attack helicopter team makes another effort to destroy the gun position also without success. It will be attacked later by an air strike with bombs and napalm.

At 0910H, while the attack on the gun position is on-going, Bravo Company's 1st Platoon moving west finds a tunnel and hooch at BT171107. The tough job of searching a dark suspected enemy tunnel is not for the faint-hearted. The soldiers who undertake this mission have been dubbed "tunnel rats" by fellow soldiers. It's not a derisive term. Tunnel rats are usually small in stature, not in courage. They must fit into the narrow spaces constructed for Vietnamese who are much smaller than the average soldier. Typically, they are armed only with a .45 cal pistol since a rifle is too cumbersome to use in such confined spaces. Sometimes they have a flashlight, sometimes they enter the dark tunnel without any light and must depend solely on feel, smell, and sounds. They are prepared to encounter anything from snakes to booby traps or enemy soldiers. Like the job of point man, not every soldier is qualified or wants to be a tunnel rat.

At 1000H, Bravo's 3rd Platoon joins with 1st Platoon. A search of the tunnel finds two males in their forties. One is missing a leg lost long ago, the stump is fully healed. There are also two women in their twenties and six children of various ages. The men are considered to be Viet Cong suspects (VCS). The women may be as well, but they are kept with the children who are understandably frightened. They will all be extracted soon by helicopter to get them out of danger.

At 1020H, a further search of the area finds several hooches about 40 m east of the tunnel. All of them appear to be storehouses for large quantities of rice and water. Upon questioning by Bravo's Kit Carson Scout, one of the women says about 100 NVA soldiers came through their location last night. The enemy often moves at night so he can't be spotted from the air. Maybe this is the same enemy force that Charlie Company faced the previous day?

Whether CPT Begley ever received this vital information about the size and location of the enemy force reported by Bravo Company is not known. In either case, it is not passed to the platoons in our company. If the information is true, the enemy force mentioned is larger than most of our companies and it may not be the only such force in our AO.

Enemy units have several advantages. They are fighting on terrain they know well having operated in the area for some time. They are difficult to track. The enemy units have no problem moving at night. They also have VC local forces assisting them in their movements and preparation of fighting positions. Everywhere we move there are concealed bunkers, mortar and heavy machine-gun positions, tunnels, and spider holes.

On the other hand, we are generally limited to daytime movement because of our unfamiliarity with the area. As said before, we also have been directed to move south essentially in one direction, so it is easy for the enemy to track our movement. Because we are normally on the move, we don't have the advantage of fighting from concealed positions.

Of course, we have significant advantages. Our capability to call in artillery, attack helicopters, and air support with bombs and napalm is a huge advantage, if we're able to use them. We also have excellent communications and resupply capabilities. Even with those weighty capabilities, in a straight-up infantry fight at close quarters, the weapons, skill, and determination of NVA infantry is equivalent to our own. The NVA soldiers have our respect as a hardened, resourceful enemy and master of small unit tactics.

At 1023H, Bravo Company's 3rd Platoon engages six enemy soldiers at BT172104, just 200 m from the heavy machine-gun position at BT174104. They are likely part of a team protecting the gun. B/2-17th Cav once again is called upon to attack the enemy soldiers. Searching the area, Bravo's 3rd Platoon spots another heavy machine gun at BT169104 along the north bank of the river. The two guns are apparently part of a larger antiaircraft network of heavy machine guns. This is another reminder such guns are usually part of an NVA antiaircraft company supporting an NVA regiment (or larger unit) with upwards of a thousand soldiers. This is an ominous sign of combat to come.

The second enemy gun is not as fortunate as the first one. A FAC flying in support of our battalion directs a twin-engine, two-seat, Marine F4E Phantom fighter-bomber to the gun position by firing a white phosphorous (WP) rocket where he wants the bombs to land. The Phantom jet carries a wide range of ordinance up to 18,000 lbs. (250 and 500 lb. bombs, napalm cannisters, and a 20 mm cannon).

The Phantom pilot drops four 250 lb. bombs on the gun position. One of the bombs scores a direct hit.

At 1340H, Bravo Company's 3rd Platoon continues its search operations at BT174107 just north of the river. They encounter another group of civilians, one woman age 30 and four children. They are moved to the Bravo Company CP which now has 25 detainees. Due to scheduled air strikes, the civilian detainees are not evacuated by helicopter until afternoon at 1500H. It will be their first helicopter ride. The children are crying and afraid of the loud helicopters. Being told by their women caretakers they are being taken to safety doesn't help. Humanitarian acts like this done by Bravo Company's soldiers to protect children are commonplace during the war.

At 1845H, an additional three women and eight children are detained by Bravo Company as they move east along a trail near Bravo's position. No one would have guessed so many civilians have remained in the area. It is notable that there are no men with these groups of women and children. Likely the adult women are also local VC, but unarmed wives and children are treated as non-combatants. They are soon released and allowed to continue moving out of the area.

Update on Other 1-501st Units

At 0800H, near to Bravo Company's location, at BT172106 Delta Company's 2nd Platoon finds a 3 × 4 ft wood cabinet in a hooch. The cabinet contains two NVA rucksacks. Documents in the rucksack appear to be training documents. Also found in the rucksacks are one AK-47 magazine, 40 rounds of AK-47 ammunition, one Chinese grenade launcher, one hand-made grenade, an NVA canteen, five 60 mm mortar fuses, one US pistol belt, several shirts, and pants, seven rockets for attachment to RPG warheads, and three pick heads without handles. The last items are a vital tool for digging tunnels and bunkers.

Soon afterwards, with our being so close to the Song Bong Mieu River, CPT Begley expects we will be crossing the river in the next day or so to continue our move south to LZ Professional. He tasks me to take a small recon team to look for a crossing site. The river is approximately 200 m away. I take my RTO, SGT Littleton, and two of his squad members. We move quietly, stopping frequently to listen and observe. It takes 30 minutes to move the short distance to the river. Once at our objective we see the muddy river has steep banks about 50 ft high. The jungle covers both banks. It's about 100 ft across and appears to be fordable at several places. We complete the reconnaissance in about an hour and report our findings to CPT Begley.

At 0918H, Charlie Company begins its day searching the enemy positions used to fire on them yesterday and last night. They find two Chinese hand grenades, one RPG round, two NVA helmets, and a black shirt typically worn by the VC. The number of AK-47 casings found scattered about indicate the attack was made by a platoon-sized enemy unit. At 1120H, Charlie Company requests a medevac for a soldier with a broken ankle. The condition of another soldier who apparently suffered a concussion injury last night has worsened and he will also be taken out on the medevac.

At 1218H, Delta Company reports we have detained ten civilians, an elderly woman, one female around 20 years old, two females thought to be 15 years old, and six children of various ages. All were found near BT174106 moving east and apparently leaving the area. Our presence in the area seems to be creating a high degree of anxiety among the local civilians who have remained here. Maybe they expect a battle will happen soon and are getting out while they can? After questioning by our KCS, this group is also released and allowed to continue leaving our area.

At 1400H, 1-501st unit locations are updated by the TOC. Alpha Company is still securing the 1st Brigade's command post at Tam Ky North. Bravo is spread out in its search operations. The CP is at BT173106 along with the 2nd Platoon. The 1st Platoon is at BT176108 and 3rd Platoon at BT174106. The platoons have not ventured far. They are all within a few hundred meters of the company CP. Delta Company remains close to Bravo Company's location and is at BT172105, now just west of Bravo Company by 100 m or so. The Recon Platoon is at BT173106 near the Bravo Company's CP. Charlie Company remains well to the northwest at BT166114. Their location will be advantageous to events tomorrow.

The scorching hot afternoon passes. Most of our units have limited their activity due to the sweltering sun and high humidity. At 1725H, Charlie Company has movement to their front and both flanks. They immediately request an attack helicopter team. Soon two LOH-6 Cayuses and two AH-1G HueyCobras arrive and begin scouting Charlie Company's front and flanks. Minutes later, Charlie Company requests a medevac for a heat casualty. The extraction is delayed due to the enemy's proximity.

End of the Fifth Day

At 1700H, while we are moving west toward our NDP, at BT164107 Delta Company discovers eight male bodies wearing khaki shorts and green shirts. The bodies are somewhat decomposed and appear weeks old. No weapons are found with the bodies, but they seem to be NVA or main force VC soldiers. A ninth body similarly clad and decomposed is found at our NDP location. Once in our NDP, we find a recently used 12.7 mm heavy machine-gun position and 60 mm mortar baseplate. The camouflage vegetation is still green.

At 1735H, Charlie Company spots four NVA soldiers in the open at BT165119 several hundred meters north of their position. As artillery is fired on their position, 15 NVA soldiers are seen scrambling into nearby bunkers. Charlie Company's FO continues to fire artillery on the enemy position while CPT Gibson requests an air strike. The air strike goes in at 1801H. No bomb damage assessment is made.

At 1910H, night defensive positions are reported. Alpha Company is preparing to move to LZ Professional to provide security there, but will remain at the 1st Brigade CP one last night. Bravo Company is at BT173107. Delta is now about a kilometer west of Bravo Company at BT163105, both companies are still just north of the Song Bong Mieu River. The Recon Platoon is at BT173105 near and just south of Bravo Company. Charlie Company remains at BT164115.

We settle in our NDP. All of us are looking forward to the cooler nighttime temperatures. Surprisingly, there have been no battalion casualties today. We've completed five days in the field. There are so many signs of the enemy's presence, we are surprised we've not had heavy contact.

Since our arrival, only Bravo and Charlie Company have had significant enemy contact. None of Delta Company's soldiers have been killed or wounded. Bravo Company has had the highest casualties. In addition to the loss of their commander and his RTO, 15 of their soldiers have been wounded in recent days plus two medics and two Recon soldiers. Charlie Company has had two soldiers killed and three wounded. Five medics from Headquarters Company supporting Bravo, Charlie, and Recon have become casualties.

We are told the enemy is present in large numbers in the Tam Ky area. Where they are and in what strength is unknown to us. So are their intentions. Are they purposely avoiding contact? Taking time to assess the combat power and capabilities of the 1st Brigade? Biding time until they can engage us on their terms or ground favorable to them? When will they choose to fight us in a sustained battle? Maybe soon.

***

Casualties and Awards

Casualty Table 5 shows the 1-501st casualties due to enemy action for the first five days in the field at Tam Ky. Heat casualties would add another 20 or so to our losses. However, most of them are soon returned to the field after being rehydrated and are not reported as casualties. We don't know the extent of enemy casualties most of which are caused by our air support and artillery.

Casualty Table 5: 1-501st 16–20 May 1969

Casualties	HHC	A Co	B Co	Recon	C Co	D Co	Total
KIA	3	0	2	0	2	0	7
WIA	2	0	15	2	3	0	22
Total	5	0	17	2	5	0	29

1-501st Soldiers Killed in Action, 16–20 May 1969

Bravo Company—2
   18 May: SP4 Lincoln Bundy, age 21, born 13 April 1948 from Redding, CA
   18 May: CPT John Pape, age 25, born 18 November 1943 from West Babylon, NY
Charlie Company—2
   18 May: PFC Rudolph Rossi, age 21, born 19 April 1948 from Howard Beach, NY
   18 May: PFC John Vollmerhausen, age 18, born 26 August 1950 from Wilton Manors, FL
Headquarters Company—3
   18 May: CPL Paul Ganun (C Co medic), age 20, born 25 September 1948 from Asbury Park, NJ
   18 May: SP4 Russell Jett (B Co medic), age 20, born 24 July 1948 from Hornbeck, LA
   18 May: SP5 Hans Mills (B Co medic), age 21, born 2 February 1948 from Sterling, IL

1-501st Soldier Awards, 16–20 May (other awards may have been made that were not mentioned in after action reports)

Silver Star—5
   Headquarters and Headquarters Company: 18 May, SP4 Charles Frank (medic)
   Bravo Company: 18 May, CPT John Pape, LT Osa Harp, and 1SG George Paulshock
   Recon Platoon: 18 May, LT Valentine Zapert
Bronze Star for Valor—14
   Headquarters Company: 18 May, SP4 Russell Jett (medic) and SP4 Daniel Thurston (medic)
   Bravo Company: 18 May, SSG Joseph Little, SGT David Holliday, and SP4 George Barnes

Charlie Company: 18 May, CPT David Gibson, LT Donald Gourley, LT Daniel O'Neill, SGT Dennis Carpenter, and SP4 Larry Slocum

Recon Platoon: 18 May, SSG Jerry Austin, SGT Gary Hlusko, SP4 Gary Craig, and SP4 Dennis Grippe

Army Commendation Medal for Valor—1

Bravo Company: 18 May, SP4 Neil Forman

Purple Heart —29 awards to those KIA or WIA

CHAPTER 5

A Brutal Day-Long Engagement

21 May

Early Morning Activity

Today is Delta Company's sixth day in the field at Tam Ky. It starts out much like the other days. We pull in our claymore mines and trip flares, check weapons, pack up our rucksacks, fix morning coffee, and get a quick bite. It is our regular routine, but an uneasy feeling hangs in the air. There is no specific enemy intelligence to inform us the enemy is close by in force. We take that for granted, but uncertainty prevails. Clausewitz speaks of soldiers "boldly advancing into the shadows of uncertainty." That is us. Uncertainty in battle, he further explains, requires trust in junior leaders, confidence in training and battle experience, and bravery in battle.[19]

As the day starts, we are still in our NDP at BT163105. Our three platoons are already awake as dawn breaks. It is our standard practice to be ready for an early morning enemy attack. That has never occurred since I joined the company five months ago. But it is a good practice, especially since we know the enemy is near. Our sister companies all follow the same procedure. Charlie is a kilometer to our north at BT164115, Bravo Company (BT173107) and the Recon Platoon are a kilometer to our east. Alpha Company will be moving from Tam Ky Airfield to LZ Professional to provide firebase security.

At 0500H, it is still dark when Charlie Company detects movement outside their perimeter and engages with M-79 grenade launchers and hand grenades. As dawn breaks, a 35-year-old woman and 10-year-old child are found dead outside the perimeter. Other women and children detained on the previous day were removed from danger. Why these two were there and what they were doing is not known. It is a sad start to the day. No soldier can be blamed for these unfortunate deaths.

At 0633H, we hear a Light Observation Helicopter (LOH-6 Cayuse) from Bravo Company, 2-17th Cavalry making a quick, first-light overflight of the battalion's immediate area of operations. The LOH draws enemy AK-47 fire from BT174104 just a few hundred meters south of Bravo Company on the far southern side of the Song Bong Mieu River. An onboard observer is wounded and the LOH goes off station. Two AH-1G HueyCobra helicopters armed with ARA engage the enemy position. Results are unknown.

At 0730H, Bravo Company's calls in an air strike at BT169104. The air strike will also be across the Song Bong Mieu River and just 600 m south of our position. Enemy movement of unknown size was detected there the previous day. Our FO ensures that the FAC knows he is to keep the bombs south of the river. The results are not reported to us.

Apparently, we will not be crossing the river today as planned. Our three 1-501st companies have been given reconnaissance in force (RIF) missions to move in a different direction. Battalion is directing all three of our companies to converge on a suspected enemy position of unknown size at BT165110. Little intelligence is available and even less is passed down within the companies. Each company will move to an assigned grid coordinate looking for the enemy. Bravo and Recon are to move one kilometer northwest to BT172109. Charlie moves due south 100 m to BT163115. Delta is to move north 500 m to BT163110.

A Morning Memory

Earlier, at first light, Delta Company's SP4 Bill Stephens and PFCs Bill "Scotty" Scott and Mike Hatzell, all 1st Platoon, awake to the heat and humidity of another tropical day. Having just come from the A Shau Valley's dense forests, high mountains, and moderate temperatures, they like others are still adjusting to the body-draining heat and humidity of the coastal lowlands near Tam Ky.

After breaking down the night defensive position they shared, they quickly prepare for the days move. Next comes breakfast. They hurriedly eat a C-Ration breakfast, avoiding the greasy canned mystery meat which makes stomachs queasy in the heat. They are starting the day with a celebration of sorts. Six months plus one day ago, they arrived together in Vietnam on 20 November1968. Scotty and Mike were in basic training together at Fort Ord, California. After finishing training, they were sent immediately to Vietnam and arrived together at Delta Company's home base at LZ Sally. That is where they met Bill Stephens who had also just arrived.

Today, all three are officially "over the hump" in their 12-month combat tour. They can begin their countdown to boarding a "freedom bird" and heading back to the "world" and home. In GI parlance they are now "short." They won't think of themselves as true "short timers" until a few more months pass. But each soldier will begin their short-timer calendar, eagerly ticking off each passing day until their DEROS (Date Expected to Return Overseas) arrives.

After breakfast, Stephens breaks out two small cans from the bottom of his rucksack that he has been saving just for this sort of worthy occasion. One olive drab can is the much-coveted, succulent yellow peach slices in their own thick, sweet juice. The other is an equally desirable can of pound cake. The two delicacies are high on the list of favored C-Ration foods, but together they are hardly enough for one soldier. The three friends with mouths already watering are happy to divvy up and share their tasty morning treat. Infantry soldiers take their pleasures where they find them.

As they sit on their rucksacks enjoying a peaceful moment, their celebration is interrupted by the dreaded familiar sounds of several enemy A-47 rifles firing short, frequent bursts only a couple of hundred meters away. Past memories are put aside. By evening, memories of today's events will be etched in their minds for the rest of their lives. At least, that is true for two of them. The tour of one of the friends will unexpectedly end today, his DEROS still many months away.

The nearby gunfire immediately gets our attention. Tension and anxiety increase. Everyone is instantly on high alert, mentally and physically. The adrenaline rush is creating that well-known feeling of "butterflies" in the pit of stomachs. There is real fear too, but no one would see it in the faces of our soldiers. What is evident is a somewhat calm, but grim, sober expression as they quickly go through weapons checks and other deliberate practiced actions as they prepare to face extreme danger.

Not waiting to be told, soldiers shoulder their rucksacks and ready for the word to move out. The orders come quickly and the pace quickens, "Hurry up, let's get moving." Not much explaining is needed. LT Black's 2nd Platoon is our lead platoon. Along with his platoon sergeant, SFC Pedro Rios, the platoon also has a full complement of three proven but junior rank squad leaders. SGT Donald Robinson's 3rd Squad will be the lead squad. SGT LC Carter and Specialist 4th Class Mike Tomaszewski follow with their two squads. The 2nd Platoon is the right choice to lead as our company moves to make certain enemy contact.

Our 1st Platoon, led by 1LT Rich Boyd and his platoon sergeant, SSG Ron Sahrle, follows 2nd Platoon in our company column. My platoon, having lost my platoon sergeant SSG Tepner to battalion, and squad leader SGT Hoffa WIA in the A Shau, is in the rear. Before Tam Ky, we had our turns being lead platoon. That was then, but things have changed. We begin moving toward the sound of firing through scattered trees and heavy brush. Few instructions have been given about our movement or what is happening. As usual, CPT Begley will give us orders by radio as the situation develops.

Bravo Company and Recon Make Contact

At 0830H, CPT John Gay, new commander of Bravo Company, passes his unit through Delta Company's position. They soon will turn north and remain close on Delta Company's right flank. They are spread out in a modified column. The terrain is now mostly open with scattered trees and brush with rice paddies here and there. Most are dry. Our maps show this area is a former large village covering several square kilometers. It has been long abandoned. Few structures of the village remain. There is only an isolated dilapidated hut here and there. They are a reminder people used to live here. The few civilians who were here are thought to have fled or were evacuated by Bravo and Delta Companies in the last two days. Charlie Company's regretful incident this morning tells us civilians may still be here.

Bravo Company's lead platoon has one squad up and fanned out. Two other squads follow in close behind in column formation. Behind the lead platoon are two more platoons also in column. The entire formation is just about 100 m long, the length of a football field. The Recon Platoon from Echo Company led by LT Valentine Zapert is moving 50 m ahead of Bravo Company screening their advance. Both units are moving cautiously expecting imminent, enemy contact.

At 0900H, Recon spots seven NVA soldiers near a 12.7 mm (.51 cal) heavy machine gun at BT163112, not more than 50 m to their front. The enemy engages the Recon Platoon with the heavy machine gun and AK-47 rifle fire. Recon is immediately pinned down with three Recon soldiers quickly wounded. This is a first indication of real trouble. The NVA has employed heavy machine guns throughout our area of operations. We know the number of guns indicates they are supporting a large unit. How many and where, we don't know. They could be anywhere. We will soon learn they are not only very close, but that they are waiting for us to get closer.

Near 0915H, CPT Gay sends Bravo Company's 3rd Platoon to assist Recon Platoon. For the next 30 minutes, both platoons come under heavy fire and are pinned down. They receive direct fire from the heavy machine gun and small arms plus indirect fire from mortars. PFC Edison Phillips, a soldier from Bravo's 3rd Platoon is killed. Three others are wounded. Delta Company commander, CPT Begley, sends our 1st Platoon under LT Boyd to reinforce Bravo's 3rd platoon.

Seven enemy soldiers scatter as they attempt to break contact with Recon and Bravo Company. One is killed outright. Five flee to the west, one to the north. CPT Gay requests artillery fire immediately to the west of the enemy heavy machine-gun position to prevent the enemy's escape. The enemy gun's position is between Recon and Charlie Company. Charlie Company, led by CPT David Gibson, has already moved to a position several hundred meters to the northwest of the Recon Platoon. Firing artillery is too dangerous with three infantry companies closing the distance between them. The proximity of friendly units will render artillery and tactical air support useless for most of the day.

Soon after, Bravo Company reports the Recon Platoon has captured the 12.7 mm heavy machine gun. It is set up for antiaircraft defense with aerial sights, a shoulder harness, and a tripod mounted, but it is still deadly firing on ground targets. The gun crew must have been surprised to abandon their gun so suddenly.

At 0940H, Bravo Company receives a volley of mortar rounds on their position at BT163112. One soldier is wounded. While under mortar fire, Bravo is engaged by some ten NVA soldiers firing from the north on their right flank. The enemy soldiers are supported by a second 12.7 mm heavy machine gun. Returning fire, Bravo kills two enemy soldiers and has two more of their own wounded.

At 1040H, Delta Company's advance on the left of Bravo Company has been held up to protect Bravo Company's flank as they, the Recon Platoon, and our 1st Platoon close with the enemy. CPT Begley still has our 2nd Platoon in front. The 1st Platoon is now a hundred or so meters to our north. My 3rd Platoon is still in the rear of our company, now closed up behind 2nd Platoon, as our company prepares for an assault on the enemy force.

All three of our platoons have dropped their rucksacks in preparation for the assault. So far, the enemy situation is not clear. As usual, neither the size of the enemy force, nor its location or intentions are known. Typically, the enemy will open fire and pull back. It's their favorite tactic. All we know is that we will move north and enemy contact is expected any moment. My platoon will temporarily stay with the dropped equipment as 2nd and 1st Platoons advance. We cannot afford to leave our equipment unguarded. It would be a treasure trove if it is captured by the enemy.

LT Black's 2nd Platoon warily advances 50 m across an open, dry rice paddy. They are moving alongside a dike toward what looks like a green island sitting in the midst of the abandoned rice fields. One hundred and fifty meters long and maybe 50 m wide, the area is slightly elevated a couple of feet above the surrounding fields. Heavily overgrown with thick, tangled brush as high as a soldier's head, scattered Crepe Myrtle-like trees rise up above the brush. A low 18" high stone retaining wall surrounds most of the elevated ground keeping dirt from washing into the rice paddies by heavy tropical rains. In earlier times, a cluster of families likely lived here as they farmed their nearby fields—a peaceful, rural setting in days gone by.

Once safely across the field, 2nd Platoon pushes a few meters into the thick brush and halts before advancing further. Already drenched with sweat, canteens come out as they await further orders. A hot tropical sun is getting hotter by the minute as it rises higher in a beautiful blue sky framed by white puffy clouds above the very green and lush landscape. SFC Rios comes up to Black's position for an update. As they talk in a low voice, Black reaches into the left chest pocket of his sweat-soaked jungle fatigues and pulls out a small, plastic, waterproof case. Within are his last two C-Ration cigarettes and a small Zippo-like metal lighter. Giving one cigarette to Rios, he takes the other. After lighting both cigarettes, without giving it any thought, by habit Black returns the lighter to the case and places it back in his upper left pocket. That seemingly insignificant act will save his life.

No sooner are the cigarettes lit, SP4 Kenneth Bowles, fire team leader, from SGT Robinson's 3rd Squad, comes up to Black and Rios from his position just a few meters in front of the platoon. Bowles says, "We have come across a bunker. Can we put a grenade in it?" He asks because we have encountered numerous bunkers in the last week without enemy contact. We have been careful not to waste grenades needlessly. Today, we may need all the grenades we are carrying.

With the enemy close by, Black gives Bowles permission to blow the bunker. Bowles smiles and turns to leave. Infantry guys like to blow things up. As he leaves, Black tells him to be careful approaching the bunker. Bowles disappears into the heavy brush back toward his advanced position in front of the platoon. Within minutes, gunfire erupts in the direction Bowles went. Black and Rios quickly recognize the sound of an AK-47 rifle firing a short, disciplined burst. For about 20 seconds all is quiet, then a grenade explodes. It is quiet again.

Enemy soldiers saw Bowles moving in a crouched position with grenade and rifle in hand toward their bunker and opened fire. Bowles was hit several times and fell to the ground. Somehow, he held on to his grenade. Lying wounded and exposed, he pulled the grenade's safety pin, and threw it into the bunker. Bowles is lying very still in the hot sun. Close to the enemy, he is barely concealed from their view among the low bushes in the bunker's field of fire. He is bleeding profusely and wondering, "How badly am I wounded?" His next thought is a common one for those seriously wounded, "Am I going to die?" In battle, the next question comes quickly, "How do I stay alive?" The will to survive is strong.

LT Black and SFC Rios immediately move a short distance toward Bowles' position, rifles ready, uncertain to what they may find. Taking cover behind a small rise in the ground, Black calls out, "Bowles, are you okay?" The answer comes back quickly, "I'm hit!" Black's and Rios' eyes meet. Both men are thinking what their next step will be. Black begins to tell Rios to hold up while he moves up his squads to provide cover. He does not want Rios to expose himself to enemy fire. But Rios is already moving in a low crouch toward Bowles with only one thing on his mind. One of his men is down and he is going to help him.

LT Black does the best thing he can do. He moves his 2nd Squad led by SP4 Mike Tomaszewski to the right flank of the enemy bunker. From there, they can engage the bunker and provide covering fire for Rios and Bowles to give them an opportunity to pull back to safety. As the squad moves into position, they begin laying down a heavy volume of fire. Immediately, the enemy opens fire and returns an even heavier volume of fire. The noise is deafening and disorienting. Rounds are whizzing by in both directions with supersonic speed, cutting vegetation, hitting the ground and trees with heavy, forceful thwacks and thuds.

Immediately it is clear to LT Black from the volume and direction of the enemy fire there are several more concealed bunkers on his platoon's right front. He directs his 1st Squad let by SGT L. C. Carter to move up on the right of Tomaszewski's 2nd Squad to flank the enemy bunkers. While Carter's 1st Squad moves into position, Black takes advantage of his platoon's covering fire to crawl closer to Bowles' position. Rios is lying nearby, killed instantly by an enemy sniper in a tree not many meters away. Despite being wounded, Bowles had quickly returned fire and killed the sniper. When Bowles exposed himself to fire at the sniper, he was hit again several times. There is nothing else Bowles can do right now for his faithful platoon sergeant who sacrificed his life trying to save him. Bowles' deep grief for his platoon sergeant will come later.

LT Black learns Bowles is alert and asks if he can crawl to safety. Bowles knows by now he has taken many hits by AK-47 rounds and may be close to dying. He says he is unable to move. (Later, medics will find seven bullet wounds in Bowles who is Kentucky bred and apparently as strong as a racehorse.) Black tells Bowles to sit tight and he will get him help.

Crawling back to his previous position on the edge of the field, Black yells to Tomaszewski to re-position SP4 Tom Higgins and his M-60 machine gun to provide additional covering fire for Bowles. In the meantime, as SGT Carter's 1st Squad moves into position on the right flank, an unseen enemy bunker on their far right opens fire. SGT Carter is hit and immediately killed, another soldier is wounded. Now, all three 2nd Platoon squads are in position, engaged in a fierce close-in firefight. They are fighting an enemy in well-concealed, expertly positioned, mutually supporting bunkers with overlapping fields of fire. Advantage enemy.

LT Black is Wounded

It is 1100H. LT Black now knows he is engaged with an enemy force beyond his platoon's capability to overcome. Likely, there are more bunkers and enemy soldiers his men have not yet encountered. He calls CPT Begley to give a situation report. It is not good. Black reports his platoon is pinned down by heavy automatic weapons fire from an unknown number of concealed bunkers. He tells Begley that Rios and one of his squad leaders have been killed. Others may be dead and several are wounded. Black requests that Begley give his platoon cover so he can pull his platoon back to a better position. Begley tells Black he will move 1st Platoon up on 2nd Platoon's right to flank and put additional pressure on the enemy bunkers pinning down Black's platoon.

LT Black's next action is to get Tomaszewski and his M-60 machine gunner, Tom Higgins, into a firing position to provide cover for getting Bowles out. Black, Tomaszewski, and the machine-gun team crawl to the position. When the gun is in place, Black calls to Bowles and tells him, "We are coming to get you!" Bowles yells back, "Stay put! I am coming out!" Somehow, SP4 Bowles musters enough strength to make a short run to cover, taking himself out of the line of fire as the M-60 opens up and puts suppressive fire in the direction of the enemy bunkers. SP4 Keith Starnes, 2nd Platoon's medic, is waiting for Bowles to get clear and immediately begins to treat Bowles' many wounds. He will survive. Yes, strong as a racehorse.

LT Black's next move is to get instructions to his 3rd Squad led by SGT Robinson. They were last told to remain in place on the left flank until they receive further instructions. As Black low crawls toward Robinson's last known position using his elbow and knees, he calls out to locate Robinson. An unseen enemy bunker ten meters to his front opens fire with a short AK-47 burst. In less than a second, Black, raised slightly on his forearms, is hit by three rounds. One penetrates Black's right boot only scraping his toes. A second slams into his chest with the force of a hard swung baseball bat hitting him just below his sternum. A third round tears into his upper left arm with such force his arm seems to be ripped off. The pain from the arm wound is intense.

Dazed for a moment by the impact of the rounds, Black realizes he has been hit. Even in combat, it always comes as a surprise. In excruciating pain, his left arm immobile beside him, Black can't move. For now, that's a good thing. He is lying exposed to the enemy who shot him and likely thinks he is dead. As he lies there, he wonders, "Is this how I will die?" Being Catholic, he makes a quick "Act of Contrition," believing his death may be near. Within seconds, the sharp shooting pain in his left arm makes Black aware he is still very much alive. He squeezes the fingers on his left hand, a rush of warm blood flows down his arm. His main concern now is to avoid bleeding to death and getting out of the enemy's field of fire.

His mind now focused by the pain, Black knows, with Rios dead, he must turn his platoon over to a squad leader. Unable to move, he risks calling out to SP4 Tomaszewski, "I'm hit! Take command!" Black's shouting draws another burst of enemy fire cracking loudly just inches from his ear, a sound he will never forget. He knows he must get to cover now or he will be killed for sure. Like Bowles before him, he somehow gathers his ebbing strength and stumbles in a low crouch to his earlier position as more bullets crack by and barely miss. Back to cover and safety, physically exhausted from shock, his wounds, and searing pain, Black collapses.

Immediately, Doc Starnes is by his side. As his arm is bandaged and immobilized, Black points to his chest and says, "I was also hit here, but it doesn't hurt like my arm." The arm bandaged and immobilized, Doc turns his attention to the Black's chest wound. Opening up his blood-stained jungle fatigues shirt, he sees the bullet hole just below his sternum. The external bleeding is not bad. The bullet does not appear to have penetrated his lung. No bubbles are obvious. Starnes seals the wound anyway just in case. He makes sure his lieutenant is in a protected position and leans him against the side of small bank providing cover from enemy fire. Black is now ready for immediate medevac just as soon as there is a break in the action. That will take some time.

Around 1115H, CPT Begley arrives at 2nd Platoon's position to see firsthand their deteriorating situation. They have lost their platoon leader, platoon sergeant, a squad leader, and it is not yet known who else. Begley's appearance lifts Black's spirits. Begley has done a brave thing getting to his platoon. What Begley doesn't yet know is just how close the enemy is. Fifteen meters, maybe closer. LT Black explains his entire platoon is "right up against an enemy entrenchment." He continues, "There are multiple concealed bunkers, supporting one another, we are unable to flank them." Black adds, "I couldn't get to Rios. He's too close to the enemy bunkers."

The loss of his much-respected platoon sergeant is an additional, heavy blow to LT Black. The two had bonded and developed a close working relationship. They had become close enough to talk about family and life after Vietnam. Rios would often talk about his children and wife at home and how he was looking forward to seeing them in September, just a few months away. His death is an emotional wound to Black that will remain long after his physical wounds are healed. Black will always remember Rios' death, wondering if he could have done more to stop him from going so quickly to help Bowles. Not likely. Rios' care for his men was a major reason his men loved him and would follow him anywhere.

LT Black's last recommendation to Begley is for his platoon to be pulled back to better cover and regroup before attempting any further engagement. CPT Begley assures Black he will get him and his platoon out and prepares to return to his company command post a short distance to the rear. At that very moment, a helicopter suddenly approaches to land nearby. It is a medevac chopper from the 4th Medical Battalion called in for Delta Company's wounded. Black yells to Begley above the noise of the rotor blades, waving his good arm to send it away, "They can't land here, the enemy's too close!" But it is too late! The medevac chopper attempts to land on the nearby rice paddy dike immediately behind Begley and Black's position.

Before his aircraft's skids touch the ground, all hell breaks loose. Heavy enemy fire is coming from every direction. The chopper is taking dozens of hits, maybe hundreds. The helicopter is quickly riddled with 7.62 mm AK-47 rounds making a loud racket as the heavy metal rounds hit the thin aluminum skin and frame of the aircraft. The pilot pulls back on his controls to lift the heavy, slow-flying HU-1 Iroquois helicopter back in the air. At tree-top level, the helicopter, too damaged by enemy fire, won't fly long or far and begins to go down. Miraculously, the pilot steers the disabled craft almost 3,000 m to the west of the fight and crash lands at BT136128. Two of the crew are wounded in the downed aircraft. Bravo Company commander CPT Gay sees the helicopter as it lifts off, trailing smoke, as it barely clears, then disappears over the trees. At 1125H, Gay reports the helicopter shot down and crashed. At 1234H, the crew is rescued by a Huey log bird pilot. More routine acts of bravery by the guys who fly.

In the meantime, SP4 "Big Mike" Tomaszewski has taken charge of 2nd Platoon. At 6 ft, 3" and 220 lbs., he has a legitimate claim to his nickname. He is also one of the most liked leaders in his platoon. He came into Vietnam as a PFC on 24 November 1968, just three days before Thanksgiving. Now one of 2nd Platoon's most experienced soldiers, if he survives, he will likely be promoted to sergeant soon. A natural leader, his men follow him regardless of his rank. We are all getting very used to having junior-enlisted men lead in positions far above their rank and time in the Army. We would be in a real fix without them stepping up to do whatever needs to be done. They are a special breed.

Tomaszewski heard LT Black's yell for him to take charge of the platoon, but Black was so quickly wounded he did not hear his reply. Big Mike is already acting to reposition his men to minimize further casualties. He first crawls forward with Higgins, his M-60 machine gunner. With both exposed to heavy enemy fire, he has Higgins place suppressive fire on the closest enemy bunkers. Now he and others can begin the long, difficult task of evacuating their wounded and attempting to recover their dead. Specialist Tomaszewski's courage and leadership under fire rallies the men in his platoon. Late in the day, Tomaszewski will take charge of withdrawing the platoon under fire. For his extraordinary leadership and courage under fire, SP4 Tomaszewski will be awarded the Silver Star.

With great sorrow, SP4 Keith Starnes, 2nd Platoon's medic, who has treated wounds and saved lives throughout the day, does not survive the fight. He is found dead from wounds in the heavy brush of 2nd Platoon's position. In the confusion of the fight, it is not clear how he was killed. He was in the very thick of things, often exposed to enemy fire treating the wounded. Words cannot express the admiration infantry soldiers have for medics like Starnes, They truly deserve high honor and recognition for their valor and commitment risking and often sacrificing their own lives to save the lives of the soldiers they so willingly serve and support.

At the Medevac Point

LT Black, SP4 Bowles, and others are carried in poncho litters to the medevac point, manned and guarded by Bravo Company. Soldiers carrying the litters are also carrying their M-16s for security. The medevac point is 150 m southeast from 2nd Platoon's position. Once there, all of the wounded, even those with serious wounds like Black and Bowles, will have a long wait. After the medevac aircraft was shot down coming in for Delta Company's wounded, there will be a two-and-a-half-hour hold on medevacs. LTC Singer, the 1-501st Battalion commander, makes the last extraction of a wounded Recon Platoon soldier at 1130H using his command and control helicopter. That happens on the east side of the bunker complex as the enemy focuses on shooting down the medevac on the southside.

The medevac point is a sobering sight. There are two dozen soldiers lying on ponchos side by side. They take up all of the available shade offered by a few small trees and bushes. Most of the wounded have blood-stained jungles fatigues and bandages. Several are coming in and out of consciousness. Seriously wounded soldiers have been given morphine, but there are frequent groans, some barely audible, and occasional sharp cries of intense pain. A few are smoking. Several medics move about the wounded ensuring they are still breathing, checking wounds for bleeding, giving quiet words of encouragement, and sometimes a prayer.

A couple of the ambulatory wounded soldiers help medics give sips of water to the parched lips of seriously wounded and try to make them as comfortable as primitive conditions allow. Another group of ambulatory patients are half sitting and lying nearby, exhausted physically and emotionally, some with blank stares. Though glad to be on their way out, many are troubled by leaving fellow soldiers in a hard fight. More wounded soldiers continue to come in. The medevac point is backing up during the long wait.

Finally at 1355H, two medevacs arrive. LT Black and SP4 Bowles are taken out. As their helicopter lifts off, flying out at tree-top level, the crack of enemy rounds is heard passing close by. Thoughts of being shot down are on the minds of wounded soldiers and crew. Soon the helicopter is safely on its way to the 27th Surgical and 325th Medical Evacuation Hospitals in Chu Lai. Relief on board is immense. The medevac pilots will return soon for another load. They and other pilots will continue their life-saving pickups late into the night.

Delta Company's 1st Platoon Is Committed

At 1200H, CPT Begley still doesn't know the size or location of the enemy force engaging his 2nd Platoon. No one does. In a 17 June 1969 after action report of the 21–22 May enemy encounter, CPT Begley writes that when his 2nd Platoon made contact with the enemy, "It was still felt that we were engaged by a small element which had been fleeing from the area where Bravo Company had contact earlier." With 2nd Platoon unable to maneuver or pull back, Begley has already told LT Boyd to have his 1st Platoon attack from east to west to seize a slightly higher rise of high ground just northeast of 2nd Platoon.

Begley's orders are understandable. Black's platoon is continuing to take casualties. They need immediate help. Unfortunately, Delta Company's situation worsens. In its attempt to flank the bunkers firing on 2nd Platoon, 1st Platoon becomes heavily engaged by other concealed bunkers. SGT Rick Halferty in 1st Platoon is wounded in his forearm by an AK 47 round. An artery is spurting blood. Boyd uses his sweatband to apply a tourniquet and stop the bleeding. Another soldier applies a bandage and Halferty is sent to the rear where wounded soldiers are awaiting medevac.

Bravo Company's 3rd Platoon and the Recon Platoon maneuver from east to west attempting to relieve enemy pressure on Delta's 1st and 2nd Platoons. The Recon Platoon under LT Valentine Zapert makes a determined effort to support Delta's 1st Platoon. They too are soon heavily engaged and pinned down within the enemy bunker complex and are taking heavy casualties. Both Bravo's 3rd Platoon and Recon are thrown back by the heavy enemy fire. Delta's 1st Platoon will be left on its own as it attacks the enemy bunkers from the east.

Though no longer participating in the assault, Bravo Company, understrength from its losses to enemy mortar fire 18 May on Hill 187, establishes a combined medical evacuation collection point at BT162108. This saves many lives as the evacuation point will be used by all of battalion units engaged in the fight, not only during the day, but well into the night.

As 1st Platoon advances toward the enemy bunkers, SSG Ron Sahrle, age 21, and platoon sergeant for 1st Platoon, is now Delta Company's senior NCO in the field. Sahrle was promoted just a couple of months ago in March while serving as a squad leader in 2nd Platoon. Delta Company should have nine staff sergeants, each leading one of our nine infantry squads. Instead, Sahrle is the only one and he was moved up to platoon sergeant because Delta Company was missing two of the three senior NCOs (in the rank of Sergeant First Class) who normally fill the key platoon sergeant positions. With Rios dead, our company has no senior NCOs in the field. Rios had been our only one since January 1969. They are in short supply in infantry companies throughout Vietnam.

SSG Sahrle is from Wayland, New York, in the state's Finger Lakes region. He married his hometown sweetheart before coming to Vietnam. A short time ago in February 1969, Sahrle and his wife met in Hawaii during his R&R. They are expecting their first child in October. He had been thinking about going home to his wife and their soon-to-be-born first child when the firing started this morning. He is due to rotate home in less than six weeks on 24 June. He will see a lot of heavy contact before he goes home.

As 1st Platoon answers the call to reinforce 2nd Platoon pinned down by enemy fire, SSG Sahrle now has only one thing on his mind, "Those are my guys in 2nd Platoon. They're in big trouble! We've got to help 'em!"

1st Platoon Continues Its Advance

LT Boyd's 1st Platoon successfully knocks out the first two enemy bunkers they encounter. As they move forward and deeper into the enemy bunker complex, they are engaged with RPGs, machine guns, AK-47s, and enemy M-16 rifles. PFC Michael Hatzell, good friend of Scott and Stephens, is killed early in the assault. During today's fight, ten other 1st Platoon soldiers are wounded including SP4 Byron "Benny" Bennett, LT Boyd's RTO. Most are wounded by shrapnel from RPGs and grenades. Several are hit by small arms fire. "Small arms" is a real misnomer when the extent of the wounds is seen. The small arms the enemy are using could kill an elephant. No, a herd of elephants.

PFC Philip Cravens is the M-60 machine gunner in 1st Platoon's second squad. His squad has become separated from the rest of 1st Platoon by 40–50 m. He sees PFC Hatzell get hit and calls for Doc Winka (SP4 Gerald Winka), the platoon medic. But it is too late. Later, when Boyd asks for volunteers to go forward with him to link up the rest of the platoon, Cravens volunteers. SGT Robert Morehouse, known as "SGT Rock" by his platoon, also goes forward and brings along one of the platoon's new guys. They move up to the stone retaining wall which marks 1st Platoon's most forward advance in its attempt to reach 2nd Platoon.

Taking up positions behind the stone wall with a steady hailstorm of rounds zinging overhead and hitting and ricocheting off the wall, Boyd and Sahrle decide a further assault is not worth the risk of more casualties. The platoon's exposed position and ability to see enemy locations is severely limited by tall grass, bushes, and trees. Boyd decides to pull his platoon back to a "safer" position where they can tend to their wounded and regroup. That is easier said than done. The enemy bunkers are everywhere and seem to cover every inch of ground with their fire.

SSG Sahrle is able to locate a depression in the ground about 30 m to the rear of the platoon's forward position. A few small trees offer a little shade. More important, the low ground makes a good collection point for the wounded as enemy automatic weapons fire sends a steady hail of bullets just over their heads. Sahrle makes several trips forward to help recover the wounded.

As 1st Platoon pulls back, they're unable to recover Hatzell's body. He lies near the front firing portal of an enemy bunker. Attempts to recover him would result in many more deaths. His position is marked and he will be recovered as soon as the enemy situation permits. Cravens also comes upon the Recon Platoon Sergeant, SSG Jerry Austin. He is badly wounded in his right leg. Cravens helps him get to the rear for medevac.

A Courageous Volunteer

SP4 Stephens and PFCs Scott and Hatzell, who enjoyed an earlier morning celebration of completing half of their year-long Vietnam tours, have been separated as 1st Platoon advanced, stopped, advanced, and stopped again. Stephens has moved forward across an old trail along the retaining wall in position to cover the advance of his squad. Scotty is holding his position to Stephens' rear some 30 or so meters.

As Scotty waits to advance, an unrecognized soldier from an unknown unit staggers toward him from out of the brush. He is wounded in the chest. SP4 Jerry Winka, 1st Platoon medic, is close by and immediately moves to render aid to the soldier. The exhausted soldier falls to the ground, relieved to be among friendly soldiers. He is suffering shock from his wounds, heat, stress of battle, and the physical exertion of getting himself to safety.

Doing what he can to stop the bleeding and ease his pain with morphine, Doc Winka decides the soldier needs to be moved immediately to the medical evacuation point some one hundred meters away and across an open, dried rice paddy Winka asks for a volunteer and looks directly at Scotty. Winka and Scotty are close friends so Scotty volunteers. He will soon regret it. Many years later, Scotty will say with a wry smile, "It is the last time I volunteered for anything in the Army!"

Doc Winka quickly constructs a hasty litter with a poncho and two bamboo poles cut with a machete. With difficulty, Doc and Scotty place the heavy wounded soldier on the stretcher. He is tall and weighs over 200 lbs. He is still wearing his web gear with its full ammunition pouches and canteen of water. Doc Winka and Scotty pick up the litter and begin to cross the rice paddy. The soldier is even heavier than expected. Halfway across, an enemy soldier takes them under fire from the enemy bunkers behind them as they move to the medevac point. Dozens of AK-47 rounds kick up dirt all around them as they continue to move. They struggle with their heavy load, tripping and falling several times along the way. The only complaint from their near unconscious patient is an occasional loud groan. Finally arriving safely at the medevac point (BT162108), they leave their wounded soldier in the care of a medic tending the wounded. They never learn the wounded soldier's name. Likely, he will never know the names of the two soldiers who saved his life at risk to their own.

With their mission complete, Winka and Scotty, separated by several feet, crouch low in a fast run back across the open field to their platoon. Almost to the other side and safety, a burst of enemy fire hits Doc Winka in his chest, spins him around, and slams him to the ground. Scotty hears Winka's loud gasp as the high velocity bullets find their mark with always surprising force. Scotty flattens himself on the ground by Doc and calls out to anyone in the nearby tree line for a medic. Seemingly, out of nowhere, a medic suddenly appears, as if an angel of mercy is already hovering close by.

Unconcerned about his own safety, the unidentified medic begins treating Winka in the open field with little protection from enemy fire. Scotty quickly tells him they must move to cover and helps drag Winka into the nearby trees. Winka is still conscious. He looks down at his sucking chest wound and sees bloody air bubbles each time he exhales. Winka calmly tells his fellow medic to make sure the plastic side of the bandage is placed on the wound. This seals the hole in his chest and ensures his lungs continue to work.

Scotty and the unidentified medic put Doc on another hastily made stretcher and all three begin the dangerous run to the medevac site. Scotty wonders if crossing the field the third time his luck will run out. He can't get that thought out of his head, but his friend's life is at stake. He will gladly sacrifice his own safety for his buddy. Winka would do the same for him. In battle, that is often what gives soldiers the courage under fire to overcome their fear of death. It is why lifelong bonds form between soldiers in combat. As Shakespeare wrote centuries ago, "For he today that sheds his blood with me shall be my brother ...." (*Henry V*, Act 4, Scene 3).

Thankfully, Scotty's third run across the field draws fire, but no one is hit. The medevac site is now still backed up with wounded soldiers. Scotty makes sure to put Winka in a shady spot. The blazing morning sun is already pushing temperatures past 100 degrees. Scotty knows his friend is in bad shape. He says a quick good-bye with a forced smile and a short prayer, uncertain Winka will survive his wounds. He takes a last look at his friend's face, thinking he may never see him again. (Years later, long after the war, Scotty will reconnect with Winka and discover he not only survived, but has a family and a successful career as a pharmacist.) Once again, Scotty and his new medic friend set out across the open field. Scotty's fourth crossing. He varies the route back and both make it to his platoon safely without drawing enemy fire. It is the end of a tough morning. A very tough day still lies ahead.

Photographing the Battle

There is no civilian news media covering the battle action at Tam Ky. That is intentional due to Hamburger Hill already causing a backlash against the Nixon administration in the US. The 221st Signal Company out of Phu Bai is supporting 1st Brigade at Tam Ky. They have decided to send one of their combat photographers to the battle. SP5 Steve Klubock is the "lucky" man who gets the assignment.

Learning he would be returning to Delta Company, he is actually glad. Klubock had spent a number of days with our 2nd Platoon recently while we were in the A Shau. Now inbound to Delta Company's location, he soon regrets his enthusiasm. Klubock's helicopter is fired on as it approaches the drop-off point near Bravo and Delta Company's casualty collection point. One of the two door gunners returns fire with his swivel-mounted M-60 machine gun. The muzzle flashes, deafening staccato, and concussion of the gun is disturbingly loud in the confines of the helicopter. Hot brass from expended rounds is clattering and bouncing around the copter's floor. The pilot is coming in fast and low for the drop off, an attractive target for enemy gunners.

The door gunner motions for Klubock to slide over to the helicopter's open door. Klubock sits in the door, holding on, nervously waiting for the aircraft to get closer to the ground. The heavy gunfire from the nearby battle adds to his discomfort. He has never been this scared on other assignments. He thinks, "I ought to be getting out of here not coming in. It can't get much worse than this!" It soon will.

Klubock is told to jump. The helicopter, still 6 ft in the air, looks to Klubock like 20. He holds on to his rucksack, weapon, and large camera bag and jumps. He lands hard, so hard a shooting pain goes up his spine. His first thought is, "I've been shot in the back." He lies still on the ground, unable to move. After a few moments, he discovers he is neither bleeding nor paralyzed.

Klubock thinks, "What am I doing here? I'm not an infantryman. I don't have the combat training to be here." Klubock again hears AK-47 and M-16 rifle fire not far away. Sitting up and getting his bearings, he decides to run to safety toward what he hopes is a group of Delta Company soldiers. Amazingly, like other soldiers, Klubock is ready to do his job despite his fear. He is a good example of what General Omar

Bradley said about soldiers in World War II, "Bravery is the capacity to perform properly even when scared half to death." Those soldiers became known as "the greatest generation." Our soldiers are the sons of those men. They have their father's legacy to uphold and are doing so quite well.

In the late afternoon, Klubock will link up with PFC Harvey Sullivan and other 2nd Platoon members whom he had met weeks earlier at Firebase Pike in the A Shau. Some of those he knew are now dead, others are wounded. In the days ahead, Klubock will do his job. He will document Delta Company's battle action at Tam Ky from 21 May to 7 June. He will take some of the only combat photographs of the fight at Tam Ky. He will also gain the respect of the infantry soldiers he photographs. He is there with us facing the same dangers, suffering the same hardships. (Stephen Klubock died in 2020 of cancer he believed to be the result of Agent Orange. Many of his official Army photographs are used in this book.)

Delta Company's 3rd Platoon Enters the Fight

As the fighting gets more intense, I radio CPT Begley for instructions, expecting my 3rd Platoon to join the action. He tells me to continue protecting the company rear from enemy attack and securing the rucksacks dropped by the 1st and 2nd Platoons as they "lightened up" to fight. My three squads are spread out about 100 m south of the enemy bunker complex. We are not visible to the enemy in the bunkers and not taking any stray rounds from enemy fire. We can hear the continuous gunfire and explosions.

It is really tough listening over the radio as our two platoons are pinned down taking heavy casualties. I keep expecting 3rd Platoon to be put into the fight, but the call never comes. By now, Begley is more concerned with getting his two platoons out of the enemy bunker complex rather than sending another platoon in. SGT Jim Littleton, my most experienced squad leader, has his squad close enough to the fighting to hear shouting coming from men in the 2nd Platoon.

Unknown to me at the time, Littleton and several of his squad members creep forward on their own initiative to see what assistance they can render. It is best I don't know they are going forward. Despite their courageous intent, I likely would have stopped them based on our orders. Once close to the fighting, Littleton lets me know where he is and that he thinks his squad can give needed assistance to 2nd Platoon. I give him the okay.

Littleton's battlefield instincts will once again prove right. He and his men are nearing the edge of the fighting. PFC Rob Sitek, a rifleman in Littleton's squad from New York, joined Delta Company in April. He is out front on point. Sitek is a rarity in Littleton's squad. Littleton, being from the swamps in Louisiana, likes to get replacements for his squad who grew up hunting, fishing, and spending time in the woods. Guys mostly from the South. But Littleton is glad to have Sitek. He grew up in a tough city neighborhood and is "street smart." After the Army, Sitek will become a New York City police officer. As they say in New York, he's got "moxie." (Moxie is a former Maine soft drink that tastes like cough medicine and is advertised to "build up your nerve.")

Sitek sees SP4 Tomaszewski on a rice paddy dike exposing his 6 ft, 3" frame to enemy fire. He and a couple of others from 2nd Platoon are trying to recover their wounded. Big Mike yells to Sitek, "We've lost a lot of guys! There're hidden bunkers everywhere. All over the place. Snipers are in trees! In holes! Everywhere! We can't get to the rest of our guys!" For two hours, Big Mike has been returning fire to help free his pinned-down platoon. He carried six 20 round magazines into the fight, quickly expending those, he then took another three magazines from one of his wounded 2nd Platoon soldiers. He is now on his third set of magazines.

When our two platoons dropped their rucksacks, their extra water and magazines were left behind. In hindsight, I and everyone else should have thought to move their water and ammunition forward. There's little shade in the enemy bunker complex. Maneuvering or even laying in the hot sun in over 100° heat and high humidity for hours is beginning to take its toll. In the early afternoon, Big Mike sees a soldier using his boot to take water from a rain puddle on the edge of the dry rice paddy. He drains the water into his canteen and throws it up to others for a sip. It takes a while for water purification tablets to work, so they risk only a sip. Some just wet their lips. Surprisingly, no one is sick later. Dysentery is the usual result of drinking untreated water with bacteria and parasites.

Littleton takes a cue from Big Mike and has his squad follow a trail along the right side of the dike to flank the bunkers. The squad moves cautiously up the trail and comes to a stand of trees on the right of the trail. Sitek, still in the lead, sees a dead NVA laying on the trail. The squad continues to move forward, bypassing the dead enemy soldier. They come upon PFC Harvey Sullivan from 2nd Platoon. He is agitated and deeply upset. With anguish in his voice, he calls out, "Hatzell and Hogan are dead!" PFCs Michael Hatzell, Edward Hogan, and Harry Sullivan were also close buddies. Only Sullivan survives today's fighting.

Before Littleton's squad moves forward again, there is a hurried discussion on whose turn it is to take the lead and go first. No one volunteers. Someone says, "It's everyone's turn!" They smile grimly in typical infantry gallows humor and begin moving together headed east along the stone retaining wall on their left. Sitek is still in front. The trail leads toward a hedgerow a short way to their front, a perfect place for an enemy bunker.

They go a few feet further and come across field telephone commo wire running along the side of the trail. It is obviously laid by the enemy. We use radios. One of Littleton's men cuts the telephone wire. Immediately, an enemy bunker opens fire from the hedgerow not 20 m away with a RPD machine gun and AK-47. The squad dives for cover in the weed-covered ditch on the left side of the trail. No one is hit, but the enemy grazing fire just inches off the ground has them pinned down. Littleton's squad returns fire. An M-60 machine gunner, likely from 1st Platoon, unexpectedly returns fire and suppresses the firing from the bunker. The assistant machine gunner takes a hit in the front of his helmet. The round spins around the inside of his steel pot nicking him in the neck. He is wounded, but still able to fight.

Littleton tells PFC Johnny Mack Pilsner, our platoon sniper, to cover the squad's rear. He knows the enemy tactic. They hit you from the front, then hit you from behind. The enemy may already be in the squad's rear. The bunker is no longer firing on Littleton's squad. Perhaps the M-60 gunner took them out. Finally able to advance, Littleton's squad comes across LT Zapert, the Recon Platoon leader whose unit is pinned down by an unremitting volume of machine-gun fire. He is trying to maneuver his platoon to the west toward 2nd Platoon. They have tried several times, but are forced back each time by the enemy's stiff resistance. Zapert has been lightly wounded by an enemy hand grenade, but continues to direct fire on the enemy and evacuate his wounded.

Littleton's men have crawled up behind a well. Things go quiet for a few moments. Seconds later, a concealed enemy bunker 20 m away on the left of the trail opens fire. Two US soldiers from an unidentified unit are in a nearby position. One of them is wounded by the strike of enemy rounds kicking up gravel like shrapnel. Soon enough, the soldier will be wounded again, next time by an AK-47 round. A 90 mm gunner appears crawling out from the bushes. On his back, he's lugging his 4 ½ ft, 37.5 lb. M67 90 mm recoilless rifle. Designed as a tank killer, the 90 mm is highly effective against bunkers. The gunner is also dragging several 90 mm rounds each 28" long and weighing 9 ¼ lbs. The gunner sets up to fire on the bunker, yelling for Sitek to act as loader. They fire several rounds, knocking the bunker out. For a few minutes all is quiet.

During the lull, those not injured apply tourniquets and bandages to the wounded. Sitek tells PFC Solomon to go back to the well and bring up some water. Everyone is thirsty. The sun now high overhead is beating down without mercy on the exhausted men. The humidity is intolerable. Water is critical. Solomon looks in the well and sees two dead NVA soldiers. Perhaps they were put there intentionally. They must fight on without water. Littleton's squad remains in position on the east side of the bunker complex the remainder of the day. They are fortunate not to have had any casualties being in the middle of the fight.

By early afternoon, CPT Begley has long since realized the enemy is much larger than he originally thought. They are also occupying an "extremely well-defended strong point."[20] Begley attempts to have his two platoons break contact so he can use artillery and air strikes to soften the enemy position. That can't happen until the two platoons are able to get their wounded out. Many of the wounded are still pinned down by enemy fire. It will take the rest of the afternoon and an assault from the west by Charlie Company to get the wounded from Delta Company out. There will be no air strikes or artillery put on the enemy's position today.

Charlie Company Attacks

At approximately 1600H in the afternoon, Charlie Company, led by CPT David Gibson, attacks across open rice paddies from the northwest in a valiant effort to relieve pressure on Delta Company. They attack with two platoons up and on line and one back. The enemy opens fire on the exposed soldiers and they quickly take cover along a rice paddy dike, reluctant to advance in the face of intense enemy fire.

The two lead platoon leaders, LT Dan O'Neill and LT Don Gourley, leave their covered positions behind the dike, exposing themselves to heavy enemy fire. They move among their men and by their personal example encourage them to continue the attack. "Follow me!" is the best battlefield command a leader can give.

SSG Kenneth Buesing and SGT Elmer Neises personally knock out enemy bunkers under heavy fire enabling Charlie Company to penetrate further into the enemy position. Another soldier, SP4 James Glemser risks his life under fire to save his wounded platoon sergeant. O'Neill receives the Distinguished Service Cross, the others including CPT Gibson all receive well-deserved Silver Stars.

Another of Charlie Company's men, 23-year-old SP4 Santiago Erevia, from Corpus Texas single-handedly destroys four enemy bunkers saving the lives of many of his fellow soldiers and enabling Charlie Company to move deep into the bunker complex. (On 18 March 2014, at age 68, Erevia from Corpus Christi, Texas is awarded the Medal of Honor. His personal valor and unselfish risk of his own life in close combat 45 years ago is finally recognized. Erevia dies two years later at age 70 on 22 March 2016.)

Charlie Company's strong push into the enemy bunkers gains the high ground Delta Company's 1st Platoon had earlier attempted to reach. By directing fire from their position on the rise, both of Delta's platoons are at last able to begin breaking contact. Delta Company takes the next two hours to extricate themselves and their wounded to safety. Unfortunately, many of Delta's dead cannot be recovered. They lie too close to still-occupied enemy positions. They will be recovered as soon as the enemy situation permits. Every soldier knows, understands, and supports the decision.

At 1620H, a log bird bringing in emergency supplies of ammunition and other ordinance, rations, and water is hit by an RPG and crashes in flames. The pilot and copilot are courageously extracted under fire with only slight injuries by a second helicopter. At 1630H, Bravo Company and Recon have enemy contact at BT165110 still at the enemy bunkers. They have four wounded. At 1815H a medevac takes the four soldiers out. Several incoming mortar rounds fall nearby during the medevac, but there are no casualties.

With the sun set and darkness not far behind, further combat in the bunkers is too risky. CPT Gibson is ordered to withdraw his company from the bunker complex. He withdraws Charlie Company out of the west end of the bunkers recovering their wounded as they pull back. At 1925H, they are hit with two RPGs as they continue to withdraw. Charlie Company suffers four killed and 16 soldiers wounded during the day's battle.

Charlie Company's attack and the courage shown by its men saved the day for Delta Company. Without their attack, it would have been impossible to get our guys out without taking many significantly more soldiers killed. Delta Company sustains the most casualties today, six KIA and 17 wounded. Charlie Company is a close second. Everyone, including Bravo Company and the Recon Platoon, gave their best effort, but the enemy fortification was just too strong to be taken by ground attacks alone. The day's battle draws to an end as neither a victory nor a defeat, just a brutal day. Much like the Vietnam War itself. But the day is not over.

By 1905H, Charlie Company completes its sweep of the enemy bunker complex pulling out under sporadic enemy fire. They withdraw to the west of the bunker complex and then south and east to set up their NDP near Bravo Company's medevac point. The sun has set, but the heat and humidity linger. So do soldiers' thoughts about the heavy fighting just completed. At 1926H, as Charlie Company moves with their casualties in the evening twilight, the rear of their column receives RPG fire from NVA soldiers observing their withdrawal. Their NDP is between Bravo and Delta Company in case the enemy makes a night attack.

***

Casualties and Awards

Total battalion casualties for today are 12 KIA and 49 WIA for a total of 61. Eleven of those killed are not yet recovered and presumed dead. Losses by unit follows:

Delta Company has 23 casualties. There are six dead and 17 wounded, all from 1st and 2nd Platoons. Delta's six dead are SFC Pedro Rios (platoon sergeant 2nd Platoon), SGT L. C. Carter, PFC Michael Hatzell, PFC Charles Hawkins (our youngest soldier KIA today), PFC Edward Hogan, and PFC James Sanford.

Delta Company's 17 wounded include: LT Ronald Black (platoon leader, 2nd Platoon); SGT Rick Haferty; SP4s Byron Bennett, Kenneth Bowles, Gary Elliot, Ronald Jones, Robert Ross, Walden Sumrow, Carl White, and Rollins Young; and PFCs Paul DiGirolamo, Robert Johnson, Charles Myers, Lowell Powers, Gary Silman, Thomas Smith, and Raymond Walker.

Charlie Company has 19 casualties. The four killed in action are: PFC Patrick Diehl, PFC Louis Fenceroy, PFC Thomas Jackson, and PFC Lee Napier. Fifteen are wounded: SFC Lester Tarkington; SGT Kenneth Buesing; SP4s James Garr, Roy Huckaby, Larry Mann, Timothy Nokleby, John Sansone; and PFCs Steven Frojen, Robert Holden, Rickie Larsen, Glenn Markovchich, Jose Mireless, John Ramirez, Gerald Rodriguez, and Adrin Zarr.

Bravo Company has nine casualties. One soldier is killed, PFC Edison Phillips. Eight others are wounded: SGT Phillip Crow, SP4s Robert Anderson, Glen Asher, Robert Dawson, Richard Sengo, Gary Singley, and PFCs Alfred Edwards and Milton Ross. Recon Platoon (E Company) has seven wounded: 1LT Valentine Zapert (platoon leader), SSG Jerry Austin (platoon sergeant), SGT Evan Mehl, SP4s George Beeton, Joel Ledbetter; PFCs Richard Costerisan, and Henry Ortivez.

HHC loses another medic killed in action. So far, this makes four medics killed at Tam Ky in a week. Killed in action today is SP4 Keith Starnes supporting Delta Company's 2nd Platoon. Two other medics are wounded. SP4 Gerald Winka supporting Delta Company's 1st Platoon and SP4 Fletcher Nowlin, supporting Charlie Company. (Nowlin is mortally wounded and will die 13 days later from his wounds on 3 June. Nowlin had previously received a Silver Star for his bravery in combat.) Casualty Table 6 summarizes our casualties today.

Casualty Table 6: 1-501st, 21 May 1969

Casualties	HHC	A Co	B Co	Recon	C Co	D Co	Total
KIA	1	0	1	0	4	6	12
WIA	2	0	8	7	15	17	49
Total	3	0	9	7	19	23	61
Total to date 16–21 May	4 KIA 4 WIA 8 Total	0 KIA 0 WIA 0 Total	3 KIA 23 WIA 26 Total	0 KIA 9 WIA 9 Total	6 KIA 18 WIA 24 Total	6 KIA 17 WIA 23 Total	19 KIA 71 Total 90 Total

1-501st Soldiers Killed in Action, 21 May 1969

Delta Company—6

21 May: SGT L. C. Carter, age 23, born 21 December 1945 from State College, MS

21 May: PFC Michael Hatzell, age 19, born 5 September 1949 from San Jose, CA

21 May: PFC Charles Hawkins, age 19, born 14 February 1950 from Philadelphia, PA

21 May: PFC Edward Hogan, age 20, born 3 September 1948 from New York, NY

21 May: SFC Pedro Rios, age 40, born 16 March 1929 from Ponce, PR

21 May: PFC James Sanford, age 19, born 8 August 1949 from Vidalia, GA
Bravo Company—1
21 May: PFC Edison Phillips, age 19, born 20 April 1950 from Plymouth, Pennsylvania
Charlie Company—4
21 May: PFC Patrick Diehl, age 19, born 5 August 1949 from Chagrin Falls, OH
21 May: PFC Louis Fenceroy, age 23, born 23 September 1946 from Bastrop, LA
21 May: PFC Thomas Jackson, age 22, born 22 September 1945 from Westbury, NY
21 May: PFC Lee Napier, age 21, born 11 January 1948 from Orchard, Nebraska
Headquarters Company—1
21 May: SP4 Keith Starnes (D Co medic), age 22, born 17 March 1946, from Charlotte, NC

1-501st Soldier Awards, 21 May 1969 (other awards may have been made that were not mentioned in after action reports)

Medal of Honor—1
Charlie Company: SP4 Santiago Erevia
Distinguished Service Cross—2
Charlie Company: LT Daniel O'Neill, SP4 James Glemser
Silver Star—16
Headquarters and Headquarters Company: SP5 Stephen Fournier
Bravo Company: CPT John Gay, SGT William Bushard, SGT Philip Crow, SP4 Robert Anderson, and SP4 Eric Nadeau
Charlie Company: CPT David Gibson, LT Donald Gourley, SSG Kenneth Buesing, and SGT Elmer Neises
Delta Company: LT Ronald Black, SFC Pedro Rios, SGT Rickey Haferty, SGT Michael Tomaszewski, and PFC Charles Sergent
Recon Platoon: LT Valentine Zapert
Bronze Star for Valor—31
Headquarters and Headquarters Company: SP4 Keith Starnes
Bravo Company: SP4 Richard Sengo, PFC Edison Phillips
Charlie Company: SGT Richard Laraway, CPL Patrick Diehl, SP4 Timothy Nokleby, PFC Louis Fenceroy, PFC Walter Hooker, PFC Bruce Johnson, PFC Thomas Jackson, PFC Curtis Lawson, and PFC John MacFarland
Delta Company: CPT Bobby Begley, SSG Ronald Sahrle, SGT L.C. Carter, SGT Larry Kirkland, SGT James Littleton, SGT Robert Morehouse, SP4 John Baldwin, SP4 Kenneth Bowles, CPL Michael Hatzell, SP4 Edward Hogan,

PFC Thomas Freece, PFC Charles Hawkins, PFC Wayne Salman, PFC James Sanford, PFC Robert Sitek, and PFC Booker Taylor

Recon Platoon: SSG Jerry Austin, PFC Richard Costerisan, PFC Joel Ledbetter, PFC Henry Ortivez

Army Commendation Medal for Valor—7

Bravo Company: SP4 Walter Michaelson

Charlie Company: SGT Robert Gaddes, SGT Donald Lewis, SGT Redford Russ, SP4 Benjamin Cryer, SP4 Daniel Richard, and SP4 Rickie Wilson

Purple Heart—awarded to all soldiers KIA or WIA

CHAPTER 6

Recovery and Review

21–22 May

Evening of 21 May

It has indeed been a long, brutal day, but the day is not yet over. Casualties must be evacuated, resupplies made, night defensive positions and security established, endless battlefield reports submitted, and plans for tomorrow completed.

At 1855H, a medevac for Delta Company occurs at Bravo Company's casualty collection point. The medevac helicopter draws ineffective mortar fire and takes out seven wounded soldiers. The medevac location has remained unchanged throughout the day due to the continuous casualty evacuations. Our medevac pilots can easily find it, but the enemy also know its location. A log bird brings in emergency resupplies for Bravo Company and is fired on by 12.7 mm heavy machine-gun fire before landing. There are no hits. The log bird takes out six more wounded soldiers without drawing fire.

The failing light conditions help cloak the helicopters flying without navigation lights. Blending into the shadows and darkening terrain, enemy gunners fire at the sound of their rotors. The pilots will soon be flying in the dark using only their well-trained eyes and exceptional skills to fly and land in the growing blackness. Two strobe lights mark the landing point. The short trip of 15 minutes to the 27th Surgical and 312th Medical Evacuation Hospitals in Chu Lai is now a well-known, well-travelled route by medevacs and log birds alike. The lights of Tam Ky serve as a guide at night.

Bravo Company has established its NDP around the medevac point (BT162108) to allow medevacs to continue into the night. Recon Platoon remains with Bravo. At 2100H, Charlie Company links up with Bravo Company to deliver its seriously wounded casualties for evacuation. Bravo Company also shares some of its earlier resupply. At 2250H, a very crowded UH-1 medevac helicopter takes out ten wounded soldiers. An armed Huey with ARA, flying cover for the medevac, survives a near miss of an enemy rocket-propelled grenade. At 2306H, the final medevac of a long day extracts several more soldiers despite drawing AK-47 fire on landing without casualties. Four lightly wounded soldiers are not evacuated due to the enemy fire. They will go out tomorrow.

Delta Company Regroups

Delta Company withdraws 600 m due west of the enemy bunker complex to BT158111and establishes its NDP. All three companies and Recon Platoon (attached to Bravo Company) have pulled back far enough to allow for air strikes the next day. Security is tight. No one has to be reminded of the danger of the nearby enemy.

LT Boyd, SSG Sahrle, and SP4 Tomaszewski with CPT Begley's approval, combine the remaining soldiers of 1st and 2nd Platoons into one platoon. Delta Company's 23 casualties today (6 KIA and 17 WIA) are the same as losing an entire platoon. SP4 Keith Starnes, 2nd Platoon medic from Headquarters Company, is not listed officially in our company casualty totals, but he is certainly thought of as a Delta Company soldier. From now on until we receive sufficient replacements, Delta Company will operate with just two platoons. LT Boyd leads 1st Platoon, I have 3rd Platoon.

When we arrived at Tam Ky, Delta Company had a field strength of five officers and 99 enlisted, a total headcount total of 104. The officer count included our artillery forward observer and the enlisted count included three attached medics. With several heat casualties in the past week and the battle casualties today, our field strength is down to four officers and 73 enlisted, for a total headcount of 77. We have had 27 losses.

After our night position is established, SSG Sahrle, SP4 Tomaszewski, and SGT Littleton are quietly working with soldiers from our two platoons to help them recover and get refocused from today's fight, ready for tonight and tomorrow. As they go from position to position, giving encouragement, their calm, professional manner helps steady our soldiers. "Recover" may not be the right word. Putting today's combat and losses out of their minds and memory for the moment is more like it. Begley does not participate in the recovery effort. He is busy with casualty reports to battalion, requests for supplies and medevacs, and working with our artillery forward observer on preplanned artillery fires in case they are needed tonight. After that, he gets battalion's new orders and completes plans for tomorrow.

Soon, our platoon and squad leaders have our guys busy doing routine soldier tasks, cleaning weapons, checking ammunition, filling up canteens, putting out claymores and trip flares. Sahrle, Littleton, and Tomaszewski also check their own weapons and equipment. Sahrle remembers he started the morning with 21 full magazines. He has fewer than three at days end.

Most of our soldiers are struggling with the loss of close friends. Some go further back than being foxhole buddies. SP4 Tom Higgins, 2nd Platoon M-60 gunner, is especially grieving over the loss of his longtime friend, SP4 Ed Hogan, killed in the fight today. Higgins and Hogan grew up together in Brooklyn, New York. After high school, they went to community college. Two years later, they graduated together having taken student deferments from the draft. Promptly after graduation on

26 June 1968, the two friends took the subway, along with Ed's dad, to Fort Hamilton in the shadow of the Verrazano Bridge. They took their oath of enlistment together. The two friends then met Larry Mulvey (now in 1st Platoon). The three were in the same basic training and advanced individual training companies at Fort Jackson, South Carolina. After graduation and pre-deployment leave, all three arrived in Vietnam on 21 November 1968 and were assigned to Delta Company. Since then, they have been with one another day and night for six months, sharing the rigors of combat. Today also marks the halfway point of their Vietnam tour. Higgins' grief is deep, with many good memories of his friend. Mulvey is also struggling. (Higgins' sorrow will still be there 50 years later. Soon, it will be compounded by the death of Mulvey on Hill 376. Memories of those days are still difficult for Higgins to recall. He does it only to honor their memory.)

SP4 Bill Stephens and PFC Bill Scott are also thinking of their close friend, SP4 Mike Hatzell. Everyone in the company knows someone who was killed or wounded. All knew and loved SFC Rios. The thought has probably crossed every mind, if an experienced soldier like Rios can get killed, it can happen to any of us.

Our soldiers begin to rally as they prepare for tomorrow. They talk in whispers in their three-man defensive positions as the night's darkness shrouds our position. C-Ration meals and clean water are welcome nourishment for exhausted bodies and emotionally drained minds. The sleep which will come easy tonight will be a brief respite from the rigors of today's combat. Sleeping in wet jungle fatigues with boots on in a hastily dug trench or hole is one of the few comforts of infantrymen in battle. There are no complaints. The rest is welcome. No doubt, similar thoughts and activities are repeated throughout Bravo and Charlie Companies and Recon Platoon as the day ends. They all have fought well, but also suffered personal losses with names and faces; losses now being reported up the chain of command as impersonal, numerical statistics—such is the grim nature of war.

At 2045H, just as many have fallen asleep, a US Air Force AC-47 "Spooky" Gunship comes on station in support of Bravo Company. CPT Gay provides target information and sequences the gunship's support with the intermittent arrival of medevacs. The slow-moving gunship spends the next two hours orbiting the battalion's night defensive positions, spotting and firing upon suspected enemy targets with its high-volume, automatic minigun cannon. The Spooky goes off station at 2240H. In the distance, at 2250H, we hear one of the last medevacs of the day taking out ten wounded guys who have had what seemed a long, anxious, and painful wait.

Finally, the end of a long day is near. Delta Company is bedded down for the night. SSG Sahrle along with other 1st Platoon members have their positions up against a stone wall. Trip flares and claymore mines are set on the far side of the wall. Just before midnight a trip flare triggers, its bright, orange-tinted light instantly flooding the wooded area. Six shadowy figures scatter. Sahrle hears them as they try to get clear in a hurry. They know what happens next.

An M-18 claymore mine immediately detonates, fired by an alert 1st Platoon soldier on security watch. The exploding mine's 700 steel balls, each 1/8" in diameter, travelling at an initial velocity of almost 4,000 ft per second, in a 60° fan, are hurled out to a lethal range of 50 m—unless they hit something or someone. The six enemy soldiers were moving along the other side of the stone wall just meters away. One is killed, the others somehow miraculously escape. Blood trails found the next morning indicate several were wounded. They were either an unfortunate enemy patrol looking for us and had stumbled into our position or just trying to leave the area after today's fighting.

The day is finally over. For almost all of our soldiers, it's the hardest day of their Vietnam tour. Very likely, the hardest day of their young lives. Those that make it home will remember today's heavy fighting the rest of their lives—a day that never seemed to end.

At the Hospital

As the medevac carrying LT Black and SP4 Bowles and others touched down on the tarmac mid-afternoon at the 27th Surgical and 325th Medical Hospitals in Chu Lai, medical teams with gurneys rush out to meet them. The hospital Quonset huts look like the temporary facilities they are on the outside, but on the inside they are first-class surgical and medical facilities. LT Black is still lapsing in and out of consciousness due to loss of blood. But the first thing he notices is how good the air-conditioning feels as his gurney enters the hospital and leaves behind the sauna-like 110° temperature and high humidity. His next thought is one of comforting relief, knowing he will now receive the medical care he desperately needs.

The doctors, nurses, and medical staff are getting well acquainted with our soldiers as they save lives, treat wounds, and prepare them for further evacuation. The doctor performing surgery on LT Black's arm and chest wound makes a remarkable discovery and eagerly visits his groggy patient as he awakens in the recovery area. First, the surgeon tells the lieutenant just coming out of anesthesia about the severe damage to his upper arm and the importance of keeping the drain line in his bicep. It will take some time to heal and likely will need another operation.

The doctor is not done. He next tells Black about the AK-47 round he removed from his liver just below his sternum. With a smile he says, "I thought you might want to have the bullet I took out of your liver as a souvenir, so I taped it to your upper chest with surgical tape." He then adds, "The round hit and passed through the plastic case and cigarette lighter we found in your left top jungle fatigue pocket." Holding up the lighter for Black to see the nice round bullet hole, he says, "This lighter saved your life!" (The 7.62 mm round fired at close range at 2,350 ft per second has enough lethal force to easily go through a man's body. Had the round gone through Black's liver, he likely would have bled out and died while waiting for the medevac. Black still has both the cigarette lighter and the AK-47 round as keepsakes from his close brush with death. He was further evacuated from Vietnam to Japan and spent two weeks at the US Army's 106th General Hospital. Afterwards, he was medically evacuated to Camp Pendleton, California, close to home, where he underwent a second operation on his severely wounded arm.)

After the doctor leaves, still in recovery and shaking off the effects of anesthesia, Black is in for yet another surprise. He hears a familiar voice greeting him as the person comes to his bedside. It is Ricardo Montalbán, the 49-year-old prominent television and film star. He is on a tour with the USO visiting hospitals throughout Vietnam to comfort and aid wounded soldiers. After asking how Black is doing, getting the report, and extending his appreciation for Black's service, he says, "Is there anyone I can contact for you when I return to the States?" Black gives him his mother's contact information.

True to his word, Montalbán calls Black's mother on his return to the US. He comforts her with a firsthand report about the well-being of her wounded son and assures her of his recovery and safety. Montalbán's mission of mercy is never publicized. (Ricardo Montalbán's own son, Mark Montalbán, just after high school volunteered for the US Army and served two tours in Vietnam in 1968 and 1969 as an operating room surgical technician. On one tour he was with the 7th Surgical Hospital supporting the 11th Armored Cavalry Regiment in Cu Chi, South Vietnam. After the Army, he married a nurse and continued a civilian nursing career until retirement in Los Angeles in his late 60s.)

Counting the Cost

After our companies pull back from the bunker complex, the three commanders begin to account for the day's losses in men, weapons, equipment, and requirements for resupply. The reports to battalion and follow-on questions from battalion and higher seem endless. Regrettably, the soldiers are not joined on the ground by the battalion or brigade commander or any of their staff. Immediately after the battle would have been an excellent time to personally meet face to face with their soldiers.

Soldiers need to know their commanders up the line are with them in the fight. Being physically present and speaking directly with them acknowledges their soldiers' hard efforts. Perhaps the six-month rotation of commanders is part of the problem. Developing relationships between commanders and their soldiers suffers. The junior leaders of "Never Quit" Delta Company are quick to pick up the slack. Their personal examples and close relationships with their soldiers are more important than senior officers showing up. Even so, a senior officer's presence on the battlefield is always welcomed and appreciated by frontline soldiers, no matter how brief, and it can reinvigorate their men.

After such intense combat, the morale of our men understandably needs a lift. Morale, or as it is sometimes called, "esprit de corps," is a French military term referring to a soldier's determination to fight and continue the unit's mission. Nothing is more important than the presence and example of effective combat leaders who lead their soldiers and units. Well-led soldiers pull together in accomplishing their mission, whatever that mission is. (A later 2018 Rand Corporation study, *Will to Fight: Analyzing, Modeling, and Simulating the Will to Fight of Military Units* concludes "the will to fight" in individual soldiers and units is one of the most important factors of combat success even though US Army tactical doctrine has not adequately acknowledged its importance.)

Tonight, the personal leadership of our junior-enlisted leaders in Delta Company steadies our men. After being bloodied today, our soldiers are no less ready to fight. Their will to fight remains as strong as ever. The Finnish have a word, *sisu,* that perfectly describes a soldier's will to fight in difficult weather, rough terrain, and against a tough enemy. In WWII, Finnish soldiers faced all three with *sisu*—extraordinary endurance in the face of adversity, persistent determination, courage, tenacity, stamina, resolve, willpower, and an indomitable spirit. That pretty much sums up what our young soldiers displayed today—their first, day-long combat at Tam Ky.

The Enemy Bunker Complex

During end of day debriefings, all three company commanders agree the size of the enemy force occupying the bunker complex was likely a reinforced company, a hundred or so men. They were well trained, highly disciplined, and tenaciously held to their fighting positions throughout the day. The extent and nature of the enemy's fortifications will not be fully known until they are searched on 22 May. The layout of the bunker complex had been well thought out, carefully constructed, and was extremely effective. Its size is impressive, some 150 m in length and over 50 m wide, much bigger than a football field. As the commanders talk, they describe what their soldiers were up against.

Some 20 bunkers were dispersed and concealed throughout the enemy fortifications. Many bunkers could easily hold 4–6 enemy soldiers. The bunkers were connected by tunnels and field telephones; reinforced with concrete and steel roofs; covered with 2 ft of dirt; and arranged to ensure mutual support and interlocking fires of automatic weapons. Camouflage made the bunkers almost impossible to detect until they opened fire. Multiple firing ports in the bunkers were located close to the ground to permit grazing fire. Fire discipline of enemy gunners in the bunkers was excellent. They held their fire, conserving ammunition, keeping their positions concealed, firing only when targets were in close range. Then, they fired in short bursts of three to five rounds.

Dozens of concealed spider holes (one-man firing positions) with trap doors to permit observation and firing were scattered strategically throughout the enemy

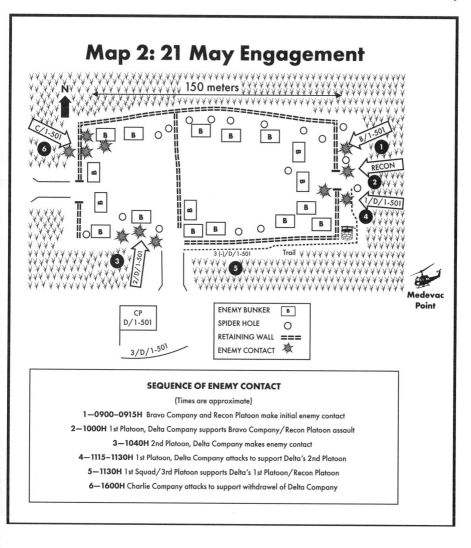

Map 2: 21 May Engagement

150 meters

N

C/1-501

6

B B B B B

B

B

B B

B B B

B B

B/1-501

1

RECON

2

1/D/1-501

4

3(-)/D/1-501   Trail

3

2/D/1-501

5

Medevac
Point

CP	ENEMY BUNKER	B
D/1-501	SPIDER HOLE	O
	RETAINING WALL	===
3/D/1-501	ENEMY CONTACT	※

SEQUENCE OF ENEMY CONTACT

(Times are approximate)

1—0900-0915H Bravo Company and Recon Platoon make initial enemy contact

2—1000H 1st Platoon, Delta Company supports Bravo Company/Recon Platoon assault

3—1040H 2nd Platoon, Delta Company makes enemy contact

4—1115-1130H 1st Platoon, Delta Company attacks to support Delta's 2nd Platoon

5—1130H 1st Squad/3rd Platoon supports Delta's 1st Platoon/Recon Platoon

6—1600H Charlie Company attacks to support withdrawel of Delta Company

position. Many were also connected by tunnels to the bunkers. Some snipers were placed in trees for better observation of advancing US soldiers. Indications are the NVA also had capability to monitor our FM radio communications during the fight. The enemy force that occupied the fortification were tough soldiers who knew their infantry tactics. We now know what we are up against.

Enemy dead is estimated at 26. The number is not confirmed because the NVA are well practiced in taking their dead with them as they withdraw from a position. They too have high regard for their dead soldiers. Three dead NVA were left behind. Their bodies are left for the NVA to recover later. The number of enemy wounded is unknown and too difficult to guess. No enemy soldiers are captured. Despite the high emphasis on body counts at higher headquarters, our soldiers have little interest in tallying an inflated scorecard of enemy casualties. It is a matter of pride for them not to overestimate enemy casualties.

Reviewing Today's Engagement

Given the estimated size of the enemy force, the enemy's tactical surprise, their well-prepared positions, familiarity with the terrain, and determined resistance, our soldiers fought extremely well. Using their favorite tactic, the enemy "grabbed our belt" and held on tightly. The close-in fight prevented our commanders from using our most effective weapons: artillery, attack helicopters, and close air support. Once our companies were engaged and pinned down, the battle became a knockdown, drag out, infantry fight to the death.

Unfortunately, prior day intelligence on 20 May, indicating a 100-man enemy force was in the vicinity of the bunker complex, did not get disseminated as sometimes happens in combat. That important information was obtained from a female civilian being evacuated from the battle area by Bravo Company. Two days ago, Charlie Company also had an afternoon engagement with a reinforced platoon or company-size enemy force fighting from bunkers.

Had this information been emphasized, more caution might have been used this morning as the three companies were directed to converge on the suspected enemy position. With civilians in the area, rules of engagement prohibited advance use of artillery preparatory fires, attack helicopters, or tactical air on the suspected enemy location. However, immediately upon initial enemy contact this morning by Recon Platoon and Bravo Company, supporting artillery and air assets could have been quickly employed. The relatively isolated target area with its vegetation-covered high ground surrounded by rice paddies would have been easy to identify, hit, and soften for a follow-on infantry assault. Hindsight is often 20/20. That is the reason after action reviews of an engagement are important.

Despite the lack of enemy intelligence, artillery, and air support, Delta Company's soldiers and those of our sister companies persevered under heavy fire. Never having experienced such an intense pitched battle, they held up well. They never faltered, were never overwhelmed by the difficult tactical situation, and never came close to quitting the fight. Their courage under fire was exceptional and commendable. Individual awards for valor were well deserved.

Today's brutal battle will be remembered by many for the rest of their lives. Some will spend a lifetime trying to forget it. Never to be forgotten are the men who died today. Today's hard fighting will influence the tactics later used on Hill 376 where employing artillery, attack helicopters, and tactical air support becomes an everyday, standard procedure by all of our infantry companies.

22 May: The Day After

After a needed, but short sleep, our company stirs. The harsh reality of so many casualties in yesterday's battle action hangs heavy over our company. The morning sunlight filtering through the trees helps dispel the gloom of our battle losses. Our dead have not yet been recovered from the nearby enemy bunker complex. It is not yet clear if the battle will be rejoined today. Hopefully, not on similar terms. Weapons and supplies, especially ammunition and water, are checked again before eating. We will be on the go soon.

At 0807H, Bravo, 2-17th Cav's attack helicopter teams spot and engage an NVA squad of about ten soldiers crossing a rice paddy moving east at BT182107. The location is about 2 km east of the enemy bunker complex of yesterday's fight. It is not clear where they are headed. (We will learn later they are headed to a mountain not far to the east, identified on our maps as Hill 376.)

A Calamitous Crash

At 0826H, an early morning medevac helicopter is in-bound to Delta Company to pick up wounded soldiers from yesterday's battle. From our position on a low ridge we can see the helicopter, still a kilometer away, approaching up the valley. Its red cross on a white circle just now barely visible to us is a reassuring sight. Flying at an estimated height of 800 ft, the Huey makes its way toward us against a beautiful blue sky. Below the copter is a lush, green-carpeted valley of trees. Some of us wonder why he is flying at such a high altitude.

As we watch, two enemy 12.7 mm heavy machine guns open up, breaking the morning calm with their rhythmic booming bursts of well-aimed fire. The medevac is caught in a crossfire from two different firing positions on the valley floor. The rounds quickly find their target. We watch transfixed as the plexiglass windshields shatter and pieces fly in every direction. The large 12.7 mm rounds chew up the helicopter's thin aluminum skin. Suddenly, the helicopter violently pitches nose up as if standing on its tail rotor. Likely, the pilot has been hit, his hand pulling back hard on the cyclic control.

The helicopter rolls over on its back, upside down. We see a crew member, probably a medic, fall from the open door of the out-of-control Huey. It is not clear if he is thrown out by the violent death throes of the helicopter or if he jumps. In either case, he falls to his death. The aircraft continues its nose-down plunge from its high altitude into the trees below. We don't see the actual impact of the crash in the valley's uneven terrain. A silent orange fireball and black smoke bursts up from the distant blanket of green followed closely by the muffled sound of the exploding Huey. The whole unsettling affair is over in less than a minute. A horrific sight, indelibly imprinted on the memories of those who see it. Previous medevacs have come in low just over the treetops, why this one did not, we will never know.

The young soldiers of Delta Company try to shrug off what they have just witnessed the best they can. It is no worse than what they experienced yesterday. They saw their buddies and fellow soldiers shot, wounded, and killed by machine guns, AK-47s, grenades and RPGs. Most handle their emotional distress by withdrawing within themselves. They show little outward display of emotion. Sometimes called "the thousand yard stare," the blank, grim set of their faces is not a good look on these young soldiers

For the moment, their psychological trauma of combat is understandably repressed. Such personally disturbing events must be set aside. A clear mind is needed to focus on the immediate, ever-present dangers constantly threatening from every quarter. Many of our men have already begun what will become a lifelong quelling of haunting memories. Some too painful to remember, others too troubling to forget. (See the extract on Post Traumatic Stress Disorder (PTSD) in Appendix 8 from the US Department of Veterans Affairs (VA).)

At 0840H, Bravo Company requests artillery fire on the two locations from where the heavy machine guns fired on the medevac. Charlie Company deploys their 2nd Platoon to locate the medevac crash site. At 1000H, they report they have found the crash and have recovered three bodies. The fourth could not be found. Later, a search team from another unit finds the remains.

Recovery of KIA Casualties

At 0940H, Bravo Company's first air strike request is made for BT165110, the enemy bunker complex and the scene of yesterday's battle. The air strikes are targeted away from where our dead are known to be. At 1006H, a second air strike goes in on the same location. In the second strike, a 250 lb. bomb make a direct hit on a 12.7 mm heavy machine gun. The FAC sees the gun thrown 25–30 ft in the air. If enemy elements remain in the bunker complex, they should be getting the idea it is time to leave.

At 1215H, there is a third and last air strike on the enemy bunker complex. At 1235H, Delta and Bravo Company sweep through the area of yesterday's battle. The sweep has three objectives. The first is to engage any remaining enemy soldiers. The second is to recover US soldiers killed in action yesterday. The third objective is to search the bunkers and destroy them. There is no enemy contact. During the night, NVA soldiers occupying the bunker complex pulled out. They have apparently taken their wounded and most of their dead with them.

Eleven US bodies are found. All have been stripped of their equipment, weapons, and ammunition. There is no indication the bodies have been mistreated in any manner. The recovery of the fallen soldiers is a somber mission. LT Boyd finds

PFC Hatzell where he had fallen. Care is taken to handle Hatzell's body and each of the bodies of the other soldiers with respect and honor. The men recovering the dead soldiers know more than anyone, these men gave their lives in hard fighting for one another. They follow the golden rule, treating their fallen comrades as they themselves would want to be treated. Members of the 2nd Platoon now assigned to 1st Platoon reverently recover the body of SFC Rios. Rios was awarded a Silver Star for his brave attempt to aid SP4 Kenneth Bowles who was wounded in action.

To aid in destroying bunkers, a combat engineer team has flown out and linked up with Bravo Company. After a quick search of each bunker, they use C-4 plastic explosives to blow them up. A US M-16 rifle and M-79 grenade launcher are also recovered. Bunker demolition continues the rest of the afternoon. An accounting of weapons is underway to see what other weapons may be missing and in the hands of the enemy.

At 1823H in the early evening, Delta Company spots four enemy soldiers at BT157109 dressed in dark shirts and shorts. They are engaged with small arms with negative results as far as we can tell. At 1910H, Bravo Company spots two NVA at BT162109 near the bunker complex. They are taken under fire with M-79 grenade launchers. One is killed, the other escapes. At 1918H, Delta Company receives six to eight 40 mm grenade rounds fired no doubt by an M-79 recently captured by our enemy. Delta Company returns fire with M-79s and M-60 machine guns. No further friendly casualties occur, as often is the case, we don't know if there are enemy casualties.

The frequent movement and contact with small elements of enemy soldiers may indicate they have dispersed to avoid large engagements. Harassing attacks by small teams of enemy soldiers are likely to continue. It is a favorite enemy tactic. They will keep us alert.

End of the Second Day

There are no battalion casualties today. NDPs are reported. Bravo Company and Recon are several hundred meters southwest of yesterday's action at BT162109. Charlie Company is at BT163114 500 m north of Bravo. Delta Company is at BT158111 300 m west of Bravo and 400 m southwest of Charlie. We are all remaining close to each other anticipating more enemy contact. There is safety in numbers.

Before dark sets in, Delta Company's two platoons set out trip flares and Claymore antipersonnel mines. Noise and light discipline measures are strictly enforced. We talk in whispers, turn down radios, limit moving around, and have no fires including smoking. We position weapons, grenades, and ammunition where they are immediately available. One man will remain awake at each three-man position. CPT Begley requests a Spooky Gunship for extra security. At 2010H, the AC-47 arrives on station. They provide quite a nighttime light show. In addition to its high volume of automatic cannon fire made visible by orange-red tracer rounds. Spooky will also be dropping illumination flares to assist ground and air observers in detecting enemy movement.

The 1st Brigade tactical operations center (TOC) notifies 1-501st and other battalions that B-52 strikes are scheduled in the next few days and US units must remain 3,000 m (1.8 mi) from targeted grid squares. Only one of the target grid squares is of concern. We will remain at an extra safe distance. At 2245H, the Spooky Gunship supporting Delta Company goes off station. A replacement is requested, but isn't available. It is lights out literally. Time to settle down for the night.

***

Casualties and Awards

1-501st Soldiers Killed in Action, 22 May 1969—none

1-501st Soldier Awards, 22 May 1969—none (other awards may have been made that were not mentioned in after action reports)

CHAPTER 7

Follow-on Operations

23–30 May

Uncertain Days

The brutal fight on 21 May is over, but no one in Delta Company or our other companies including the Recon Platoon thinks heavy enemy contact is at an end. The unexpected intensity of the day-long firefight under a scorching tropical sun and our high US casualties is an eye-opening, sobering experience. We are all anticipating more of the same. It seems not a matter of if, but when. Anticipating "when" is an added high stress factor on our soldiers and those who lead them.

Infantry always fights on a battlefield of uncertainty. The term "fog of war" has long been used to describe the difficulty of having sufficient information or "situational awareness" to fight a battle successfully. At all levels (squad, platoon, company, battalion, and higher) there is always uncertainty. For example, here are three important areas (not the only ones) where information may be lacking or even wrong:

- First is the enemy situation. Where is he, what is his strength, his intentions, capabilities, current activity?
- Second, what is our friendly situation? What is our higher headquarters wanting us to do? Today? Tomorrow? How is the best way to get our mission done? How will our chain of command respond to battlefield developments? How will we?
  - What are our sister units, our other companies, doing? How does what they do affect accomplishment of our mission and we theirs?
  - What about our supporting arms and our supplies? What is available? When? Where? How do we get it?
- Third, what is the terrain and weather like, how do they affect our operations? How will our unfamiliarity with the terrain and fighting in unaccustomed weather conditions complicate our operations? How will it change tomorrow?

These questions are just a start, with the information and answers constantly changing. Exchange of information through our communication and coordination channels does not always flow smoothly or on time. In short, battle is complex at all levels and leaders and commanders must work continuously to stay abreast of both enemy and friendly situations. The best combat leaders understand the coordination and communication required and learn to operate in the midst of uncertainty, anticipating what may or may not happen.

But to be clear, just because battles can be chaotic it would be wrong to think infantry units operate in total chaos. Perhaps it might be best to say a battlefield is a dynamic environment and agility of mind and capabilities are always at a premium. There is an old saying that even a good battle plan doesn't survive the first enemy contact. That adage is linked to the uncodified Murphy's Laws based on an original premise "if anything can go wrong it will." A corollary to Murphy's Law adds, "and at the worst possible time." Murphy, some think, was an infantry grunt. (The term "grunt" to describe infantryman is of unknown origin with many anecdotal stories about how it came to be. The bottom line is "grunts" do grunt work which has been described by others as thankless and menial work that lacks glamour or prestige. When infantrymen call themselves "grunts," it is a term of endearment and pride.)

The infantry, like other combat arms, undergoes intensive combat training. There is no end to infantry doctrines, standard operation procedures, practices, tactics and techniques that provide the framework for infantry combat operations. All help reduce the chaos. Basics like soldier values, training, teamwork, discipline, physical conditioning, good morale, and leadership are also critical to successful infantry combat operations. Yes, it is a complicated profession.

A Summary of the Next Eight Days

Delta Company's soldiers who were in the middle of the 21 May fight are just beginning to recover from their physical and emotional fatigue. That is most of our company, our commander, his headquarters element, the 1st and 2nd Platoons and Littleton's squad from 3rd Platoon. Though we are still combat effective, after such a strenuous effort, our company could use a brief time to recover and regroup before continuing our mission.

Delta, Bravo with Recon, and Charlie companies are remaining close to one another for the time being. We are still near the 21 May battle area. CPT Begley is wisely not pushing our company hard. Our movement over the next few days will be limited, but we are keenly alert to enemy activity.

Begley hasn't communicated much about our company's mission or given us an updated enemy situation. He likely hasn't been told much. Most of us in Delta Company, with the possible exception of CPT Begley and maybe his FO and RTOs aren't aware of what is happening in our sister companies. More information would help us better understand what we should expect next. This is not a complaint. The reality is we are in an infantry unit and there will always be less information than we want or need. That is when good leaders earn their pay.

Over the next week, we will continue to conduct RIF and search operations looking for the enemy. Having tasted firsthand the enemy's capabilities in close infantry combat, we are much better prepared. "Forewarned is to be forearmed" is a military saying from the 1500s, originally in Latin, *praemonitus, praemunitus*. No doubt, like Murphy's Law, this saying was coined by an infantryman.

A brief summary of Delta Company and our battalion operations over the next eight days follows. The summaries are by no means a complete account, the intent is to keep them brief, but touch on the extent of our engagement with the enemy.

Though not included in the following day-to-day summaries, each of our four companies are making constant use of supporting arms. US Navy and Marine F-4 Phantoms provide close air support with air strikes (bombs, napalm, and 20 mm cannons). A US Air Force Forward Air Controller (FAC) directs the air strikes and a "Spooky" gunship is also on call at night. Bravo Troop, 2-17th Cavalry adds their scout and attack helicopters (with mini-guns, rapid-fire 40 mm grenades launchers, and aerial rockets). Artillery, "the king of battle" has multiple firing batteries providing immediate on call artillery fires from 105 mm, 155 mm, and 8" howitzers and 175 mm guns. All are critical in supporting the infantry mission of closing with and killing the enemy.

Another matter not detailed in the summaries is that all of our units are continuously receiving harassing fires from enemy snipers, small team ambushes, and mortars. Generally, these enemy activities are mentioned only when US casualties result. Each of our 1-501st companies are in enemy contact one way or another just about every day.

1-501st Battalion Operations, 23–25 May

23 May. At 1353H, Bravo Company's command post is once again hit by enemy fire. Reports are not clear whether the weapon was a lone mortar or RPG round. Three soldiers are killed in the explosion, one from Bravo, SGT Roy Newsome, and two from Recon, PFCs Robert Boese and Robert Randall.

Eight are wounded. This includes the new Bravo Company Commander CPT John Gay, First Sergeant George Paulshock, and Platoon Sergeant SFC Gonzalo Tapia-Flaw. Four other Bravo soldiers are wounded: SP4 Carl Noeler, PFCs Larry Cherry, Walter Michelson, and Raymond Norris, along with a medic from Headquarters Company, SGT Frederick Ellis.

Charlie and Delta Company search suspected enemy mortar locations without results. Delta Company assists Bravo Company with the evacuation of the wounded. NDP positions are: Bravo and Recon along with Charlie Company are at BT160113; Delta is at BT157110. A Company is OPCON to the 1-46th Inf battalion at LZ Professional. CPT Walter Shelton is flown in as the new Bravo commander.

24 May. At 1449H, Bravo Company and the Recon Platoon receive sniper and mortar fire. A Recon soldier is killed by a sniper, SP4 Charles Jones. Two Recon soldiers are wounded by the sniper: SP4 Peter Coyer and PFC Alvin Carrington. Alpha Company is released from the 1-46th Infantry and is conducting RIF Operations to BT172080, north of LZ Professional. Bravo Company and Recon are at BT160112 just 200 m west of the enemy bunker complex fight on 21 May. Both Charlie and Delta Company are close by. NDP locations are: Alpha at BT164098 a little more than a kilometer south of the three other companies but on the south side of the Song Bong Mieu River. Bravo and Recon are at BT161115; Charlie is also at BT161115; and Delta at BT162110. No US casualties occur beyond the one KIA and two WIA in Recon.

25 May. At 0739H, a LOH from 2-17th Cav is shot down. Both pilot and co-pilot are hurt in the crash. The downed helicopter is secured by the 2-17th's Aero-Rifle Platoon and a medevac picks up the two pilots. All four 1-501st companies conduct saturation patrols in assigned grid squares. Each grid is one kilometer square, all are adjacent to another company. Alpha Company is assigned BT1609; Bravo and Recon, BT1511; Charlie, BT1610; and Delta BT1611. At 1717H, Alpha Company engages an enemy 82 mm mortar crew, captures the mortar squad leader and mortar, kills the crew, and several other NVA soldiers. In the fight, Alpha company has two soldiers killed: SP4 Ralph Vitch and PFC Mario Lamelza. At 1840H, while engaging an enemy bunker, two from Bravo Company are wounded: SGT Wayne Burton and PFC Robert Hughes. The most important event for Delta Company today is the arrival of a new artillery forward observer. At 2000H, NDP locations are: Alpha Company, BT165098; Bravo and Recon BT158115; Charlie at BT164115; and Delta BT163106.

Delta Company's New Artillery Officer

LT Paul Wharton, age 23, born in New Haven, Connecticut, is of average height and build, but packs a big punch with his artillery skills. His talents are not yet known to Delta Company. In combat, an infantry company commander and his artillery forward observer are a close-knit team practically joined at the hip. But when Wharton arrives at Delta Company on 25 May, he is not exactly welcomed with open arms by the commander.

CPT Begley has just recently lost his long-time FO due to an assignment rotation. Begley knows he is ending his company command the last day of May and he and Wharton won't be working together but for a few days. Wharton doesn't know Begley is leaving and neither do other members of Delta Company.

How Wharton made it to Delta Company is an interesting saga. He reached Vietnam on 6 May 1969 after a 19-hour flight from Travis Air Force base in San Francisco. He has just over nine months active duty which began 1 August 1968. Like most lieutenants, he is on his first tour of duty in the Army and his first combat assignment. His short active duty time includes the Field Artillery Officer Basic Course followed by Airborne and Ranger training. With Ranger training just completed, Wharton is in great shape mentally and physically. He will need to be.

Wharton was first assigned to the 25th Infantry Division on arrival in Vietnam. He was changed to the 101st Airborne Division in part because he is an airborne lieutenant. The division had also been having heavy enemy contact and losses both on Hamburger Hill and at Tam Ky. After being flown to Camp Eagle, the Division Artillery Headquarters and 1st Brigade's home base, Wharton was told by the division's artillery commander to head over to the helipad for a familiarization trip to one of the 101st firebases. Unfortunately, the next helicopter was going to FSB Airborne. It's a small artillery firebase (25 m wide and 200 m long) on the eastern side of the A Shau Valley's northern tip.

Wharton arrived at Airborne the day before it was hit with a massive, all-out attack at 0330H 13 May. He fought with the battery to repel the enemy assault though NVA sappers using satchel charges destroyed four 105 mm howitzers and the artillery fire direction center (FDC). Wharton began to wonder what his next assignment would be like. His "familiarization" tour completed, he flew out the next morning.

Back at Eagle, he was told to go to LZ Sally, the home of Alpha Battery, 1-321st Field Artillery Battalion. Once at Sally, he was attached to the 1-501st as an artillery forward observer (FO) and flew to Tam Ky by Huey to link up with the battalion. The chopper had an inflight problem and the pilot autorotated the Huey into an open, unsecure field. As the crew, Wharton, and other passengers evacuated the helicopter, it burst into flames.

Fortunately, another helicopter accompanying Wharton's helicopter quickly landed, took on the additional passengers, and left the Huey burning in the field. They soon arrived at LZ Professional, the 1-501st headquarters at Tam Ky. After a brief orientation and overnight there, the next day he was attached to Delta Company as their new forward observer.

Taken by Huey to Delta Company's field location on 25 May, he arrives just days after the company's hard fight on 21 May. Finally, he is with an infantry company ready to do the job he most wants to do in combat. Begley's RTO, Ed Medros, and other soldiers bring him up to speed on recent battle activity.

1-501st Battalion Operations, 26–30 May

26 May. Bravo and Recon continue operations in grid square BT1511 with two Bravo Company soldiers killed by sniper fire: PFC Euan Parker and PFC Eric Nadeau. Two from Bravo are wounded: SP4 Richard Slinkey and PFC James Dodge. Alpha Company continues RIF operations near BT165058 and has two soldiers wounded by snipers, SP4 Anthony Tucker and PFC Harvey Newman. Alpha Company is picked up and flown north across the river to a location near Delta Company. Delta Company conducts a detailed search of its area without casualties. At 1855H, NDP locations are Alpha and Delta Company co-located at BT163106; Bravo Company, Recon and Charlie Company are co-located at BT163115. Charlie Company has two hand grenades thrown into its NDP after dark with two soldiers wounded: PFC George Jones and PFC Clarence Parker.

27 May. A quiet day. More RIF operations. No enemy contact. No casualties. NDP locations are Alpha, Bravo and Recon are at BT154113; Charlie and Delta are co-located at BT164116. The 1-501st companies continue to locate close to one another in anticipation of heavy enemy contact.

28 May. Another quiet day. There are no US or known enemy casualties. Alpha, Bravo with Recon, Charlie and Delta Companies conduct detailed search operations in the vicinity of BT154113, BT155115, BT164116, and BT164116 respectively. Alpha and Bravo are 200 m from each other. Charlie and Delta Company are co-located. At 1755H, they receive sniper fire and employ air strikes on the suspected enemy area. NDP locations are: Alpha, Bravo Companies and Recon co-located at BT165115; Charlie and Delta Company co-located at BT164116.

29 May. All companies continue RIF operations. No US casualties occur. We receive ineffective sniper fire, a reminder the enemy is still nearby. The lack of significant enemy contact seems strange. Tension is high. The question at our level is always, what's next? Where is the enemy? When do we engage him next? Several air strikes are called in. Delta and Alpha Company find a total of three NVA dead in two different air strike bomb damage assessments. Bravo Company finds a previously reported downed Huey at BT160118 with tail number #616118. Though the aircraft is completely destroyed, two damaged M-60 machine guns and one M-16 rifle are found in the burned out wreckage. They are removed and further destroyed. NDP locations are Alpha Company BT159114; Bravo Company and Recon close by at BT159112; Charlie and Delta Company are co-located at BT163112.

After we set up our NDP, I remember today is my birthday. In the field the days run together, so I almost missed that I am now 24 years old. Without mentioning it to anyone else, I say to myself. "Happy Birthday, LT Sherwood! Wonder if you'll make it to 25?" I scrounge a can of C-Ration pound cake, a delicacy favored by all, carried in my rucksack for just this occasion. I open it with the indispensable, 1 ½' long P-38 can opener every infantryman carries attached to his dog tags chain. I eat the dry canned cake along with a drier chocolate "lifer bar" and gulps of water from my canteen to avoid choking. I have the amusing thought that choking to death on birthday cake would be a sad way for an infantryman to die in combat.

30 May. A fourth day of no enemy contact and no casualties, friendly or enemy. Today, the National Liberation Front (NLF) announces a 48-hour cease fire in honor of Buddha's birthday. (The NLF is the Viet Cong's senior political headquarters in South Vietnam.) Bravo Company and Recon are picked up by helicopter and flown to Tam Ky North for a one-day stand down. Alpha Company conducts RIF operations near BT160113 and begins an in-the-field stand down. Charlie and Delta also remain in the field and begin to stand down near BT163112.

Memorial Day—Remembering Our Dead

Today is also Memorial Day. No one in our company mentions it. For us, it is a day like all other days and that is just as well. Delta Company's six soldiers killed in action on 21 May were our first at Tam Ky. They are still very much on our minds. All total since our initial combat assault on 16 May, two weeks ago, our battalion has lost 27 soldiers KIA. Alpha Company, two KIA; Bravo, six KIA; Charlie, six KIA; and Recon three KIA. Our medical platoon in our Headquarters Company has lost four medics KIA. By comparison in the ten weeks prior to Tam Ky, our battalion had seven soldiers KIA.

I mention this only because we are now in a new phase of combat. The cost in terms of lives has increased four-fold in two short weeks. Our battalion has had 119 total casualties including killed and wounded since 16 May, enough to field another infantry company. Few replacements are coming in to make up our losses. Enemy casualties are not usually known, but are likely high due to our heavy and frequent use of artillery, air cavalry, and air support. (This is confirmed later by captured enemy soldiers.)

Back in the States, next of kin have only just recently learned of the death of their loved ones. Unknown to our soldiers, Memorial Day received mixed reviews back home. The focus is mostly on honoring World War I and II dead. There are still many living WWI veterans of "The Great War." Most are in their seventies and eighties and still able to participate in the nation's Memorial Day ceremonies. WWII veterans, from "The Greatest Generation," are just hitting late middle age. They are the largest group of veterans still living. Honoring WWII dead is an appropriate major focus. Korean War dead and veterans are fewer in number, but they too get attention.

The 33,000 dead from the Vietnam War receive a lot of negative attention from war protesters across the nation. They have a three-part message. The war is unjust, the dead are dying in vain, and the war dead are victims, not heroes. Some hatefully add, the Vietnam war dead should not be honored at all. Further adding to the tragedy of Vietnam War deaths, the year 1969 is a turning point for the war on the home front. Over 50% of American adults don't think the US should send troops to Vietnam. The numbers among mothers are likely much higher.

The protests against the war doesn't stop hundreds of towns and cities across America from honoring their Vietnam War dead though they are more recent and certainly more painful to many. Protests of the war are increasing. The American public is souring on the war. Our own government says they are not for a military solution and some public officials are openly denouncing on-going US military operations. Memorial Day is a hard day for families who have lost sons, brothers, husbands, and fathers. It will be for years to come.

In the meanwhile, soldiers in Vietnam fight on.

Casualty Table 7: 1-501st Casualties, 22–30 May 1969

Casualties	HHC	A Co	B Co	C Co	D Co	Recon	Total
KIA	0	2	3	0	0	3	8
WIA	1	2	12	2	0	3	20
Total	1	4	15	2	0	6	28

***

Casualties and Awards

1-501st Soldiers Killed in Action, 23–30 May 1969

Alpha Company—2
25 May: PFC Mario Lamelza, age 21, born 28 February 1948 from Philadelphia, PA
25 May: SP4 Ralph Vitch, age 20, born 4 March 1949 from Tampa, FL
Bravo Company—3
23 May SGT Roy Newsome, age 20, born 9 August 1948 from Somers, CT
26 May: PFC Eric Nadeau, age 20, born 12 November 1948 from Grand Forks, ND
26 May: PFC Euan Parker, age 22, born 18 August 1946 from Brigham City, UT
Echo Company (Recon)—3
23 May: PFC Robert Boese, age 22, born 29 December 1946 from Marion, KS
23 May: PFC Robert Randall, age 19, born 9 March 1950 from Miami, FL
24 May: SP4 Charles Jones, age 20, born 6 June 1948 from Calhoun City, MS

1-501st Soldier Awards, 23–30 May 1969 (other awards may have been made that were not mentioned in after action reports)

Bronze Star for Valor—21
Delta Company: 28 May, PFC James Dodge
Headquarters Company: 18 May, SP4 Russell Jett (medic) and SP4 Daniel Thurston (medic). 25 May, SP4 Henry Wolfe (medic)

Alpha Company: 25 May, LT Larry Gottschalk, SGT Andrew Arguello, SGT Michael Brateen, SGT Gerald Gillette, SGT Terry Lucarelli, SP4 Ralph Vitch
Bravo Company: 23 May, LT Osa Harp, SGT Frederick Ellis, SGT Philip Wolter, SGT George Cohen, SP4 David Yamamura. 25 May, SGT Dorsey Brewer, SP4 Richard Fuller, PFC Euan Parker
Recon Platoon: 23 May, PFC Robert Boese, PFC Robert Randall. 24 May, SP4 Charles Jones
Army Commendation Medal for Valor—1
Bravo Company: 23 May, 1SG George Paulshock
Purple Heart—28 awards to those KIA or WIA

CHAPTER 8

A Broken Cease Fire

31 May

Buddha's Birthday Continues

Today is the second day of the cease fire announced by the NLF in honor of Buddha's birthday. US forces are still standing down for the cease fire. No US combat operations are taking place throughout Vietnam. At least, that is the plan. Delta Company remains in the field at BT163112 with Charlie Company close by. The company's defensive perimeter is in a lightly wooded area on the gentle slope of a low hill next to a rice paddy.

Each of the company's two platoons have put out three-man observation posts (OP) in opposite directions. The 3rd Platoon's OP is 250 m north of the company. The OP is on the edge of an open area, able to observe enemy movement near or toward the company. In the last eight days since the big fight on 21 May, no one in Delta Company has been killed or wounded. Other companies haven't been so fortunate. All is quiet. We are glad to have a slow day.

Arrival of a New Commander

Unknown to most in the company, today is CPT Begley's last day as company commander. He is finishing a five-month command tour which began on 1 January 1969. For unknown reasons, he has been quiet about it. Perhaps it is difficult for him to leave so soon after we've had so many casualties and the company is expecting further heavy combat. The standard tour length for company, battalion, and brigade commanders is about six months. Begley's time is up because his 12-month Vietnam tour is ending.

CPT Leland Roy has been selected to take over Delta Company. Roy didn't learn he was taking the company until this morning, just a few hours in advance of joining the company, LTC Singer, the 501st Battalion commander, tells him, "You're going to a good company. It has the three best platoon leaders in the battalion." Singer may not be aware that LT Black, our 2nd Platoon leader, was seriously wounded on 21 May and is no longer with the company. Whether his high opinion of our platoon leaders is true or not, as events unfold in the next two days it won't make any difference.

Roy comes out on an early morning log bird a day in advance of taking command. He wants to get a feel for the company and learn as much as he can before assuming command tomorrow. A few replacements come in with Roy. With the company hunkered down in the field for the cease fire, it seems a good day to get acquainted with his new company.

CPT Begley introduces Roy to three key men in the company: LT Paul Wharton, artillery FO, SP4 Ed Medros, RTO, and SP4 Mark Moses, an RTO who acts as "field-first," handling all company logistics, manning, and medevacs. They are all critical to the company's combat operations.

Roy is not introduced to the two platoon leaders or their platoons. LT Boyd and I are not even aware he is present or that this is Begley's last day as our commander. Roy will get a close-up opportunity to meet us soon. Begley doesn't provide Roy much information about the company except that the company's current field strength is little more than half its normal number and the company now has only two platoons. Not much is said about the 21 May fight and the heavy casualties, though so far it is the company's most intense combat action at Tam Ky and is still fresh in the minds of the company's soldiers.

Soon after CPT Roy's arrival, at 0935H FAC comes on station flying the familiar US Air Force two-engine Cessna O-2 Skymaster. The pilot, a USAF forward air observer, also has an artillery FO on board. The FAC team coordinates tactical air and artillery support with each company's "on the ground" artillery FO. It is always good to have a FAC overhead. They are our eyes in the sky, keeping watch for enemy activity. Slow day or not.

Unexpected Enemy Contact

With the FAC coming on station, SP4 James Parvin and PFC John Bishop from 3rd Platoon take a VS-17 Aircraft Marker Panel out to our OP. The 24" × 70" nylon panel is high-visibility orange. The panel is laid out on the ground to mark the OP's position just in case USAF tactical air support or Army Air Cavalry attack helicopters are needed.

At 0937H, automatic weapons fire is heard from the direction of the 3rd Platoon's OP. The gun, identified by sound, is a US M-60 machine gun. Everyone looks toward the OP, but nothing can be seen since the OP is concealed in some bushes. First thoughts are the OP has opened fire on an enemy target. A report comes in over the radio. The OP has received enemy fire from a previously captured US M-60 machine gun. PFC Paul Scouten has been hit. More accurately, his M-16 rifle's composite plastic stock has been hit and the splinters gouged Scouten's side. The wound is serious enough to require medevac.

When the enemy opens fire with a US weapon, there is momentary confusion. Infantry soldiers are accustomed to quickly identify both enemy and friendly weapons fire by sound. The machine gun was likely captured during earlier attacks on South Vietnamese Army units. Soldiers at Tam Ky learned to expect the unexpected. Take nothing for granted. The enemy position is reported to be across an open area 200 m north of the OP. SGT Littleton, 3rd Platoon squad leader responsible for the OP, immediately goes out to the OP to check on his men and assess the situation. He doesn't have to be told to go. He just goes.

Minutes later, CPT Begley tells me to have 3rd Platoon conduct a sweep toward the location from where the enemy machine-gun fire came. Alerted by the gunfire, we are ready to move. We quickly leave the company perimeter and move forward past the OP. I see Scouten has been bandaged. He is hurting but will survive. Littleton, Parvin, and Bishop join our formation as we begin our sweep up the slight slope of a hill covered with knee-high scrub brush. PFCs Johnny Pilsner and Rob Sitek remain at the OP to cover our rear.

As my platoon moves up the hill in the direction of the enemy machine-gun fire, our adrenaline is flowing full throttle. The anticipation of immediate enemy contact has all of our senses on full alert. Every man in the platoon including me is making his own personal estimate of our situation as we move. Where is the enemy located? Was this a hit-and-run attack? Is the enemy trying to draw us into an ambush? What is the size of the enemy element we'll encounter? What actions will we take on enemy contact? When will they open fire with the machine gun?

Our platoon is exposed as we continue up the slope, moving toward a tree line 100 m away. We spread out as we move making ourselves a harder target to hit. It is likely we will soon receive fire from the tree line from the same enemy M-60 machine gun that opened up on our OP. All eyes are peeled to our front and flanks for any signs of the enemy. We are moving at a steady, fast walk, weapon's safeties off, ready to return fire at the first indication of enemy contact.

Halfway up the slope, an explosion 30 m behind our advancing platoon gets our attention. It is not clear if the round is a 60 mm mortar or a 40 mm grenade fired from a captured US M-79 grenade launcher. It doesn't matter. No one is hit. My first instinct is to yell, "Keep moving, let's go!" If we stop and hit the ground, we will become an easy target.

A few seconds later, another explosion occurs closer behind us. Again, no one is hit. I yell again. "Let's move! Faster!" The tree line is not more than 50 m away. The enemy may be waiting until we get closer to open fire. If so, they will likely open up any moment. We need to keep going. If we can make it to the trees, we will be safer than in the open.

We cover the distance quickly and enter the tree line without receiving fire. Just inside the trees is an old 4 ft high stone wall. Moss and dead leaves cover much of the wall's large black stones. Vegetation on the far side of the wall and to our left and right flanks makes visibility difficult beyond 20–30 m. An old trail follows along our side of the wall. The platoon spreads out along the wall taking up firing positions and providing security.

SGT Littleton's squad is on the right, SGT Horan's on the left. We take a short breather, quietly listening and looking. It is eerily quiet. I can hear my heart thumping. A foreboding feeling adds to the suspense. Several men in Littleton's squad advance beyond the wall slowly, walking softly, deliberately placing each foot to minimize noise. They see two dilapidated huts, but hesitate to check them out. They realize they may have advanced too far. None of us brought our rucksacks. We don't have all the ammunition we normally carry. They wisely decide to pull back to the wall.

I make a radio call to CPT Begley. "Delta-Six, we've reached the top of the slope and have taken up positions along a stone wall." He tells me to explore along the wall. I reply, "We're checking it out. I'll report back soon." In the meantime, Littleton's squad is back at the wall. He is observing the two dilapidated huts some 20–30 m from the wall when he sees movement from one of the huts. It is an NVA soldier. Littleton fires at him. The enemy soldier disappears.

Request to Pull Back Denied

It seems clear we have come upon an enemy position. The size is unclear. We likely will not know the location of any concealed positions until they open fire. The 21 May firefight is uppermost in my mind. The last thing I want to do is get my platoon trapped in an enemy bunker complex. I call Delta Six again. This time I recommend we pull back and pound the enemy position with artillery. Delta Six refuses my request. He says we should attempt to flank the enemy position in an effort to take out the positions and kill the enemy soldiers.

I am uncertain how that can be done without losing some of my men. The position can't be flanked if we don't know the enemy's size or where other bunker positions may be located. Are they drawing us into an ambush on ground that gives them the tactical advantage? Delta Six says, "1-6 is bringing his platoon up on your right flank." LT Richard Boyd's platoon is made up of what is left of 1st and 2nd Platoons after the 21 May day-long firefight.

Again, Delta Six says he wants me to attack the enemy position. Rather than refusing a battlefield order, I say, "Delta Six, I don't see how it can be done without getting a lot of our guys killed. Request you come forward and take a look at our situation. Show me what you want done and I'll do it." He replies with some irritation, "On my way!"

Infantry soldiers know it is serious to disobey a direct order in combat. It is drilled into our heads to follow orders. To disobey a direct order is an unpardonable sin

In my mind, I haven't ever disobeyed Delta Six's orders. I don't intend to now. My intent is to get him to better understand our situation. He can't know what we are facing several hundred meters back at the company CP.

Three thoughts guide my actions. First, we have a mission to accomplish. Pulling back and hitting the enemy position with artillery before attacking will also accomplish the mission. Second, if at all possible, we should try to accomplish the mission without getting our guys killed. If that is not possible, we should at least try to minimize casualties. Third, a close-in ground attack on a hidden bunker complex with an enemy of unknown size seems a bad idea, especially so when artillery and air support are immediately available. Once we are engaged close in with the enemy position, we won't be able to use our artillery or air support. Thought we had learned that on 21 May.

In this situation, I would rather be criticized for being too careful and protective of my men than getting them pinned down and needlessly chewed up within another enemy bunker system. When I took the platoon in January, I told them, "I've been with the Ranger Department at Benning for the last seven months, two in training and five as instructor, but I'm new here. You guys know more about combat than me. All of you want to go home alive and in one piece. A big part of my job is to get you home safely. If you see me doing something dumb, tell me!" So far, no one has been killed in 3rd platoon. That will soon change.

1st Platoon Moves Up

Before CPT Begley arrives at our position, LT Boyd's platoon nears the top of the slope on our right. When I first see them, they're only 20 m or so from what we believe might be an enemy bunker. I yell, "Boyd, down! Enemy!" motioning downward with the palm of my hand then pointing in the direction of the enemy position. Automatic weapons fire immediately erupts at 1st Platoon's front. Boyd's RTO, PFC Philip Pratt, is killed outright by a burst of AK-47 fire.

As Boyd drops to the ground, he sees Pratt get hit. Boyd yells to a nearby soldier to put a grenade in the bunker from where the firing came. The enemy gunner takes quick aim at Boyd. One round hits in front of him. A second round shatters the bones in his right hand and lodges in his wrist between two arteries. He is bleeding badly and not sure how seriously he is wounded. The grenade forces the enemy gunner to pull back through a tunnel connected to the bunker. Boyd moves to cover. The 1st Platoon medic bandages his hand and wrist to stop the bleeding. SSG Sahrle takes over the platoon and begins repositioning his platoon.

PFC Pratt had been 1st Platoon's sniper since 21 May when LT Boyd's RTO, PFC Byron "Benny" Bennett was wounded. Pratt reluctantly took over the radio. He was a good soldier, willing to help where he can. PFC Phil Cravens was next to Pratt when he was hit. He saw him fall, killed instantly. They were close friends. Cravens wasn't hit but fell forward to take cover. He is now inside the bunker complex. Each time he moves, he takes fire. In 3rd Platoon we hear him call out. Thinking he is wounded, we begin working on how to get him out.

Cravens, meanwhile, is working to get himself out. An enemy soldier in a dark green NVA uniform tosses a grenade his way. Cravens picks up the grenade and throws it back. He doesn't know if he killed him. What he knows is he must get out of there quick. Cravens pops a smoke grenade and throws it toward the enemy position. The smoke screens his escape. He scrambles out and rejoins his platoon which has pulled back some 50 m. A too close call.

A Forced Decision

PFC Johnny Mack Pilsner, the 3rd Platoon's sniper, is in SGT Littleton's squad. He has been called forward from the OP. He is kneeling behind the stone wall. His M-21 sniper rifle is positioned in a small opening. PFC John Meade is to Pilsner's left. They are buddies. Meade crawls over to get a drink from Pilsner's canteen. PFC Booker Taylor is lying just under Pilsner. He is also trying to spot the enemy through a hole in the wall.

Knowing the enemy is close by, Littleton tells them to spread out. Pilsner spots movement through his high-powered sniper scope. He thinks he may see an enemy soldier looking through an enemy bunker firing port. Pilsner tells the others. They continue to gather with Pilsner behind the wall to see what he sees. It is a regrettable mistake.

CPT Begley arrives at our position. Unknown to me or our platoon, CPT Roy accompanies Begley forward. Roy is kneeling 10 m to the rear of Littleton's squad. Begley and I huddle to talk each on one knee. We are a short distance from the wall, maybe 20 m to the side of Pilsner's position. As I begin to brief Begley of our situation, Roy notices the men bunching up at Pilsner's position and tells them to disperse.

Before they can move, the enemy fires an RPG directly at Pilsner's position. The loud whoosh of the 40 mm rocket travelling 300 m per second gives no time to react. The exploding RPG is deafening. The heavy explosive RPG round which can penetrate 5 ft of brick wall smashes the 2 ft thick wall in front of Pilsner. He is knocked back, calls out and dies from his wounds. Taylor, directly below Pilsner, is wounded and bleeding and should be dead. Miraculously, he won't need a medevac. Meade still on Pilsner's left is dazed. Littleton on the right is knocked out by concussion. CPT Roy is wounded in his left shoulder by RPG fragments.

When the RPG hits, CPT Begley and I have barely begun to talk. Neither of us are wounded. The explosion knocked us over. A large dust cloud hangs over our platoon. Gathering my senses, I look to see what happened. Begley yells at me over his shoulder as he immediately departs, "Get your wounded and pull your platoon back!" I yell back, "Hold 1st Platoon in place to cover us!" Begley doesn't answer or turn around. Perhaps he doesn't hear me. At least, he knows our situation first-hand now.

The quicker we leave the position, the better. Several soldiers are already on their feet preparing to carry Pilsner. He is a big, muscular man, well over 200 lbs. It takes four men. Another gets Pilsner's weapon. Several more provide security. My greatest concern as we begin our pull back is the enemy will discover we are leaving. If they do, they will fire on us as we move back over open ground carrying Pilsner off the hill. We have to move quickly.

We reach the edge of the tree line and enter the open area we must cross to get back to our company perimeter. Several hundred meters away, I see 1st Platoon already off the hill. They are arriving back at the company's position. Apparently they didn't get word to cover our withdrawal. We are on our own. As Pilsner is carried back, we provide our own security. Pratt's body couldn't be recovered by 1st Platoon without getting more men killed. He will be recovered as soon as the enemy situation permits.

As we get back to the company, we leave Pilsner at the company command post. He will be evacuated with LT Boyd and PFC Scouten. Though wounded in the shoulder, CPT Roy remains in the field overnight. He will stay with the company and take command tomorrow as planned. His coming forward with Begley and staying with the company after being wounded are early signs we are getting a good new commander.

PFC Johnny Mack Pilsner will be missed. We called him "Tex." Good natured, he always had a smile. A good attitude even in difficult situations. Pratt will also be missed. Especially by his best friend Cravens. Tomorrow when the company sweeps through the bunker complex, it will be Cravens who finds Pratt and carries him back to the company for evacuation.

In combat there is little time to mourn loss of fellow soldiers. Pilsner is the first soldier killed in action while I've had the platoon. I am thankful more didn't die today. I will never forget Pilsner or regret delaying the attack on the enemy position. It is the hardest and maybe best decision I make as a platoon leader. Calling in artillery first before attacking the bunkers still seems the right call.

Each soldier's death takes a toll on everyone in the unit. The full impact of a fellow soldier's death is sometimes not immediate. Good company commanders, platoon leaders, and squad leaders feel responsible for their men and they are. Soldiers sense that same responsibility for their buddies. At company and below, the men killed are often well known. They are not numbers on a board. Memories of them last a lifetime.

For two families, Pilsner's in Alleyton, Texas and Pratt's in Fremont, New Hampshire, their mourning will soon begin. More brave men will fall. The fight at Tam Ky is not nearly over.

An Air Strike Goes Wrong

At 1500H, CPT Begley's last combat action as Delta Company commander is to call for an air strike on the bunker complex. We hear the call over our radio. I wonder, "Why we didn't we do this an hour ago?" The FAC is still on station. He shoots a marker rocket where he wants the bombs to land. When the rocket explodes, white phosphorus smoke identifies the target, making it easy for a "fast mover" to see. We get a single Marine F-4 Phantom for the strike. It's enough. The two-engine attack fighter carries a heavy bomb load.

Delta Company puts out a visual marker panel to identify our forward position from the air. The FAC tells the Phantom pilot the location of the bomb-target line. That is the flight path he must take to avoid dropping bombs on friendly troops. The line is parallel to Delta Company's position and 500 m to our front. If he stays on the bomb-target line, the Phantom pilot will never have to fly over Delta Company.

Any air strike closer than 600 m to friendly troops is called "danger close." With our actual distance about 500 m, we have a front-row seat. The first pass is flawless. It is a dry run for the pilot to get his bearings. The Phantom comes in on the bomb-target line in a steep dive. He pulls out at 300 ft with his afterburners roaring. We look on with admiration and awe.

On the second pass, the pilot drops a 500 lb. napalm cannister near the bunker complex. It is a close miss, but a miss. Still, we feel the heat of the jellied-gasoline blast from our position of safety. Napalm doesn't explode but burns extremely hot and fast, terrifying targeted enemy soldiers. Casualties occur from intense heat (up to 2000°) and suffocation when oxygen in the air is instantaneously burned up.

On the third pass, the Phantom will drop its bombs. We wait lying flat on the ground. The Phantom is out of sight. We barely hear him. A minute or so passes. Suddenly, we hear the thundering roar of the twin-engine fighter-bomber behind us. We look up. He is off the bomb-target line. The target smoke has been obliterated by the napalm. Misoriented, the pilot is in a steep dive coming right at us! There is no time to react. His altitude is only a few hundred feet as he levels his aircraft and releases four 250 lb. bombs. We see the bombs detach from the racks under his wings and the fins of the high-drag bombs snap open. The bombs are falling nose down toward our position. There is no time to take cover. A nearby soldier shouts a loud expletive.

The bombs pass just over the trees above us. Their forward momentum pushes them a mere 100 m past our position. The explosion is indescribable. The shock wave in the air and through the ground throws us up in the air and slams us down. Shrapnel, dirt, debris, and dust fall all over us. Those in the company command post closest to where the bombs hit are buried in a layer of dirt. LT Wharton, our FO, urgently calls to the FAC, "Abort air strike! I say again "Abort air strike!" The FAC hears his call. The air strike ends. No one is hurt. All are shaken by the near miss.

There is lots of nervous laughter and cursing. Had the pilot hit the bomb release a second sooner, we would be dead.

Moments after the last bomb run, we see six enemy soldiers running hard from the bunker area. They are 300–400 m from our position. They survived two bomb runs and aren't hanging around for another. Taken under fire, one is killed. The others get away. We are not the only ones who escaped death today. As things settle down, the next order of business is to get a medevac in for LT Boyd and PFC Scouten. PFC Pilsner will be flown out too. It is mid-afternoon. A "slow day" at Tam Ky.

At 1920H, night defensive positions for the 1-501st are Delta Company at BT163115 co-located with Alpha Company; Bravo Company and the Battalion Recon Platoon are at BT163112. Charlie Company is now attached to 1-46th Infantry Battalion and pulling security at LZ Professional.

Tonight, CPT Begley's command ends. The next morning, he will take an early morning chopper back to the rear. He makes few farewells to the soldiers he has led for five months. Though it has been a very tough two weeks, it is not Begley's fault he's leaving. Likely, he doesn't feel good about his soldiers being left behind in a hard fight.

Begley's departure points to a major failure of the personnel system and senior Army leaders who set the policy. What could be right about a company commander giving up command of his infantry company in the midst of heavy combat simply because he has completed five months of command and his 12-month Vietnam tour? Not much. Tomorrow we will wake up with a new commander. As Scarlett O'Hara famously said in Gone with the Wind, "Tomorrow is another day." Maybe it will be a better day.

***

Casualties and Awards

Casualty Table 8 shows the number of casualties suffered by Delta and its sister companies over the last ten days (22–31 May) since our biggest battle on 21 May and since the beginning of combat operations at Tam Ky on 16 May.

Casualty Table 8: 1-501st Casualties, 22–31 May 1969

Casualties	HHC	A Co	B Co	C Co	D Co	Recon	Total
KIA	0	2	3	0	2	3	10
WIA	1	3	12	2	4	3	25
Total	1	5	15	2	6	6	35
Total to date 16–31 May	4 KIA 5 WIA 9 TOT	2 KIA 3 WIA 5 TOT	6 KIA 35 WIA 41 TOT	6 KIA 20 WIA 26 TOT	8 KIA 21 WIA 30 TOT	3 KIA 12 WIA 15 TOT	29 KIA 96 WIA 125 TOT

1-501st Soldiers Killed in Action, 31 May 1969

Delta Company—2

31 May: PFC Johnny Mack Pilsner, age 22, born 30 April 1947 from Alleyton, TX

31 May: PFC Philip Pratt, age 20, born 20 April 1948 from Fremont, NH

1-501st Soldier Awards, 31 May (other awards may have been made that were not mentioned in after action reports)

Bronze Star for Valor—1

Delta Company: SP4 James Parvin

Army Commendation Medal for Valor—2

Delta Company: SP4 Arthur Gale, PFC John Meade

Purple Heart—awarded to all soldiers KIA or WIA

CHAPTER 9

Change of Command

1–2 June

1 June: A New Commander

Early morning 1 June, we learn CPT Roy is now in command. Yesterday, CPT Begley had not made us aware CPT Roy had flown out to join the company and was taking command the next day. I was also unaware that yesterday he had come forward with Begley and had been wounded in the shoulder by the same RPG that killed Pilsner. But here he is taking command of his first infantry company in combat. How he got here is an interesting story, but first things first.

CPT Roy calls for me and SSG Sahrle to come to the company CP. We are meeting him and he is meeting his two platoon leaders for the first time. Sahrle is now acting platoon leader of 1st Platoon (including what remains of 2nd Platoon) and is the most senior NCO in our company. He was promoted to Staff Sergeant just a few months ago. He is on his first term of enlistment and graduated from PNCOC (the same course Tepner attended) before coming to Vietnam in June 1968. Roy doesn't know Sahrle's background or mine.

I can imagine what Roy is thinking, "This is all I've got for platoon leaders? These two guys don't even have platoon sergeants and their squad leaders are all first-termer, junior sergeants leading understrength squads." He is not discouraged. Roy's been in the infantry long enough to know you play the hand you are dealt. He will make do with what he has. After a brief introduction and cordial exchange, Roy is ready for us to get on with our first mission of the day. We are to recover PFC Pratt who was killed yesterday. That is his top priority, a fact that will be quietly noted with satisfaction and appreciation by our soldiers.

Our two platoons are to sweep through the bunker complex and find Pratt. Sahrle's platoon will lead since Pratt was a 1st Platoon member. Roy reminds us that even though we saw enemy soldiers leaving the area of the bunkers yesterday, we don't know if the bunkers were reoccupied during the night. We are to approach the bunkers cautiously. When we find Pratt, we are to take care that his body isn't booby-trapped. Once we recover Pratt and check the bunkers, we are to return to our current location. With clear guidance, we brief our platoons and are soon ready to move out.

Our two platoons move back up the hill to the enemy bunker complex. We approach cautiously, but as expected the enemy has evacuated the position. Blood trails indicate they took casualties. PFC Pratt is found and carried back by PFC Cravens to the company CP. Pratt will go out this morning on the same chopper as CPT Begley. Our mission is completed in less than an hour. CPT Roy notifies LTC Singer that Pratt has been found and there are no enemy contact or casualties. Singer is pleased to get the word and commends Roy for his first mission accomplished.

Later that day, CPT Roy and I have a brief talk. He puts his hand on my shoulder and says, "Ed, take care of yourself. You're my last platoon leader." I smile and say, "Yes sir, that's my plan." It is a good gesture on his part. We are all in need of encouragement. During the remainder of the day, Delta Company conducts limited combat patrols under the new leadership of CPT Roy.

Questions About Our New Commander

In combat, soldiers have little opportunity to get an advance look at the background, character, knowledge, and capabilities of a new commander like Roy. They will watch him closely to learn as much as they can as soon as they can. Their battlefield success, not to mention their lives, depends on his effectiveness as a combat leader.

The soldiers of Delta Company have many unspoken questions about their new commander. How does he respond to stress and pressures in battle? Is he physically tough? Mentally and emotionally stable? Does he instill confidence so his men want to follow him? Can he quickly make right decisions in the heat of battle? Is he technically competent in infantry skills?

There is more. How does he talk with his officers, NCOs, and soldiers? What level of respect and concern does he have for those he leads? What motivates him as a commander? Is he outwardly motivated merely trying to impress senior officers? Or, is he internally motivated as a soldier and leader to do the right thing? These questions and others will be answered in the days ahead.

The Army trains its infantry captains quite well to lead infantry companies. As a group they consider themselves better than average officers. A good number are excellent. Some of course are better than others and in combat, soldiers want the best. It won't be long before they will begin to have their many questions answered. If the soldiers of Delta Company knew about Roy's background and experience, their minds would be put at ease. They will soon discover they are getting just the commander they need for the difficulties that lie ahead.

The Right Man for a Tough Job

CPT Roy, age 28, was born 6 December 1940 in the rural town of Evangeline, Louisiana. Evangeline is in the state's southwest corner in bayou country. It is best known for having the first oil well in the state. His family had limited money. His father abandoned his family when Roy was an infant. He grew up in a time when single parent families were not common. His life as a young boy was spent outdoors hunting, fishing, playing sports, and spending time in the swamps. As a young man, he began to think of becoming a Marine.

World War II was not long over when Roy reached his teens. As high school graduation approached, he and a close friend decided to join the Army under its new "buddy plan." His friend backed out at the last minute, but Roy enlisted anyway in 1959. He was 18 years old. Roy volunteered for airborne because of the extra "jump pay." He sent most of his paycheck home to support his mother.

Roy completed basic training at Fort Jackson, South Carolina, followed by advanced infantry training at Fort Benning, Georgia, and jump school at Fort Bragg, North Carolina. He was assigned to the 82nd Airborne Division's 2nd Airborne Battle Group, 501st Infantry (Airborne) at Fort Bragg. For his first years, Roy was an infantry heavy weapons specialist. During those early years, he volunteered for and successfully completed the Special Forces Qualification Course.

Soon after graduation, he was recommended for Officer Candidate School (OCS) at Fort Benning. He waited a year for a slot in the school and finally graduated as a Second Lieutenant in 1965. After OCS, Lieutenant Roy went to Vietnam as an individual replacement from January 1966 to January 1967. He saw extensive combat as an infantry platoon leader with Bravo Company, 1-327th Infantry, 1st Brigade, 101st Airborne Division. Roy was seriously wounded during operations on 4 March 1966 in Tuy Hoa located in the coastal plains of central South Vietnam. He was walking behind his three-man point team near the front of his platoon. An enemy machine gun firing from their flank hit all three point men and Roy. A round passed through the back of his helmet. Multiple rounds impacted his rucksack. One round hit his lower back penetrating deeply from side to side.

A medevac took Roy to an Army Field Hospital then he was flown to Japan for major surgery. There his back was wired together. He remained in Japan recovering prior to being returned to the States. His healing went well. Instead of going home, he volunteered to go back to Vietnam. He was allowed two weeks convalescence leave before returning to Vietnam, but refused, eager to get back to his platoon.

Once in-country, he purposely by-passed the Army replacement center and made his way back to the 1st Brigade of the 101st and his old battalion. MAJ David Hackworth, his Battalion Executive Officer, was surprised, but pleased to see him. Knowing Roy was just out of the hospital, Hackworth offered Roy any job in the battalion. Roy asked to get his old platoon back. Hackworth said "Done!" (Hackworth later became a battalion commander and GEN Creighton Abrams, commander of military forces in Vietnam, called him "the best battalion commander I ever saw." COL David Hackworth, one of the most decorated soldiers of the Vietnam War, later authored *About Face: Odyssey of an American Warrior*, Simon& Schuster, 1990, offering a biting critique of the conduct of the Vietnam War.)

Roy was flown out to his old platoon operating independently near Phan Thiet. His friend who took over his platoon after Roy was wounded willingly relinquished it. He told Roy, "Welcome back! In two hours, your platoon will be on Hawk Flight standby as the ready reaction platoon for the battalion. You don't have much time to get ready." Roy smiled and said, "It's good to be back!"

Roy completed seven months as an infantry platoon leader and then moved to Charlie Company as executive officer for several months until the end of his tour. In that position, Roy who was now a 1st Lieutenant, became a "Fighting XO," often going on combat patrols with his company commander, each leading two platoons. He wasn't much for staying safe in the rear area.

In January 1967, his first Vietnam tour completed, Roy returned to the States and was assigned as a senior tactical officer at OCS. His leadership was recognized by the graduating officer candidate class which dedicated their yearbook to him. Roy decided to seek a Regular Army commission. With no infantry slots available, he reluctantly accepted a branch transfer to the Military Police Corps. Now promoted to Captain, Roy's first assignment as a military police (MP) officer was command of the MP company in the 82nd Airborne Division. His boss there was LTC Eugene Murdock, Provost Marshall for the division. During his command tour, Roy decided he wanted to return to the infantry, applied, and received a branch transfer back to infantry.

In September 1968, CPT Roy received orders for Vietnam and arrived in October 1968. LTC Murdock, who would be promoted to Colonel and take command of the Military Police Group at Long Binh, appointed Roy as his Assistant S3. Out of loyalty to Murdoch, Roy served seven months with the group until Murdock's tour ended.

In May 1969, when Murdock departed, Roy was finally free to seek an infantry assignment in Vietnam. His first choice was to return to the 1st Brigade, 101st Airborne Division. Unfortunately, the first week in May he had a major appendicitis attack and emergency surgery at the Army Hospital in Long Binh. Released from the hospital with two weeks convalescence leave, he decided instead to make his way north to join the 101st Airborne Division and his old unit. Arriving at the 101st, for six days he was first assigned to the 3rd Brigade and 2-501st who had just finished fighting in the Hamburger Hill battle which was now over.

With the 1st Brigade heavily engaged in a new fight near Tam Ky, CPT Roy was reassigned to the 1-501st due to the battalion's heavy casualties and recent loss of two company commanders. He was flown by Huey to LZ Professional and joined the battalion. At first, he was considered for the S-3 Air position responsible for coordinating air assets used by the battalion. A few days later on short notice, LTC Singer told Roy he would immediately replace Begley in Delta Company. Finally, he would command an infantry company in combat with the 101st Airborne Division, the position he most wanted.

CPT Roy is 28 years old as he takes command. He is the oldest young man in Delta Company and certainly the most experienced. More importantly, he is the right man for the tough job of leading an understrength infantry company short of officers and NCOs. The men who serve under CPT Roy in the days ahead will respond well to and appreciate his leadership. Many will owe him their lives and attribute their survival in combat to him.

2 June: Preparation for Hill 376

A "Never Quit" Commander

In his second day in command, CPT Roy's shoulder wound is hurting and worse than expected. My platoon medic looks at his wound and sees it is getting infected. He advises CPT Roy to get it treated by the medical staff at LZ Professional. Roy reluctantly agrees. Before going in, he calls LTC Singer to let him know his plans to return to Professional in the next hour. Singer agrees and tells him not to worry about the company. He and his operations officer, Major MacDiarmid, will keep an eye on it.

Roy takes a helicopter out in the early afternoon. It is the last time I'll see CPT Roy for 46 years. Landing at the dusty helipad at Professional, he goes straight to the 1st Brigade's well-staffed and equipped clinic. As the medic said, infection is beginning to set in. The wound is cleaned and rebandaged. A strong course of antibiotics is prescribed.

LTC Singer comes in to see him. He's concerned about Roy's ability to take the company into combat. He tells Roy he has a replacement company commander ready to go and Roy does not have to go back out. Roy doesn't tell Singer that he's also only three weeks out from his recent appendectomy. He is confident it won't hurt his performance. He has been getting stronger every day.

Roy refuses to give up his new command. He tells LTC Singer, "I'm both willing and able to get back to my company, I can fly out first thing next morning." Singer tells him, Delta Company will be making a combat assault in the morning, likely into a hot LZ. Roy responds, "I'm ready to go. The shoulder wound is painful, but only a temporary setback." Finally, LTC Singer relents, impressed by Roy's resolve. Though Roy and Singer may not be thinking it, Roy is the personal embodiment of Delta Company's motto, "Never Quit!"

Roy knows Delta Company is both understrength and short of officer and NCO leaders. He rightly believes his previous combat experience is in dire need. What he saw and briefly learned about the company was positive despite the manning issues. His decision to return and resume command is an unselfish decision. His experience, combat leadership, and "Never Quit" fighting spirit will be needed more than Roy knows.

Once his wound is treated, CPT Roy heads over to the battalion's TOC to get a detailed update on events. He talks with one of the older TOC operations NCOs. He learns more about the 21 May combat and how brutal it was. The NCO says the battalion's four companies have tended to operate close to one another since taking heavy casualties. It is understandable.

Roy talks briefly with MAJ MacDiarmid, the battalion operations officer, about plans for tomorrow. He learns this afternoon Bravo Company (1-501st) is conducting a combat assault to rescue an Aero-Rifle Platoon from the brigade's Bravo Troop, 2-17th Air Cavalry. The platoon was attacked by a large number of NVA immediately after landing on Hill 376 and took heavy casualties. Tomorrow morning, Delta and Alpha Companies will be inserted on Hill 376.

The Fight on Hill 376 Begins

For the past two weeks whenever brigade helicopters fly near or over Hill 376 they take enemy fire. Sometimes light caliber weapons, but often .51 caliber heavy machine guns in an antiaircraft role. This eventually raises the question, "Why does the enemy have heavy guns there? What are they protecting?"

Since noon on 2 June, the 1-501st TOC has been listening to the developing situation on Hill 376. The 1st Brigade commander inserted a small 18-man Aero-Rifle Platoon from Bravo Troop, 2-17th Cavalry at BT210128 on the east side of the mountain. Dropped off by helicopter, their mission was to determine the size and location of the enemy which may be there. They found out soon enough. The enemy was waiting for them in force. Within minutes of the helicopters lifting off, the platoon is pinned down by withering enemy fire. Surrounded and under attack by what is reported to be hundreds of NVA soldiers, the platoon quickly has four killed and four wounded.

SP4 Joseph Guy LaPointe Jr. is the medic for the Aero-Rifle Platoon. He immediately answers the call "Medic!" from the wounded. Going forward to locate the wounded soldiers, he runs through heavy enemy fire then begins to crawl directly in view of the enemy bunker. As his platoon attempts to provide covering fire to suppress the enemy bunker, LaPointe administers first aid to one wounded soldier and protects a second soldier with his own body. Fire from the enemy bunker wounds LaPointe, knocking him to the ground. Though wounded, he returns to the two wounded men and continues to give them aid until an enemy hand grenade kills all three men. For his bravery under fire, SP4 LaPointe is awarded the Medal of Honor posthumously on 25 January 1972. LaPointe was a conscientious objector who chose to serve in the military to save the lives of others.

The 1st Brigade commander soon realizes "we've kicked a hornet's nest." He alerts the 1-501st and assigns the battalion the mission of relieving enemy pressure on the 2-17th Cavalry's platoon. In fact, it is a rescue mission. Bravo Company at Tam Ky North securing 1st Brigade's command post is designated the immediate reaction force. At 1440H, the 1st Platoon from Bravo Company, 1-501st is inserted into an LZ near BT203126 to link-up with the Aero-Rifle Platoon. The timely arrival and bravery of the platoon leader (name is withheld by his personal request) and his platoon reinforces and saves the Aero-Rifle Platoon from being overrun and certain death.

At 1745H, CPT Walter Shelton comes into Hill 376 with the rest of Bravo Company and the battalion's Recon Platoon attached. At the end of their first day on Hill 376, Bravo has only one wounded soldier, SGT David Holladay. Apparently, the enemy has decided to lay low and not take on a larger unit in direct combat. Alpha and Delta companies are on standby alert to conduct combat assaults into

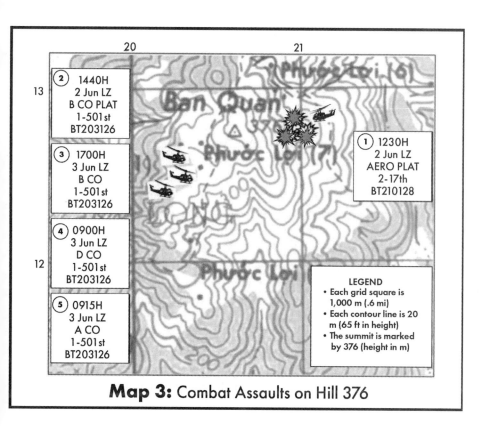

Map 3: Combat Assaults on Hill 376

Bravo's LZ the next morning (3 June). Once alerted, the two companies monitor the on-going battle on their radios and turn their attention to tomorrow's combat assault. The fight for Hill 376 has begun.

In the afternoon, Delta Company moves to its pickup point at BT164109 for tomorrow's combat assault. Our two platoons are making routine combat assault preparations. They know the drill. Checking weapons, ammunition, grenades, radios, batteries, food, and water. So far, no additional information on the enemy situation is available other than what is picked up on the radio. What is clear—there is a large, well-armed NVA force on Hill 376. The fighting is likely to be intense. There is also no information on the battalion's concept of operations. The only thing known, and it's a guess, is that Delta and Alpha Company will likely be put down on the Hill somewhere close to Bravo Company.

Fortunately, Bravo Company takes only one casualty on their first day on Hill 376, SGT David Holladay is wounded in action. The Aero-Rifle Platoon's four KIA casualties include SSG Jimmie Reed, SSG Emmanuel Saunders, and SP5 Richard Brech. As previously mentioned SP4 Joseph LaPointe the attached medic was also killed. (Soldiers WIA were not identified in the Bravo Troop, 2-17th Cavalry after action report for *Operation Lamar Plain* and could not be identified in other records.)

My Last Day in the Field

As evening closes in, my attention is on tomorrow. Not enough on our current situation. A costly mistake. We have been in our current position all afternoon. Our claymore antipersonnel mines and trip flares are not yet out. Typically, we do that just before dark. As dusk approaches, we begin to feel secure. We have had no enemy contact in two days. A quiet stillness settles over our position. We begin to implement our nighttime security procedures. Talking in low voices. Turning radios down. Making as little noise as practical checking weapons. No fires for heating chow. My platoon's position is within a stand of small scrub trees and brush. They are just tall enough to conceal my 6 ft, 3 in frame. I am busy checking our positions. Most of my guys are already dug in for the night.

Suddenly, the quiet is shattered by an explosion just a few feet from where I'm standing. I'm thrown some 20 ft into an open area and land like a sack of potatoes. A second explosion follows the first. Both rounds are preceded by the characteristic "bloop" of an M-79 grenade launcher. I hear neither. Closely following the two explosions there is a long burst of AK-47 fire. Then quickly, again all is quiet!

I'm lying still. Not sure what has happened. I look down at my legs. My jungle fatigue pants are saturated with blood. My legs are numb. I can't move them. Like other wounded soldiers, at first I have no idea how bad I'm hit. I look over and see the head of our platoon medic ("Doc") pop up from a foxhole dug for the night. Calmly, he says, "3-6, I'm coming out to get you."

I am not about to let Doc come out in the open to treat me. I tell him to stay put. I will come to him. I begin a slow crawl over to his position using my elbows to push myself along. Half-way there, my leg gets caught on a clump of grass. I look down and see what looks like a jagged bloody stick coming out of the top of my boot. Thinking it's my legbone, I reach down to free myself. It comes loose easily. Just a bloody stick lodged in the top of my boot. Relieved and somewhat amused, from that moment on I figure I will be okay and crawl the rest of the way with renewed strength. Doc comes out and pulls me the rest of the way and begins to treat my wounds.

The bravery of medics in combat is a much under told story. My platoon's medic is as brave as they come. Tall, lean, and muscular, he could probably take anyone in our platoon in a hand-to-hand fight. But here he is, a black conscientious objector, serving as an unarmed medic alongside soldiers in an infantry platoon armed to the teeth. (He joined us after our arrival in Tam Ky. I heard his name when he first came into the platoon two weeks ago, but we all have called him "Doc" out of respect and admiration. I am sad to say that none of the veterans in our company can recall his actual name 50 years later. In research for this book, I have tried numerous efforts over a three-year period to find him to no avail with the support of other members of Delta Company and our battalion. We won't give up until we find him.)

Days earlier I had given Doc my personal Colt Commander .45 caliber pistol. It wasn't government issue. I purchased it from my former platoon sergeant, Gary Tepner, just before he left the platoon for the battalion TOC in the A Shau. I told Doc, "Please take this for your self-protection." He took it with a smile of appreciation. Years later, I learned he carried it unloaded in the bottom of his rucksack. Clearly, he was a man of firm conviction.

As Doc bandages my wounds, I listen on the radio as a nearby medevac helicopter is called. He asks about the enemy situation near our location. He is told we have just received fire from a close-in enemy, and I hear his quick refusal to make the pickup. I can't blame the pilot. Two medevac helicopters from his unit have been shot down in recent days.

A log bird hears the refusal. He immediately volunteers to make the pickup. His instructions are simple. Put a strobe light in a hole and he will land on it. He is less than five minutes out. Log bird pilots flying in support of infantry often seem fearless. They too are usually young men in their early twenties. Many risk their lives to carry infantry soldiers to battle and bring them ammunition, water, and other needed supplies. They have a major role in evacuating wounded and flying out the bodies of dead soldiers. Like medics, helicopter pilots have the greatest respect and appreciation of infantry soldiers and we them.

While waiting on the log bird, one of my men does a quick crater analysis of the round that wounded me. Gold colored metal fragments reveal it was a 40 mm M-79 round, an American weapon. The crater shows the round had come in at an angle of 45 degrees. From my wounds it is easy to see it exploded on my left side. The round has a lethal radius of 5 m from the point of impact if it drops straight down. I was only a meter or so away from where it exploded. It wasn't my time.

We hear the log bird well before we see him. The enemy can hear him too. The dark olive-drab helicopter body blends with the shadows as he comes in low and fast, skimming the treetops. We expect he will take fire coming in, but he doesn't. The Huey's noise is always deafening as it hovers just inches off the ground. Another soldier, PFC Ron Kohler, and I are put on the floor of the empty helicopter. Kohler has also been wounded by shrapnel from the other M-79 round. He is alert and sitting up.

With his two passengers on board, the pilot revs his engines for lift off. They whine with the weight of the aircraft. The roar of the engines and rotors drown out all conversation. The pilot looks back, gives a quick thumbs up, lifts off and pitches the helicopter nose down and accelerates forward. My immediate thought is nearby enemy soldiers are holding their fire until we lift off. I'm expecting we will be hit. Hopefully we won't crash. Again, nothing happens.

I take a last look in the direction of my platoon. A few unrecognizable green-clad soldiers blend in with the shrubs and increasing darkness. Not soon enough, we are at a thousand feet and climbing enroute to Chu Lai and the 312th Evacuation Hospital. I'm glad to be alive. My thoughts briefly turn back to my guys. I'm leaving them in a tough spot. Knowing I was going out, I turned my platoon over to SGT Jim Littleton. I lay my head back on the floor of the helicopter. There is nothing I can do to help them now. SGT Littleton has the platoon. He is still my best combat leader.

Back at LZ Professional, CPT Roy receives word of the brief enemy attack. He has lost two more from his already undermanned company, PFC Kohler and his last officer platoon leader. It doesn't change his resolve to rejoin his company. His combat experience and leadership skills are needed now more than ever. Delta Company will conduct its combat assault on Hill 376 tomorrow as planned.

***

Casualties and Awards

As the 1-501st enters combat on Hill 376, its casualties in the first 26 days of combat at Tam Ky are shown in Casualty Table 9.

Casualty Table 9: 1-501st Casualties as of 2 June 1969 (Before Hill 376)

Casualties	HHC	A Co	B Co	C Co	D Co	Recon	Total
KIA	4	2	6	6	8	3	29
WIA	5	3	36	20	23	12	99
MIA	0	0	0	0	0	0	0
Total	9	5	42	26	31	15	128

2-17th Soldiers Killed in Action, 2 June 1969

Aero-Rifle Platoon, Bravo Troop, 2-17th Cavalry—3
  2 June: SP5 Richard Brech, age 21, born 10 February 1946 from Cottonwood, SD
  2 June: SSG Jimmie Reed, age 25, born 3 January 1944 from Tacoma, WA
  2 June: SSG Emmanuel Saunders, age 22, born 25 August 1946 from Washington, DC
Headquarters Company, 2-17th Cavalry—1
  2 June: SP4 Joseph Guy LaPointe Jr. (medic) age 20, born 2 July 1948 from Dayton, OH
1-501st Units—0

2-17th Soldier Awards, 2 June 1969 (other awards may have been made that were not mentioned in after action reports)

Medal of Honor—1
  Headquarters Company: 2 June, SP4 Joseph Guy LaPointe Jr. (medic)
Purple Heart—awarded to all soldiers KIA or WIA

PART 3

The Decisive Battle at Tam Ky

3–12 June 1969

"I love the infantry because they are the underdogs. … They have no comforts, and they even learn to live without the necessities. And in the end, they are the guys that wars can't be won without."—Ernie Pyle

CHAPTER 10

Hill 376

The Final Challenge

A Final Test of Courage

The intense fighting on 21 May resulted in unexpected high friendly casualties for Delta and its sister 1-501st companies. No one-day battle action at Tam Ky has been fiercer. But it is only a warm-up for the battalion's sustained ten-day fight on Hill 376. The men of Delta Company will once again show their courage under fire and "Never Quit" spirit.

Hill 376 is a low coastal mountain lying 20 km (about 12 mi) southwest of Tam Ky, then capital of Quang Tin Province (now Quan Nam Province). The mountain's 376 m summit (1,268 ft) is broad, relatively flat, and heavily forested. On a military map with a grid scale of 1:50,000, the mountain covers about four square kilometers (or just about 1.5 sq mi). Numerous spurs and ravines radiate from the flat mountain top with a scattering of large boulders and rock formations. A wide, well-travelled trail runs from northeast to southwest with multiple trail junctions allowing rapid movement across the mountain. The mountain's terrain and somewhat isolated location make it an ideal location for concealing a large enemy force.

By late May, elements of the enemy's 2nd NVA Division are consolidating forces on the mountain and nearby. Their intentions are unclear. They may be considering a last offensive operation against US forces, perhaps to be followed by a withdrawal further into the mountains west, southwest, and southeast of Tam Ky. The Laotian border is only 50 miles to the west. Units from the division's 2nd or 3rd NVA Regiment and 1st Main Force Regiment may be located on and around the summit of Hill 376. Indications are they may be accompanied by elements from other main force and local force battalions and augmented with heavy weapons such as 12.7 mm machine guns. The size of the enemy force on Hill 376 may be as high as 600–800 enemy soldiers. See Appendix 2.

At first, COL Bresnahan, the 1st Brigade commander, and his operational staff, do not realize Hill 376 is a major enemy stronghold. As they will later find out, the 2nd NVA Division headquarters may have been there along with an NVA field hospital. It is likely that the mountain served as the operational base from which the 2nd NVA Division was planning to launch its attack on Tam Ky.

The battle-hardened soldiers of the 2nd NVA Division are well trained and equipped. Armed with Soviet and Chinese infantry weapons and fighting from well-established defensive positions, they can hold their own in a close-in fight with US infantry units. Earlier, they overran South Vietnamese Army units, capturing many US Army weapons (rifles, machine guns, grenade launchers, and hand grenades).

They practice sound infantry tactics and are masters of camouflage and conceal-ment. All are hardy soldiers. Despite often operating with a lack of food, shelter, transportation, and medical supplies, their morale and fighting spirit is high.

The enemy has the capability to occupy sections of a large defensive perimeter around the top of Hill 376 creating a formidable bunker complex roughly 1,000 m in diameter. Main force Viet Cong units probably built and occupied the mountain fortress unopposed for many months in anticipation of the 2nd NVA Division's arrival in early May. The positions are well concealed, complete with concrete, steel-reinforced bunkers with over-head cover and interconnected with tunnels and commo wire. Other bunkers are reinforced with large logs and stones. The bunkers are dug deep in the ground with firing ports no more than 10" above ground level with good fields of fire. Their hardy construction enables protection against artillery, attack helicopter rockets, and air strikes.

The defensive network also includes hundreds of "spider holes" located on the forward slopes of the mountain interspersed with the enemy's bunkers. These one-man fighting positions resemble the hole of a "trapdoor spider." The concealed trap door is opened slightly to allow observation or permit firing of a weapon. The enemy positions are dispersed in depth across the mountain. Enemy units and soldiers can move quickly to any point on their perimeter to engage attacking US forces to halt their advance.

Part of the enemy's preparation of the mountain stronghold includes numerous primary and alternate firing locations for 82 mm and 60 mm mortars. The NVA and main force units are equipped with mortars in large numbers. The 82 mm mortar has an effective range of 4,200 m (2.6 mi). Its high trajectory allows firing over mountains and trees to hit attacking US forces. Prominent terrain features such as trail junctions, ridge lines, open areas, and approaches to the summit are identified and registered as preplanned targets to enable quick and accurate indirect fires from the enemy mortars.

Elements of the 2nd NVA Division on Hill 376 are supported by an anti-aircraft battalion equipped with more than a dozen 12.7 mm (.51 cal) heavy machine guns. The guns are located on Hill 376 and the terrain surrounding the mountain. The guns have an effective range of 1500 m against aircraft and 2000 m against ground targets. They can fire 600–700 rounds per minute. Each round is almost 6" long in its brass case and the bullet is over .5" in diameter. The gun crews also have pre-planned primary and alternate firing positions and can constantly move to avoid targeting. Any US aviator flying in support of ground troops at Tam Ky can testify to their effectiveness.

Delta Company's Combat Status

The enemy is not the only challenge Delta Company will face on Hill 376. The large number of Delta Company casualties suffered on 21 May along with loss of all three platoon leaders in the two-week period prior to Hill 376 has left the company and its sister units much reduced in fighting strength. Having arrived in Tam Ky two weeks ago with a field strength of five officers and 95 enlisted, Delta Company has taken 20% casualties before Hill 376. Bravo and Charlie Companies have fared just as bad or worse. Replacements have been slow in coming.

Field Strength Table 2 shows estimates of how the 1-501st's field strength has dropped based on casualties it has sustained since 15 May and its arrival at Tam Ky. The table doesn't show the replacements which have trickled in. Also not shown are the small percentage of soldiers who have non-life-threatening, superficial wounds. Those soldiers may soon be returned to the field after their wounds are cleaned and treated with sutures, sterile dressings, and antibiotics. Heat casualties are also not shown. Normally, following medevac they are rehydrated and returned to the field in a matter of days.

The lieutenants who normally lead Delta Company's three platoons have all been wounded and not replaced. The 2nd Platoon leader, LT Ron Black was WIA on 21 May, the 1st Platoon leader, LT Richard Boyd, on 31 May, and me, the 3rd Platoon leader, 2 June. As mentioned previously, the 1st and 2nd Platoons have been combined into one platoon led by SSG Sahrle. The 3rd Platoon is led by SGT Jim Littleton. The lack of officers is not the only issue.

As previously said, all soldiers except the company commander are "first termers" on their first enlistment in the Army. About a third are draftees, others enlisted voluntarily sometimes to avoid the draft, but often to serve their country in time of war. Just to repeat as a matter of emphasis, there are no staff sergeants (grade E-6) to lead squads or Sergeant First Class platoon sergeants (grade E-7).

Severe shortages of airborne qualified NCOs exist in all five airborne brigades in Vietnam (the three 101st brigades, the one brigade from the 82nd Airborne Division; and the 173rd Airborne Brigade). As the Vietnam War has dragged on for

Field Strength Table 2: 1-501st, Start of Hill 376, 3 June 1969						
Field Strength	A Co	B Co	C Co	D Co	E Co	Total
Officers	5	3	3	2	0	13
Enlisted	79	54	55	60	10	258
Total	84	57	58	62	10	271

years, the Army can't keep up with the numbers of airborne NCOs needed to man these brigades. The short 12-month tour for soldiers, reliance on the draft, and the individual replacement system are also major contributing factors.

In his book, *A Better War* (p. 288 ff.) Louis Sorley explains that the lack of experience later in the war was largely due to President Johnson's administration's decision to not activate large numbers of Army Reserve and National Guard units. They chose instead to rely on the draft and an individual replacement system which was not adequate to meet Army needs.

Further complicating our manning was the heavy casualties by infantry battalions in the Hamburger Hill battle. Junior-enlisted soldier replacements with the Military Occupational Specialty 11B – Infantrymen were also in short supply and priority of replacements was going to them not us. The 101st Airborne Division's *Operational Report – Lessons Learned, Period Ending 31 July 1969* states, "During the month of May the 101st sustained increased casualties in operations in the A Shau Valley. Assignment priorities were modified emphasizing the operational missions of the infantry battalions giving highest priority to those units engaged in heaviest contact with the enemy."[21]

When the 101st transitioned from an airborne to an airmobile division in 1969, non-airborne NCOs began to be assigned. SSG Sahrle was one of the first "leg" (non-airborne) sergeants to be assigned to Delta Company. He takes a lot of ribbing for not having his jump wings, but at Tam Ky he quickly earned the respect of those he leads and his company commander. (The shortage of NCOs was so severe that the availability of NCOs did not improve until 1971 and 1972 after the division was pulled out of Vietnam.)

The bottom line is that Delta Company will go into the fight on Hill 376 with the soldiers they have—and CPT Roy will lead them. His junior leaders will willingly accept the higher levels of responsibility placed on them. As good soldiers, they will give their best effort. That is what is expected of infantrymen, They, like CPT Roy, do not back down from the daunting challenge ahead.

Having just taken over command of the company, Roy has little time to prepare for the upcoming battle. The company is not only in need of replacements, but it has not had a break from combat operations since arriving in Tam Ky. Before that, Delta's last stand down was two days in February. No one in Delta Company is complaining. They know they are at Tam Ky because the Americal Division needs help.

Delta Company's battle action on Hill 376 begins 3 June with a combat assault and ends 12 June when the company is extracted. For those who fight and survive, it will be remembered simply as "the Hill."

CHAPTER I I

Combat Assault and First Contact

3–4 June

Day One on Hill 376

The Combat Assault

CPT Roy flies out early the morning of 3 June with his wound bandaged, but still painful. Delta Company's combat assault is scheduled for 0900H. He arrives just an hour or so before the scheduled assault. After a hasty meeting with his two acting platoon leaders, SSG Sahrle and SGT Littleton, he hurriedly readies Delta Company for its pickup. Understrength or not, it is going into battle.

SGT Littleton is leading 3rd Platoon for the first time. He has been in the field with the platoon for ten months and unashamedly says fear is his constant companion in combat. He is right. A soldier without fear endangers himself and others. Training, confidence in fellow soldiers, and raw courage makes it possible to overcome fear in combat. Another big motivation is not letting your buddies down. Time and again, infantry soldiers sacrifice their own safety and their lives to protect one another. That is why those who survive Hill 376 will have a lifelong bond.

Delta Company is picked up where they spent the night (BT164109). Five Hueys come in on each lift. Three lifts are needed to move the company. The battalion's AAR will later show the company lift included 85 soldiers. That number may include five replacement soldiers. A second flight of five helicopters follows close behind the first. As each of the five lifts quickly load, they lift off nosedown, gain speed and fly at 80 knots just above the treetops.

Hill 376, only 4 km (2.5 mi) away, is immediately in sight. Its towering green mass looms menacingly over the surrounding terrain. The morning sun is already hot, shining brightly in a brilliant blue sky. Gathering storm clouds are seen in the distance. Temperatures and humidity are already high and rising. Dark sweat stains saturate the jungle fatigues of each soldier as they labor in the heat and humidity under their heavy combat loads. The day has just begun. It will soon get much hotter.

CPT Roy is in the third helicopter of the first lift with his artillery FO, Lieutenant Paul Wharton. Also, on board are his two RTOs, Specialists Ed Medros and Mark Moses, and the company medic, now the former 3rd Platoon medic. Roy chooses

June Back in the World	
1 Jun	Top hit *Get Back* by Beatles
1 Jun	Bomb blast at Univ of Michigan ROTC building after earlier antiwar protest
2 Jun	General Omar Bradley attends D-Day's 35th anniversary at Normandy
2 Jun	US Supreme Court rules 7-1 against banning blacks in non-private clubs
3 Jun	GOP legislators report unexpected unrest at 50 major US universities
3 Jun	Last episode of original *Star Trek* series airs
6 Jun	Anniversary of 1968 assassination of presidential candidate Robert Kennedy
8 Jun	Brown Univ graduating class turns back to Dr. Kissinger at commencement speech
11 Jun	*True Grit* released (#8 '69)
18 Jun	Weathermen forms, later bomb NYC police HQ, US Capitol, and Pentagon
20 Jun	Grateful Dead's 3rd album *Aoxomoxoa* captures angst of deadheads
28 Jun	NY City Stonewall Riots begin modern LBGT rights movement

to go in on the first lift with his FO and RTOs in the likelihood they encounter enemy contact on landing. Being first on the ground, he can size up the enemy situation and immediately call for artillery, gunships, and air strikes.

The LZ on Hill 376

The first lift is off at 0855H. The LZ at BT203126 is on the southwest side of Hill 376, 400 m from the summit's highest point. This same LZ was used the previous day by Bravo Company. As they approach and land, the young Huey pilots are keenly aware they are prime targets of lurking NVA 12.7 mm (.51 cal) anti-aircraft heavy machine guns. Infantry soldiers in back give that threat only passing concern. Their thoughts are fixed on what they will soon face at the landing zone.

Flight time to the LZ is short. The 4 km takes just a few minutes from lift off to landing. The first five Hueys swoop in to the small LZ, flying fast and low. Rotor blades make the familiar, loud, distinctive "whop-whop-whop" announcing their arrival to friend and foe. The Aero-Rifle Platoon and Bravo Company are relieved to hear reinforcements are landing.

The LZ has been prepped with ARA from Cobra gunships. The acrid smell of explosives is still strong. Smoke hangs on the mountain's side clinging to trees. CPT Roy scans the LZ. He sees a burst of green tracers fired toward his flight. It quickly ceases. Likely fired, he guesses, by an over eager NVA soldier. The enemy has learned quickly when they fire on helicopters with small arms, return fire from Cobra gunships or artillery is deadly. Better to wait until the US units are on the ground. A close-in fight from bunkered positions will give them much better odds.

Private First Class John Meade in 3rd Platoon sits with his squad in one of the Huey's two open doors ready for a quick exit. Getting close, they stand on the helicopter's skids. Balancing their heavy combat loads, they jump off as the Huey hovers several feet off the ground. In a matter of seconds, all six soldiers exit—a practiced skill used by soldiers in each helicopter. Both soldiers and pilots know a hovering helicopter is a big, easy target. Rules for landing infantry units are simple. Get off, get down, get security, get moving! The rule for Huey pilots is much simpler—get in and get out fast!

No further fire is taken as Delta Company lands. Enemy units are certainly close by. Likely they have observed the arrival of the two infantry companies. They wait for a more opportune time to make their presence known. Specialist Rob Sitek, a rifleman in 3rd Platoon, sees four body bags lined up as he enters the tree line near the LZ. They are soldiers from the 2-17th Cav Aero-Rifle Platoon killed in yesterday's heavy fighting. A grim welcome to Hill 376. One of the dead is SP4 Joseph LaPointe, the medic who gave his life treating two wounded soldiers.

Lifting off, the five empty choppers of each lift pitch forward in choreographed sequence, increase speed, and roar back into the sky, banking sharply to avoid tall trees guarding the LZ. The second lift is already inbound just minutes behind. The first lift helicopters circle back to pick up the third and final lift, completing Delta Company's move to Hill 376 at 0913H. Twenty minutes total. The speed of an airmobile combat unit insertion on a battlefield is a hallmark of the 101st Airborne Division. The work of the Huey pilots and co-pilots is not yet done. Next, they bring in Alpha Company, completing their three lifts at 0931H to the same LZ used by Delta Company.

What remains of the Aero-Rifle Platoon boards the Hueys from Alpha Company's last lift. Their four dead comrades accompany them on the choppers, their duty done, but sorrowfully ended. Now begins their long trip home. Families are not yet notified of the loss of their son, brother, or husband. Others will soon follow. Casualties on Hill 376 will mount quickly for both US and enemy forces.

On the Ground

The brigade commander's intention was for the 1-501st to immediately insert an infantry company to rescue his Aero-Rifle Platoon which was in imminent danger of being overrun. That was readily done by Bravo Company which was immediately available at Tam Ky North, securing the 1st Brigade's headquarters. Now Delta and

Alpha Company have been inserted today because of the intensity of the enemy force the Aero-Rifle Platoon had encountered.

Neither the battalion nor the brigade commander know the strength of the enemy force on Hill 376 or what they may be doing on the mountain. The plan is for the 1-501st to conduct reconnaissance in force missions to develop the enemy situation. In short, the battalion, as is often the case, is going in blind with little information about enemy strength, capabilities, or intentions. All that is known is from the Aero-Rifle Platoon's report. The NVA are there in force.

The battalion plan is to spread the three infantry companies out to increase the likelihood of locating the enemy. The separation of the companies also permits freedom of movement and fires. It is unclear why none of the companies are sent to occupy the summit of Hill 376 only 400 m away from today's LZ. Since the NVA are believed to be on the mountain in force, the three 1-501st companies are kept close enough to support one another if a company runs into trouble. "Trouble" will become Hill 376's middle name.

The platoon leader, who successfully led the Bravo Company platoon in yesterday's rescue of the Aero-Rifle Platoon, is waiting for CPT Roy on the edge of the LZ as Delta's first lift arrives. He has been transferred from Bravo to Delta Company due to Delta's shortage of platoon leaders. Roy assigns him to lead his 1st Platoon which still includes the remnants of 2nd Platoon. Roy is happy to get him. SSG Sahrle, who has done a great job as interim platoon leader, reverts to his role as platoon sergeant.

Security is Delta Company's first concern upon landing. As they take up hasty defensive positions near the LZ, CPT Roy accounts for his men and confirms his map locations and bearings. He is ready to move his company to the southeast toward their assigned objective at BT207123. Alpha Company coming in last to the LZ will move to its objective at BT205121. (Alpha Company grid coordinates for 3–5 June in the 1-501st *Operation Lamar Plain* after action report are incorrect and have been changed to more accurately reflect the unit's location.) Bravo Company's objective is BT206124. Initially, all three companies move laterally across the southern slope of Hill 376, moving towards the area where the Aero-Rifle Platoon was first attacked yesterday.

Delta Company's Initial Move

Delta Company's move over unknown, difficult ground is understandably slow. The size and location of enemy forces is not yet known. Given the enemy's favored tactic of ambush, enemy contact may occur any moment. Delta's soldiers heard the report from yesterday of the Aero-Rifle Platoon encountering "hundreds of NVA soldiers." The four dead soldiers on the edge of the LZ are mute testimony that the enemy is here on the mountain in large numbers.

Three veteran soldiers are leading the company, a "point man" and two "slack men" walking some 5 m or so behind the point. As mentioned previously, point man is one of the toughest jobs in the infantry. No one is more likely to get shot or killed. Their eyes scan the terrain ahead for any sign of the enemy. Their ears are listening, their hearts pounding. Every sense is acutely tuned to the slightest hint of the enemy's presence. Fear is another enemy of the point man. It is true what many have said, "Courage is not the absence of fear, but overcoming fear despite great danger." Point men are courageous men.

Point men usually volunteer for the job. They are typically the most experienced soldiers in the unit. They are not prima donnas. That doesn't work in combat. They want the job because they believe they can best protect the men who follow behind them. Some soldiers seem gifted to perform this extremely dangerous duty. Nothing gives a moving infantry unit more confidence than to know they have a point man out in front who has earned their trust and is on his game.

The slack man, whether one man or two, walks behind the point man, protecting him just far enough back so he is not hit if the enemy fires on the point man. He is also another pair of eyes and ears looking and listening for signs of the enemy. The slack man also must motion to the following unit to stop, take cover, or move based on the point man's hand signals. Soldiers who walk slack are also experienced. In Delta Company, like in most infantry units, the point man and slack man trade out positions. Being on point is mentally exhausting work. A point man's mind and all his senses must stay on full alert.

Bravo Company Has Enemy Contact

Late morning at 1000H near BT203127 and only 400 m from the LZ, Bravo Company receives sporadic small arms fire. The fire is from enemy positions located 100 m to their east. The lead platoon returns fire. Artillery is called in. CPT Shelton maneuvers another platoon against the position. A US Air Force FAC requested by Bravo Company comes on station at 1035H to search for targets and direct air strikes. The FAC is a single pilot and artillery observer flying a Cessna O-2 Skymaster. The slow-flying, dual-engine (front and back propellers) aircraft can circle for hours high above target areas, providing intelligence and directing air strikes or artillery fires. They fly high because they are a lucrative target for enemy 12.7 mm heavy machine guns.

Bravo's air strikes by two F4 Phantoms are made at 1135H and 1140H near BT208128 using napalm and 250 lb. bombs. There is one secondary explosion, seven bunkers and three hooches are destroyed. One destroyed bunker is 10 ft long × 8 ft wide × 6 ft high, made of concrete and with a steel-reinforced roof. It is buried and concealed in the mountain side so it is virtually invisible to advancing soldiers. Well-constructed bunkers are a clear indication the enemy has occupied Hill 376 for many months.

Delta Company is close enough to hear the small arms fire in Bravo Company's engagement. The gunfire is soon drowned out by the thunderous ear-piercing roar of the Phantoms as they make their tree top bomb runs. The danger to nearby friendly troops is high. The Phantom pilots don't know where our units are located. Everyone remembers the close call just three days ago when the bombs were almost dropped right on Delta Company. The air strikes are an unneeded, further reminder Hill 376 is a dangerous place.

Bravo Company's 3rd Platoon conducts a bomb damage assessment (BDA). As they approach the area, they receive small arms fire return fire and kill one NVA soldier. Two soldiers are wounded. One from Bravo Company, SP4 William Swain and one from the Recon Platoon, PFC Antonio Lopez. A medevac chopper picks up Bravo Company's wounded and two more, a heat casualty and a soldier with a badly sprained ankle. A third air strike is completed at 1504H near BT203128 with two secondary explosions and destruction of one small 6 ft × 8 ft hooch and numerous spider holes. While the air strikes go in, Delta, Bravo, and Alpha Company limit their movement and take cover where they can.

End of Day One

Delta Company has no contact or casualties their first day on Hill 376. Captain Roy reports the company's NDP as BT207123. The day's move covered some 700 m. Delta soldiers are tired. Not so much from the physical effort expended or distance covered. The adrenaline drain from being on continuous alert long hours in the face of imminent danger is a factor. The NDP position for Bravo and Recon is BT206124. Alpha's NDP is at BT205121,

Stopping for the night is welcome relief. Moving by foot for seemingly endless hours over new ground in enemy territory expecting contact at any moment is more stressful than many can imagine. In combat, that is what infantry soldiers do day in and day out. They are called "ground pounders" and "foot soldiers" for good reason. They have a close, intimate awareness of the ground upon which they are fighting. The ground is their friend when the enemy is near. It is their protection when fired upon. Digging in at night offers protection from both enemy direct fire and mortars and after a long hot day the cool ground is a comfortable place to sleep.

The soldiers in Delta Company follow their long-practiced, careful routine in setting up a night defensive position. Captain Roy first positions his two platoons to cover likely approaches by an enemy attack. M-60 machine guns are positioned on those approaches. Sectors of fire are cleared. Weapons are checked, loaded and ready. Grenades and flares are laid out within easy reach. Positions are camouflaged. Claymore anti-personnel mines and trip flares are set out in front of fighting positions. Security watches are set up. Light and noise discipline is enforced. Radio volumes are turned down. Whispers are used instead of normal voices. Movement is limited.

Map locations are verified. Artillery preplanned targets are set. Radio contact with platoons and battalion are confirmed.

As always, these NDP procedures are done quickly and from habit by soldiers without being told. The cool night is helpful. Sleep comes easy for those not on watch. A light poncho liner is all that is needed. The cool damp earth is restful. Air mattresses and sleeping bags are for guys in the rear. The night is dark and quiet. Morning will come too soon.

Day Two

First Enemy Contact

Day Two, 4 June, on Hill 376 will be a different day. At 0715H a psychological operations (PSYOPS) team sets up portable speakers with Bravo Company. They begin booming out their "Chieu Hoi" (open arms) message in the general direction of the enemy. The intent is to encourage defections. It does not work. A second attempt is made in the Delta Company area. Still no results. PSYOPS is generally ineffective against hardened NVA soldiers. It is the same for main force VC soldiers, at least for now.

Around 0730H, Alpha, Bravo, and Delta Companies conduct local combat patrols out from their NDPs. The battalion's Recon Platoon is attached to Delta to make up for its shortage of soldiers. The patrols move slowly on purpose. Enemy locations are unknown. What is known is that they are nearby and ready to fight. Terrain favors the enemy. They know the area quite well. Their extensive defensive network with its prepared fighting positions offers them good protection from small arms fire and limited protection from artillery, aerial rockets, and air strikes. The positions, as usual, are well concealed and are undetected until the enemy opens fire.

At 0830H, a 2-17th Cav scout helicopter conducting reconnaissance receives 12.7 mm heavy automatic weapons fire from BT203123. The enemy position is engaged with mini-guns and rockets. There are no friendly casualties. Enemy casualties are unknown. A FAC is on station. He makes frequent reports during the morning of enemy sightings near Hill 376's summit. Multiple air strikes and artillery are called in throughout the morning into early afternoon.

In the afternoon, the weather worsens. Dark clouds roll in and torrential tropical rain pelts the mountain in sheets. Winds come from the west at 35 knots. Lighting strikes hit all around. Radios, the communications lifeline in battle, are turned off for protection. Delta Company headquarters has four radios including the one for the artillery FO. Each of the platoons have two. The PRC-25 radio is a lightning magnet with its 24 lb. metal box, large battery, transmitter, receiver, and antenna. The RTOs carrying the radios are happy to turn them off until the storm passes.

The bad weather doesn't stop the fighting, it just makes it more difficult. Noises are muffled, visibility is worse, footing is terrible, wet equipment and uniforms are heavier, and every piece of metal rusts. Infantry soldiers on both sides operate in all types of weather. They have no choice. Their mission continues day and night, no matter the weather.

At 1555H, Bravo and Delta Company are mortared. Captain Roy identifies them as 82 mm mortars, definitely not the smaller 60 mm mortars. The distinctive sound of the incoming rounds and their explosive force are clear indicators. He remembers them well from his first combat tour. He says it is not something you ever forget or mistake!

As the mortar rounds explode, Delta Company's 1st Platoon receives heavy automatic weapons fire from several close-in firing positions no more than 30 m away. They're AK-47 rifles (7.62 mm) fired on full automatic with disciplined fire in short bursts. Enemy RPD machine guns soon join in. The volume of fire is horrendous. The noise is deafening and momentarily disorienting.

Walking point for 1st Platoon, PFC Gary W. Silman, is killed instantly. The platoon returns fire and hugs the ground. Enemy grazing fire just inches off the ground pins the platoon down. It is difficult to see the location of the well-concealed bunkers and their firing slits hidden just above the jungle floor. Hundreds of enemy rounds continue to snap and whiz by with lethal force—another sound combat soldiers never forget. SP4 William Scott, "Scotty" to his platoon, is pinned down close to the enemy position. Enemy rounds are impacting just inches from his head. He flattens himself on the ground unable to move or return fire. If he moves, he will be killed.

LT Paul Wharton, the company's artillery FO learns 1st Platoon has been cut off from the rest of the company and is taking casualties. Wharton leaves his covered position at the company command post to aid the separated platoon. He runs across an open area covered by enemy automatic weapons fire. The rounds follow close behind him kicking up dirt. Upon reaching the platoon he calls in an attack helicopter. Just as Scott thinks he has no choice except to move and risk getting killed, a Cobra attack helicopter hovers low over the platoon and begins to fire aerial rockets into the enemy position.

The rockets explode less than 30 m to the 1st Platoon's front. The thunderous explosions shake the ground and throw shrapnel, dust, and debris in every direction. Wharton directs the pinned-down men to return fire. The enemy ceases fire. Scott and the rest of the platoon have the brief moment they need to pull back.

Wharton helps treat the wounded and leads them back to the company. He will later be awarded the Silver Star for his bravery under fire. In the absence of his normal complement of infantry officers, Wharton routinely assists CPT Roy in company leadership roles well beyond that expected of an artillery forward observer. Later, Roy puts Wharton in for a coveted Combat Infantryman Badge (CIB). Despite a first denial, Roy successfully ensured the award was made. Wharton values his CIB more than his Silver Star. He deserves both.

1st Platoon hurriedly moves back. Silman can't be reached due to the heavy enemy fire. Now the exploding rockets make it impossible. Captain Roy directs Wharton to call in artillery to further aid 1st Platoon's withdrawal. Delta Company pulls back from its location at BT202122 to a new position several hundred meters away. The 1st Platoon remains separated, but close to the company. They are safe for now—as safe as it gets in the midst of battle.

Earlier, during the initial enemy contact, SGT Ed Flood, a 1st Platoon squad leader, was hit and spun around falling on his back. Fortunately, the AK-47 round hit one of the two extra ammunition bandoliers he wore across his chest. The round destroyed two full M-16 magazines, but didn't penetrate any further. Flood would later discover a huge bruise on his chest. Still under heavy enemy fire, Flood crawled forward to return fire and maybe throw a grenade.

Flood hadn't moved but a short distance when another round slammed into and destroyed the sturdy black composite stock on his M-16 rifle. The rifle was now useless. As Flood pulled out his .45 caliber Colt Commander pistol, he saw a nearby exploding mortar round hurl a fellow soldier into the air. Knowing the soldier was likely severely injured, Flood quickly moved to him, running in a low crouch through the enemy fire. The soldier was lying face down, unmoving, and maybe dead. Flood rolled him over and was both surprised and glad to see the half-smiling, half grimacing face of PFC Forest Smith, the platoon's RTO.

Smith was holding his leg wound with his hand, applying pressure to stop the bleeding. Flood checked the leg for an exit wound or other shrapnel wounds. There were none. More mortar rounds exploded. AK-47 rounds were hitting close by. One ricocheted off Smith's radio. Before Flood could hoist Smith on his shoulder in a fireman's carry, Smith reached up and pulled a long shard of Flood's rifle stock out of his bleeding shoulder.

Flood carried Smith back toward the company and away from the enemy as Smith fired his M-16 to cover their withdrawal. Bullets from the enemy continued to fly. Flood made it back to a tree line. Smith was still bleeding. Flood and Smith were seemingly alone. Flood was not sure which way to go. Two NVA soldiers appeared nearby. Just as they began to shoot at Flood and Smith, a M-60 opened up and killed the two enemy soldiers.

Travelling further down a trail, Flood and Smith finally heard English voices. Suddenly, several friendly soldiers appeared. They had reached Delta Company's defensive position and safety. A medic team treated their wounds, gave them a needed drink of water, and readied both soldiers for evacuation. Soon they would be back in the rear. Smith would be further evacuated and returned to the States. The war was over for him. SGT Flood would return to his Delta Company platoon and the fight on Hill 376.

End of Day Two

Bravo Company assists Delta Company's withdrawal and movement of their wounded. A medic from Bravo Company, SP4 Roy Gargus, is killed by enemy fire while running forward to give aid to PFC Silman from Delta Company. Delta Company's 1st Platoon Leader sees Gargas' unselfish act in the heat of battle. Later, he will recommend Gargas for the Medal of Honor, but he is awarded the Silver Star. Delta Company has one KIA, PFC Silman, and six WIA. SGT Ed Flood and PFCs Forest Smith, Richard Moore, Robert Ter Vree, and Patrick Petersen all receive fragmentation wounds. PFC Dale Stewart is wounded by small arms fire.

Today's enemy contact is characteristic of NVA tactics. On Hill 376 in almost all cases, the enemy will initiate the contact on terrain of their choosing, usually from concealed positions at the very close range of five to ten meters. They engage for a short time and then may withdraw, usually pulling back quickly before artillery and attack helicopters hit their position. The tactic is often successful in slowing down the movement of US forces by inflicting casualties requiring medical care and evacuation. It is a pattern that Delta and its sister companies will experience all too frequently.

It has been a long afternoon. Dusk falls as Delta Company and the Recon Platoon attached reach their position for the night at BT205126. It is still raining. The bad weather and declining light mean no medevac will come in until morning. Alpha Company's NDP is at BT205121. Bravo Company is at BT206127. Restful sleep is difficult in the rain with everything wet. Hasty poncho shelters are put up by some. Others just sleep under a draped poncho thrown over themselves and their ruck. There is no enemy contact during the night. Maybe they were trying to stay dry.

***

Casualties and Awards

1-501st Soldiers Killed in Action, 3–4 June 1969 (Days 1 and 2)

Delta Company—1
  4 June: PFC Gary W. Silman, age 20, born 21 February 1949 from West Monroe LA

Headquarters Company—2
  3 June: SP4 Fletcher Nowlin (Co C medic), age 20, born 29 September 1948 from Rochdale Village, NY (died from wounds on 21 May)
  4 June: SP4 Roy Gargus (B Co medic), age 22, born 2 July 1946 from Lancaster TX

1-501st Soldier Awards for Hill 376, 3–4 June (other awards may have been made that were not mentioned in after action reports)

Silver Star—3

Headquarters and Headquarters Company: 3 June, PFC Christopher Bean (medic). 4 June, SP4 Roy Gargus (medic)

Delta Company: 4 June, LT Paul Wharton (FO)

Bronze Star for Valor—3

Bravo Company: 3 June, PFC William Swain

Delta Company: 3 June, PFC Leonard Baldauf and PFC Larry Mulvey

Army Commendation Medal for Valor—3

Bravo Company: 4 June, PFC Alan Hinz

Delta Company: 3 June, PFC William Ayers. 4 June, PFC Edward Medros

Purple Heart—awarded to all soldiers KIA or WIA

CHAPTER 12

Trouble on the Hill

5 June

Day Three on Hill 376

Early Morning Medevac

The third day on Hill 376 begins early. At 0710H, CPT Roy requests a medevac and gunships to provide cover during the extraction of yesterday's wounded. The pickup of wounded with the enemy close by is never easy. Two AH-1 Cobra attack helicopter gunships provide close air support near the LZ prior to the medevac's arrival. They locate and attack an enemy 12.7 mm antiaircraft heavy machine-gun position with aerial rocket artillery, 40 mm rapid-fire grenade launchers, and 7.62 mm miniguns. The mini-guns have a death-dealing rate of fire up to 6,000 rounds per minute.

A FAC circles overhead ready to identify enemy activity and suppress enemy fire as the Huey medevac chopper comes in. The bright red crosses on the nose and sides of the helicopter are no restraint for enemy gunners. They have shown repeatedly they will fire on medevac helicopters.

The wounded soldiers huddle close to the LZ to minimize the helicopter's time on the ground. As the flying ambulance sits down, the soldiers make their way to the waiting aircraft. Some carried, some hobbling, some helping others. Safely on board, they are glad to be leaving Hill 376, but have mixed feelings leaving their buddies behind. Enemy contact expected during the medevac does not occur.

Five of the wounded are evacuated to the 27th Surgical Hospital in Chu Lai. The most seriously wounded soldier is flown directly to the 312th Medical Evacuation Hospital also in Chu Lai. Both have medical staff and facilities fully capable of handling severe wounds.

No One Left Behind

The medevac complete, CPT Roy turns his attention toward retrieval of PFC Silman's body. Silman is on everyone's mind. His recovery is a top priority. The enemy situation did not allow his recovery yesterday. He had fallen directly in front of the enemy position and 1st Platoon could not get to him without taking more casualties and getting others killed.

Recovering a fallen soldier during on-going enemy contact is one of the toughest tasks and hardest decisions in battle. It is particularly hard when the enemy has ambushed a unit and the enemy still controls the area where the soldier fell. The truth is no soldier wants his unit to be shot up trying to recover his body once he has died. But every soldier wants and expects his body to be recovered as soon as it can be done. That is an unwritten, but well-understood rule—leave no one behind.

At 0931H, CPT Roy's air strike request is delivered by the circling FAC putting bombs near the previous day's enemy contact (BT204107). The intent is to kill enemy soldiers in the area near Silman's body or failing that persuade them to leave. Two F4 Phantoms each drop four 500 lb. bombs and two napalm cannisters. The two aircraft rake the area using their 20 mm Vulcan cannons firing ten-second bursts each of 1,000 rounds. The air strike is close. The roar of the jet's after burners as it pulls out of its dive, the ground-shaking explosions of the bombs, the heat of the napalm, and the hammering of their cannons is unsettling to close-by friendly infantry. No one thinks about how terrifying it is to the enemy soldiers being targeted. It doesn't seem possible that anyone can survive the constant air attacks even in reinforced bunkers. Many do not.

At 1010H with the air strike is complete, CPT Roy moves Delta Company into the area (BT204107) to retrieve Silman's body. The air strike missed the target area Roy had requested, but the recovery will continue anyway. At 1015H, the FAC reports two bunkers, one unknown structure damaged and one destroyed. No enemy casualties are reported though they likely occurred. The bomb damage is good, but it is in the wrong area for the recovery mission.

At 1100H, CPT Roy reports his unit has spotted "a lot of movement" south of their location near BT196102. He turns to his FO, LT Paul Wharton, for artillery support. Roy will later say Wharton is the best FO in Vietnam. Most Delta Company soldiers don't yet know him. He will save their lives more than once. He is also responsible for a large share of Delta Company's enemy casualties on Hill 376. On this occasion, Wharton requests anti-personnel "firecracker rounds" designed to kill enemy soldiers caught in the open. (The technical name for artillery firecracker rounds is Controlled Fragmentation Munitions (COFRAM). Fired by M110 (self-propelled) or M115 (towed) 8" Howitzers, each 200 lb. round contains 108 bomblets or grenades ejected 400 m above ground to disperse them over a wide area. They then explode 6 ft off the ground. The howitzers can fire the round 16.8 km or 10.5 miles. M102 (105 mm) and M114A1 (155 mm) howitzer batteries are also capable of delivering similar, though scaled-down, versions of COFRAM rounds.)

Around 1150H, Delta Company moves toward the location (BT201122) where they expect to find Silman's body. Suddenly, 3rd Platoon receives two long bursts of enemy small arms fire from a concealed position 50 m away. The platoon immediately takes cover and returns fire. CPT Roy has Wharton call in artillery again. Delta

Company's movement is held up while the artillery is fired and walked back to the enemy location. By 1210H, the company is slowly moving again, anticipating further enemy contact at any moment.

At 1230H, Delta's 3rd Platoon is close to Silman's last known location. Again, they come under small arms fire. The company takes up hasty defensive positions, returns fire, and waits. Once more, artillery is requested. This time it is much closer to the company's position. Moving again, the going is slow. The weather is getting worse. By 1530H, heavy thunderstorms with lightning and high winds strike the mountain. Movement and visibility are more difficult. The mission continues despite the miserable weather. It is not the company's chief worry. As the company prepares to recover Silman, the unit again comes under a heavy volume of small arms fire.

A Good Soldier Goes Missing

While the firefight is on-going, another element of 3rd Platoon is some 100 m away checking a clearing to see if it is suitable for an LZ to extract Silman. The team is led by squad leader, SGT John Horan. Other team members are SP4 James Parvin, PFC John Meade, and PFC Steven Strand. They are stopped on the edge of the clearing. Dropping their rucksacks, they take a drink from their canteens. Horan is the only one standing. He is scanning the clearing, not more than 30 m away, when an enemy soldier pops out of a spider hole on the other side of the open area. The enemy soldier begins to run into the forest away from Horan's team.

SGT Horan fires at the running enemy soldier. His aim is difficult because of the trees. Horan quickly crosses the clearing. He is gone before his men have time to react. SP4 Parvin calls for him to stop. Horan continues to chase the enemy soldier. Parvin then sees six or so enemy soldiers get up from spider holes on the far right side of the clearing to chase after Horan. In seconds, they disappear into the woods close behind Horan.

Instinctively, Parvin takes up the pursuit of the enemy soldiers. He catches brief sightings of them and fires his M-16. They return fire. The enemy soldiers are also firing at Horan. Horan takes cover jumping into a hole only to find it occupied by another enemy soldier. After a brief struggle, Horan frees himself and runs deeper into the forest. The enemy soldiers chasing him are closing in.

PFC Strand has followed Parvin across the clearing. He catches up to him just in time. Strand sees an enemy soldier coming out of a hole just to Parvin's front. He throws a hand grenade and yells, "Parvin grenade, get down!" Parvin flattens himself. The grenade explodes killing the enemy soldier. Parvin gets up hurriedly making sure he is dead. Looking into the hole, Parvin sees Horan's M-16, sweat band, scarf, and cigarette lighter scattered about. He picks up the M-16 and notices the magazine is empty. Horan was out of ammunition.

Parvin no longer hears any firing. He has pursued the NVA for 100 m and decides he can't go further. The chase is over. Just minutes have elapsed. Everything happened quickly. Parvin's effort to rescue Horan ends. Parvin gathers Horan's weapon and personal belongings. He, Strand, and Meade head back to the company. Parvin turns in Horan's rifle and personal gear and makes a brief report. He notices the lighter has an engraving. Just under Horan's name are the words, "I know I am going to heaven because I have spent my time in hell—Vietnam 1968–1969."

Back at the company, someone mentions Parvin's attempt to save Horan should get him a medal. Parvin is briefly irritated. He replies, "I lost him. I didn't do anything to deserve an award." Parvin will later think it was Horan's action that saved the men in his team. The enemy soldier Horan chased likely was trying to draw Horan's men into the clearing. The hidden NVA soldiers on the right of the clearing were in perfect position to easily cut them down.

CPT Roy has his men conduct a brief search for SGT Horan. The enemy situation does not permit a long search or coverage of a large area. SP4 Parvin replaces Horan as squad leader and is promoted to Sergeant. Months later, as Parvin prepares to leave Vietnam he turns in his rifle and other equipment. The serial number of his rifle is checked. It is Horan's weapon. Parvin discovers he had mistakenly kept Horan's rifle. His rifle is already listed as turned in. His mind immediately flashes back to that fateful day. He will remember the loss of SGT Horan the rest of his life.

Presumed captured, days later on 16 June, SGT John Horan is found dead by a South Vietnamese Army unit over 10 km from Hill 376. Whether SGT Horan escaped capture or had been taken some distance away by his captors is never determined. His body is recovered and returned home to his family. They will grieve his loss and always wonder how his life ended. That may never be known. This is known: SGT Horan died doing his duty. A soldier fighting a tough enemy, remembered by the men he led.

The Booby Trap

In the meanwhile, CPT Roy assigns a five-man team the task of recovering Silman. Like Silman, they are all from 1st Platoon. The platoon leader and his RTO, PFC George Dennis, accompany the five-man team. They include SP4 Robert Ruttle and PFCs William Ayers, Kevin Crowe, Larry Mulvey, and Vincent Earley. Roy reminds the team leader to be careful. The body is likely booby-trapped. This is a common enemy practice. Roy tells the team to have one man tie a rope to Silman's leg. Grappling hooks Roy requested earlier have not arrived. The team is to take cover in case of an explosion, then drag Silman clear of the immediate area before attempting to carry his body.

The platoon leader gives the team an additional warning about the likelihood the body is booby-trapped. The team moves out with their platoon leader. They have some 100 m to go. Expecting enemy contact each step of the way they move slowly with great caution. It takes almost 15 minutes to reach the location where Silman lies. Once at the location, the platoon leader and his RTO withdraw. The team moves in. The sight of their fallen comrade laying alone where he fell in the previous day's combat is tough. It is a vivid reminder the enemy is close by. Understandably, they are in a hurry to retrieve the body. Their first thought is to get Silman and get out of there before the enemy discovers their presence.

PFC Vincent Earley takes up a security position to cover the other four soldiers as they move in. They huddle around Silman. As they pickup Silman, there is a deafening double blast which reverberates down the mountain to the company's position. Two booby-traps explode in quick succession with devastating results. The four soldiers are killed outright.

Earley is seriously wounded with deep fragmentation wounds in his right arm, right leg, and face. In a moment, the recovery of one fallen soldier becomes the recovery of four more and one wounded soldier. Earley escapes death because he is 15 ft or so further away than the others in a kneeling position pulling security. The blast picks him up and throws him backwards, knocking him out. He regains consciousness as a second team of soldiers arrive to check out the explosion. They recover all five bodies. Earley, half conscious, is half carried, half dragged back to the company's position. The company medic treats his wounds, bandages him, and gets him ready for medevac.

PFC George Dennis heard two explosions in quick succession. It may well be that the booby-trap was made up of two explosive charges wired in tandem. No one really knows what type of booby trap was used. Earley, the only survivor, believes it was a large mortar or artillery round. Perhaps an 82 mm mortar round or even a 105 mm shell concealed and detonated at close range. Earley's wounds are caused by sharp, jagged metal fragments. How the round was triggered is not known. The firing mechanism could have been connected to the body by commo wire or some other means. It was tripped as soon as the body was picked up.

SP4 Phil Cravens looked at a helmet from one of the soldiers who was killed. It had round holes like ball bearings, characteristic of a US claymore mine. US claymores are packed with 700 ball bearings that would produce such holes. Chinese claymores have short cylindrical rods and their hole pattern is different. If there were two explosions, it is possible both a mortar or artillery round and a claymore mine were used.

Later, as PFC Earley is bandaged, he explains to "Doc" the company medic what happened during Silman's recovery. Doc tells CPT Roy. Roy is working on getting the medevac in, accounting for his men, making a report to battalion on what happened, and checking to make sure his soldiers are alert should the enemy decide to follow-up with an attack. Earley tells CPT Roy that in their hurry to get Silman out, they didn't tie a rope to Silman's body. They knew the enemy was likely nearby and they expected enemy contact at any moment. Just as they picked up the body, the explosions went off. A tragic mistake.

An Early Evening Medevac

Daylight fades, the faint, familiar sound of a flight of helicopters is heard in the distance. A medevac escorted by two Cobra gunships is in-bound. Help is on the way. As usual, both friend and foe can hear the choppers. The gunships are in a protective role. No medevac is ever routine. Pilots are accustomed to flying in and out of remote, hastily prepared LZs. Each one different and dangerous. The unlevel ground often has many obstacles. Sometimes rotor blades clip branches of nearby trees. The enemy is usually nearby. Time is always short.

Those who fly medevacs have the utmost respect and admiration of infantry soldiers, their most frequent customers. Both medical and logistical pilots and crews give top priority to picking up wounded soldiers. They know lives depend on their efforts. They see firsthand the weary, mud-crusted, bandaged soldiers, uniforms stained with sweat and blood. The wounded are sometimes carried or helped by their fellow soldiers to the waiting helicopter's open bay doors. Those same fellow soldiers are still in the fight. They may be the reason for their next medevac flight.

The medevac is a log bird this time. Light is fading fast. The weather is bad and getting worse. As soon as the helicopter touches down three of the soldiers KIA are loaded aboard. The remaining two soldiers KIA must be taken out the next morning. All five had been laying side-by-side on the edge of the LZ in the rain. Army-issue ponchos carried by each soldier serve as body bags. Wrapped in the rubberized, olive-drab colored nylon, the soldiers are indistinguishable. Each one a stark reminder that young men, courageous and committed men, are giving their lives in battle in the mountain forest just beyond the LZ. They are men who won't be forgotten. Those who survive and make it home will remember and honor them the rest of their days.

PFC Earley is asked if he's okay to go out on the helicopter with three of the soldiers killed in action. He doesn't hesitate. He is badly wounded and uncertain he can make it through the night. Earley is helped on board, the helicopter takes off without receiving fire. Earley's destination is the 312th Medical Evacuation Field Hospital in Chu Lai. In minutes, he will be in the care of men and women dedicated to serving wounded soldiers fresh off the battlefield. The other five soldiers are taken to the Graves Registration Detachment also at Chu Lai. Delta Company reports the medevac complete at 1842H.

A Bitter Fight

Day Three on Hill 376 has begun and ended with a medevac. Casualties are mounting. The numbers are blunt testimony to continuing stiff enemy resistance. A determined, well-armed enemy fighting from fortified defensive positions on familia ground. Alpha, Bravo, and Delta companies are likely outnumbered in terms of soldiers. Perhaps by double. The enemy's defensive advantage is also significant. Delta Company and its sister companies must constantly move and expose themselves to find and engage the dug-in, concealed enemy. Avoiding frontal attacks by flanking enemy positions is extremely difficult due to the circular layout of the enemy's defense and the mountainous terrain's ridges and ravines.

In hindsight, years after the battle, the frontal attack tactics forced on the rifle companies on Hill 376 seem at best questionable. The combat leaders at battalion and above were Korean and World War II veterans. Their tactics seem reminiscent of those times. Vietnam is a different war with much more powerful weapons available to infantry units. As was done at Hamburger Hill, making repeated frontal attacks against a dug-in enemy in a string of reinforced bunkers seems an unwise tactic. Sometimes it is possible to flank a bunker. Most often it is not. The question arises, "Why not pull the infantry companies back and use B-52s to level the mountain?" A formation of three B-52s could easily take out a box approximately a quarter mile wide and a mile long. It is expensive in terms of ordinance and air assets, but not in lives lost.

Another factor led to infantry frontal attacks on Hill 376. The battalion and brigade commanders directing the attacks at Tam Ky typically are flying at 5,000 ft high above the battlefield. High enough to be safely out of the range of 12.7 mm anti-aircraft guns. Unfortunately, they are too high to see the battle close-up. They are far removed from the ground combat of their units. They can't see the terrain and other obstacles faced by their soldiers. Essentially, they know only what they are told via radio communications by those on the ground.

Airmobile doctrine is still evolving. The tactical separation of battalion commanders from their company commanders and soldiers seems a big mistake. Few infantrymen ever see their battalion commander. The tour of a battalion commander lasts no more than six months. Soldiers are in the field longer than their commanders, often up to ten to twelve months. Not only do tactical operations suffer, the bond between battalion commanders and their men never develops. Such were the conditions at Tam Ky.

The battle action on Hill 376 is being fought by company commanders, junior officers, and junior-enlisted men they lead. The young soldiers of the 1-501st are both determined and courageous. They don't back down from a fight, but keep constant pressure on the enemy. It is a typical, classical, tough infantry mission. Close with, kill, or capture the enemy. A mission with very high costs.

The enemy's defensive advantages are many, but they are not decisive. The battalion's soldiers have the tactical advantage. Their leaders know how to call in air strikes, attack helicopters, and artillery and they are quick to do it. They continue to pound the enemy for the next seven days. Though the NVA is taking heavy losses, CPT Roy and the other company commanders aren't interested in reporting enemy body counts. There is not time to "keep score." The bitter fighting is too intense.

End of Day Three

At 1930H, the night defensive positions are reported. Delta Company is at BT201122 and BT204129 several hundred meters away. Alpha Company's position is BT205123, Bravo Company at BT206125. The units prepare their positions for the night, looking forward to a short rest despite miserable weather and the nearby enemy. Security is tight. There is no let up to the unrelenting stress and fatigue of the battle

At 2310H, 1st Brigade reports that a reliable agent has revealed the enemy will be conducting a general offensive against all friendly units in the Tam Ky area commencing at 0400–0500H 6 June, tomorrow. That is in just five hours. The message is passed to each company. The battle may soon get tougher. For now, the rest of the night is quiet.

***

Casualties and Awards

1-501st Soldiers Killed in Action, 5 June 1969 (Day 3)

Delta Company—5
5 June: PFC William Ayers, age 21, born 29 February 1948 from Austin, TX
5 June: PFC Kevin Crowe, age 21, born 9 April 1948 from Malden, MA
5 June: PFC Lawrence Mulvey, age 19, born 10 January 1950 from New York, NY
5 June: SP4 Robert Ruttle, age 23, born 11 August 1945 from Hatboro, PA
5 June: SGT John Horan, age 20, born 8 July 1948 from New York, NY (on this date SGT Horan is MIA. He is later found on 16 June, presumed KIA on 5 June)

1-501st Soldier Awards for Hill 376, 5 June (other awards may have been made that were not mentioned in after action reports)

Bronze Star for Valor—3
Delta Company: PFC William Ayers, PFC Kevin Crowe, PFC Lawrence Mulvey
Purple Heart—awards were made to all soldiers KIA or WIA

CHAPTER 13

The Move to the Top

6 June

Day Four on Hill 376

Then and Now

Today is the 25th anniversary of D-Day, the invasion of the Normandy coast by Allied forces fighting Nazi Germany. The landing on the western coast of France and the ensuing fighting is one of the most decisive battles of World War II. The 501st Infantry Regiment, 101st Airborne Division had a key role in the invasion, parachuting well behind the enemy beach defenses to secure bridges and block enemy reinforcements. So began the storied history of the 501st. No one on Hill 376 is thinking about those distant days. They are in their own desperate fight.

Vietnam is a different war. From a historical perspective, it is neither decisive nor popular. What is similar is the courage, competence, reputation, fighting skill, and commitment of the young officers and soldiers who fill the ranks of the 101st Airborne Division. These young men are upholding the honorable legacy passed to them by those who were first to serve in the Screaming Eagles.

Vietnam is an infantry war and the infantrymen of the 501st are serving their nation well. They are making a worthy contribution to the lineage of the 101st as a premier fighting force of the United States. No one on Hill 376 is thinking about this either. Most of the young soldiers are thinking and praying about surviving, not letting their buddies down, and getting back home in one piece. 6 June on Hill 376 is just another day much like others. The days run together like one long interminable day. An unending, long, slow, murderous slog in the mud and mountain jungle forest punctuated by frequent, sudden, small unit engagements initiated by enemy ambush.

Another Medevac

This day starts with another medevac to pick up the two remaining soldiers killed in action the day before. CPT Roy makes the request at 0725H. As often happens, a Huey "log bird" used for logistics resupply of ammunition, water, food, or whatever is needed, makes the extraction. The Huey "flying ambulances" with their red crosses are usually reserved for seriously wounded soldiers. Understandably so. They are equipped with life-saving medical supplies and equipment and medics who can apply advanced, immediate, life-saving aid. They are a premium enemy target. Typically, they don't make extractions with enemy forces close by.

On the other hand, log bird pilots often come in no matter the enemy situation. They have a special affinity for the infantry soldiers they support. Log birds sometimes have only a single pilot. They usually take more risks. Not only do they evacuate the wounded and the dead, but they are also the carriers of life-saving supplies essential to an infantryman's survival. The pilots are mostly in their early twenties, not much older than the young soldiers they support. They have a mutual admiration society for sure. The Vietnam Helicopter Pilots Association says there were 2,202 helicopter pilots killed in Vietnam. Out of the 12,000 helicopters of all types flown in the Vietnam War, over 5,000 were destroyed.

An Air Cavalry team comes on station at 0730H in support of Delta Company. The team is made up of one light observation helicopter (LOH-6 Cayuse) and two AH-1 Cobra attack helicopters. Because of its LOH designation, the Cayuse quickly picked up the slang name "Loach." The team's mission today is twofold. First, they look for targets that threaten the medevac. Second, they scout the area in advance of Delta Company's planned movement to the top of the mountain. The LOH sneak-and-peak missions at tree-top level to search out lurking enemy are extremely dangerous. The light but heavily armed helicopter was first introduced to the Vietnam theater in 1966. Of 1,419 Cayuse helicopters sent to Vietnam, 842 were destroyed by ground fire. Many more were shot up and spent days in repair.

The Move to the Top Begins

At 0745H, CPT Roy has his company ready to move. The mission is difficult and dangerous. Conduct a reconnaissance in force moving up the mountain. Find, engage, and determine the strength of enemy forces defending the mountain to the company's front. Alpha and Bravo Companies have similar missions. Delta begins moving at 0830H as the Cav Team screens their movement from above.

CPT Roy has not forgotten the brigade's intelligence report received last night. The major enemy offensive against US units is to begin this morning. It is overdue. Delta's lead platoon is moving slowly, cautiously. The platoon is in a modified column. The column formation is dictated by the terrain. There is no room to move on a broader front. As usual, a point man from the lead platoon is out front with two slack men slightly behind and to the flanks. All three are immediately ready to return fire in case of ambush.

Nothing shows the courage of young infantrymen more than moving in difficult terrain knowing enemy contact is imminent. Contact by a hidden deadly enemy who is ready to fight and die if need be. The only thing unknown is when, where, how many, and with what weapons the enemy will open fire. That is a lot of unknowns. The routine bravery of young infantry soldiers in Vietnam is often overlooked. It was not mentioned in *The Vietnam War*, the 2017 18-hour, 10-part series documentary by Burns and Novak.[22] Only an infantryman really knows what it is like to fight an infantry battle.

The entire company now moves toward the mountain's summit. By 0900H, the company has moved 100 m to the vicinity of BT201123. They are nearing the top. So far so good.

At 0915H, the 1st Brigade S2 (intelligence staff) gives an unconfirmed report that there is a major enemy position near BT206119. It includes six hooches, eight bunkers, with connecting trench and fighting positions. Another enemy camp is seen at BT208121. No enemy forces are sighted. Likely, they are already deployed in fighting positions to attack approaching 501st infantry units. The general enemy offensive that is meant to have begun today at 0400–0500H has not happened. The day is still early.

Ambush Near the Top

At 1025H, the battalion's three companies report their positions: Alpha, BT209126; Bravo, BT209122; and Delta, BT201124. They are all closing in on the mountain top. Moments later, Delta Company receives automatic weapons fire from a hooch 100 m to their front. They hold their position and return fire. The gunner for the company's M67 90 mm (3.5") recoilless rifle is called forward and readies his weapon to fire. The heavy (37.5 lb., 53" long) shoulder-fired weapon's round is 28" long and has an effective range of 400 m. The back blast of the recoilless rifle is powerful enough to kill. Capable of taking out tanks, a wood hut is no problem for the 90 mm.

Quickly checking that his back blast area is clear, the gunner takes aim and fires one round into the enemy position. The round explodes out of the barrel and swooshes toward its target covering the 100 m in a fast second. The detonation is spectacular. No more hut. The lead platoon flanks the target and soon arrives at the smoking remains. No enemy casualties or blood trails are seen. Apparently, the enemy soldiers decided to withdraw when they saw the 90 mm being readied to fire. It was a good decision on their part. At least the gunner got to fire his weapon. It is way too heavy to lug around the mountain and never use it.

At 1335H, the Cav Team flying in support of Bravo Company takes small arms fire from the area of BT204115. After attacking four enemy ground positions with rockets, the LOH is hit by enemy small arms fire and goes off station. At 1355H, a FAC comes on station. All unit movement halts. An F4 Phantom air strike is requested by Bravo Company at BT207118. The strike is complete at 1450H. Bravo Company can't make a bomb damage assessment. At 1620H, the FAC reports that he has engaged and battered an enemy 12.7 mm machine-gun position but didn't destroy it. At 1622H, he goes off station and is replaced by a new FAC. The pounding continues.

At 1620H, Alpha and Bravo Companies are near BT202121. Delta Company with the battalion's Recon Platoon still attached is at BT203123. Delta has covered approximately 600 m since morning. That is a straight-line distance of over six football fields. But there are no straight-line movements on Hill 376. It is all up and down and back and forth. The distance may not seem far to those who haven't served with infantry, but it is a good day's work on a mountainous battlefield crawling with enemy soldiers. Each man is carrying a full combat load of 75–100 lbs. The mountain forest is often thick with trees and other vegetation and it is hot and humid with no breeze unless it's raining.

Delta is now near the mountain's top and the enemy likely knows it. They are located near the high-speed trail that crosses the summit of Hill 376. The trail has a junction to the southwest with one fork headed due west and the other fork headed south. There is no doubt from the tracks that the enemy has been using this trail frequently. CPT Roy knows to keep clear of the trail junction which is a likely an enemy pre-planned target.

Enemy Resistance Increases

At 1715H, the lead element of Delta Company receives small arms fire from a small hit-and-run enemy team. They return fire. CPT Roy maneuvers a platoon to flank the area from where the firing had come. The enemy pulls back. The brief contact is a reminder that no part of the mountain is uncontested. This time no casualties enemy or friendly occur. CPT Roy's suspicion that the enemy is protecting something important on the summit of Hill 376 is growing. The closer Delta Company comes to the mountain top, the more enemy resistance stiffens. Perhaps cornered on the mountain, the enemy commander may be fighting a holding action to allow his units time to exfiltrate back to Laos or into the mountainous areas to the west and southwest. Anywhere to get away from the relentless "white chicken" men. (101 soldiers wore a distinctive colored patch with a fierce-looking, white-headed "Screaming Eagle" on their left shoulder. Enemy soldiers, not knowing about eagles, thought it was a "mean white chicken." Even after subdued patches in black and olive drab came out, the 101st wore the colored patch so the enemy would know who they were fighting.)

During the firefight, storm warnings are reported by battalion. They are always the same. Heavy rain, lightning, and high winds. An infantry soldier's interpretation—more mud, everything wet, soaked uniforms and equipment, rust on weapons, less visibility, bad footing, bone-chilling cold nights, and interrupted sleep. Situation normal. The mission continues.

At 1800H, Delta Company makes its last push of the day to the top of the mountain. An enemy position abruptly opens up with intense high volume "grazing fire" from an RPD machine gun. The RPD's rate of fire is 700 rounds per minute. The trained enemy gunner is firing controlled bursts of three to six seconds. Enough to keep everyone's head down. Grazing fire is the deadliest of automatic weapons fire. The stream of 7.62 mm rounds is fired not more than ten inches above the ground. Even a prone soldier may be hit. Every fold in the ground becomes a welcome haven. A pack or radio on a soldier's back is easily hit. A raised head or butt is certain to be shot. The lead soldiers "hug the ground" and return fire. Due to the unit's quick reaction, only two soldiers are lightly wounded. Neither requires evacuation.

The brief engagement stops Delta's advance. CPT Roy decides the move to the top is over for the day. Light is fading. The company begins to prepare its hasty defensive positions. Roy wants to resume the advance in the morning. The battalion commander tells CPT Roy he wants the enemy machine-gun position taken out. CPT Roy isn't sure why. He calls for SGT Parvin and tells him to take his squad and do his best to take out the gun position. Parvin asks if he can try it with just two men rather than risking his entire squad. Roy okays Parvin's request.

Parvin asks PFC John Meade if he will volunteer to go with him. Meade agrees and the two of them talk over how they plan to neutralize the gun position. Their plan is simple. They will slowly crawl up to the position and throw grenades in the bunker. Their plan works. It takes about 30 minutes, but the gun position is knocked out without any US casualties. Parvin is awarded a Bronze Star for Valor. Meade is awarded an Army Commendation Medal for Valor.

In the meantime, MAJ MacDiarmid tells CPT Roy to pull his company back several hundred meters for the night. Though outranked, CPT Roy argues strongly against the pull back. His company has worked hard and suffered casualties to get to its present position. Every foot the company pulls back is another foot that it will have to regain in the morning. And likely, the enemy will booby trap the area and be lying in wait.

CPT Roy faces an all too common problem for infantry units in Vietnam. As mentioned previously, battalion operations officers, and battalion commanders for that matter, are usually in their staff or command positions for only six months. Few operate on the ground with their infantry companies. Flying high overhead in a helicopter or looking at a map back at the battalion command post, it is too easy for them to "direct" the movement of units on the ground. To move up, back, sideways, or forward for any distance seems simple for those who don't have to execute the movement. After making his case, CPT Roy prevails. He has a habit of doing what is best for his company.

End of Day Four

The night defensive position for Delta Company and Recon is BT202123. Alpha is at BT206124, Bravo at BT210121. As Delta Company prepares its defensive positions for the night, an enemy attack by a sizeable force is still expected. The company and platoon command posts are set up to communicate and control any battle action during the dark of night. The defensive set up is accomplished quietly and quickly with little direction or correction. The young sergeants leading the platoons are proven combat soldiers, showing time and again they know what to do.

Probable enemy approaches are identified. Platoons are positioned in two- and three-man teams close enough to see from one position to the next. Each position is set with an eye toward communicating and controlling the fight should the enemy attack at night. Interlocking fields of fire are cleared, machine guns and grenade launchers are located at critical points, claymore mines and trip flares are set up to cover enemy approaches. All of this is a standard, oft-repeated practice.

It is getting dark quickly. There are no night vision devices. Soldiers do it the old-fashioned way, allowing their eyes to adapt to the dark night. The pupils of the eyes enlarge exposing the eyes rods which are sensitive to low levels of light. In about 40 minutes each soldier's eyes gain about 80% of their best ability to see at night. It takes hours to reach 100%.

At 1940H, brigade intelligence reports information from a captured NVA soldier. He says he is a member of a battalion from an NVA regiment located at BT190128 just west of Hill 376. That location is only about 2,000 m or just over a mile from the current positions of the three 501st companies. He further states his unit's twofold mission is to engage US units and obtain rice for his unit. He says his unit has received extensive training in small unit tactics including ambushes. The men of Delta Company have observed that firsthand.

Reluctantly, he reveals his battalion's strength has been reduced to 160 men divided into three companies. If true, they have been decimated, losing two-thirds of their men. They are still fighting and have been using mostly hit-and-run tactics. Lastly, the enemy soldier confirms the earlier report of an upcoming attack. They are preparing for a major offensive on 10 June to be conducted throughout the American Division's area of operations. This includes the 1st Brigade and the 501st operational area. The report signals a coming increase in the intensity of operations. Later at 2220H, it is reported the captured enemy soldier's battalion is part of the 2nd NVA Regiment.

The storm on the mountain continues into the night. Radio calls are limited to essential traffic. At 2050H, there is a report the brigade's Signal Operating Instructions (SOI) have been compromised. The enemy probably has it and can listen in on 501st radio transmissions. On the good side, Delta Company and its sister companies have had no casualties today. A good day! Rain or not, it is time to sleep. Maybe it will be a quiet night.

***

Casualties and Awards

1-501st Soldiers Killed in Action, 6 June 1969 (Day 4)—none

1-501st Soldier Awards for Hill 376, 6 June (other awards may have been made that were not mentioned in after action reports.

Bronze Star for Valor—5
> Bravo Company: 6 June, PFC Carlton Lang, PFC Lino Pacheco, PFC Dale Wilson, and SGT Steven Romano
> Delta Company: SP4 James Parvin

Army Commendation Medal for Valor
> PFC John Meade

Purple Heart—awards were made to all soldiers KIA or WIA

CHAPTER 14

Nearing the Top

7 June

Day Five on Hill 376

More Enemy Contact

As usual, Delta Company is awake at first light. Sleep has been a brief respite. The fatigue of constant combat is draining. The first conscious thoughts of waking soldiers are, "I am still on the Hill. Nothing happened while I was asleep. Got to get up. Get going. Be ready. Stay alive. Keep my buddies alive! I'm hungry. Have to take a leak." Perhaps not always in that order.

At 0730H, a familiar, reassuring sound is heard. A Cav Team's throbbing rotors announce the arrival of a LOH-6 and two AH-1 HueyCobras. After checking in over the radio with CPT Roy, the Cav Team begins to recon to the front of Delta Company's intended movement up the Hill. Roy knows they are very close to the top. Another hundred or so meters and the company will be up on the broad flat top of the mountain which consists of a 200 m wide ridge running from the southwest to the northeast. Once there, it is a straight 500 m shot to the summit's highest elevation.

Likely any final enemy defensive fortifications, facilities, or command posts will be on or around the flat portion of the summit. The highest point might have a communications antenna. Right now, all of this is only speculation. CPT Roy's intent is to get Delta Company up there today and find out what the enemy has been defending. He briefs his key leaders to anticipate immediate contact once they begin their move toward the top. Roy tells them the enemy has a purpose in its dogged, determined defense of the summit. Something big is there. It might also be that the enemy could be assembling its forces and planning a breakout through Delta's Company's sector in an effort to escape back to Laos. As usual, there are a lot of unknowns.

At 0800H, as Delta begins to move north out of their night defensive position, they immediately receive heavy automatic weapons fire. Again, it is an enemy RPD machine gun accompanied by an unknown number of AK-47 rifles. Well concealed as usual and dug in on the side of the hill, the enemy positions weren't seen by the Cav Team. The enemy soldiers held their fire and knew better than to open fire on the helicopters.

The NVA positions were obviously prepared many weeks if not months earlier. The well-hidden bunkers are reinforced with concrete, steels, and tree logs. Brush has been selectively cleared in the enemy gunner's sector of fire to better see approaching US forces and improve the effectiveness of their weapons.

Delta's lead platoon is pinned down and unable to maneuver as the enemy machine gunner directs bursts of 7.62 mm fire in their direction. The machine gunner and AK-47 riflemen demonstrate they are well trained and disciplined as they continuously fire short bursts of 5–6 rounds every few seconds to preserve their ammunition and keep targets to their front unable to move. Two soldiers of the Recon Platoon attached to Delta Company are killed in the opening bursts: PFC Stephen Larsen and PFC John Lewis. Three Recon soldiers are wounded: SGT Raymond Cooney, PFC David Shotwell, and PFC Emmett Richards.

Immediately upon the enemy opening fire, members of the lead platoon dive for cover behind trees, boulders, and every fold in the ground and return fire. CPT Roy is not far behind the pinned-down platoon. He requests the Cav Team hovering just above the treetops behind Delta Company move forward and take out the enemy positions.

Delta's soldiers, unable to pull back, continue to return fire. The battle noise is always deafening. There is the loud, rhythmic staccato of the enemy RPD and AK-47s firing, the LOH's mini-guns and rotors, the two nearby attack helicopters, and the Delta platoon's returning fire. Hundreds of bullets snap and crack and whish by at supersonic speeds making a loud sharp "thwack" in rapid succession as they hit trees or ground. Ricochets off rocks add high-pitched whines as they skip in every direction. Tree limbs and brush are shredded by gun fire. The firefight's intensity goes beyond what words can describe.

The rounds from the Cav Team are impacting only meters away from the pinned-down platoon. Soldiers in the platoon can only keep their heads down. It seems if they are not killed by the enemy gunners, they will be killed by the supporting helicopters. CPT Roy uses the suppressive fire of the Cav Team to maneuver a platoon to the east side of the hill to flank the enemy gun position. As the team's LOH makes a close-in gun run with mini-guns blazing, it is hit by enemy fire. The pilot is wounded, but manages to keep his aircraft flying. Not knowing how badly he or his copter has been hit, he goes off station and returns to base.

The Push to the Top Continues

At 0915H, Bravo Company led by CPT Shelton pushes forward up the mountain. They receive small arms fire from several bunkers at BT209119 some 50–100 m to the south and rear of their position. The enemy has gotten in behind them. They return fire and engage the position with their 81 mm mortar. The company commander moves a platoon toward the bunkers. Results are not reported. No friendly casualties occur. Enemy casualties are unknown.

By 1005H, the three 501st companies report their locations: Alpha is at BT204123; Bravo at 209119; and Delta at 202123. All companies are making good progress. Having neutralized the enemy position with the aid of the Cav Team, Delta Company awaits a medevac for their five Recon casualties. They hold up so the Cav Team can scout ahead and for Bravo Company to request an air strike.

At 1015H, the Cobra identifies two enemy 12.7 mm heavy machine-gun positions at BT201112 and BT202118 to the west and southwest of Delta Company. With fuel running low, the pilot chooses not to engage the positions. A new Cav Team will soon come on station.

At 1045H, Bravo Company is again moving. They reach the high-speed trail that runs across the mountain top and begin to follow it. There are recent footprints on the trail. Many of them. Almost immediately, they are engaged by an enemy RPD machine gun. Three soldiers from Bravo are killed immediately by the enemy fire: SP4 Raymond Talburt, SP4 Michael Callahan, and PFC James Rundle. Two are wounded: 1LT Lester Dixon and PFC Carlton Lang.

CPT Shelton has his FO tell the supporting artillery battery to stand by to fire. The Cav Team fires rockets into the RPD position close to Bravo's most forward friendly soldiers. Two Bravo soldiers sustain concussion injuries from the explosions.

CPT Shelton follows up with his air strike request to the circling FAC. By 1210H, the air strike is completed. There is no bomb damage assessment. An unknown number of enemy are probably killed. The enemy continues its repeated tactic of moving just ahead of the advancing 1-501st companies to set up ambushes at every opportunity. Bravo Company once again begins its move firing artillery ahead of its advance.

At 1210H, a log bird waiting to resupply the three advancing 1-501st companies returns to base. Multiple air strikes, the close proximity of enemy forces and continuous enemy engagements, medevacs, and the constant movement of the companies has worked against the resupply. The log bird remains on call. It will be needed soon. Ammunition and water are running low.

Alpha Company's Extended Firefight

At 1320H, Alpha Company receives small arms fire from the area south of BT205123. One Alpha soldier is killed, three are wounded. The firefight continues. Soon two more soldiers are wounded. Ten minutes later the company receives incoming 82 mm mortar fire from an unknown enemy location, wounding an additional two soldiers who receive concussions. At 1350H, the Cav Team leaves Delta Company, refuels and rearms to begin support of Alpha Company. At

1415H, the Cav Team returns to Alpha Company's area, but departs just after firing its aerial rockets due to extremely bad weather with high gusting winds and low visibility.

At 1440H, CPT Patrick McGuire reports Alpha Company is still in contact receiving small arms and RPG fire. They have taken three more wounded casualties and now have two soldiers killed and ten wounded. Killed were SGT Frederic Davis and SGT Michael O'Leary. Ten soldiers were wounded: SSG Jerry Nowack; SGT Neil Bishop and SGT Robert Jacobs; SP4s Hayward Barnes, Hargrove Bunting, Jose Gonzales, Donald Schilling, and Hugh Yerke; and PFCs Glenn Franze and James Medlin.

An hour later at 1540H, Alpha Company is receiving only sporadic fire. The enemy contact ends at around 1600H. CPT McGuire sends a team to locate an LZ to evacuate his wounded. There is a break in the weather. Medevacs can fly. Alpha Company reports six confirmed NVA dead, five AK-47s captured. Finding NVA dead is unusual. The enemy puts a high priority on removing their dead and preventing US units from knowing about their losses.

At 1630H, Delta Company completes its medevac of three wounded soldiers from Recon. They are taken to the 312th Medical Evacuation Hospital in Chu Lai. At 1700H, the soldier KIA is taken out by the log bird that brings in an emergency resupply of ammunition and water and Delta's first and only replacements on Hill 376. The small group includes LT James Bryant and PFCs Jessie Harris, George Dennis, and Ken Hornbeck. Bryant is only the second officer replacement Delta Company has received since the fight on Hill 376 began.

This is LT Bryant's first combat assignment. He meets briefly with CPT Roy who hopes this means the replacement stream is finally opening up, but there won't be any others. He assigns LT Bryant to lead 3rd Platoon, led by SGT Jim Littleton up to now. Being dropped into the middle of a hot fight is tough for all new replacements. There is no "warm up" time. A lieutenant doesn't have time to get to know his platoon and maybe worst, the platoon's soldiers have no time to get to know him.

Both leaders and those being led are again experiencing firsthand the failure of the individual replacement system in Vietnam. It undermines teamwork. Teamwork on a battlefield is critical. Infantry squads and platoons fight as a small unit team. It takes time to know and trust the guys on the team. Time is in short supply on Hill 376. The new guys and old guys don't even know each other's names, their experience, or their abilities. Both must do the best they can. Hill 376 is not the best place for on the job training.

End of Day Five

At 1850H, night defensive positions are reported. Delta Company and Recon are at BT202123, Alpha at BT206124, and Bravo at BT210119. It's been a tough day. At 2347H, Delta Company in a coded report says it has received two 82 mm mortar rounds 100 m south of their night defensive position. The three companies settle down for the night.

LT Wharton has a discussion with a nearby Delta Company infantryman. The topic "What's the best way to sleep? In wet jungle fatigues or skivvies?" It is the kind of important discussion soldiers have in combat on a dark night after being awoken by enemy mortar rounds exploding close by. Since everyone is always wet on Hill 376, there are only two choices. Infantrymen typically sleep in their wet jungle fatigues with boots on. At night they wrap up in a poncho liner and are dry by morning. If there is enemy action at night, they are ready to fight.

Wharton being an artilleryman is somewhat more refined. He prefers to strip down and put on dry skivvies and dry socks, his boots off but close by. His jungle fatigues are hung nearby to dry. He figures the comfort of sleeping dry is worth the risk. If startled awake by enemy action in the middle of night, he will call in artillery in his skivvies. They are Army green of course. Wharton adds, he always sleeps with his head toward north and his feet south. If aroused from deep sleep, he is immediately oriented. The infantryman laughs and concedes the argument. He will still sleep in his wet jungle fatigues with his boots on!

***

Casualties and Awards

Battalion casualties for today, 7 June, are high. Delta Company has no KIA or WIA, but Recon Platoon fighting with Delta Compony has two KIA and three WIA. Alpha has three KIA and 10 WIA. Bravo reports three KIA, two WIA and two soldiers with concussions. Total enemy casualties are unknown. The seven NVA KIA confirmed are believed to be a fraction of those killed and wounded.

1-501st Soldiers Killed in Action, 7 June 1969 (Day 5)

Recon Platoon (attached to Delta Company)—2
    7 June: PFC Stephen Larsen, age 21, born 23 November 1947 from East Ely, NV
    7 June: PFC John Lewis, age 21, born 19 November 1947 from California Hot Springs, CA
Alpha Company—2
    7 June: SGT Frederic Davis, age 21, born 26 October 1947 from Union Lake, MI
    7 June: SGT Michael O'Leary, age 23, born 18 May 1946 from Kokomo, IN
Bravo Company—3
    7 June: SP4 Michael Callahan, age 21, born 11 April 1948 from Wildwood Crest, NJ

7 June: PFC James Rundle, age 26, born 14 November 1942 from Kingston, NY

7 June: SP4 Raymond Talburt, age 24, born 26 October 1944 from Wichita, KS

1-501st Soldier Awards for Hill 376, 7 June (other awards may have been made that were not mentioned in after action reports)

Silver Star—3

Alpha Company: 7 June, PFC Robert Garcia

Bravo Company: 7 June, LT Lester Dixon, PFC James Rundle

Bronze Star for Valor—21

Headquarters and Headquarters Company: 7 June, SP4 Gregory Weisner (medic)

Alpha Company: 7 June, CPT Patrick McGuire, SFC Marvin Grandsinger, SSG Jerry Nowak, SGT Frederic Davis, SGT James Day, SGT Gerald Gillette, SGT Roger Long, SGT Michael O'Leary, SGT David Saulter, SP4 Robert Guyse, SP4 Edward Pettit, and PFC Tommy Hale

Bravo Company: 7 June, CPT Walter Shelton, SP4 Dorsey Brewer, PFC Michael Callahan, and PFC Raymond Talburt

Recon Platoon: 7 June, SP4 Norris Arrowood, PFC Stephen Larsen, PFC John Lewis, and PFC Harrel Stearns

Purple Heart—awards were made to all soldiers KIA or WIA

CHAPTER 15

Unexpected Setbacks

8 June

Day Six on Hill 376

On this day, President Nixon makes his first US troop withdrawal announcement after meeting with South Vietnam President Nguyen Van Thieu on Midway Island. A first increment of 25,000 military personnel will be withdrawn from Vietnam in August 1969. Planning for troop withdrawals has been secretly underway since the end of 1968. It has been kept hidden so as not to encourage the enemy, affect the US position at the Paris Peace talks, or adversely affect soldiers fighting on Vietnam's many battlefields.

Fortunately, the news of the announcement won't make it to Hill 376. It would be a certain morale killer. The first thought of US soldiers would be, "Why should I risk my life, if we're going to be sent home soon?" Instead, Delta and its sister companies remain locked in mortal combat. For their NVA enemy, the news will come as welcome relief. The Americans are leaving! No better reason to hold on and continue fighting!

The 501st soldiers on Hill 376 are far removed from stateside news reports, the politics of war, protests at home, and the president's announcements. No cameras or microphones are recording events on Hill 376 for televisions back home. They continue fighting in anonymity, not seeking glory or even the thanks of their nation as they fulfill their commitment and duty as soldiers. Their most pressing concern is staying alive.

A Day of Unrest Begins

Before Day Six dawns, at 0325H an Alpha Company soldier on night watch spots movement in their defensive perimeter. Tension mounts. A trip flare triggers. A single NVA soldier is illuminated. He is carrying an RPG launcher. An Alpha soldier blows a claymore. Those who are sleeping are startled awake. Others begin to engage with rifle fire. An M-60 machine gun erupts. After a few minutes, the firing dies down.

There are no further signs of enemy activity. No friendly casualties occur. Enemy casualties are unknown.

Delta and Bravo are alerted by Alpha Company's early morning firing. They closely monitor the action on their radios at lowered volumes. Security is increased. Soldiers on watch anticipate action in their sectors. Those who were awakened settle down again for needed sleep. The rest of the night is quiet.

Later at 0630H, welcome light seeps in among the still, dark trees. One dead NVA soldier is found. Another dazed enemy soldier is captured along with the RPG launcher, several RPG rounds, a K-50M rifle, and seven hand grenades. Others could have been killed or wounded, but were likely moved, dead or alive.

No one knows it, but at the end of today this ten-day battle action has reached its mid-point. Total 1-501st casualties are 14 KIA and 25 WIA. The number of friendly casualties will almost double in the next two days. The NVA continues to take even heavier casualties which becomes evident later. The expected enemy attack on 10 June is still two days away.

Today is Sunday on Hill 376, but it won't be a day of rest. Delta Company is already stirring. As explained earlier, 501st companies "stand to" each morning ready for an enemy attack at first light, though no early morning attacks have yet occurred. The days continue to run together. The first five days on Hill 376 have melded into one continuous, long grind. Today is expected to be more of the same. It will prove much worse.

The Only US Military Female KIA

Early this morning at 0555H, Army nurse, LT Sharon Ann Lane, is the first and only US military female killed by hostile fire in Vietnam. She has just finished the 12-hour graveyard shift at the hospital and is sitting briefly on an unoccupied bed for a quick rest. It is her 40th day in country.[23]

Upon arrival in Vietnam on 29 April 1969, LT Lane was first assigned to the Intensive Care Unit (ICU) of the 312th Evacuation Hospital in Chu Lai. It is the same hospital where 1st Brigade's seriously wounded casualties are taken by medevac from nearby battlefields. Later, LT Lane was transferred to the hospital's Vietnamese Ward 4B, where she cared for wounded, injured, and sick civilians including children. LT Lane worked in the civilian ward five days a week,12 hours a day. In her "free time" she volunteered to return to the ICU and care for US soldiers. She helped save the lives of many and saw many die.

When I was wounded on the evening of 2 June, I was taken by medevac to the 312th. I don't know if I ever met or saw LT Lane in my short two-day stay there before continuing my journey to a hospital in Japan. I do have several distinct memories upon waking up the next morning from a deep sleep after my evening surgery. The first was the comfort of the air-conditioned ward and a soft bed and pillows with clean sheets. All quickly noticeable after sleeping in the field for nearly five months.

The second memory is that of an attractive, young female nurse who came through our recovery ward wishing us a good morning with a bright smile and the happy news a hot breakfast was on the way. After the nurse left, a wounded Huey pilot in the bed next to me exclaimed, "Wow, I could spend the rest of my tour right here!" as he tenderly patted the sheets on his bed. "Not me." I replied. I feel a little naked without my M-16. If I can't be armed, I'd just as soon be on my way. The quicker the better.

Last week, LT Lane had written to her concerned parents telling them not to worry, "They haven't mortared us in weeks." A few days later at 0555H on 8 June, a NVA 122 mm rocket slammed into Ward 4B and exploded, instantly killing LT Lane and a 12-year-old Vietnamese girl. Twenty-seven others were wounded. LT Lane was buried with full military honors in North Canton, Ohio. The recovery room of Fitzsimmons Army Hospital in Denver Colorado where Lane served before going to Vietnam was renamed and dedicated in her honor. In 1973, Aultman Hospital in Canton, Ohio, where LT Lane trained to be a nurse erected a 7 ft bronze statue of Lane in her jungle fatigues with the inscription, "Born to honor, ever at peace." In 1986 the hospital established the Sharon Lane Woman's Center. The names of 110 local servicemen killed in Vietnam are on the base of the statue. In 2002, the Sharon Lane Foundation established a women and children's clinic near Chu Lai Vietnam. LT Lane's name is listed on the Vietnam War Memorial in Washington DC, panel 23W, line 112.

The Fear of Dying

No soldier in Delta Company thinks he is safe from being wounded or killed. They know better. They have already seen too many soldiers they know die. In this battle, like all battles, death is an everyday reality. It seems a random thing. The Grim Reaper prowls Hill 376, not fussy about his prey. Even the best of soldiers are being killed.

The fear of dying briefly darts in and out of soldier minds. Surrounded by death, few soldiers dwell on it. They can't afford to. A few put it out of their minds altogether. Some take on a fatalistic bent. If it happens, it happens. Others pray for their safety and the safety of others. "Dear Lord, please get me through this!" For most soldiers, thoughts focus on the mission at hand. "Stay alert! Stay alive. Don't let your buddies down." This thinking helps many through tough spots. They will need such thinking today.

Delta's new replacements have no previous combat experience. They have had no opportunity to get introduced or accustomed to combat over a period of weeks or even months. Dropped in the middle of an intense battle on Hill 376, they are understandably more vulnerable to later suffering Post Traumatic

Stress Disorder (PTSD). Any soldier can suffer PTSD, but those in a fierce battle for an extended length of time without having developed personal relationships with other soldiers are more susceptible. (See the brief discussion on PTSD in Appendix 8.)

The amazing thing about Delta Company's young soldiers is their seemingly endless ability to overcome their fear in battle. Some say "the fight or flight" response is built into the psychological makeup of every human. That may be so, but time and again, Delta's soldiers at Tam Ky choose to fight not flee. They are anxious in battle and as SGT Littleton said, "scared all the time," but they aren't immobilized by fear or so terrified they are panic-stricken. They are doing their duty in deadly combat. As an old Army adage says, "Doing your duty is not part of the job of a soldier, it is the job."

Relief for Delta Company

At 0655H a FAC comes on station to direct air strikes for Alpha Company. A Cav Team arrives on station at 0745H but stands off while the air strikes are completed. By 0830H, three "danger close" air strikes are completed on or near the summit of Hill 376 using a combination of 500 lb. bombs and napalm cannisters. No bomb damage assessment can be made. The intensity of the three air strikes just several hundred meters apart likely causes significant enemy casualties. At 0910H, the Cav Team goes off station to refuel. Another will return soon.

Early morning plans are made by the 1-501st Battalion commander to insert Charlie Company on Hill 376 in relief of Delta Company. Since 31 May, Charlie has been pulling security at LZ Professional. Delta came into the Hill 376 battle not yet recovered from its heavy casualties in the major firefight on 21 May. It has since taken many more casualties. Replacements haven't been available to make up for the casualties and bring the company up its normal fighting strength. The attachment of the half-strength Recon Platoon on 4 June with its 12 or so soldiers to Delta Company boosted its troop count some. They too have taken many casualties. Roy welcomes the opportunity for a brief stand down. Though Delta Company hasn't lost its fighting edge, they are ready for a short break.

The plan to extract Delta Company seems simple at first—move south from its present location at BT203125 along the southern fork of the high-speed trail to a pickup point at the base of the mountain near BT205108. The planned move will cover over 1,000 meters. CPT Roy is not in favor of the battalion commander's plan. As the commander on the ground of a much understrength infantry company, he knows firsthand the difficult terrain and obstacles they will face. The 1,000 m move along the trail will expose his company to enemy ambushes and needless casualties. He believes the enemy has already moved in behind and below his company on Hill 376. Further, if the enemy is massing for a planned attack as earlier reports indicate, he wants to be in a defendable location. His current location is tactically sound and a nearby area is suitable for an LZ.

Another important factor in staying put is both Alpha and Delta Company haven't been resupplied for the last two days due to continuous enemy contact. Before Delta Company can move, it needs the essentials—ammunition, water, and rations. At 0910H, the resupply log birds are on standby until today's scheduled air strikes are completed. Both Delta and Alpha companies are remaining in place for now. Roy will express his concerns about the move more vigorously later.

Multiple Air Strikes

At 0920H, all units update their location prior to the close support air strikes soon to occur. The unit updates are critical for safety. Bombs were dropped recently on friendly soldiers during the Hamburger Hill battle. Everyone wants to avoid that—especially the soldiers on the ground. Delta and Recon are at BT203125. Alpha is nearby at BT206124 and Bravo at BT210119.

Once locations are confirmed, Delta Company's previously requested two air strikes go in at BT202123. The target is just 200 m southwest of Delta's current position, really close. Soon F4 Phantoms make their runs on a bomb target line from east to west each dropping a full rack of four 500 lb. bombs. As anyone who has attended an air show knows, the sound of a jet fighter-bomber swooping low to the ground is louder and longer than can be imagined. The simultaneous earth shaking, bone rattling explosion of 2000 lbs. of bombs a short distance away is in a class all by itself.

Artillery and a Cav Team standby to follow the air strikes. CPT Roy's FO, LT Paul Wharton, is controlling the air space above his battle area to avoid catastrophic accidents. He can't employ tactical air support, artillery, or the Cav Team on the same targets at the same time. The sequencing is critical. When the air strikes are complete, artillery will be fired next. Unfortunately, the Cav Team is no longer available. It left to refuel and a second Cav Team has yet to arrive.

At 1245H, a window opens for a log bird to evacuate Bravo Company's four wounded soldiers and three soldiers killed in the previous day's battle action. Alpha and Delta are still waiting for an opportunity to resupply. First priority goes to the planned air strikes for Delta and Alpha Company. Both strikes are again close, a couple of hundred meters from each company's location. The air strikes are critical. They are designed to hit enemy forces which reports say may be massing to attack US units. Bomb damage assessments can't be made to see if they are successful.

A Tragic Incident

At 1600H Delta Company still hasn't initiated its directed move south. They haven't been resupplied and are still short ammunition and water. Food can wait. Ammunition and water can't. Suddenly, they receive machine-gun, small arms, RPG, and M-79 grenade fire from several bunkers just north of their position. It is not clear whether the enemy has recently slipped into the bunkers or has been there all along, waiting for the right moment to open fire.

The volume of fire is the heaviest contact Delta Company has yet encountered. In returning fire, 1st Platoon attempts to maneuver against the enemy position. Two Delta Company soldiers are wounded. Another soldier, PFC Jessie Harris, one of the new replacements, is just in front of an enemy position when it opens fire. In the heavy vegetation, others in the platoon lose sight of him. Harris is believed to be dead. No one can get to him because the enemy fire is too intense.

LT Wharton, the FO, gets the artillery firing. Rounds soon begin to fall close, almost too close, to Delta Company's positions, but squarely on the enemy positions. CPT Roy requests a flamethrower team from battalion to deal with the bunkers. At 1720H, the two-man team from Echo Company arrives by Huey, along with a couple of replacements. The two wounded soldiers are taken out. The two soldiers with the flamethrower don't seem familiar with their weapon. Apparently they have received only a brief impromptu training session on the seldom-used weapon just before being put on a helicopter. CPT Roy tells the flamethrower team to standby. He intends to give them specific instructions and accompany them to their target area.

With his men still under heavy fire, Roy is on the radio with Apache 6, the battalion commander. Flying high above the battlefield, Apache 6 can't see what's happening, but he can hear the firing over the radio. He presses Roy to begin his move south along the trail even though Delta Company is currently engaged in a heavy firefight. Precious minutes go by. Roy hurriedly and impatiently attempts to get off the radio to attend to the more immediate business of the on-going firefight.

While Roy is tied up on the radio, the flamethrower team, hearing the heavy firing a short distance up the hill, decides to move up the hill on their own without Roy. They don't have far to go. One hundred meters up the slope, 1st Platoon is heavily engaged returning fire against enemy positions 20 to 30 m to their front. The platoon's M-60 machine gun is laying down a steady stream of fire attempting to suppress the enemy fire coming from a nearby bunker.

Maneuver against the enemy position is difficult. The expertly concealed bunkers are hard to detect until the enemy fires. Both sides are putting out a heavy volume of fire. The noise is deafening. The platoon leader cautiously leads a small group of his platoon and the flamethrower team around to the right flank of the enemy positions. The flamethrower team is positioned forward to fire on the bunker. The flame will cover a wide area out to 30 m and give the platoon an opportunity to destroy the bunker.

As is often the case in a fast-moving combat situation in close contact with the enemy, things happen too quickly to be certain of all the details. There are differing accounts from the soldiers present, but all agree the platoon leader was holding a grenade just before it explodes. Whatever happened, he should be dead. Six others, including the flamethrower team, are also wounded. The M2A1-7 flamethrower is hit by shrapnel and destroyed. Mercifully, the four gallons of napalm-like, jellied gasoline in the two tanks doesn't explode. Platoon Sergeant, SSG Ron Sahrle, and PFC George Dennis are the only soldiers not hit. Both are in a prone position not far behind the platoon leader when the grenade explodes. Dennis, who came in as a replacement just a few days before, makes the radio call for help.

The first soldier to arrive is PFC Ken Hornbeck. Hornbeck is also a new replacement who came in with Dennis. Hornbeck sees Dennis writhing in pain on the ground and thinks he is wounded. Dennis tells him that a hot casing ejected from the nearby machine gun hit his helmet and then went down the collar of his jungle fatigues, blistering his back. (He will be able to laugh about it later, but it isn't funny now.)

Sahrle, Dennis, and Hornbeck help the wounded back to the company. The platoon leader and one other soldier must be carried. (The name of the other soldier who is seriously wounded is not known, though his name may be listed with the wounded at the end of this chapter.) The wounded soldiers able to walk make their way back as best they can. CPT Roy has heard the explosion and soon sees the wounded flamethrower team being helped down the hill.

After checking the wounded, Roy is relieved to learn no one was killed. Next, he gathers information from the survivors and forwards his report to battalion. Roy had hoped the flamethrower would allow Delta Company to break through the enemy's chain of bunkered positions. Once they broke through, the way to the summit of Hill 376 would most likely be open. Unfortunately, it won't happen today. SSG Sahrle once again assumes leadership of the remaining elements of 1st and 2nd Platoons, now with five fewer men.

Having made sure the wounded are being treated and a medevac has been called, CPT Roy immediately turns his attention to recovering PFC Jessie Harris, who has been reported as missing in action. Darkness is approaching and a search will be difficult. The enemy bunkers north of Delta Company's position are not neutralized and remain a danger.

Missing in Action

After the unresolved heavy firefight earlier in the day and the grenade incident, Delta leaders from squad to company level account for their men. Twenty-year-old PFC Jessie B. Harris Jr, a new replacement from Port Chester, New York, is missing. Although Harris' body hasn't been recovered, he is believed to have been killed in action during today's earlier intense firefight. Before pulling back, members of 1st Platoon had called out Harris' name several times. There was no answer. A further search couldn't be made due to the enemy situation. Harris is then reported as MIA. Unknown to Delta Company, Harris has been captured during the close-in fight in Hill 376's dense vegetation with the enemy sometimes only a few meters away. The following account is told as it happens.

Harris is lying wounded, his right elbow and forearm shattered by enemy AK-47 rifle fire. The enemy continues to fire at him with AK rifles and a captured M-79 grenade launcher. Protected behind a tree trunk, he can't move without being killed. Soon after Harris' platoon pulls back, two NVA soldiers move up to where he is lying. Harris sees them coming and plays dead. A couple of hard rifle butts to the head force him to breathe and they see he is alive.

The two enemy soldiers decide to set up an ambush using Harris as bait. It is a favorite enemy tactic. Harris realizes what they are doing. Soon, there are several calls from soldiers in his platoon, "Harris where are you? Are you okay?" Harris hears them and wants to be rescued, but knows if he calls out to them they and he are likely to be killed. He keeps quiet. His platoon again pulls back. After an hour, the enemy soldiers give up their trap and pull back with their prisoner.

Harris is taken to an enemy camp likely on the back or northside of Hill 376. For three days he is kept isolated and guarded in a small hooch surrounded by concertina wire. Alone, in excruciating pain, and scared, his greatest fear is he will soon be killed. He battles hard against losing hope. He repeats The Lord's Prayer over and over to keep his mind from focusing on how bad his situation is. He knows if he doesn't get help soon, he will likely die alone in the jungle mountains. His family may never know what happened to him.

Harris finally asks one of his guards, "Are you going to kill me?" He gets an abrupt one word answer, "No." The guard, a former South Vietnamese soldier, knows a little English. Harris is at a camp with a small 8' × 14' hooch used as a primitive and poorly equipped hospital. Apparently, a doctor or maybe just an experienced medic has recently arrived. He tells Harris' guards to bring him in for surgery. For the first time, Harris has hope they intend to let him live.

Without anesthesia, his wounds are cleaned, sewn up, and bandaged. When his wound is probed for bullets and other debris, the excruciating pain causes Harris to let out a loud yell. Gathered around the operating table on three sides just a few feet away, are a large group of small children from kindergarten age down. They have been watching the surgery on this US soldier with keen interest. When Harris yells in pain, the children laugh in a nervous response. To the children's delight, Harris smiles at them and keeps his attention on the children, making faces and talking to them until his surgery is over. It is the best anesthesia he has available.

The presence of children means his captors are local Viet Cong, rather than NVA out of Laos. The Viet Cong provide all kinds of support to the NVA so they can focus on fighting. Harris also spots women in the various camps to which he is moved.

One woman in particular is easy to identify. She has extensive burn scars all over her face, body, arms, and legs. She appears to have been severely burned by napalm.

During his 135 days of captivity, Harris is moved several times, but always kept in the mountains southwest of Tam Ky either on or near Hill 376. At one temporary camp with an NVA officer is charge, Harris is interrogated for the first time. He is asked some simple questions like, "Are you married?" Harris refuses to answer any of the questions. At one point a VC guard picks up a large stick and walks menacingly toward Harris. His threatening look shows he intends to punish his failure to answer. The interrogator stops him. Being a new replacement and junior enlisted soldier, the enemy soon learns Harris doesn't have any useful military intelligence information.

Harris had made up his mind early not to collaborate with the enemy. His Geneva Convention training taught him that he should not divulge more than his name, rank, and serial number. But he has another important reason. He doesn't want to embarrass or dishonor his family. He knows his mother, brother, and two sisters are praying for him. Harris is unaware they have already been notified he is missing. His mother will never believe he is dead. In fact, months after he is reported missing, she will refuse to take the insurance benefit offered by the US Army. For her to do that, the Army would have to change his status from missing to missing and presumed dead.

No harm comes to Harris via torture or mistreatment, but staying alive is itself a major struggle. Being alone and afraid, his high pain level, his infected wound, malaria, dysentery, and being so cold at night his body shakes, are all part of his suffering in captivity. He is in a different battle now against a deep feeling of hopelessness. What gets him through many lonely days and nights is the hope he will survive and return home to his family. In one camp at night, he can see the distant flickering lights of Tam Ky, which remind him to hold on another day.

Harris' sparse diet of water and rice doesn't help his condition. He knows his captors don't get much more to eat than him. They are all fed meager portions of rice and water. Harris is the only US soldier being held captive by the enemy in 1st Brigade's area of operations, but his captors hold 25 Army of South Vietnam (ARVN) soldiers. Harris is kept separate from them and couldn't talk with them anyway. They don't speak English.

As time goes by, Harris is getting weaker. His captors know he won't survive long. The NLF controlling Viet Cong activities in South Vietnam decides to release several US POWs being held by their units in 1969. PFC Harris is released in October, three others are released in November, and two more in December. Indications are the releases are to gain support of the US war protest movement. Three of the POWs released praise their former captures and question the war on the front page of the *Chicago Tribune*.[24]

Harris neither praises his captors nor participates in protests against the war, but he's thankful they kept him alive, didn't torture him, and decided to release him. On 2 October 1969, he is taken to an area near a small South Vietnamese Army outpost on Highway 9 where he is freed. In rough shape mentally and physically, Harris makes his way to the gate. When he is challenged by the guards, he calls out with all the strength he can muster, "I am an American!"

He is searched and taken inside the compound. Two US advisors at the camp are alerted and soon appear. Harris identifies himself and his unit. A medic is called. Food and water are brought in but with his weakened body and dysentery, Harris can't eat much. The two US advisors ask him a few questions about where he was and who were his captors. He can't give much detail. When asked if he knows why he was released all he can say is they knew I was dying. Soon, he is airlifted by helicopter to the 312th Evacuation Hospital at Chu Lai. He will stay there for two weeks as he gets medical treatment and strength for the long flight home.

Before leaving the Army's Chu Lai medical facilities, a scheduled call is arranged with Harris' mother, brother, and two sisters. It is not a long call. Harris is too exhausted for that. He tells his mother how much he loves her and misses her. She is elated to hear his voice. God has answered her many prayers! Before the call ends, Harris says to her "I told you when I left home, I'd be back." It is a promise he's eager to keep.

PFC Jessie Harris was born in Tuscaloosa, Alabama. His family moved to Port Chester, NY, when he was young. Growing up, his mother instilled in him as a young black man he had responsibilities to his country and to his people. After high school, Harris took a civilian job, but soon decided if his country was at war, he wanted to do his part. He enlisted in the US Army on 13 December 1968. Like many young soldiers, he knew he could be killed, but wanted his life to count. In a time of growing racial unrest, he believed it was important to show others, that young black men were willing to die for their country and deserved to be fully accepted by it. PFC Harris proved to be right. His honorable service and the faithful service of hundreds of thousands of men like him, during the Vietnam War and since, has resulted in increased understanding, greater freedom, protection of rights, and opportunity for blacks and other minorities in our country. The path has been uphill, but always forward.

On 1 November 1969, PFC Harris lands at Kennedy Airport in New York City and is taken by ambulance to the US Naval Hospital in Saint Albans, New York. After an additional six months of hospitalization, he is released from the hospital and allowed to go home on convalescence leave. A year later after his arrival home, now SP4 Jessie Harris receives an honorable discharge and medical retirement on 13 October 1970 and returns to Port Chester New York, a much-changed young man.

End of Day Six

The day has not ended well for Delta Company on Hill 376. Unexpected events have caused a change in plans. Long ago, Julius Caesar, a Roman general before he became an emperor, said it well, "No one is so brave he's not disturbed by something unexpected." Today's unexpected setbacks (the grenade incident, the wounding of ten men, and the loss of PFC Harris) are troubling. The enemy contact also prevented Charlie Company's arrival and ended CPT Roy's plan to get his company to the top of the hill. With their extraction delayed, the men of Delta Company will spend another night on Hill 376.

At 1840H, the logistical helicopter on standby most of the day is released. It will return tomorrow to complete needed supply drops. At 1900H, the medevac for Delta's wounded is complete. Five are flown to the 312th Evacuation Hospital at Chu Lai. Two are dropped off at the 27th Surgical Hospital in Chu Lai. Others remain in the field since their wounds are not life threatening.

At 2120H, NDP locations are Delta and Recon at BT203125; Alpha BT206121, and Bravo BT209118. Delta Company remains in the same position in which it began the day. It is much too late to move south to the proposed extraction point. The new plan is to secure an LZ near Delta's current position.

There are several bright spots. No Delta or Echo Company soldiers were KIA today. Delta Company didn't make the long, risky, solo move south to the extraction point. Though further reduced in strength and in the midst of a tough fight, they are still combat effective, willing and able to continue engaging the enemy they face.

As Delta Company beds down for the night with today's casualties on the minds of many, they have survived another day. Sleep is a welcome respite. There is hope for a better tomorrow. But tomorrow will be one of Delta Company's toughest days at Tam Ky.

***

Casualties and Awards

Day Six casualties for Delta Company include eight WIA: the 1st Platoon Leader (name withheld by his request), and PFCs Leonard Bauldauf, Arthur Briggs, David Cauign, Vernon Elliot, Ronald Hauge, Randall Lefever, and Jack Vacca. PFC Jessie Harris is missing in action. Echo Company (the flamethrower team attached to Delta Company) adds another two WIA: PFC Michael McAndrews and Jose Masa.

Total US casualties for the 1-501st Battalion's six days on Hill 376 are 14 KIA, 35 WIA, and 2 MIA. Enemy casualties are also high, but accurate reports are not available. No one in Delta Company really cares. Body counts are a poor way to keep score.

1-501st Soldiers Killed in Action, 8 June 1969 (Day 6)—none

1-501st Soldier Awards, 8 June 1969

Bronze Star for Valor
  Delta Company: CPT Leland Roy, PFC Edward Medros, and LT Paul Wharton

CHAPTER 16

Turning Point

9 June

Day Seven on Hill 376

Today will be a turning point, not an easy day, but a pivotal change for the better in the fight on Hill 376. Of course, no one knows it. Nothing in the last six days of fighting gives any hint that a breakthrough is about to occur. It is the nature of warfare. The decisive moment a favorable turn in a battle's outcome occurs is often not recognized by those in the throes of fighting. Early morning events are a bad start for the day.

Early Morning Mortars

At 0320H, Alpha Company is shaken awake by the booming of 15 enemy 82 mm mortar rounds exploding in rapid succession. Sleep-deprived soldiers instinctively react to the unwelcome wake-up call. "Get down! Stay down! God please let me survive!" is the common thought. There is a collective sigh of relief when it is clear the rounds aren't on target. The enemy gunners have overshot Alpha Company's position, but not by much. No friendly casualties occur.

Each 82 mm mortar round has a lethal blast radius of 30–35 m. In open terrain, a single round's blast can cover almost half the size of a football field. In mountainous, forested terrain the lethal blast area is reduced. Fifteen rounds are still a deadly barrage. Had it landed on Alpha Company, casualties would be high. Captain McGuire, the company commander, has his forward observer call for artillery in the area from where they suspect the mortars were fired. Likely, the enemy mortar crews have already moved. They know return artillery fire will arrive soon.

At 0350H, Alpha's artillery request is fired. An incoming 105 mm round falls short and explodes in Bravo Company's position. The bursting shell kills three soldiers: SGT William Bushard, SGT William Sparks, and PFC Larry Gilbertson. PFC David Bleeker is wounded and needs immediate care. A nighttime medevac is requested. At 0425H, the medevac is cancelled due to dangerous flying conditions.

CPT Roy hears the enemy mortars hitting Alpha Company over the battalion radio net. The delayed muffled booms rapidly echo across the mountain side. It is an ominous, unwelcome sound. He recalls the enemy attack mentioned in the recent intelligence report. The attack is to begin tomorrow, 10 June. Maybe this is it, a day early. If he is right, the battle action on Hill 376 will soon get more intense. The early morning hours before sunrise are peacefully quiet. It is an illusion.

Choosing an LZ

Finding an LZ for Charlie Company is the first of Delta Company's morning tasks. Soon after first light, CPT Roy adds several Delta Company soldiers to the attached Recon Platoon (now no bigger than a reinforced squad). He sends them out 200 m to the southwest of Delta Company's position at BT203125 to search for a suitable LZ. The battalion plan from yesterday to have Charlie Company relieve Delta Company was postponed. Delta Company's enemy contact prevented their move south to the proposed pick-up point. CPT Roy still believes the solo move south by his understrength company is too risky with an enemy attack expected soon.

The Recon element moves out of Delta's perimeter to see if a long ridge line running southeast off Hill 376 may be a suitable LZ. It seems capable of handling 5 or 6 helicopters at a time and it will take 15 Hueys to bring in Charlie Company. As each of Charlie's lifts arrive, Delta will load up the empty helicopters with their own men for extraction. At least, that is the plan.

While Recon is still scoping out the potential LZ, the air commander responsible for Charlie Company's movement vetoes the location. He tells CPT Roy the proposed LZ on the ridge line will expose inbound and outbound helicopters to the enemy's 12.7 mm heavy machine-gun fire. CPT Roy then quickly recommends and gets approval for using a much smaller, one-ship LZ adjacent to his company's position.

The approved LZ is small and cramped, only one Huey can land at a time and after unloading must do a 180° turnaround to fly out. With some needed brush cutting, it will have to do. The LZ has two advantages. It is close by Delta Company's position at BT203125 and can be covered by fire from the company's perimeter. It is also in a swale with high ground immediately to its north and south which provides protection from enemy observation and antiaircraft fire. The Hueys can approach the LZ from the south and fly out on the same route.

SSG Sahrle, who is once again leading the remnants of 1st and 2nd Platoons, takes on the task of clearing brush to widen the LZ and enlists SGT Littleton in 3rd Platoon to provide a three-man team with machetes. Littleton will also take a security team several hundred meters to the west of the LZ to cover the likely direction from which an enemy attack may come.

SGT Robert Clouatre, SP4 Terry Rada, and PFC Steve Strand, all from 3rd Platoon, begin work with machetes clearing the west end of the LZ. Some 20 m away and just above them on the high ground to their north is a berm running parallel to the LZ from east to west. It is 70 m long and 8–10 ft high. Overgrown with vegetation, the berm is part of an abandoned terraced area once used for farming.

Initial Enemy Contact

At 0715H, the morning's humid temperature is rising. Clearing the LZ is hot work. Rada is sitting down for a short break, Strand is standing 6 ft behind him, Clouatre is standing near to the side of Rada. Their weapons are nearby. Without warning, an enemy grenade explodes just in front of Rada, killing him instantly. It is thrown from a concealed enemy position on the west end of the berm up above the LZ. Strand and Clouatre are both wounded, Clouatre seriously. He will survive, but will require hundreds of stitches and several operations.

CPT Roy is on the LZ checking progress of the brush clearing just 30 ft to the east of the brush clearing team when the enemy grenade explodes. Doc, the company medic, bolts out from the company perimeter to the wounded men. Roy knows the medic and the wounded men are in danger and yells for them to pull back to the company's perimeter. Soldiers on the company's southwestern perimeter begin providing suppressive fire on the berm to cover their withdrawal. Strand and the medic help move Clouatre to safety. Rada is carried by others who have come out to help.

The enemy position near the west end of the berm is continuing to fire AK-47s. Roy estimates by the firing there are several enemy soldiers, maybe more. Fortunately, the enemy is not positioned on the military crest of the hill. They are unable to see directly down to the wounded soldiers on the LZ or take them under fire as they make their way back to Delta's defensive position. The suppressive fire from Delta's perimeters keeps them from improving their position, Otherwise, there would be several more casualties.

Once within the perimeter, Doc treats Clouatre with Strand's help. It takes more than a few minutes since Clouatre is bleeding badly from multiple shrapnel wounds. Doc makes sure he hasn't overlooked any life-threatening wounds and applies bandages to the worst of them. When done, Doc notices Strand has bled through his jungle fatigues jacket. His rolled-up right sleeve is saturated with dark red blood. Once bandaged, Strand is surprised when Doc tells him he will also go out on the next medevac. That won't happen until the enemy contact has ended. In the meantime, SGT Littleton's security team is told to return and they make it back without incident.

While Strand waits for a medevac, his thoughts turn to Rada. They were good friends. Rada was well-liked by his platoon members. Before Tam Ky, he was a top-notch RTO for SSG Tepner, 3rd Platoon's former platoon sergeant. His slight, wiry frame and average height belied his strength. Rada could easily carry his 50 lb. rucksack and 35 lbs. of radio and batteries even in mountainous terrain. He wore military issue, heavy, black-framed glasses, had reddish, short-cropped hair, and a quick wit. When he returned from R&R a few weeks back, he asked to give up his RTO job and be a rifleman in the platoon with the guys. He got his wish. He was a great soldier, fondly remembered by all who knew him. SSG Tepner will soon hear of his death at battalion with deep regret and sorrow.

The Expected Attack Occurs

CPT Roy and LT Wharton, Roy's cracker-jack artillery observer, take up a position on the south western edge of Delta's perimeter next to a huge rock that towers over them. The top of the rock is a perfect place for locating the large international orange panel that marks their position for friendly aircraft. From their vantage point, both Roy and Wharton can observe the enemy position on the berm about 50 m away. The enemy continues to fire sporadically. For a welcome change, it is not well-aimed. No one is hit. For once, they have strangely encountered enemy soldiers who can't seem to shoot straight.

The Recon element is still out. Roy radios for them to immediately pull back and take cover. Just as they begin to withdraw, no more than 50 m away they spot a large enemy force of undetermined size moving east among the trees. The enemy also sees Recon and begins to fire at them with small arms and RPGs. Recon knows their small element is in great danger of being overrun. PFC Ken Hornbeck, a Delta soldier serving as the Recon RTO, calls in and yells they are surrounded by a "horde of enemy soldiers." This is likely part of the enemy's general offensive that has been expected. It may be more than expected.

Later, it is estimated the enemy is a reduced-in-strength battalion from the NVA regiment defending Hill 376. Perhaps it is as many as 200 soldiers, maybe more. A recently captured enemy soldier reported their casualties had reduced their companies to around 60 men. The enemy's location, numbers, and direction of movement indicate they are likely massed for an attack on Delta Company's position.

The enemy attack from the berm seems to have been a diversionary attack, a planned distraction to allow the larger enemy force to make a surprise attack from a different direction. The easterly movement by the main enemy force indicates they are getting into position to attack Delta Company from the north. It appears the firing from the berm began too early, before the larger force was in position to attack. A fatal mistake.

As Recon makes their way back, they are firing and moving. Reaching a position in the tree line near the eastern end of the berm, they can go no further. They are a hundred or so meters from Delta Company's defensive position and safety. The two medics in Recon, SP4s Gary Winkler and Daniel Thurston, are in trouble. They normally are at or near the rear of Recon when the unit is moving. In case a Recon soldier is wounded, they can easily go forward to treat the soldier. This time they are the ones in danger.

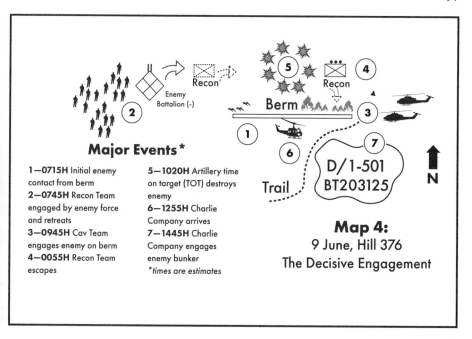

Major Events*

1—0715H Initial enemy contact from berm

2—0745H Recon Team engaged by enemy force and retreats

3—0945H Cav Team engages enemy on berm

4—0055H Recon Team escapes

5—1020H Artillery time on target (TOT) destroys enemy

6—1255H Charlie Company arrives

7—1445H Charlie Company engages enemy bunker

*times are estimates

D/1-501
BT203125

Map 4:
9 June, Hill 376
The Decisive Engagement

Thurston is wounded and unable to move. In the rush to pull back, no one sees that he is hit. He has not made it to the tree line with the others. He calls out to his fellow medic and close friend, SP4 Gary Winkler. Winkler stops and quickly decides to stay with Thurston. It is an unselfish act typical of medics whose first instinct is to stay with, treat, and protect the wounded.

Cavalry to the Rescue

The enemy continues to advance from the northwest on Delta's position, hidden from direct observation from Roy and Wharton's position. They quickly overrun Thurston and Winkler's position and are closing in on Recon's position. Just then, the Cavalry arrives, just like in the movies. This time it is for real.

LT Wharton is on two radios. Handset in each hand. One held to each ear. He has been talking with the Air Cav team which was loitering nearby. On the other phone is the artillery fire direction net. He is also setting up and sequencing artillery fires. The immediate target is the enemy position on the berm, 50 m to their front. Wharton directs the Cav Team to make several runs along the berm with mini-guns from east to west. As usual, the fires are danger close to Delta Company and the Recon Team. Wharton uses the berm to direct their fires. The Cav Team is to keep its fires along the berm and not extend its firing beyond the two ends of the berm.

The high-decibel onslaught of the Light Observation Helicopter and two AH-1 HueyCobra attack helicopters is much louder that the uninitiated could possibly imagine. The rotors, engines, and deep-throated roar of almost continuous minigun fire is impossible to describe. Movies, television, or video games aren't even close. To say it is oppressively loud and violent is only a start. The air reverberates with ear-splitting sounds.

A fire started by mini-gun tracers breaks out on the berm. It spreads quickly, fanned by the rotor wash and wind and soon engulfs the length of the berm. Smoke and dust clouds along the berm are blown by the rotors and the wind. Smells of cordite, splintered and torn vegetation, and newly over-turned earth permeate the air. Time and again well-bunkered NVA soldiers survive such attacks, but not this time. The enemy firing from the berm quickly ceases. At 0845H, the Cav Team goes off station to rearm and refuel.

While the Cav attacks the enemy position on the berm, the enemy force stops its advance and takes cover. Once they begin moving again, the Recon Team is in danger of being overrun. The burning berm is between Recon and Delta Company. Recon requests permission to drop their rucksacks and make a run for it. They will run through the smoke and flame just as soon as the Cobra helicopters finish their attack. CPT Roy gives them the okay.

As the Air Cav helicopter team completes its attack, SSG Sahrle and a small group of his soldiers higher up on the hill within Delta Company's perimeter can see the Recon Team. Behind the team, they catch sight of enemy soldiers moving in the trees and closing in on Recon. They are heavily camouflaged with vegetation stuck in their helmets, web gear, and packs, and practically invisible until they move. From Sahrle's position, their easterly movement is from left to right in an attempt to flank Delta Company's position on the north before beginning their attack.

SSG Sahrle and his men begin yelling at Recon, "Get out of there! Run for it! Let's go!" The Recon soldiers drop their rucks and sprint as hard as they can go the 100 m to Delta's perimeter. Only afterwards is it known the Recon's two PRC-25 radios are purposely left behind by the RTOs to lighten their load. At least they remembered to twist the dials to make sure the enemy couldn't detect the radio frequencies being used. As soon as the Recon Team is clear of the hill, Sahrle and several others open fire on the enemy force with their M-16s. The enemy doesn't return fire. They are still not wanting to disclose their position in the trees as they close in for the attack.

PFC Lyle Stoner is with 3rd Platoon in Delta Company's perimeter. He sees the Recon team's frantic flight through the heat of the burning berm fire and broiling sun. They are exhausted. Several suffer from heat exhaustion. They collapse inside the perimeter. Doc enlists Stoner to help treat those who are in the worst condition. He tosses a saline solution bag from his medical kit to Stoner. He points to a prostrate soldier and tells him to plug it into his arm.

Stoner looks at the bag, the soldier, and then back to Doc. He has never done an IV before. Doc reassures him, "I'll talk you through it." One step at a time, Stoner follows the medic's instructions, "Put the tourniquet on his upper arm good and tight. Next, find a vein on his arm below the tourniquet. Should be one around the inside of his elbow. Take the needle and stick it in the biggest vein you see." Stoner complies. It takes him three sticks to get a vein. The barely conscious soldier is too exhausted to complain. The needle is in. Stoner tells the medic, "Nothing's happening!" Doc tells Stoner, "Loosen the tourniquet." That works. The saline solution begins to flow. Twenty minutes later the soldier comes around.

Jokingly, Doc tells Stoner, "I'll put you in for a Combat Medic Badge!" Stoner smiles and gives a quick, "No thank you!" Quietly, he is glad he could help. That is what good soldiers do. Whatever it takes. The Recon Team is done. They are still suffering effects of heat exhaustion. They are also without their equipment and radio. CPT Roy decides to put them on the next helicopter out. They've performed a vital mission. Their early identification of the enemy force moving toward Delta Company saved many lives.

The enemy force is now less than 100 m from Delta Company's perimeter. Advancing behind the hill on which the berm is located, they can't be directly observed by CPT Roy and LT Wharton. Thanks to Recon's earlier report, the approximate location of the advancing enemy is already known.

Artillery Saves the Day

Meanwhile, the attack helicopters have stopped firing on the enemy position in the berm, CPT Roy tells LT Wharton to crank up the artillery from nearby supporting firebases. Wharton is already on it. He is planning a time-on-target (TOT) shoot. This is artillery speak for massed fires of several batteries. The fires will be coordinated so all rounds land on the target at the same time plus or minus three seconds from the planned time of impact. Fuses on the rounds will be set for both airburst and ground impact. It is the most effective use of available artillery for the situation at hand. The intent is to smother the attacking enemy under a large, deadly blanket of artillery.

Napoleon once said, "God is on the side with the best artillery." Rudyard Kipling, the well-known British author, expressed a higher thought in his poem *Ubique* as he wrote admiringly of British artillery in World War I, "The guns, thank Gawd, the guns!" (*Ubique* is the Latin word for "everywhere", motto of the Royal Artillery.)[25] It is a view all infantrymen should have. In today's fight, artillery will strike the decisive blow against the enemy on Hill 376. Artillerymen, like infantrymen, are rightly proud of what they do. Someone has quipped they divide all people into just two groups, artillerymen, and targets. Good natured rivalry aside, artillerymen know they couldn't do what they do without infantrymen finding and engaging the enemy. Both need each other to win battles.

As soon as the helicopters cease fire and as the Recon Team runs in, LT Wharton runs out to the berm. He wants to make a quick visual check on the target location. He hurriedly peeks over the berm. The enemy force is close and closing. He scampers back to the company grinning because he already has pre-planned artillery fires targeted on the area the enemy is approaching.

Wharton is planning to use three different artillery batteries at two firebases. He has kept the gun–target line, the line between the guns and the target, for each battery in mind as he plans fires. He won't use a gun battery if friendly troops (including Delta Company) are in proximity to the target end of the gun target line. A round falling short or long on friendly troops is an avoidable disaster. In the heat of battle, it is easy to get things confused and out of sequence, but Wharton doesn't make that mistake. He never has. Still the fire mission will be "danger close."

While Wharton makes final plans for the artillery shoot, an unknown caller comes over his radio net identifying himself as "Popeye." Wharton asks for his grid coordinates to identify the location of the guns and the gun–target line. As he unfolds his map, he sees the location is well east of Tam Ky out in the South China Sea! It is a US Navy ship, part of a naval task force assigned to provide naval gunfire to ground forces ashore. Wharton asks the fire direction center (FDC) to add the naval guns to the time-on-target. The guns are in range, barely.

In the next minutes, Wharton's quick planning will soon come to fruition, demonstrating his mastery as a forward observer. Unable to directly observe the enemy force, the TOT will cover a target area the size of three football fields. The three batteries include: C Battery, 1-14th Field Artillery located at LZ Professional with six 105 mm howitzers; C Battery 2-320th Field Artillery (also with six 105 mm howitzers) from FSB Young (BT188158); and B Battery 3-18th Field Artillery at FSB Young with four 8" (203 mm) howitzers. The latter are the heavy hitters shooting shells weighing a death-dealing 200 lbs. Each gun can fire two rounds per minute with pinpoint accuracy ranging out to 12.5 miles.

The Navy 5" gun (127 mm) has a range of 24 km or near 15.4 miles and it will be firing near its maximum range. The location of their gun–target line is especially critical. Accuracy decreases at maximum effective range. Unlike Army howitzers, it is a stabilized, automated gun capable of firing 16–20 rounds per minute with 500–600 rounds in its ready rack.

With an up from the FDC all is ready, Wharton gives the command "Fire!" The "danger close", massed fires of three batteries, plus the Naval destroyer, is the most awesome firepower display Delta Company soldiers have ever seen, heard, felt, or even imagined. The high-pitched, wailing shrieks of hundreds of incoming shells are followed immediately by thunderous explosions sending continuous shudders through the earth. Violent shock waves throb the air, accompanied by the constant whining and buzzing of deadly shrapnel flying into Delta Company's position. It is all over in what seems like an interminable ten minutes. The smell, smoke, and dust that boiled up hundreds of feet into the air hangs like a shroud over the target area.

The fires are enough to cower nearby Delta Company soldiers in their relative position of safety. For enemy soldiers in the target area the artillery barrage is a hellish nightmare, a violent maelstrom of fire, explosions, shrapnel, and death. Those who survive are marked for life, physically or emotionally by its horror and intensity. The results of the destructive force of massed artillery fires won't be known until tomorrow. What is obvious immediately is the enemy attack hasn't and won't reach Delta Company's position. Yet unknown is just how effective the fires were. Those not killed have fled the battle area in terror.

CPT Roy is not taking anything for granted. Who knows whether this was just a first attack? Perhaps the enemy will try again. This is not a time to be complacent. It is not yet noon, the day is not yet half done. But things began to quieten down. It is a sober time. Delta conducts a headcount of its soldiers, makes situation reports to battalion, checks ammunition status, adjusts its defensive perimeter, and readies itself for another attack. SP4s Thurston and Winkler are listed as missing in action and presumed dead. The fast-moving enemy situation doesn't permit an immediate search for the medics. The next order of business is to prepare for Charlie Company's arrival. A medevac is called in for SGT Clouatre and PFC Strand and now two other wounded soldiers, PFC William Moore and PFC David Tarrant.

Charlie Company Arrives

Sometime around noon, CPT Roy receives word Charlie Company is soon leaving LZ Professional where it has been providing firebase security. They will use the one-ship LZ at Delta's location. Charlie Company is still commanded by CPT David Gibson. His company like Delta Company took significant casualties on 21 May. Their brief stay at Professional gave them a little respite from the daily grind in the field. Delta is still looking forward to its first short break.

Giving Delta Company a breather has figured large in LTC Singer's thinking. He still plans to pull Delta Company off the hill. Surprisingly, today's enemy contact hasn't changed his mind. It may be the full impact of Delta Company's morning fight and the likely early start of the enemy's general offensive hasn't yet sunk in at battalion. They weren't present during this morning's battle action. The plan is still to extract Delta Company at 1515H once Charlie Company is fully operational on Hill 376.

At about 1245H, Charlie Company's first pickup from Professional occurs. Five Huey's are used. CPT Gibson is on the first lift with his RTOs and artillery forward observer. Having monitored the battle action on Hill 376 for several days, Charlie

Company knows they are joining a tough fight. It won't take long. The flying time to the LZ is five minutes.

At 1250H, as Charlie Company is enroute to Hill 376, Alpha Company receives another ten to fifteen 82 mm mortar rounds. This too seems part of the general attack against the 1-501st. Alpha company employs their own 81 mm mortar in response then adds artillery fires and a Cav Team in reply. The Cav Team comes in at 1308H remaining until 1325H and leaves only after expending its aerial rockets and mini-gun ammunition.

Charlie Company's first ship arrives at Delta Company's LZ. Other helicopters orbit out of sight from enemy gunners. Each one takes its turn flying into the cramped space. They deposit their load of combat ready soldiers, turn around to exit, and return to orbit. What is left of the Recon Platoon is standing by on the LZ for extraction. CPT Roy has decided with their casualties and loss of equipment they are no longer combat effective. Their major contribution to today's battle is done. Early sighting of the enemy force was critical to the outcome of today's battle. It only takes two helicopters to pick up what is left of Recon. In half an hour, Charlie's last lift is complete. Charlie is in, Recon is out, and Delta is still on Hill 376.

Upon their arrival, operational control (OPCON) of Charlie Company passes back to LTC Singer and the 1-501st. While pulling security at LZ Professional, they operated under the control of the American Division's 1-46th Infantry Battalion which is itself under the operational control of 1st Brigade. Today is the first time the Geronimo Battalion has all four infantry companies on Hill 376 together. The plan is still for Delta Company to be extracted. LTC Singer wants it to happen this afternoon around 1515H, enemy situation permitting. It won't.

Charlie Company passes through Delta Company and temporarily occupies the north and east side of Delta's defensive perimeter. SSG Sahrle notices a grim look on several of the Charlie Company soldiers who pass his location. It is a look frequently seen on Hill 376. With Delta's much-reduced strength (now less than 60 soldiers), it occupies a position little more than 60 m long and 40 m wide. With another attack likely, Charlie Company is a much-welcome addition.

Charlie consolidates their position and prepares to conduct tomorrow's RIF mission. The Delta Company medevac for their wounded is completed after the last lift from Charlie Company. SP4 Rada is put on the same helicopter. He begins the first leg of his long trip home.

Company locations are reported to battalion. Delta is at BT203125. Charlie Company is co-located with Delta Company and has taken up positions just north of Delta. Alpha is at BT 204121 some 200 m southeast of Delta Company; Bravo is at BT209118 another 400–500 m to the southeast of Alpha Company. The four companies are in quick supporting distance of each other should the enemy launch another major attack.

Afternoon on the Hill

During the intermission in enemy contact, an aerial PSYOPS team makes several passes over Delta and Charlie's location in a Huey equipped with loudspeakers. The blaring message is in Vietnamese to whoever is on the hill, "Attention soldiers of the 2nd and 3rd Regiments. Your regiments have been badly mauled. Your only hope is to surrender. You will receive fair treatment, food, clothing, and medical attention. Either you can die unknown and never see your family again or you can start a new life in South Vietnam." This is a catch-all message to any unit within hearing.

The message sounds persuasive, but has little effect on NVA or main force soldiers for several reasons. First, they are hardened combat soldiers. Second, political officers within their ranks keep tight control of soldiers. Third, their fight has been going on for decades. First they fought against the French and now they fight against the US in what they call "The American War." They have lost many hundreds of thousands of soldiers without being defeated. Peace talks are underway in Paris. The enemy on Hill 376 likely already knows the US president intends to pull American troops out of Vietnam and they believe if they can hold out, they will win after the Americans leave—and they are right.

At 1440H, LTC Singer reaffirms his plan for Delta Company to be picked up at 1515H. They have sustained additional casualties further reducing their combat strength. Five minutes later at 1445H, Charlie Company receives heavy small arms, RPG, and mortar fire from fortified positions on the north side of the position of the two companies. This is the same area in which Delta Company had contact and casualties the previous day. On Charlie Company's arrival, CPT Roy gave CPT Gibson a heads up to watch out for that particular enemy position.

Gibson maneuvers a platoon led by LT Don Gourley against the position and is successful in eliminating it, despite numerous casualties. One soldier is KIA, PFC Donald Hartman. Ten are wounded: SGT Raymond Searcy, SP4 Larry Mann, PFCs Ronald Wiley, Albin Garland, Claude Hamilton, Val Reynolds, Paul Tenkamn, Norbert Jackson, Thomas King, and Ernest Trujillo.

With this latest enemy contact and the casualties from Charlie Company and those mentioned earlier from Bravo Company, plans to extract Delta Company are quickly cancelled. Sporadic enemy mortar fire is received throughout the afternoon. Alpha unfortunately suffers the loss of their executive officer, LT Waldemar Geiger. He came out from the rear to check on soldiers in his company. He is killed in the late afternoon by a sniper. Another medic PFC Christopher Bean, supporting Charlie Company is also killed. Bean is the fourth medic to be killed in seven days of fighting on Hill 376.

End of Day Seven

At 1825H, Delta Company requests an emergency ammunition and water resupply and it is completed before dark. Not long after Charlie Company's afternoon enemy engagement and the battalion's additional casualties, an unexpected warning order from the battalion TOC is sent out to all 1-501st companies. Planning is underway to extract all four companies from Hill 376. No time or reason is given.

The preliminary order is well received but raises several questions. The enemy on Hill 376 has taken heavy casualties, but their destruction may not be complete. There are likely other reasons. Unknown to the infantrymen on Hill 376, political considerations high up the chain of command are weighing heavily in the decision to extract the battalion.

No one at brigade, battalion, and the soldiers on Hill 376, knows it yet, but today 9 June (Day 7 on the Hill) is the turning point in our fight at Tam Ky. Not just on Hill 376, but throughout the entire 1st Brigade's area of operations. Today, a large enemy force on Hill 376 of yet unknown size has been routed and likely destroyed. From this day forward, enemy contact and resistance in the 1st Brigade's area of operations will slacken and remain light until *Operation Lamar Plain* ends on 13 August 1969. More soldiers will die, but US casualties will be much reduced. The NVA will no longer threaten Tam Ky.

Tomorrow is a New Day

Attention tomorrow will be given to recovering Thurston and Winkler and assessing the size and damage to the enemy force. Over the next two days, focus will be on extracting the battalion from the site of its toughest, extended battle action at Tam Ky. At days end, there is increased confidence among Delta Company's "Never Quit" young soldiers and junior leaders that they have not only endured a tough seven days of hard combat on the Hill, but prevailed over an enemy force much larger than their now seriously understrength company. Despite the loss of many of their fellow soldiers, some express regret they will not have the opportunity to make it to the top of Hill 376.

There is also renewed confidence in knowing all four companies of the battalion are located close to each other. They have come through the fight at Tam Ky together. All have fought hard. All have taken many casualties. The battalion settles in as darkness falls. All companies remain alert. SITREPS to battalion are negative the rest of the night. The men of Delta Company and their sister companies will sleep hard tonight, a well-deserved rest.

***

Casualties and Awards

Terry Rada is Delta Company's only casualty KIA today. SGT Robert Clouatre, PFCs Steve Strand, William Moore, and Daniel Tarrant, all from Delta Company, were wounded. Attached to Delta Company, the two Recon medics from the Headquarters Company Medical Platoon (SP4s Daniel Thurston and Gary Winkler) are presumed dead. Five other Recon soldiers are wounded: SP4s Mario Vernali and Norris Arrowood and PFCs Robin Donaty, Ivan Reid, and Dale Werner.

Casualty Table 10 shows the casualty figures for today (9 June), the cumulative casualties on Hill 376 from 3–9 June, and the cumulative casualties since the initial combat operation of *Operation Lamar Plain* on 16 May. As explained earlier, Charlie Company has only been on Hill 376 only one day, otherwise their casualties would likely be much higher.

Casualty Table 10: 1-501st Casualties 9 June 1969

Casualties	HHC	A Co	B Co	C Co	D Co	Recon	Total
KIA	3	1	3	1	1	0	9
WIA	0	3	1	7	4	5	20
MIA	0	0	0	0	0	0	0
Total	3	4	4	8	5	6	29
Total Hill 376 3–9 June	5 KIA 1 WIA 0 MIA 6 TOT	3 KIA 13 WIA 0 MIA 16 TOT	6 KIA 4 WIA 0 MIA 10 TOT	1 KIA 7 WIA 0 MIA 8 TOT	6 KIA 19 WIA 2 MIA 27 TOT	2 KIA 11 WIA 0 MIA 13 TOT	23 KIA 55 WIA 2 MIA 80 TOT
Total to date 16 May–9 June	9 KIA 6 WIA 0 MIA 15 TOT	5 KIA 15 WIA 0 MIA 20 TOT	12 KIA 39 WIA 0 MIA 51 TOT	7 KIA 27 WIA 0 MIA 34 TOT	12 KIA 36 WIA 2 MIA 50 TOT	5 KIA 23 WIA 0 MIA 28 TOT	50 KIA 146 WIA 2 MIA 198 TOT

1-501st Soldiers Killed in Action, 9 June 1969 (Day 7)

Delta Company—1
 9 June: SP4 Terry Rada, age 20, born 23 September 1948 from Geddes, SD
Alpha Company—1
 9 June: LT Waldemar Geiger, age 25, born 5 March 1944 from Cleveland, OH
Bravo Company—3
 9 June: SGT William Bushard, age 23, born 13 February 1946 from Mancelona, MI
 9 June: PFC Larry Gilbertson, age 22, born 25 July 1946 from Mora, MN
 9 June: SGT William Sparks, age 20, born 19 October 1948 from Stout, OH

Charlie Company—1

9 June: PFC Donald Hartman, age 21, born 19 December 1947 from Independence, MO

Headquarters Company—3

9 June: SP5 Daniel Thurston (medic supporting Recon Platoon), age 22, born 7 February 1947 from Ambler, PA

9 June: SP4 Gary Winkler (medic supporting Recon Platoon), age 20, born 9 October 1948 from Babylon, NY

9 June: PFC Christopher Bean (medic supporting Co C), age 20, born 26 August 1948 from Rockland, MA

1-501st Soldier Awards for Hill 376, 9 June (other awards may have been made that were not mentioned in after action reports)

Silver Star—3

Headquarters and Headquarters Company: 9 June, PFC Christopher Bean

Bravo Company: 9 June, SGT William Bushard

Recon Platoon: 9 June, SP4 Lee Turner

Bronze Star for Valor—7

Headquarters and Headquarters Company: 9 June, SP4 Daniel Thurston (medic) and SP4 Gary Winkler (medic)

Alpha Company: 9 June, LT Waldemar Geiger

Bravo Company: 9 June, SGT William Sparks, PFC Larry Gilbertson

Charlie Company: 9 June, PFC William Ingle

Delta Company: 9 June, SP4 Terry Rada

Purple Heart—awards were made to all soldiers KIA or WIA

CHAPTER 17

Aftermath

10 June

Day Eight on Hill 376

Counting the Cost

Early in the morning just after first light, CPT Roy and the 3rd Platoon under LT Bryant and SGT Littleton moves cautiously out of the company's perimeter. They are heading to the area where yesterday the massive artillery fires targeted the large enemy force moving to attack Delta Company. The first order of business is security. A reinforced or reconstituted enemy may have used the cover of darkness to return and take up ambush or new attack positions.

Roy has several security teams checking likely enemy locations. One team checks the berm. Another checks the tree line. A Cav Team overhead makes wide circles looking for signs of the enemy's presence. Once the area is secure, there are just two priorities. The first is to find the two missing medics presumed killed during the enemy's attack on the Recon Platoon. Second, Roy wants to assess the effectiveness of the artillery fire. How much damage did it do?

They don't have far to go. Less than 100 m north of their company's position, they encounter the forward edge of the area targeted by the artillery barrage. The artillery craters are too many to count as far as the eye can see. As Roy and the search teams move further into the area, it is obvious the artillery did its job. CPT Roy will later report to LTC Singer, the battalion commander, "There's blood and guts everywhere!"

The carnage spreads out over a football field-size area. Only seven enemy bodies are found. All were killed by artillery. Many more were likely removed during the night. The NVA always make it a priority to recover their dead and they have had all night. The smell of death hangs in the air. NVA soldier equipment is strewn over the area—damaged weapons, ammunition magazines, medical supplies, helmets, and assorted web gear.

The NVA usually do a better job of battlefield clean up. They need every piece of equipment they can recover. The chaotic scene indicates the large enemy force was decimated. In Roy's own words, "the artillery broke their back." The truth of that

208 • COURAGE UNDER FIRE

statement will be evidenced by the fact there will be no further large-scale enemy attacks on Hill 376 or anywhere else in the 1st Brigade's area of operations.

The two PRC-25 radios and several rucksacks dropped by Recon are also recovered. All the gear including the radios was damaged by the fire on the berm that spread out from there. Soon afterwards the two Recon medics, SP5 Daniel Thurston and SP4 Gary Winkler are found. They are side by side in a depression in the ground where they courageously tried to fight off the NVA. The inseparable friends died from gunshot wounds doing their best to protect one another as the enemy closed on their position. They likely held off the enemy advance just long enough to keep the Recon Team from being overrun. They saved others even as they gave up their own lives.

Winkler and Thurston are recovered with solemn, respectful care. They are carried back by fellow soldiers to Delta Company's perimeter where they will be taken out by helicopter later in the morning. It is a somber moment. The two men were not only the best of friends, but the best of soldiers.

Winkler had plans to be a medical doctor. He came from a working-class family in the New York City borough of Queens. He couldn't afford college and medical school, so he enlisted and planned to use the GI Bill for schooling after Vietnam. Like his buddy Thurston, he had a real love for helping soldiers who needed medical care. Both earned the respect and affection of the men they served in Recon and Delta Company. They could be counted on to show up whenever a soldier was hurt. With great pain, their families will soon learn of their deaths. Both men were awarded the Bronze Star for Valor in combat,

The Enemy Dead

Not much thought is given to the NVA dead in combat. That is understandable. It is better to think of them as "the enemy"—the enemy you are trying to kill before he kills you. It is the best that can be expected of soldiers in the heat of battle. It is a reality of war that there's no time for compassion if an enemy is shooting at you. The enemy is given derogatory or demeaning names like "gooks" or "dinks" to further dehumanize them. It is likely American soldiers also have derogatory names given by the enemy.

Some soldiers develop a hatred for enemy soldiers. They reason, "They're killing my buddies, they're trying to kill me! I wouldn't be in this God-forsaken place if it weren't for them!" Such sentiment dies slowly for some, even after the war. Most soldiers don't hate the enemy and others who do often work hard to put the hate aside.[26] Many infantrymen even develop a grudging respect for the enemy, especially if the enemy puts up a good fight and doesn't mistreat US soldiers.

As a matter of pride and honor, Delta Company's leadership and soldiers have a reputation as a disciplined unit. They do not abuse the bodies of dead enemy soldiers or mistreat those captured alive. Most often, when dead enemy soldiers are found on the battlefield, our soldiers lay the enemy dead aside in a location where they can be found by their recovery teams. If the enemy soldier has a poncho or rain sheet, our soldiers may even wrap them up in it.

US and NVA soldiers have much in common. The average NVA soldier is also a draftee or soldier who enlisted to avoid the draft. Most are 18–22 years old. Many are from rural areas of North Vietnam. (See Appendix 2). They too have left their families behind and have been sent to fight the Americans. Most are also well trained in infantry skills and are disciplined soldiers. Unlike US soldiers, mail from home for NVA soldiers serving in South Vietnam is sparse to non-existent.[27] Often NVA soldiers fight in the south until they are killed or incapacitated by wounds.

Another thing NVA soldiers have in common with our soldiers is when they are killed, they too will be remembered and grieved by mothers and fathers or other family members. War is a horror to mothers no matter what side you are on. Notifications of soldier deaths will be terribly slow in reaching North Vietnam. Many families will never learn of the fate of loved sons, brothers, husbands, and fathers who were sent to fight in South Vietnam.

In time, many of our own soldiers who fought on Hill 376 will likely see their former enemies as soldiers doing their duty much like themselves. For some, that may never happen.

Long ago in 1902, Thomas Hardy, the renowned English author, published his famous poem, *The Man He Killed* which tells the story of two men who met on a distant battlefield as enemies. A shortened extract is shown:

> But ranged as infantry
> And staring face to face,
> I shot at him as he at me,
> And killed him in his place.
> I shot him dead because,
> Because he was my foe,
> Just so: my foe of course he was;
> That's clear enough although
> He thought he'd enlist, perhaps,
> Off-hand like, just as I
> Was out of work, had sold his traps
> No other reason why.

The Fight Slackens

As 1st Brigade's after action report (dated 15 September 1969) will later state: "10 June 1969: Enemy activity slackened around Hill 376 as the 1-501st continued to search the battlefield while the 1-46th Infantry Battalion (attached to 1st Brigade) continued to move north to block any enemy forces attempting to withdraw from or reinforce the contact area."

The brigade's AAR for the rest of June records the daily decrease in enemy activity throughout its area of operation with these words: "Activity decreased, sporadic activity continued, activity was light, activity continued to decrease, the enemy continued to avoid contact, the brigade AO was quiet ...." Not only June, but July and August will continue to see light enemy activity. Indications are that after the final battle action on Hill 376 on 9 June, the NVA elements of the 2nd NVA Division began to break up into small groups and withdraw to the west, southwest, and southeast to avoid further contact with US forces. The emergency at Tam Ky is over.

Back on Hill 376

At 0901H, 1-501st companies are reported at the following locations. Alpha company at BT204121, close to and linked up with Charlie Company. Bravo Company is nearby at BT210118. Both Charlie and Delta are still located at BT203125. Planning is still underway by battalion to extract the four companies from Hill 376.

An hour later around 1005H, Alpha Company discovers a set of enemy documents at BT204119. One paper appears to be some type of operations sketch. No immediate intel is gained from it. A dead NVA soldier found nearby was apparently killed by a napalm air strike. Two burned up AK-47s are a few yards away. No telling how many additional killed and wounded casualties may have occurred. Both documents and weapons are sent out an hour later on the next log bird. The intelligence officers at battalion and brigade will give them a close look.

At 1135H, a low-flying Air Force FAC with an artillery forward observer on board spots a group of six NVA carrying heavy loads and moving west at BT184108. Another group of five are spotted hiding among nearby trees. This element appears to be exfiltrating out of the Hill 376 area of operations. Likely it is only one of many small groups making their way out of the 1st Brigade's area of operations. The NVA on Hill 376 have finally had enough. Thankful to be leaving, they are not home free yet. The FAC and observer fire artillery on the enemy location and follow up with an air strike.

In the meantime, the four 1-501st companies having been resupplied and are preparing to move south to their extraction point. They are all close to one another. At 1350H, company positions are reported. Alpha BT202119; Bravo BT207116; Charlie BT201123; and Delta BT202124. With major enemy action decreased and the companies in close proximity to one another, it is an excellent time for the battalion commander to drop in and visit his troops on the ground. Perhaps even spend the night with them.

Soldiers like to get a visit from their commander when they have been through a tough time. It is important for a battalion commander to walk among his men in the field, look them in the eye, shake their hand, tell them what a good job they've done, and let them know he appreciates their effort. It hasn't happened during the entire Tam Ky operation. Unfortunately, it doesn't happen now. A lost opportunity. The company commanders and junior-enlisted leaders don't expect a visit. They are busy taking care of their soldiers. They will be the ones remembered after the war.

Late in the day, around 1655H, as Delta Company repositions its 3rd Platoon, a sniper hits new platoon leader LT James Bryant. It is a minor wound in the shoulder. Bryant will remain with his platoon until the extraction. He has been in the field just a few days and will recover from his wound. Long after the war, I asked Jim Littleton, my longtime squad leader and later acting platoon leader, how he made it through ten months of combat with the same infantry platoon without having so much as a scratch. With his customary smile, he says without hesitation, "I stay away from lieutenants!" Good advice. Delta Company has lost five lieutenant platoon leaders in less than three weeks. All wounded in action.

At 1730H, near BT204118, Alpha and Charlie Companies receive small arms fire from a small enemy element. They return fire. CPT Dave Gibson takes advantage of an on-station Cav Team. The two attack helicopters and light observation helicopter make short work of the enemy position. No friendly casualties occur.

With what is left of the NVA units exfiltrating from out of the 1st Brigade's operational area, Main Force and local Viet Cong units are left behind. They are already home. Though much decreased in number, their purpose now seems limited to giving the badly mauled NVA units time to escape. As far as the enemy knows, the 1-501st is massing for a large, final attack. They don't know the battalion is preparing for extraction.

End of Day Eight

At 1950H, the four 1-501st companies report NDP positions. Alpha, Charlie, and Delta are linked up at BT203120. Bravo is at BT206115 some 400–500 m southeast of the others. The battalion TOC issues verbal frag orders for each company to begin moving south tomorrow morning to grid square 2010 for extraction. The distance to be covered is approximately 1500 m. A long slog by Hill 376 standards even downhill. No matter. Everyone is looking forward to getting off the hill. "One more night, one more wake up. Then we are outta here!" Maybe.

Between 2135H and 2240H, 15 enemy 60 mm mortar rounds land within the defensive perimeter of the three co-located companies. There are no casualties. CPT Roy and the other commanders never report that rounds have landed within their perimeter even if it is true. The enemy is likely listening to the battalion's radio traffic. No need to let them know their mortars are on target.

The mortaring will not go unanswered. At 2255H, CPT Roy requests a USAF AC-130 Spooky. At 2335H, just before midnight, the four-engine turboprop, a converted Lockheed transport, arrives on station. It is anything but a cargo plane. Those that went back to sleep after the mortar attack will soon be wakened.

The Spooky (an Air Force name) is a night-flying, specially equipped aircraft with advanced targeting and fire control systems. A large gunship equipped to attack ground targets at altitudes from a 1,000 to 5,000 ft. The danger of 12.7 mm heavy machine guns seems to have lessened. It flies in a circular pattern as if on a pylon. Unlike a straight-line strafing attack, the AC-130 gunners can keep a continuous stream of high-volume fire on enemy targets.

The aircraft's armament is two 7.62 mm mini-guns with six barrels, air-cooled and electrically driven. A machine gun on steroids. Each gun can fire 3200 rounds per minute (rpm). Both guns are electronically linked and can fire together at 6400 rpm. Spooky is also armed with two M-61 20 mm Vulcan cannons. Each six-barreled gun can fire a staggering high 6,000 rpm, each (100 rounds per second).

As the gunship fires, the guttural rip and roar of the mini-guns shatters the night quiet, another unforgettable sound of battle. The burning tracer ammunition from the guns creates an unbroken bright ribbon of fire extending from the aircraft to the target like a flame-breathing dragon. Soldiers have aptly named the winged gunship "Puff the Magic Dragon," often shortened to "Puff." When Puff comes calling, there is "no frolicking in the autumn mist." Enemy soldiers know what to expect. They quickly dig their holes deeper or flee the area.

For 30 minutes, Spooky works over the area where the enemy mortars were believed to be set up. Of course, the enemy mortar crews fire and move. Spooky knows that and extends its fires to cover a wide area. Mission finished, the aircraft goes off station. The rest of the night is quiet. Sleep comes easy.

***

Casualties and Awards

1-501st Soldiers Killed in Action, 10 June 1969 (Day 8)—none

1-501st Soldier Awards, 10 June 1969—none (other awards may have been made that were not mentioned in after action reports)

CHAPTER 18

Coming Off the Hill

11 June

Day Nine on Hill 376

Time to Go

Moving day has finally come! At 0520H Charlie Company gets a going away present. Fifteen rounds of 82 mm mortar rounds fall in quick succession inside their perimeter. Incredibly, again there are no casualties. Charlie Company's FO is quickly given the okay by CPT Gibson to answer the mortar attack with artillery. The artillery is fired and the mortars remain silent.

CPT Roy has mixed feelings about the extraction. So do his men. Though they made a good effort and were close, they never made it to the top of Hill 376. Roy's other thought is his men are tired. They are still combat effective, but combat fatigue is an increasing problem. Not to be confused with PTSD, combat or battle fatigue is a temporary condition. PTSD is longer-term trauma. Combat fatigue doesn't necessarily lead to PTSD but it may. (See Appendix 8)

The young soldiers of Delta Company are both mentally and physically fatigued. The stress of continuous combat takes its toll. They have earned a rest. They have been hard on the go since 16 May without a break. The last eight days seemed endless. Days ran together, enemy contact or the expectation of enemy contact was continuous for 192 hours. There is some renewed strength in the tired young men as they learn their time on Hill 376 is nearly over.

Before pulling out from Delta Company's position high up on Hill 376, PFC Cravens in 1st Platoon has been planning for this moment for a while. He has decided to leave a memento of Delta Country's presence on Hill 376. Rummaging around in his rucksack, from the bottom of his pack he pulls a rumpled, but properly folded American Flag. He has been carrying it the entire time at Tam Ky. He unfolds the flag, holds it up for others to see, and explains what he has in mind.

He gets an enthusiastic response. With the help of a couple of platoon buddies, the 3 ft by 5 ft flag is hung high on a tree in sight of the surrounding countryside. It is a victory flag of sorts. Not like the famous flag raised on Iwo Jima, but one perfect for this war and just right for the battle action on Hill 376. Once the flag is up, it flutters proudly in the breeze, the red, white, and blue standing out in the morning sun. With deep respect and a few tears, Cravens and the other soldiers render a brief salute and then load up for the move off the hill.

The Move Begins

By 0730H, all companies are moving south. The 1500 m move to the extraction point is expected to take most of the day. Bravo is on one route several hundred meters to the east with Alpha following. Charlie leads out on a separate parallel route with Delta following. The companies are moving with platoons in column one behind the other and each platoon in a single file.

In Delta Company, SSG Sahrle's combined 1st and 2nd Platoon is in the lead. CPT Roy tells Sahrle to keep the tail end of Charlie Company in sight so the two units don't become separated. LT Bryant, still nursing a shoulder wound, is with 3rd Platoon providing rear security during the movement. SGT Littleton serving as acting platoon sergeant and squad leader moves at the rear of the platoon. His experience is needed there. If the enemy follows Delta Company off the hill, they are likely to hit the rear of the unit first. Enemy contact is expected. All Delta platoons are told not to chase after individual enemy soldiers. They may expose themselves trying to get US soldiers to follow them and draw them into an ambush.

The four companies follow this movement order most of the way to the extraction point. Charlie and Delta Company move along a ridgeline running southeast. They are following a well-travelled trail, but there is no hurry going down. Everyone is moving with caution. The terrain on the southern slope of Hill 376 is forested. Openings in the trees are encountered along the way. All are ideal places for ambushes. The weather is cooperating. There is no rain and it is not especially hot. A good day for a walk off the mountain—as long as the enemy cooperates.

At 0840H, after moving only 200 m, Charlie Company surprises a lone NVA soldier on the trail near BT203118. He is fired on and killed by the advance element of Charlie Company. Moving quietly always pays off, a lesson every infantry company in combat learns or pays for it if they don't. All four companies report their location prior to nearby air strikes scheduled at 0955H. Bravo is at BT206115 with Alpha 200 m behind at BT205117. Charlie is at BT203116 with Delta 100 m back at BT203117.

At 1000H, an air strike goes in at BT215125 in the area northeast of Alpha and Bravo Companies. The target is a trail to the east that trends south generally parallel to the direction the four companies are moving. There are several hooches and what appears to be a small enemy camp located there. The strike is intended to discourage enemy elements from using the trail to get ahead of and ambush the withdrawing US companies.

At 1130H, Bravo Company stops while their lead element fires several machine-gun bursts at an enemy trail watcher. They fire artillery to their front to clear their path for the next few hundred meters. As they resume their advance, both Bravo and Alpha Companies cross the first checkpoint marking their progress toward the extraction point.

At 1155H, location reports are Charlie at BT203114 and Delta still following at BT203116, 200 m behind Charlie. SGT Jim Littleton with the 3rd Platoon's last squad bringing up Delta Company's rear is listening for signs that the enemy may be following them down the mountain. They are. An enemy grenade is hurled from an unseen enemy soldier. It explodes, wounding PFC Robert Palagios who has the distinction of being the last 1-501st soldier wounded on Hill 376. No medevac is required.

On the other axis headed south, Bravo is at BT207111 and Alpha is 100 m behind them at BT207112. Charlie and Delta have moved just 200 m south in the last two hours. Bravo and Alpha have moved south approximately 400 m. The going is slow on purpose. It is not a race. All units are making sure they do not walk into an ambush.

At 1305H, Charlie Company reports pursuit of an enemy soldier with commo wire and an entrenching tool at BT203112 south of their location. No report is made of the outcome. Might be that he was intent on rigging a booby trap ahead of Charlie Company's advance. With all four companies closing in on the extraction point, battalion makes final plans for the extraction, but it won't happen today. Perhaps that has been the plan all along. Once at the extraction point, the battalion will be off the Hill. They will spend one more night in its shadow.

Arrival at the Extraction Point

At 1400H, Delta passes their first checkpoint. Fifteen minutes later, at 1415H Charlie Company reports reaching their first checkpoint. Delta Company went ahead of Charlie Company while they were pursuing the enemy soldier. At 1405H, Bravo reaches their second checkpoint as they near the extraction point. At 1420H, battalion reports company locations as follows: Bravo at BT207105, Alpha still following 200 m back at BT207107. Both have reached the grid square where the pick-up will be made. Delta reports they are at BT203107 and Charlie Company is 300 m back at BT203110. Delta has also arrived at the 2010 grid square. Charlie is minutes away. The extraction point has been reached without incident—and without further casualties.

At 1625H, company locations are again updated. Alpha and Bravo are at BT205105. Charlie's at BT204105, and Delta BT204106. Delta's position is in a stand of trees. With just under 50 men left in Delta Company and not many more in each of the other companies, the battalion occupies a smaller area that usual. The four companies are now adjacent to one another. All are within a perimeter not more than 250 m in diameter. After arriving at the extraction point, each company completes its linkup with units on their right and left, sets up their night defenses, checks weapons and equipment, eats, and organizes for tomorrow's pickup.

End of Day Nine

The battalion is now in a valley at the base of Hill 376. The sun begins an early descent behind surrounding hills. The good weather is still holding. It is hot and humid in the valley, but bearable. The weather seldom changes except during frequent thunderstorms. After a storm passes, the humidity is visible in the air like vapor in a steam bath.

Each unit makes a quick reconnaissance near their positions then settles in for the night. At 1730H, Charlie Company's lead element spots a lone enemy soldier. As they fire at him, he takes off running, dropping his rucksack to escape. Sweeping the area, Charlie recovers the rucksack. It is standard NVA equipment. Inside is one AK-47 magazine, 60 AK-47 rounds, civilian clothes, one poncho and poncho liner, a raincoat, and a bag of rice. Soon they discover the body of the dead NVA soldier and recover one full RPD machine-gun magazine, 40 12.7 mm heavy machine gun and 80 AK-47 rounds. The ammo looks new, right out of the can. This is an unneeded reminder that though the units are off the Hill, the enemy is still close by.

Each company goes through standard procedures for setting up its security and defensive measures. Weapon placement, fields of fire, and artillery target registration are especially important tonight. With the presence of other units in the battalion's perimeter, care must be taken not to fire on friendly units. NDPs are reported. Alpha at BT205105, Bravo at BT206105, Charlie at BT204104, and Delta at BT205104.

There is noted optimism among Delta Company soldiers. It is the same in their sister companies. In Delta Company, the soldiers have broken out their chow. There is quiet talk in each position. Not so much about the last nine days on the Hill. There is talk of home, getting back to the States, and the break they are looking forward to tomorrow.

As dark sets in over the valley, the soldiers prepare for sleep. They are finally off the Hill. The night passes quietly. No one is disappointed.

***

Casualties and Awards

1-501st Soldiers Killed in Action, 11 June 1969 (Day 9)—none

1-501st Soldier Awards, 11 June 1969—none (other awards may have been made that were not mentioned in after action reports)

CHAPTER 19

Extraction

12 June

Day Ten in the Shadow of Hill 376

The Pickup Zone

Delta Company awakes at first light. Everyone is quickly packed up and ready to go. A company headcount is taken. All are accounted for. The number is 44. Not much more than a full-strength rifle platoon. Delta will be the last company out. The PZ is a short distance from the battalion's NDP. It is a flat, wet, open area surrounded by trees. Some of it is old rice paddies.

The open area is about 100 m wide and 100 m long. A scattering of low bushes and small plants dotting the PZ pose no hazard to the choppers. The area is just big enough to land five Hueys in a box formation with one helicopter at the top of the box. Each company will be taken out in two or three lifts of five helicopters. The lifts will come in one behind the other.

At 0723H, Apache 6, the battalion commander, arrives from LZ Professional in his Command & Control helicopter. It flies high above the PZ so not to interfere with the lift helicopters. A FAC comes on station at 0735H and flies a wide circular pattern looking for signs of nearby enemy. He radios all clear. The FAC will remain in overwatch until the extraction is complete.

Alpha Company is first to move to the PZ. They position five groups of six to seven soldiers at each landing point. Alpha's extraction begins at 0801H. The entire company is at LZ Professional by 0821H. Flight time is short, just about five minutes. Charlie is next out. Their pickup begins at 0825H. They too are flown to Professional. Their lifts are complete at 0857H. Both companies now fall under the operational control of 1-46th Infantry Battalion located at Professional. The 1-46th, has been an important part of the 1st Brigade's fight since its arrival at Tam Ky in mid-May.

Bravo Company quickly lines up on the PZ. Their first lift is at 0911H. They are being taken to the Tam Ky airstrip to be re-missioned. Delta Company, the smallest of the four companies, is last out. Delta moves to the PZ. They will be taken out in two lifts of five helicopters. There are smiles all around, but no loud talking or yelling. They are still conditioned to move quietly, a practice which has saved many lives.

CPT Roy will be on the last helicopter of the last lift by design. There are two good reasons. First, he wants to make sure every man gets out. Second, should the enemy make a last attack as his understrength company is extracted, he'll have his FO and RTOs to communicate with artillery, the FAC, and if need be, a CAV Team. Today they won't be needed.

The helicopters are heard well before they are seen. It won't be long now. Adrenaline is flowing once again. Minutes before the helicopters arrive, Delta Company fires a pre-planned "mad minute" into the tree line surrounding the PZ. All the company's weapons fire for a full minute—rifles, machine guns, and grenade launchers. It is a precautionary measure. There are indications the enemy followed the battalion's move off the Hill. Are they planning a surprise going away present? No return fire is received. The first lift for Delta is at 0925H.

The 3rd Platoon will have the distinction of being the last out. Their mission is to pull security for the first lift. As the first lift comes in SGT Littleton spots a uniformed NVA soldier. He has moved to within 150 m of the PZ to observe the extraction. It seems he is only watching. Littleton and two other soldiers take him under fire. It is not clear if he's hit. The shots aren't heard by others due to noise of the approaching helicopters.

Delta's first lift of five helicopters comes in. The familiar sight and sound of the Huey's approach always increases anxiety in soldiers. There is more relief than anxiety this time, unlike the combat assault on 3 June heading into battle. Tired soldiers from 1st and 2nd Platoons laden with heavy rucksacks heave themselves and their weapons quickly on board. Many are still smiling. They have made it through the roughest ten days of their young lives.

As the first lift rises from the PZ, most of the soldiers take a last look at Hill 376. There is some shouting back and forth and some laughter. Some congratulate each other. A few men in 1st Platoon look high up on the mountain. They see it! The red, white, and blue colors still flying! They shout and point toward the mountain. Tears well up in hardened young soldiers' eyes on seeing the symbol of their sacrifice, the emblem of their duty as soldiers, and the flag of their fallen buddies and loved ones back home.

Soon, Tam Ky can be seen in the distance. Talk fades, for a couple of minutes thoughts turn inward. All are grateful for making it off the Hill. Some briefly reflect on past days of combat. Some silently offer a prayer of thanks. Others think of those who didn't make it. Those who make it out of Vietnam will carry the memory of Hill 376 with them the rest of their lives. They leave Hill 376, not knowing PFC Jessie Harris is alone, still held captive in the nearby mountains.

By 0950H, much fewer in number, Delta Company is back at the Tam Ky airstrip from where their first combat assault was launched. It seems a lifetime ago.

After a head count and weapons check they are eager to board the waiting trucks for transport to the Americal Division's Rest and Recreation Center at Chu Lai. They have more than earned a well-deserved break from combat operations. Their mission on Hill 376 now complete.

Stand Down

The Americal (23rd Infantry) Division Headquarters is at Chu Lai. So too are the 312th Medical Evacuation Hospital and the 27th Surgical Hospital. Since 15 May, all serious casualties of 1st Brigade units have been taken to the medical facilities here. But that's not where Delta Company soldiers are headed today. The Americal Division's Rest and Recuperation (R&R) Center is here too—a much more desirable destination for the weary Delta Company soldiers.

Above all else, most of Delta's soldiers are looking for a hot meal and hot shower, enjoyed well away from the constant threat of enemy ambush. Some want a cold beer (or two) first. They are scheduled to be here three days. The billets are palatial, five-star accommodations for infantrymen compared to sleeping in the field. They are un-airconditioned, temporary buildings with corrugated sheet metal roofs; plywood sides and floors; large, wrap-around, screened windows; and best of all, beds with mattresses, pillows, and sheets. They will sleep soundly tonight with little worry about the enemy, comfortable in their dry skivvies and for a short while, out of their wet jungle fatigues and muddy boots.

Delta Company's First Sergeant Purcell has been at the rest center well ahead of the arrival of his company. He has everything set up for his troops. Once billets are assigned, some head off for the bar, lunch for them can wait. Others tired of eating field rations head for the mess hall for their favorite meal—a coke, juicy hamburger, and fries with ketchup!

After lunch many go back to their billets for a nap or just some bunk time, a luxury not available in the field. The mental and physical fatigue of extended combat is wearing. These young men are in good condition. Lean and strong from the carrying a heavy pack in hot, humid weather in the mountains, if they had to, they could have gone further and longer in the field. But over time, their combat effectiveness would slip. A three-day rest will make a big difference.

The Americal sergeant managing the center requests that CPT Roy maintain control of his company, so they don't "tear the place up." This is apparently a frequent occurrence as combat units come fresh out of the field. Airborne units are known for their rowdiness. CPT Roy tells him not to worry, "that won't happen with my guys"—and it doesn't.

Once Delta Company is checked in at the center, CPT Roy goes straight to the 312th Evacuation Hospital to check on his former 1st Platoon leader. Having seen his wounds before his medevac, Roy doesn't know if he is still alive. He is relieved to find him still listed as a patient though he hasn't been further evacuated due to his severe wounds. Almost all other wounded Delta soldiers are already at or on their way to Cam Ranh Bay or have been further evacuated to hospitals in Japan. A few lightly wounded soldiers have been returned to LZ Sally.

Roy finds his platoon leader by asking the ward nurse for his bed number. He is unrecognizable, literally bandaged from head to toe. His face and upper body took most of the grenade's blast and shrapnel. He is completely covered except for his eyes, nose, and mouth. Though sedated with morphine, the young officer is conscious and able to talk. They speak briefly about his wounds, medical care, and how soon he will get to go home. Satisfied that he will live, Roy says good-bye and rejoins his company.

The lieutenant will not only survive his extensive wounds, but 14 months later he is again sent to Vietnam though in his own mind he is uncertain that he is fully recovered. Having made Captain while he was healing, he is sent to Tien Phuoc near Tam Ky to command the Special Forces camp which serves as the base for a South Vietnamese Ranger Company, the very camp which was in danger of being overrun when the 1st Brigade showed up at Tam Ky.

End of Day Ten

Recreational facilities are available, but most Delta soldiers want to hang out at the "refreshment" stand where they can take it easy with their buddies. Some just want to sleep and turn in early. Others stay up talking late into the night. Talk of going home, their former civilian life "back in the world," and already "war stories" about the Hill.

For a few days, the men of Delta Company are free from the rigors of combat. Their short rest out of the field is a needed tonic. Battle fatigue is quickly gone. They are enjoying just being with one another. They have survived the long fight on Hill 376 and the day-long battle on 21 May. They are bonded as their own band of brothers for the rest of their lives.

Unfortunately, the battalion commander once again misses an opportunity to visit his battle-weary soldiers and commend them for a job well done during their three-day stand down. Certainly, he must be attending to other important matters related to his command. Perhaps he is having to account for his battalion's large number of casualties or he is involved in planning the 1-501st's next operation. The "Never Quit" soldiers of Delta Company are glad that CPT Roy, the commander who led them on Hill 376 is with them.

***

Casualties and Awards

1-501st Soldiers Killed in Action, 12 June 1969 (Day 10)—none

1-502st Soldier Awards, 12 June 1969—none (other awards may have been made that were not mentioned in after action reports)

CHAPTER 20

Final Thoughts on Hill 376 and Tam Ky

In the previous chapters, it has been my privilege to share details of the Tam Ky battle never before disclosed publicly and rarely mentioned in Vietnam War official records and publications. As this final chapter ends and before the epilogue, I summarize my more important research findings and personal thoughts about what I have learned and hopefully have conveyed to readers. This last chapter is divided into four sections.

Section 1: Hill 376, The 1-501st's Decisive Fight at Tam Ky
Section 2: 1-501st Combat Operations After Hill 376
Section 3: The Conclusion of *Operation Lamar Plain* at Tam Ky
Section 4: Observations and Conclusions

July–August Back in the World

1 Jul	Top hit *Love Theme from Romeo and Juliet* by Henry Mancini
3 Jul	Rolling Stones guitarist drowns during alcohol/drug binge
4–5 Jul	National Mobilization Committee to End the War in Vietnam established
4 Jul	Zodiac serial killer begins public reign of terror murdering and threatening murder, never caught
14 Jul	*Easy Rider* released (#4 movie in '69)
16–24 Jul	Apollo 11, first moon landing, Neil Armstrong and Buzz Aldrin first to walk on moon
17 Jul	*NY Times* retracts ridicule of scientist Goddard for predicting space travel in 1920
18 Jul	Senator Ted Kennedy's car plunges into Chappaquiddick
31 Jul	Elvis performs live first time in 8 years before 2,000 fans in Las Vegas
1 Aug	Top hit *In the Year 2525* by Zager and Evans
3 Aug	Creedence Clear Water Revival releases *Green River*, 2nd of 3 albums in record-breaking year
8–9 Aug	Manson's cult kills eight people including actress Sharon Tate

12 Aug	Outbreak of 30 years of violence in Northern Ireland
14–17 Aug	Hurricane Camille hits the Mississippi coast killing 259
15–18 Aug	Woodstock Festival in Bethel, New York, 400,000+ attend

Section 1: Hill 376, The 1-501st's Decisive Fight at Tam Ky

The 1st Brigade commander's early description of the fight on Hill 376 as "a hornet's nest" was accurate. The enemy had quite a sting. The 1st Brigade's after action report dated 15 September 1969 accurately describes the ten-day fight on Hill 376 as the decisive battle at Tam Ky:

> Following contact with the 1-501st Infantry near Ban Quan (Hill 376) at BT2012 during the early part of June in which they [the enemy] took heavy casualties, the enemy began to conduct defensive operations. … The enemy suffered heavy losses due to artillery, air strikes, and aerial rocket artillery causing him to disperse into small groups …. Throughout the operation, the enemy withdrew to the southeast, southwest, and west in order to reorganize, resupply, and retrain.[28]

The same AAR makes it clear that after the fight on Hill 376, enemy activity "continued to decrease," "slackened," "was sporadic," and "remained light" until *Operation Lamar Plain* ended. Though no record could be found formally stating when the tactical emergency ended which brought the 1st Brigade to Tam Ky, for practical purposes the emergency was over with the end of the fight on Hill 376 though the combat was not yet at an end.

Enemy Casualties on Hill 376

There are no accurate estimates of enemy casualties during the ten-day battle action on Hill 376. It is safe to assume they were significantly higher than 1-501st casualties. Not long after the 1-501st was extracted, a South Vietnamese Army battalion found 188 graves on the summit of Hill 376. Some were mass graves. The number of enemy wounded would of course be much higher as well. As previously noted, most of the enemy casualties were the result of artillery, air cavalry, and close air support, but even those casualties could not be achieved without infantry finding and engaging enemy forces on the ground.

The American Division's Operational Report commenting on *Lamar Plain*'s success adds this: "The period of low-level enemy activity that was witnessed during July 1969 continued until 11 August when VC/NVA forces completed their period of retraining and resupplying."[29] The report goes on to say elements of the 2nd NVA did mount further attacks primarily by indirect mortar and rocket fire in Quang Tin province in late August and September 1969 after the 1st Brigade (101st) departed. However, it concludes that after the enemy took further heavy casualties, the enemy attacks could not be sustained and the enemy turned their efforts to harassing attacks, food gathering, and disrupting local pacification efforts.

1-501st Tactics on Hill 376 Leading Up to 9 June

Combat on Hill 376 by all the companies of the 1-501st was characterized by frequent close infantry-against-infantry combat with heavily inflicted casualties on both sides. US casualties were heavy primarily for two reasons. First, the enemy was determined, skilled, and experienced. They almost always fought from concealed bunkers and consistently used ambush and hit and run tactics.

Second, the 1-501st units on Hill 376 were given orders by battalion and brigade to move straight up the mountain. The mountainous terrain offered little opportunity to maneuver and flank the ring of enemy bunkers on the forward slopes of Hill 376. It did not take company commanders long to confirm what they already knew, attacking straight up the mountain worked to the enemy's advantage.

There were no easy tactical answers. Infantry units were forced to move up slowly, often in heavy vegetation until the enemy opened fire on them. The standard battle drill was to take cover, return fire, call in artillery, air cavalry, or close air support, then move out and repeat the deadly drill all over again. This was a major difference from the fight on 21 May when the enemy engaged our soldiers from close range and artillery and attack helicopters were not used. On Hill 376, both artillery and attack helicopters fires were placed on enemy positions very close to friendly units.

During the latter half of the ten-day fight on the hill, company commanders adopted the tactic of waiting the enemy out. Rather than making direct frontal attacks, they chose to remain on defendable terrain and use their advantage of artillery, attack helicopters, and close air support to repeatedly hit the enemy. They also wisely stayed off or away from terrain features such as trail junctions or ridges lines which the enemy may have already registered as mortar targets.

Perhaps in hindsight, the initial combat air assault and landing of the battalion on Hill 376 should have been followed by an immediate attack on the summit. The LZ was very close (400 m) to the top. However, the mission of the initial combat assault was designed to reinforce Bravo Company and engage the large enemy force threatening Bravo Company, not to seize the summit. The point may be argued by old veterans, now armchair tacticians, current combat-experienced infantrymen still serving, or even younger soldiers who have not yet been in their first battle. However, after coming off Hill 376, those who fought did little second guessing about what was done, not done, or could have been done. They had accomplished their mission.

Commenting on the extensive artillery and bombing the enemy took, SGT Jim Littleton, always willing to share his soldierly wisdom with humor, observed, "With the amount of ordinance we dropped on Hill 376, it should be renamed Hill 346. Its height was lowered by at least 30 meters!"

Delta Company's Role on 9 June

Delta Company had an important role in bringing the Hill 376 fight to a decisive conclusion on 9 June. The battalion's Recon Platoon attached to and augmented by Delta Company soldiers was the first to discover the attacking enemy force which intelligence reports had long predicted. The enemy, estimated to be what remained of an NVA battalion, was clearly positioning itself to make a daylight attack from the high ground north of Delta Company's position. Caught moving in the open, the time-on-target barrage directed by CPT Roy and expertly coordinated by his forward observer, LT Wharton, was fired by multiple batteries including naval gunfire. This was the decisive blow on Hill 376 which resulted in the enemy's defeat. See Chapter 16.

The Leader and the Led

CPT Leland Roy, the new Delta Company commander who led his soldiers all ten days on Hill 376, recalls the fighting as his toughest in his two combat tours with the 101st Airborne. He came away from the battle with great admiration for his young "first-termer" soldiers who fought there. Reflecting on his understrength company due to casualties and its severe shortage of officer and senior NCO leaders, Roy says his junior-enlisted soldiers rose to the occasion. "Their courage under heavy enemy fire was impressive. I was honored to lead them in combat. They fully lived up to Delta Company's motto, 'Never Quit.' Likely few in Vietnam ever fought harder or with more determination!"

Soldiers who fought on Hill 376 under CPT Roy also admired his "Never Quit" leadership in battle. None knew beforehand his background or his determination. No one knew he was just weeks into a recovery from a serious medical operation. Neither did they know he was wounded in action on 31 May just before taking command. And for certain, they did not know Roy could have stayed in the rear and allowed an already-designated replacement commander to take his place. He chose to rejoin "his soldiers" and take them into what he knew was going to be a strenuous fight. What Roy's soldiers did come to see and know firsthand in hard combat, they could not have been led by a better commander and many owed their very lives to him.

***

Casualties and Awards—Hill 376

The 1-501st casualties on Hill 376 are evidence of the battalion's decisive fight and major combat role at Tam Ky. Battalion losses on Hill 376 were 23 KIA, 2 MIA, and 56 WIA, almost the current field strength of one of the battalion's infantry companies. Most of those casualties occurred in a three-day period from 7–9 June (15 KIA, 2 MIA, and 43 WIA). See chapters 14–16. The individual names of casualties were provided in previous chapters. Casualty Table 11 summarizes the casualties by unit.

Casualty Table 11: 1-501st, Hill 376, Summary, 3–12 June 1969

Casualties	HHC	A Co	B Co	C Co	D Co	E Co	Totals
KIA	5	3	6	1	6	2	23
WIA	1	13	4	7	20	11	56
MIA	0	0	0	0	2	0	2
Total	6	16	10	8	28	13	81
Total to date 16 May–12 June	9 KIA 6 WIA 0 MIA 15 TOT	5 KIA 15 WIA 0 MIA 20 TOT	12 KIA 39 WIA 0 MIA 51 TOT	7 KIA 27 WIA 0 MIA 34 TOT	12 KIA 36 WIA 2 MIA 50 TOT	5 KIA 23 WIA 0 MIA 28 TOT	50 KIA 146 WIA 2 MIA 198 TOT

A Special Tribute to 1-501st Medics KIA

Nine medics were killed during 23 days of combat (18 May to 9 June) supporting the 1-501st Battalion's infantry companies at Tam Ky. Three were KIA on 9 June, the day of the decisive battle on Hill 376. Once the battalion returned home to LZ Sally, a group of 1-501st infantry soldiers had a stone memorial plaque made to honor the memory of the nine medics killed in action. The memorial was a tribute not only to the nine 1-501st medics, but was dedicated to honor all medics who died sacrificing their lives for their fellow soldiers. As usual, the medics were in the thick of the fighting. The memorial stone still hangs in the headquarters of the 1-501st Infantry.

Each of the nine medics has been mentioned in previous pages of this book, but are listed here by the date of their deaths: SP4 Paul Ganun, 18 May; SP4 Russell Jett, 18 May; SP5 Hans Mills, 18 May; SP4 Keith Starnes, 21 May; SP4 Fletcher Nowlin, WIA 21 May, died 3 June; SP4 Roy Gargus, 4 June; SP4 Christopher Bean, 9 June; SP4 Daniel Thurston, 9 June; and SP4 Gary Winkler, 9 June. See Appendix 6 for photographs and additional information. (The index may be used to locate the combat action in which they were killed.)

The Effect of 1-501st Casualties on Field Strength

Another name for field strength is "fighting strength." The fighting strength of the 1-501st already depleted on 21 May without sufficient replacements, declined

Field Strength Table 3: 1-501st, Ending 12 June 1969

Unit	A Co	B Co	C Co	D Co	E Co	Total
Officers	5	3	3	2	-	13
Enlisted	60	50	55	44	-	209
Total	65	53	58	46	-	222

further on Hill 376. Having begun at Tam Ky on 15 May with 19 officers and 399 enlisted soldiers (418 total), the battalion's field strength at the end of Hill 376 is estimated at little more than 13 officers and 209 enlisted soldiers. In other words, when the fighting on Hill 376 ended the battalion's fighting or field strength had declined 53% due to battle losses at Tam Ky.

Ending field strength totals are estimated based on the strength at the start of *Lamar Plain*, the reported casualties and the small number of replacements received during the operation.

Echo Company's Recon Platoon attached to Delta Company was essentially no longer combat effective at the conclusion of Hill 376 due to casualties and exhaustion. Having fought well and played an important role in detecting the NVA attack on 9 June, CPT Roy, Delta Company commander, had them taken out by helicopter to recover and regroup.

Unfortunately, neither the 1st Brigade nor the 1-501st after action reports show the field strength of the battalion immediately after Hill 376. They show the assigned strength of 1-501st and other battalions following large numbers of replacements during July 1969 weeks after the heavy fighting was over. In other words, they do not identify the low point of the field strength during the period of heaviest fighting. However, the 1st Brigade's AAR does refer to the severe shortage of replacements in saying, "In the critical 11 Series MOS (Infantryman), losses exceeded gains by 297 during the operation."

The shortage of infantry replacements at Tam Ky was not unique to the 1-501st or its sister battalions. The 101st Airborne Division was short almost 1,000 MOS 11B Infantryman. (See *Operational Report—Lessons Learned Headquarters, 101st Airborne Division, Period Ending 31 July 1969*, dated 9 December 1969). A second factor was the priority of replacements initially and appropriately went to 101st units who fought at Hamburger Hill and suffered high casualties.

1-501st Soldier Awards for Hill 376, 3–9 June (other awards may have been made that were not mentioned in after action reports). Silver Stars, 9; Bronze Stars for Valor, 39; Army Commendation for Valor, 4; Purple Hearts, 81.

Section 2: 1-501st Combat Operations After Hill 376

Combat operations for the 1-501st continued after Hill 376. Following Delta Company's standdown at Chu Lai, they moved by CH-47 helicopter to LZ Professional and along with Alpha Company were under the operational control of the 1-46th Infantry Battalion. Bravo Company again picked up the security mission at 1st Brigade's headquarters at Tam Ky North. Charlie Company went to Chu Lai for a short stand down.

Delta Company remained at or near LZ Professional providing firebase security and conducting local patrolling around the base until 3 July. Delta and Alpha Company then returned to the 1-501st and all companies conducted local combat patrols and RIF missions until the end of Operation Lamar Plain. Battalion deaths due to hostile action declined significantly after Hill 376 which ended the first 28 days of combat at Tam Ky. Having made it through the heaviest fighting, more young men gave their lives, more families suffered loss of loved ones.

***

Casualties and Awards: After Hill 376

Casualties during the remaining 60 days at Tam Ky from 13 June to 12 August 1969 included nine soldiers KIA and 27 WIA. Those casualties are identified here:

JUNE

14 June: Alpha Company WIA: 1LT James Judkins and PFC Jack Jasiszembowski

16 June: Recon Platoon KIA: PFC Harrel Stearns, age 25, born 21 September 1943 from Nacogdoches, TX

25 June: Bravo Company KIA: SGT Carl Janowsky, age 21, born 2 June 1948 from Ithaca, NY

27 June: Bravo Company WIA: SP4 Richard Langley

Casualty Table 12: 1-501st, 13 June–12 August 1969 (60 days)

Casualties	HHC	A Co	B Co	C Co	D Co	E Co	Totals
KIA	0	1	5	0	2	1	9
WIA	0	9	5	3	4	6	27
MIA	0	0	0	0	0	0	0
Total	0	10	10	3	6	7	36

JULY

4 July: **Recon Platoon WIA:** SSG Truman Owens, SP4 Jerry Cameron, SP4 David Hare, and PFC David Dunson

5 July: **Delta Company WIA:** SP4 Gerena Nieves and PFC Leroy Gordon

8 July: **Alpha Company WIA:** SP4 Johnny Conroy, SP4 Johnny Frazier, PFC Larry Darnall, PFC William Jones, PFC Harvey Newman, and PFC Steven Purdy

8 July: **Recon Platoon WIA:** SP4 Norris Arrowood

9 July: **Charlie Company WIA:** PFC Thomas King and PFC Ernest Trujillo

13 July: **Recon Platoon WIA:** PFC Freeman Hill

16 July: **Delta Company WIA:** PFC Gordon _____ (last name not determined)

16 July: **Delta Company KIA:** SGT John Horan, age 20, born 8 July 1948 from New York City, NY (SGT Horan was previously listed as MIA from 5 June 1969)

20 July: **Delta Company KIA:** PFC Robert Sanford, age 18, born 25 August 1949 from Kent, WA

AUGUST

2 August: **Bravo Company KIA:** SP4 David Ball, age 24, born 9 February 1945 from Austin, TX;
SP4 William Campbell, age 20, born 24 October 1948 from Gibson City, IL;
PFC Richard Lewis, age 20, born 2 October 1948 from Escanaba, MI;
PFC Dwight McKeathon, age 23, born 23 June 1949 from Detroit, MI;
PFC Alexander Pomeroy, age 21, born 2 February 1948 from Great Falls, MT

2 August: **Bravo Company WIA:** SP4 Donald Fuller, SP4 George Barnes, and PFC Bruce Windcroft

3 August: **Delta Company WIA:** PFC Jimmy Phifer

8 August: **Bravo Company WIA:** SSG James A Homburger (spelling may not be correct)

14 August: **Alpha Company Non-Hostile Death:** PFC Michael Deragon, age 22, born 14 November 1946 from Brewer, Maine

1-501st Soldier Awards, 13 June–13 August 1969 (other awards may have been made that were not mentioned in after action reports)

Silver Star—5

Bravo Company: 2 August, SP4 David Ball, SP4 William Campbell, PFC Richard Lewis, PFC Dwight McKeathon, PFC Alexander Pomeroy

Bronze Star for Valor—6

Bravo Company: 2 August, SSG Samuel Perez, SGT Lee Edmundson, SP4 Larry Musgrave, PFC Richard Langley

Charlie Company: 23 August, SP4 Dennis Mattox

Recon Platoon: 2 August, SGT Gary Hlusko

Army Commendation Medalfor Valor—1

Bravo Company: 2 August, SGT Donald Fuller

Purple Heart—36 awards were made to include all soldiers KIA or WIA

Section 3: The Conclusion of *Operation Lamar Plain* at Tam Ky

Casualty Table 13 summarizes the 1-501st casualties for the entire 90 days at Tam Ky by each phase of *Operation Lamar Plain*. Delta Company and the Recon Platoon (Echo Company) were the only units that were in the field continuously from 16 May through 12 June. That was the time of the heaviest fighting. Neither unit had the opportunity to secure the Tam Ky Airfield, 1st Brigade Headquarters, or LZ Professional. This contributed in part to their higher friendly casualty count. Bravo Company which had the second most days in the field also had a high casualty count. These statements take nothing away from the extensive combat Alpha and Charlie Companies saw nor the heavy casualties they sustained. All fought hard, all sustained significant casualties.

Casualty Table 13: 1-501st, *Operation Lamar Plain* at Tam Ky

Casualties	HHC	A Co	B Co	C Co	D Co	Recon	Total
First 18 Days	4 KIA	2 KIA	6 KIA	6 KIA	8 KIA	3 KIA	29 KIA
15 May–2 June	5 WIA	3 WIA	36 WIA	20 WIA	23 WIA	12 WIA	99 WIA
	0 MIA	0 MIA	0 MIA	0 MIA	0 MIA	0 MIA	0 MIA
	9 TOT	5 TOT	42 TOT	26 TOT	31 TOT	15 TOT	128 TOT
Next 10 Days	5 KIA	3 KIA	6 KIA	1 KIA	6 KIA	2 KIA	23 KIA
Hill 376	1 WIA	13 WIA	4 WIA	7 WIA	20 WIA	11 WIA	56 WIA
3–12 June	0 MIA	0 MIA	0 MIA	0 MIA	2 MIA	0 MIA	2 MIA
	6 TOT	16 TOT	10 TOT	8 TOT	28 TOT	13 TOT	81 TOT
Last 60 Days	0 KIA	1 KIA	5 KIA	0 KIA	2 KIA	1 KIA	9 KIA
To Operation End	0 WIA	9 WIA	5 WIA	3 WIA	4 WIA	6 WIA	27 WIA
13 June–13 August	0 MIA	0 MIA	0 MIA	0 MIA	0 MIA	0 MIA	0 MIA
	0 TOT	10 TOT	10 TOT	3 TOT	6 TOT	7 TOT	36 TOT
Lamar Plain	9 KIA	6 KIA	17 KIA	7 KIA	16 KIA	6 KIA	61 KIA
90 Days	6 WIA	25 WIA	45 WIA	30 WIA	47 WIA	29 WIA	182 WIA
15 May–13 August	0 MIA	0 MIA	0 MIA	0 MIA	1 MIA	0 MIA	*1 MIA
	15 TOT	31 TOT	62 TOT	37 TOT	64 TOT	35 TOT	244 TOT

SGT John Horan changed from MIA to KIA

Combat Operations of the 1st Brigade, 101st Airborne Division at Tam Ky

A detailed review of the 1st Brigade's combat operations including those of the 1-502nd and 1-46th Infantry battalions and supporting units is well beyond this book's scope. However, battle records show the entire brigade fought valiantly and suffered significant losses during *Operation Lamar Plain*. After action reports for the 1st Brigade and the two battalions as well as other units like the 2-17th Cavalry are listed in the bibliography and are available at various internet sites. Interested readers may also find information about these units on the internet. For example, the 101st Airborne's 2nd Brigade Combat Team (BCT) "Strike History" listed in the bibliography provides additional information on *Operation Lamar Plain*, Both the 1-501st and 1-502nd infantry battalions were assigned to the 2nd Brigade in Vietnam, but were under the operational control of 1st Brigade at Tam Ky. The cross attachment of battalions between brigade headquarters was a common occurrence in Vietnam due to the fluidity of airmobile operations.

A Closer Look at 1st Brigade Casualties

The 1st Brigade sustained 120 KIA, 404 WIA, and 1 MIA in *Operation Lamar Plain* at Tam Ky. The 1st Brigade's after action report dated 15 September 1969 shows only 116 KIA. However, a detailed review of the updated and more accurate Coffelt Database for the same period shows an additional four KIA not included in the brigade's AAR. The brigade's WIA (404 soldiers) and MIA (1) are taken from the 1st Brigade AAR. It is possible, that the 404 wounded soldiers may include some soldiers who were returned to the field after being treated for their wounds. That number is believed to be relatively small, but could not be verified. (The one MIA is the Delta Company POW who was released in October 1969.)

Of the 1st Brigade's 120 KIA, the three infantry battalions had 105 KIA (88% of those killed). The 1-501st had 61 KIA; the 1-502nd, 30 KIA; and 1-46th, 14 KIA. (The 1-46th suffered a significant number of casualties before they were placed under the operational control of 1st Brigade. Those casualties are not recorded here, because they were not then part of *Operation Lamar Plain*.) The 1-501st had 51% of the brigade's KIAs and 45% of the brigade's WIA. The remainder of the 1st Brigade's 15 KIAs were from the brigade's headquarters (1); Bravo Troop 2-17th Cavalry (7); A Company. 101st Assault Helicopter Battalion, (4); A Battery 4-77th Aerial Rocket Artillery (1); and A Company 326th Engineers (2).

Enemy Casualties at Tam Ky

Enemy losses are estimated in the 1st Brigade After Action Report as 477 KIA with 13 Main Force Viet Cong and 8 NVA captured. No account of enemy wounded is provided though reasonable estimates may be as high as three to four times enemy killed in action. There were 3 defectors from enemy units. There were 61 civilian detainees, usually thought to be family or persons in support of local main force Viet Cong units. Another 278 innocent civilians were taken out of or relocated in the brigade's area of operation for their safety. A total of 439 children were processed by the Provost Marshal's military police collection point.

Redeployment from Tam Ky

Redeployment of Delta and its sister companies from Tam Ky began on 10 August. The next day, 11 August, the 1-501st was flown on an hour flight to Camp Evans, 24 km northwest of Hue. From there, on the last leg of their journey, the battalion was trucked to their home base at LZ Sally. This was not a mere change in location. The men who returned from fighting at Tam Ky had undergone the hardest challenge of their young lives. Knowingly or not, they were transformed by their recent combat experience. Most, for good. Whatever they would later do in life would in some way be affected by their arduous, combat experience.

Section 4: Observations and Conclusions

My greatest satisfaction in researching and writing *Courage Under Fire* was reconnecting over four decades later with veterans from my former 101st unit. Many have become close friends. Also important was finally letting the veterans of Tam Ky (and their families) learn of the battle they valiantly fought so long ago. In the following paragraphs I share some personal thoughts about what I have learned and hopefully conveyed to readers.

First, in my research it became clear that in 1969 there were valid strategic military and political reasons for not immediately disclosing the 101st Airborne's battle at Tam Ky. President Nixon had been newly elected by the American people to bring an honorable end to the Vietnam War. Just as Nixon announced on 14 May, the US would no longer seek a military solution to the war, the 101st Airborne fought two major battles from mid-May to mid-June with over a thousand casualties. With Hamburger Hill casualties already causing a major political backlash in Washington DC and in the media, the report of a second major battle with high casualties would likely have had severe consequences, jeopardizing Nixon's plans to bring the war to an honorable end.

Second, more time was needed to implement Nixon's top priority Vietnamization initiative to turn the ground war over to South Vietnam's government and military. If successful, that would allow increased US troop withdrawals planned in March 1969, announced in June, and begun in August. Continued support of Nixon's conduct of the war by the American people was essential to implement the Vietnamization strategy.

Third, once *Operation Lamar Plain* was successfully kept from the media, war protestors, and political adversaries, there was no benefit to the Military Assistance Command Vietnam, the Joint Chiefs of Staff, or the Nixon administration to disclose that a major battle with high casualties had been hidden from the American people. Indeed, disclosing the battle during the war would likely cause a further loss of support for the war. For certain, it would further the belief that the American people were not being told the truth about the war and in some cases they weren't.

Fourth, the fighting at Tam Ky was a major battle in every military sense: the mission, enemy encountered, the scale and length of the operation, the terrain, the intensity of fighting, and high number of casualties. In fact, it was one of the last large US offensive operations of the Vietnam War. There is no doubt General Abrams, commander of the Military Assistance Command Vietnam, acted prudently in not publicly disclosing the battle at Tam Ky immediately on the heels of Hamburger Hill's high casualties.

Fifth, it is clear the decision to keep *Operation Lamar Plain* undisclosed had nothing to do with the valiant combat performance of the soldiers who fought at Tam Ky or with the top outstanding leadership of the 101st Airborne Division. As was often the case in the Vietnam War, political considerations outweighed and overshadowed recognition of military accomplishments and the valor and sacrifices of soldiers in battle.

Sixth, the US Army Center of Military History has not yet recognized *Operation Lamar Plain* and the fighting at Tam Ky as one of the last major US offensive operations in the Vietnam War. The battle at Tam Ky is absent from almost all of its otherwise excellent publications. It needs to be included as part of the history of the war in 1969 as President Nixon became commander-in-chief and charted a new course for the war. I am hopeful that will be remedied in the near future.

Seventh, despite overarching political considerations, the leadership of the commanders and the courage and tenacity of their young infantry soldiers fighting at Tam Ky showed they are worthy of being remembered. They were part of the 101st Airborne's long tradition as a premier infantry fighting force in the Vietnam War. Veterans of Tam Ky describe their fight on 21 May and the ten-day fight on Hill 376 from 3–12 June as "a continuous bloody grind of intense combat where days ran together with no end in sight." Many soldiers didn't expect to survive Tam Ky without being wounded or killed—and many didn't.

The soldiers of "Never Quit" Delta Company and their sister units did not give up, but persevered under difficult battlefield conditions and struck the final decisive blow against a determined enemy. The "Never Quit" commander who led Delta Company certainly had a major contribution to their victory. But just as important, the soldiers did not quit because of who they were. Many were sons, grandsons, and nephews of "the greatest generation," veterans from World War II and the Korean War. A high standard had been set for them as soldiers and they met it. They came from all over America, from farms and urban centers, small towns and big cities, representing just about every ethnic heritage of our nation. They were young men, draftees and volunteers, many in their teens ineligible to vote, not many older than 23.

What made them special, beyond their youth, physical conditioning, superb training and combat skills? They were committed to one another, not willing to fail their fellow soldiers in combat, dishonor their families and friends back home. They had pride in who they were and what they were doing. They were infantry soldiers, "Screaming Eagles" in a famed division of the US Army with a long tradition of courage in combat. They could not quit!

The Story Continues

The story of Delta Company and their sister companies continued long after the war. Soldiers who died in combat became men who will forever be honored and remembered though their young lives were sadly cut so very short. For soldiers who returned home, no matter what they or others thought about Vietnam, either then or years later, their memories and experience at Tam Ky would always be a part of who they are and what they became. Appendix 9 provides a brief look of the life they resumed when they returned home.

For those who returned to civilian life as most did, or continued serving as soldiers as few did, every soldier knew he had been tested at the very core of his being. Despite constant fear, fighting as infantry against a tough enemy, under rugged battlefield conditions in an unpopular war far from home, the young soldiers of Delta Company and the Geronimo Battalion prevailed. Undaunted, they passed their young life's most severe test—with great courage under fire.

Looking Back Over 50 Years Later

Tragic Consequences of the Vietnam War

Looking back over 50 years after the Vietnam War, a fair question to ask is, "Was it worth it?" The war cost 58,220 American lives, mostly young men.[30] There was untold suffering of families who lost loved ones and of the seriously wounded, whether physically or emotionally. Of course, the tragic consequences of war extended well beyond our nation and included both our allies and enemy. The South Vietnamese Army had between 200–250,000 deaths. The Viet Cong and North Vietnamese Army had 1.1 million deaths. Two million Vietnamese civilians in North and South Vietnam were killed.

Deaths were not the only lamentable result of the war. The war divided our nation. In 1971 *The Pentagon Papers*, a top secret US Defense Department study of Vietnam political and military policy from 1945 to 1967, was openly printed in *The New York Times*. The information revealed the Kennedy and Johnson administrations had not told the truth about the war to the American people. Progress in the war was not as it was often reported and that was mostly due to political agendas and objectives, not military considerations. Young combat soldiers like those in Delta Company (as well as their families), bore the brunt of those political decisions.

Soldiers and their commanders fighting in Vietnam knew nothing of the hidden political agendas of the war. Presidents Kennedy, Johnson, and Nixon often kept the Joint Chiefs of Staff, the nation's top military leaders, well removed from their political calculations and maneuvering. As a result, opposition to the war increased in and out of government and advanced the view the war was an ill-chosen effort which wasted too many lives.

A Larger View

Viewing the Vietnam War from a larger, global perspective is helpful by placing the war in its proper historical and political context. In the turmoil after World War II ended in 1945, there was an explosive, worldwide expansion of communism. The long "Cold War" between the western nations and the communist nations began. Russia extended its totalitarian control over eastern Europe and began to exert considerable influence globally. China, with the world's largest population, became communist in 1949 and reached its tentacles into all of Southeast Asia.

In 1950, with the backing of China and the Soviet Union, communist North Korea invaded South Korea. In 1956, Egypt, with close political ties to Soviet Union, nationalized the strategic Suez Canal and threatened to shut off Persian Gulf oil to Europe and the US. In 1959, Fidel Castro's revolution established communism in Cuba and in 1962, the Soviet Union tried to base nuclear missiles in Cuba 90 miles from Miami. Other communist-led insurrections were occurring elsewhere in South America, Central America, and Africa. And so on it went, communism seemed an unstoppable worldwide force for evil.

Some historians estimate that under Stalin's brutal rule in the Soviet Union and Mao Zedong's tyrannical reign in China, tens of millions of civilians were brutally killed for political reasons. Others place the number well over a hundred million with worldwide civilian deaths caused by communists even higher. South Vietnam was just one of many countries in communism's looming shadow.

The Kennedy administration chose South Vietnam as a strategic location for the US to take a stand against communism. Several books in the bibliography cover the decision to become engaged in Vietnam and pursue the war during the Kennedy, Johnson, and Nixon administrations. *The Best and the Brightest* by David Halberstam and Susan Wright is a good place to start for those interested in the decisions made by Presidents Kennedy and Johnson. There were views for and against fighting there. Despite the political issues and restraints, US military forces fought well in Vietnam. The case can be made that under General Abrams' leadership, beginning in June 1968, the tide had truly turned from a military standpoint. The US decision to end the Vietnam War was a political one with dire consequences.

A Disgraceful End

Though the Cold War led to the Vietnam War, it is fair to acknowledge our government's mistakes and deceptive behavior first in entering the war and later in the conduct of the war. South Vietnam's government also contributed to the political failure of the war. Harry Summers says in his review of *Dereliction of Duty*, that H. R. McMaster (the author, a former Army general and US national security advisor) rightly concludes the war was not lost on the battlefields in Vietnam, but in Washington DC.[31]

The war ended as it did in 1975 because the American people tired of the increasingly high casualties of a war that had lasted twice as long as World War II. Politically, the American people and their government lacked the will to continue fighting and paying the high costs of a seemingly endless war. By unilaterally pulling out of the war and with the US Congress cutting off funding and other support, our nation abandoned our South Vietnam ally to our communist enemy.

The momentous fall of South Vietnam and its capital, Saigon, on 29 April 1975 is a harsh, shameful memory. A now notorious, iconic news video captured the dramatic event which came to symbolize the war's tragic end. An over-crowded helicopter is evacuating desperate Vietnamese civilians from a Saigon rooftop. North Vietnamese Army tanks are reported to be entering the city. The rumble of artillery can be heard. The civilians fear the worst. They fight and push to get on the helicopter to be carried to waiting US ships in the South China Sea. Failure to get on may result in captivity or death. For those who fought in Vietnam, it is a heart-rending scene—and memory.

The final surrender of South Vietnam occurred on 30 April 1975. Tens of thousands of civilians are believed to have been killed. Some 90,000 were evacuated by the US State Department and military in the last days before Saigon fell. Hundreds of thousands were sent to re-education camps. Over the next few years, a mass exodus of two million South Vietnamese refugees by boats and other means extended the discomfort of many Americans, especially Vietnam veterans, who watched the refugees' plight with deep regret and sorrow.

Yes, the Vietnam War had a bitter end. Two decades later, the 1994 official account of the successful effort of the US military and its allies to free Kuwait from Saddam Hussein's invasion, had a telling title, *Certain Victory: The US Army in the Gulf War.* In the report, Brigadier General Robert H. Scales Jr. bluntly contrasted how the two wars ended and painted a bleak picture of the post-Vietnam Army. He writes: "The American Army emerged from Vietnam cloaked in anguish. In the early seventies, it was an institution fighting merely to maintain its existence in the midst of growing apathy, decay, and intolerance."[32]

But there is another better and greater story about the post-Vietnam military that is largely unknown. The US military and particularly the US Army purposed to rebuild and prepare for future wars and engagements. Al Santoli's 1993 book, *Leading the Way: How Vietnam Veterans Rebuilt the US Military* gives an excellent account.[33] Santoli makes a strong case that the Vietnam veterans who stayed in the Army for the next 20 or so years transformed the US Army into a remarkable fighting force. That Army became the center piece of a coalition of 30 nations that fought The Persian Gulf War in 1990 and 1991. The end of the invasion of Kuwait by Saddam Hussein and the Iraqi Army was done quickly and decisively. Since then, the quality of our "all-volunteer" Army has remained unequaled in the world.

Coming Home

Mistreatment of our young soldiers as they returned home (including turning a blind eye or deaf ear to their experiences) added to our nation's embarrassment and shame following the end of the Vietnam War. The soldiers, especially the junior-enlisted men in their late teens and early twenties, were mostly citizen soldiers. They were the very ones most deserving honor and appreciation for their faithful service, especially so, those killed in battle. Whether draftees or enlistees, the vast majority of young soldiers, particularly those in frontline combat units, performed their battlefield duties admirably, faithfully, and courageously—just like soldiers have done in our past wars and those since Vietnam. The American public as a whole sometimes seemed unaware of the sacrifice of its young soldiers in Vietnam.

Rich Kolb, who wrote the foreword to this book, shared this with me. When *Life Magazine* published its disturbing 27 June 1969 issue, the cover headline said, "Faces of the American Dead: One Week's Toll." The close-up photos of the faces and names of 242 mostly young soldiers reported to have been killed in action from 28 May through 3 June hit a raw nerve in the nation. Suddenly, the hundreds of deaths reported each week were particularly and individually personal. In stunned reaction, one *Life* reader naively wrote: "I guess I never realized 19 year olds have to die." The reader had no clue 19 year olds had been dying since 1965. From that age group alone, a total of 8,283 died by war's end!

The *Life Magazine* edition published right after the heavy media coverage of Hamburger Hill gave the impression to civilians that all the soldiers pictures or mentioned were killed in that battle. In fact, it included those killed throughout South Vietnam including *Operation Lamar Plain*. SFC Pedro Rios from Delta Company is one of the names listed without a photograph.

A Homecoming That Wasn't

The anguish of the post-Vietnam era was not just an institutional matter. Many young soldiers experienced firsthand the hostility by some, or more likely the ambivalence and lack of concern of others. As they were discharged and returned to civilian life, they were not always welcomed home with warm greetings by others. That was especially true from 1968 to the war's end as the conflict became increasingly unpopular. Author James Wright in his book *Enduring Vietnam* gives an account of a returning soldier that illustrates the experience of many others.

> One came home, just before Thanksgiving and at a large family celebration he expected to be "bombarded by questions and stuff," but no one mentioned Vietnam to him. So, he never talked about it to them—for the next 40 years.[34]

Some soldiers endured far more negative experiences with many attempts to shame them for fighting in the war. It seemed all the hate and blame for the war was projected unfairly and directly on the backs of our young fighting men. No wonder many Vietnam veterans remained quiet long after the war.

Those who fought as young infantry soldiers (or with them in close support) came home changed men. They had travelled alone from home, many for the first time. They joined a new unit as a stranger on a distant battlefield. Many arrived during intense battles. They saw and did things for which their past training and experience did not fully prepare them. In constant danger, they overcame ever present fears. Challenged by harsh battlefield conditions, scorching temperatures, brutal humidity, and unfamiliar, difficult terrain, they hunted and killed tough enemy soldiers who were hunting and bent on killing them.

They saw and heard their buddies and fellow soldiers being killed and wounded. They felt helpless as many died, some screaming in agony, some writhing in pain, others silently slipping away. The thought they could be next was never dismissed from their minds. They lived with uncertainty day to day, week to week, month after month, always under pressure not to fail their fellow soldiers. By 1969, the burden of combat leadership fell squarely and heavily on these young "first-termer" soldiers and they steadfastly rose to meet the challenge.

Finally their time was up. They came home with great relief, glad to be back "in the world." Memories and stories came with them. Many good memories of the men with whom they bonded in combat, fellow brothers in arms. Sometimes they carried guilt and regrets of things done wrong or left undone. But, underlying all this was a well-earned sense of pride, "I fought as an infantryman and did my duty despite great hardship and survived!" Their hard experience remained fresh in their minds and hearts ever since—and made them better men.

Concluding Thoughts

Now over 50 years later, many in our nation are acknowledging the faithful service of Vietnam War veterans. There is finally realization that Vietnam veterans are not the homeless, anti-social, psychotic, violent drug users they were often made out to be. Nor were they the caricatures featured in so called "award-winning," anti-Vietnam War films like *Platoon, Apocalypse Now, Full Metal Jacket,* and others.

What some may not have yet learned is that the young infantry soldiers who fought at close quarters with a much-underrated enemy could be numbered with the best soldiers our nation has ever produced. They fought in a tough, unpopular war not because they relished going to war, but because they willingly answered their nation's call in time of war. They responded just as their fathers, uncles, grandfathers, and forefathers had done before them—with a strong, patriotic sense of duty to serve their country, often at great sacrifice.

That sacrifice is not well known by many in our nation. I wince mildly (but only inwardly and briefly) when I hear the now customary, "Thank you for your service." Those who genuinely say it mean well and their sentiment is appreciated. But often, without intention, the phrase is said with limited understanding of the heavy cost that combat veterans of any war have endured. A veteran's best reply is a genuine smile and a subdued, "Thank you." Not much else is expected or needed. It is best to take it for what it is, an attempt by others to show they care about the past service of veterans—all veterans including those who served in Vietnam.

For me and many other Vietnam veterans, Memorial Day and Veterans Day are adequate for saying "thank you" and remembering those who died and those who served honorably. Many Vietnam Veterans would prefer to see the March 29th National Vietnam Veterans Appreciation Day dropped altogether. Vietnam veterans can make do with the traditional 11 November Veterans Day in which all veterans are recognized. Maybe, instead of a "thank you for your service" on Veterans Day and Memorial Day, I and other veterans would much prefer to hear the words, "Remember our fallen!" That is the kind of recognition most combat veterans I know would appreciate the most.

On the whole, the Vietnam veterans who fought in *Operation Lamar Plain* at Tam Ky do not want to be recognized as heroes. More than anything else, they just want their story to be told. Told accurately and without exaggeration. When I first started writing *Courage Under Fire* for Delta Company veterans in 2016, the public telling of their story was a hurdle for those I interviewed (and for me as well). I overcame my hesitation and that of others with the reminder this untold story of combat veterans at Tam Ky is to be passed down to families long after we are gone—a legacy of honorable service in the best traditions of the Army's 101st Airborne Division and infantry soldiers in any unit.

A second common remark I heard from Delta Company's veterans was, "I am no hero, the guys that didn't make it are the real heroes." To that I replied, "This book will be dedicated to them. You and I are part of their story. When we tell our story, we will also be telling their story." That point was brought home to me early in my writing by former Sergeant and my close friend, Jim Littleton. Jim died in October 2018 and now stands muster with the Lord he loves. In one of our first conversations about the book, Jim looked me straight in the eye and said, "I hope you're not going to call anyone in your book a hero. I don't like the way that word is too often thrown around. We weren't heroes, we were just doing our duty and often scared to death doing it!" That remains my favorite definition of courage under fire. In agreement with Jim and to honor his request, I reserve that word to describe those who gave their lives for their fellow soldiers and their country.

Final Questions

I end this story of young infantry soldiers in combat during the Vietnam War with the often-asked question about the cost of lives lost, "Was it worth it?" That question is much more complicated than it first seems. It is difficult, if not impossible, to give one answer for everyone to that question. Each soldier and soldier's family will have their own answer. I no longer think it is even the right question to ask of veteran combat soldiers. The better question is: "Did our young soldiers faithfully serve their country in Vietnam and do their duty with honor and courage when they were called upon?"

For the veterans and families of "Never Quit" Delta Company and others who fought valiantly in 1969 and other years, that answer is a resounding and heartfelt "Yes!"

Operation Lamar Plain: A Hidden and Almost Forgotten Battle

As the author of Courage Under Fire: The 101st Airborne's Hidden Battle at Tam Ky, *I did extensive personal research of archival records to determine why* Operation Lamar Plain *was not publicly disclosed during the Vietnam War, how it was kept hidden, and who was responsible. This is what I found.*

The Intriguing Question. The 101st "Screaming Eagles" is one of America's best-known fighting divisions. Those interested in military history may be intrigued to learn how one of its last major offensive operations, that began 15 May and lasted until 13 August 1969, could remain hidden and largely unknown during and even well after the Vietnam War? This question has long been of interest to the 101st combat veterans who fought it. They prevailed in harsh conditions against a tough enemy; lost fellow soldiers and friends; many were seriously wounded; some still suffer battle trauma over 50 years later. Also interested are family and friends of the veterans of *Lamar Plain* especially if they lost loved ones. Then too, all 101st soldiers and veterans may want to discover this largely unknown chapter of their division's valiant past. So what then is the answer?

A Simple, But Surprising Answer. A quick answer is the operation was never covered by US media in Vietnam and therefore, never reported to the American public. In the summer of 1969, other newsworthy political and military events in and out of Vietnam held the media's attention. But this is not the full story. Keeping the battle out of the public eye was the work of the top US military command in Vietnam. There were understandable strategic, military, and political reasons on the home front for the battle to remain undisclosed not only to the press, but more important, kept from the impatient, critical, political opponents of newly elected President Nixon. Time was needed to implement major new war policies to bring the increasingly unpopular war to an honorable end. As a result, the hard, bitter fighting by the 101st troopers remained unknown even beyond the war's end. It lies until now almost forgotten among the declassified war files of our national archives and in the often-troubled memories of those who fought.

A Contentious Political Environment. As Nixon, himself said, the Vietnam War was three wars in one, "the battlefield, the Saigon political war, and US politics."[35]

Battlefield events in Vietnam affected US political events, but US political considerations were by far the controlling factor in fighting the Vietnam War. There is no
better example than the 1968 spring Tet Offensive. Tet was a clear military defeat
for North Vietnam, but for the US, it was a significant political and psychological
setback, a turning point in the war. The surprising, large-scale, country-wide enemy
attacks ended President Lyndon Johnson's bid for reelection just as the presidential
campaign season began. Tet continued to affect subsequent political and military
events. On 5 November 1968, President Nixon, a Republican, won the presidency
on a promise to end the war. Assuming office on 20 January 1969, Nixon immediately faced stiff opposition from former Democrat administration officials, a still
Democrat-controlled Congress, and a raucous anti-war movement.

Questioning of US Military Strategy. In Washington DC, during late 1968 and
early 1969, a high-level political battle was waged over how to fight the war. At
issue was the current US military war-fighting strategy of "maintaining maximum
pressure on the enemy." General Creighton W. Abrams, the top military commander
in Vietnam, had successfully employed the strategy since 10 June 1968 when he
assumed command of US Military Assistance Command Vietnam (MACV). MACV
(pronounced "MAC V") was the senior, joint forces headquarters in Saigon of about
3,000 persons with about two-thirds being Army personnel. "Maximum pressure"
meant conducting large offensive US ground operations to keep the enemy off-balance
inside Vietnam and when approved, bombing enemy bases and resources outside
of Vietnam in Cambodia, Laos, and North Vietnam.

Nixon Continues the Maximum Pressure Strategy. In the first months of his
presidency, Nixon's political opposition and the already large anti-war protest
movement was hardening. His brief post-election honeymoon ended quickly.
Those opposing Nixon believed the US should take up a defensive posture, reduce
offensive operations, and bring a quick end to the war. In their thinking, offensive
operations were causing unnecessary and high US casualties.[36] Immediately following
his inauguration, President Nixon consulted his Secretary of Defense Melvin Laird
and his top commanders: General Abrams at MACV; Admiral John S. McCain Jr.,
head of US Pacific forces, and General Earle G. Wheeler, Chairman of the Joint
Chiefs of Staff (JCS). They all agreed, as did Nixon, of the necessity to continue
maximum pressure on the enemy. That decision set the stage for the major ground
operations in the first half of 1969.

The Transitioning Military Environment. The year 1969 was a year of major US
military strategy and policy transition in Vietnam.[37] Even as the Nixon administration
decided to maintain its present strategy of offensive action, they realized large offensive
ground operations did cause high US casualties. However, assuming a defensive
posture would cause even more. Big multi-battalion offensive ground operations also
gave the wrong impression that the US was escalating the war contrary to Nixon's
aim to end it. Such perceptions jeopardized Nixon's newly restarted Paris peace

talks, further decreased already fading US public support for the war, and energized Nixon's political adversaries limiting his domestic and foreign policy alternatives.

Troop Withdrawal Planning Begins. In March 1969, while visiting Vietnam, Defense Secretary Lairdgave General Abrams directions to begin planning the first unilateral withdrawal of American combat troops to begin that same year. After Laird returned and gave his trip report to the president, General Wheeler sent an immediate message advising Abrams that US troop withdrawals were now "an exceedingly hot topic."[38] He further warned Abrams that high US casualties would make any announcement to withdraw American combat forces look like a retreat forced by the enemy. Discussions were already underway to decide when Nixon should announce the first withdrawal, including how many and which troops would be first to be pulled out. Ideally, the withdrawals were to be announced and made during a lull in combat action.

Avoiding a "Too Speedy" Withdrawal. Nixon, his top advisors, and commanders knew that continuing high casualties would significantly increase pressure for a rapid settlement of the war.[39] But stopping the war too quickly and prematurely would derail Nixon's goal to achieve peace with honor. Polls showed the American public supported Nixon's approach to ending the war, but pulling troops out too fast would be viewed as a humiliating defeat. US credibility would be damaged globally for decades. Nixon's own credibility would be impaired early in his first term of office and he would go down in history as the first US president to lose a war.

The Secret Bombing of Cambodia. Nixon had authorized the secret bombing of enemy bases in Cambodia under Operation *Menu* to begin on 18 March in response to the enemy's 1969 Tet Offensive. A week later, a headline appeared on the front page of *The Washington Star* about the restart of US bombing. General Wheeler, concerned about accusations the US is escalating the war, immediately sent a stern note to General Abrams criticizing MACV's lack of information security. Abrams responded that the news article had been "a disaster bearing directly on the functioning of the [MACV] command" and made assurances that more leaks would not occur.[40] They did not and the bombings, made with tacit support of Cambodia, were camouflaged as bombing attacks in Vietnam to protect the neutrality of Cambodia. *Operation Menu* continued without interruption until April 1970.

The Strategic Importance of Vietnamization. The new policy of "Vietnamization" was the center piece of Nixon's plan to first reduce US involvement in the war and then end it entirely. Nixon had already quickly decided to begin transitioning US responsibility for fighting the war to the South Vietnamese government and its military. That required time, more than a year and likely longer. Time was limited and already fast running out, risking the successful implementation of Vietnamization on which withdrawal of US troops depended.

US Casualties Are a Top Concern. Continuing and increasing US casualties in what was then America's longest war were a major problem for Nixon's strategy to end the war. High US casualties threatened to drastically shorten the time available to successfully hand off the war to South Vietnam. In a 3 April 1969 message from Wheeler to Abrams, sent during a lull in enemy engagements and a corresponding brief respite in US casualties, the top US general expressed his deep concerns:

> The subject of US casualties… is being thrown at me at every juncture: in the press, by the Secretary of Defense, at the White House and on the Hill. I am concerned that decisions could be made in response to strong pressure inside and outside the administration to seek a settlement of the war which could be detrimental to our objectives or to adopt a defensive strategy in South Vietnam.[41]

Abrams reinforced the urgency of Wheeler's message two days later at his 5 April MACV Commander's Conference. He instructed his top commanders to continue pressuring the enemy by offensive operations, but with awareness that needless American casualties are detrimental to their efforts.[42] Abrams could have said, "high casualties of any kind" are detrimental and he would have been right. A later 1996 study by RAND, *Casualties and Consensus: The Historical Role of Casualties in Domestic Support for US Military Operations* quoted the conclusions of other studies that showed:

> Casualties, especially war dead, had increasingly become the single most troubling aspect of the Vietnam War. By March 1969, the number of battle-related deaths had risen to over 34,000—the final toll of the Korean War—and nearly two out of three said they would have opposed the U.S. entry into the war if they had known the costs of that conflict.[43]

Hamburger Hill and President Nixon's 14 May Address. In May 1969, concerns about strategy, casualties, Vietnamization, and troop withdrawals defined the military and political climate. On 10 May, the 101st Airborne Division's 3rd Brigade began *Operation Lamar Plain.* On 14 May, while heavy fighting is raging on Dong Ap Bia or Hill 937 (soon known as Hamburger Hill), President Nixon made his first nationwide television address to outline his new, long-awaited Vietnam policy. Four months had passed since his inauguration. The American public and his political opposition were eager to hear Nixon's plan for ending the war. Others were also listening, including North Vietnam's top leaders in Hanoi and their negotiators in Paris. Much was riding on his speech.

Nixon's New War Policy. Nixon's 14 May address was the most important speech in the beginning months of his presidency. However, it is not apparent from research for this book that Nixon knew the size or intensity of the 101st battle already underway. Whatever he knew, he certainly did not yet know the extent of US casualties in the battle or the political consequences that would result. In describing his new war policy, Nixon said, to the surprise of friend and foe alike, "We have ruled out attempting to impose a purely military solution on the battlefield."[44] Days later, when the fighting on Hamburger Hill became public, the size of the battle and its high US casualties seemed to directly counter Nixon's just-announced US war policy. There was extensive media coverage of the hard, heroic fighting of the 101st Airborne Division's 3rd Brigade soldiers and the casualties they suffered. This caused an abrupt challenge to Nixon's conduct of the war. Other recent battles in Vietnam also had high casualties, but none had worse timing and such high visibility. The one exception, Tet 1968, had well-known, disastrous political consequences. The following describes the central issue of high US casualties:

> The public was tired of seeing body bags. Abrams, who had rejected calls the previous year to reduce U.S. casualties, could no longer defy the mounting pressure. From now on, he and his subordinates would have to exercise greater restraint in undertaking actions that put Americans in harm's way.[45]

Kennedy's Immediate Criticism. Senator Ted Kennedy's 20 May angry denunciation of Hamburger Hill on the US Senate floor received wide attention. His harsh words, particularly in the last two paragraphs below, characterize the relentless, sharp, political assault Nixon faced:

> After the cessation of bombing last November, the President issued an order to the field that American military forces were to maintain a constant and steady pressure upon the enemy. As a result, the levels of combat and casualties did not remain the same but actually increased. The number of U. S. offensive actions making contact with the enemy grew significantly; the total number of U. S. battalion-size operations was raised; the amount of bomb tonnage dropped in the South rose to a total greater than the amount of bomb tonnage previously dropped on the North and South. In effect, the President's [Johnson's] order of last November to maintain steady and constant pressure has not only been carried out by our military commanders in the field, it has been carried out to the letter and then some.
>
> President Nixon in his April 18th press conference reaffirmed President Johnson's earlier directive by stating that he has not ordered, nor did he intend to order, any reduction of our activity in Vietnam. He explained that this was in the interest of maintaining the strength of our bargaining position in Paris.
>
> I am compelled to speak on this question today for I believe that the level of our military activity in Vietnam runs opposite to our stated intentions and goals in Paris. But more importantly, I feel it is both senseless and irresponsible to continue to send our young men to their deaths to capture hills and positions that have no relation to ending this conflict.
>
> President Nixon has told us, without question, that we seek no military victory, that we seek only peace. How then can we justify sending our boys against a hill a dozen times or more, until soldiers themselves question the madness of the action. The assault on "Hamburger Hill" is only symptomatic of a mentality and a policy that requires immediate attention. American boys are too valuable to be sacrificed for a false sense of military pride.[46]

The National Media Amplifies Kennedy's Criticism. Kennedy's jarring remarks, though widely reported, were not well received by everyone. Especially disturbing to many was his reference to American solders being "sacrificed for a false sense of military pride." Others were quick to say Kennedy's accusations against commanders and soldiers in the field were out of place and inappropriate. He had certainly failed to recognize the bravery of young soldiers who faithfully fought in one of the war's toughest battles. Kennedy grudgingly acknowledged commanders were following agreed-upon military strategy in a war fully sanctioned by Congress and two previous presidents. He did not mention it was his brother, President John Kennedy, who significantly increased US involvement in Vietnam. Nevertheless, the senator added more weight to calls to reduce US offensive operations and casualties and bring a quick end to the war:

> Kennedy's comments won immediate support from newspapers such as the *Baltimore Sun,* the *New York Post,* the *Boston Globe,* and the *St. Louis Post-Dispatch,* which stressed in their editorials the need to stop the fighting. Other papers-the *Wall Street Journal,* the *New York Times,* and the Hearst syndicate questioned Kennedy's criticism of military tactics but agreed nonetheless that it was time to lower the level of violence in South Vietnam.[47]

Operation Lamar Plain Begins. This second major fight by the same 101st Airborne had begun on 15 May, just five days after the 10 May start of the ten-day battle on Hamburger Hill still being bitterly fought on Hill 937's steep mountain slopes. *Operation Lamar Plain* was located 100 miles to the south near Tam Ky, capital of Quang Tin Province. This was out of the 101st normal area of operations and in that of the American Division. Led by the 101st Airborne Division's 1st Brigade, the US force included two 101st infantry battalions (the 1-501st and 1-502nd) and a third infantry battalion (the 1-46th) from the American's 196th Infantry Brigade. MACV had summoned the 1st Brigade, long known as "the Fire Brigade," to respond to a tactical emergency declared by the American Division. The brigade's mission was to find and destroy elements of the 2nd North Vietnamese Army (NVA) Division threatening Tam Ky, US firebases, and South Vietnamese Army camps. They arrived with combat troops on the ground within 24 hours of being called. The 1st Brigade brought a full array of military support by air and sea. Included were tactical air; ground and air artillery; attack helicopters and scouts; medical units; combat engineers; and a full complement of logistics units. By all measures, *Lamar Plain* was another large (3,000 soldier-strong), multi-battalion, offensive operation by the same 101st Airborne Division already fighting at Hamburger Hill. This second intense fight would last longer and have heavy casualties.

Lamar Plain Not Covered by the Media. Extensive media coverage of Hamburger Hill continued until 7 June when *Operation Lamar Plain* ended. *Lamar Plain's* heaviest fighting occurred during its first few weeks and decreased significantly after 10 June. This helped keep it out of the media's spotlight and out of view of the American public. More important, Nixon's vocal political adversaries, including the growing anti-war movement, knew nothing about the battle or its casualties. For Nixon, keeping the battle undisclosed was exceptionally helpful for the implementation of the new administration's plans. *Lamar Plain* would have given the media an attractive follow-on story to Hamburger Hill. One can only imagine the firestorm Nixon's adversaries would have made of the high casualties of the two operations together. But media attention on Hamburger Hill was not the only reason *Lamar Plain* did not receive media attention.

Media's Focus on Other Events. Two other significant events garnered media attention at the same time as *Lamar Plain*'s most intense combat. On 21 May, the very day of the fiercest 101st fighting near Tam Ky, a surprise White House press release was released. President Nixon will go to Midway Island on 8 June to confer with South Vietnam President Thieu. Feverish speculation about what might happen quickly eclipsed even Hamburger Hill.[48] Rumors and speculation began about what major developments were in the works. Media coverage further intensified as Nixon and Thieu met. Soon, Nixon's momentous announcement of the first US combat troop withdrawals from Vietnam blanketed all other news. For weeks, the media was preoccupied with what units would be first to go and the effects on both South Vietnamese combat operations and the Paris peace talks. *Lamar Plain* stayed well out of the news.

A second major event from 23 June to 2 July was the central highlands battle of Ben Het near Dak To along the South Vietnam border with Laos and Cambodia. Fought just before the first US troop withdrawal in August, North Vietnam radio broadcasts claimed Ben Het would be another Dien Bien Phu, the final 7 May 1954 French defeat in Vietnam. The battle was closely watched in Vietnam and Washington DC as a first test of Nixon's Vietnamization policy. A US Special Forces camp at Ben Het was attacked by 6,000 to 7,000 NVA soldiers. Over-matched, the camp had just two US-led irregular forces battalions made up of Montagnard tribesmen, a US artillery battery, and standby US airpower. A South Vietnamese Army commander led a seven-battalion force to reinforce and save the beleaguered camp. There were friendly losses of 200 KIA (the majority South Vietnamese, some US many from the artillery battery) and heavy NVA losses of over 1,700 dead. Because this was such a show that Vietnamization was working, Deputy MACV Commander General William B. Rosson personally briefed reporters on the "exceedingly favorable" results of the battle.[49]

Media Battle Fatigue Is a Factor. By late 1968, the US media in Vietnam had begun to experience "journalist battle fatigue" and were eager to turn their attention from ground combat operations to other matters.

> After the November 1968 bombing halt and the beginning of the negotiations, the attention of television news began to point away from combat in South Vietnam and toward subjects that explored the implications of an American disengagement.[50]

Both television and print media were cutting back on ground combat coverage. Clearly, Hamburger Hill with its extensive media coverage was a singular major exception and likely because of expectations resulting from Nixon's election. In any case, many veteran journalists had seen or at least reported on enough ground combat to last a lifetime. They were not on the lookout for more ground combat stories. Close-up coverage of young, courageous soldiers fighting lacked the emphasis of earlier years as the war has become much less popular in the US. War protesters were now portraying all soldiers as "baby killers" and "village burners," a grossly exaggerated, false charge still resented by Vietnam veterans today.

Media Controls at MACV Headquarters. The media's lack of attention to *Operation Lamar Plain* was not just a matter of the higher priority of other events or lack of attention by the media. General Abrams, a wise and astute general, was well aware of the political consequences of Hamburger Hill's casualties in the US. He was also quite attuned to how a second media frenzy might take place over *Lamar Plain's* casualties or any other battle for that matter. He knew the political consequences that might follow would certainly undermine US plans to end the war, lead to more anti-war opposition, and further harm American public support of the war. All those consequences could result in higher US casualties in the long run or bring about a dishonorable end to the war. These were consequences he could not ignore.

MACV Efforts to Keep Lamar Plain Undisclosed. Ever since the previously mentioned secret Operation *Menu* was publicly disclosed, General Abrams and his chief information officer at MACV headquarters had imposed strict procedures to limit media access to combat operations. Hamburger Hill is an obvious breakdown. Given General Abrams' understanding of the strategic political and military consequence of battlefield information, the following information is strong evidence MACV deliberately kept *Operation Lamar Plain* undisclosed. In the following paragraphs is a review of what extant MACV and other documents revealed.

MACV's Office of Information Delays and Sanitizes Press Releases. Every MACV monthly summary of significant combat activities for May, June, July, and August 1969 was delayed until two weeks after *Lamar Plain's* end date, 13 August 1969. Each release cover letter was dated 1 October and had the same wording: "This release has been prepared to present a review of significant events occurring in this command during (insert month) 1969." In addition to being delayed, none of the MACV monthly summaries identified *Operation Lamar Plain* by name and in each release, operational details are missing or vague concerning units involved, locations, and casualties. (Copies of each MACV press release were reviewed during research for this book.)

US Combat Operations Are No Longer Identified by Name. The Joint Chiefs of Staff were critical of MACV's failure to promote Vietnamization and the contribution of South Vietnamese forces in the Hamburger Hill and Ben Het battles in the summer of 1969. There was growing concern in official US channels that South Vietnam's role was understated to the detriment of upcoming US troop withdrawals and continuing Vietnamization efforts. Once made aware of this, General Abrams personally instructed his MACV Chief of Information "to play down the role of US forces in large operations." A quiet revision of MACV policy was made. Names of US operations in progress were no longer released. Briefers were "merely to state that fighting has occurred at such and such a place so many miles from Saigon or some other large city."[51]

Limited Media Coverage of Lamar Plain. Research of newspaper archives found only two short print articles announcing the start of *Lamar Plain.* One is in *The New York Times (NYT)* and the other in *The Stars and Stripes-Pacific Edition.* Neither article was on the front page. The *NYT* article does not mention *Lamar Plain* by name. It is from an Associated Press release, so likely other similar versions of the story were printed, though none were found. The *NYT* article on page 3 was dated 27 May, 12 days after *Lamar Plain* began. Friendly and enemy battle casualties in the article are not accurate, being much understated. The article says, "news of the two operations … had been held until now for security reasons." The comment suggested there was nothing new to see here, this was old news.

A photo of a 101st soldier sitting on Hamburger Hill overlooking the A Shau Valley accompanies the *NYT* article. Anecdotally, families of 101st soldiers killed or wounded in *Lamar Plain* often initially thought their loved ones were casualties of Hamburger Hill. As far as they knew, the 101st was engaged in only one battle. The portion of the *NYT* article covering *Lamar Plain* is printed here:

Two New Offensives Under Way in Vietnam. SAIGON, South Vietnam, Tuesday, May 27 (AP) – The United States Command disclosed two new offensives yesterday and said they were directed at eliminating the enemy in South Vietnam's northern provinces and destroying enemy installations there.

The command said that news of the two operations, one eighteen days old and the other eleven days, had been withheld until now for security reasons. It said 142 North Vietnamese had been killed in the drives.… One of the two new offensives has accounted for most of the action since it was launched by the United States 101st Airborne May 16 in foothills 45 miles south of Da Nang. The command said that 113 North Vietnamese and 26 Americans had been killed and 102 Americans wounded.

The offensive was designed to ease pressure on the key provincial capital of Tam Ky where there has been sharp fighting in recent weeks. …[52]

Clearly, information about the start of *Lamar Plain* did slip through MACV's strict media controls. But MACV recovered. These were apparently the last news articles describing the operation. After 27 May, news was limited to only vague, mostly indirect, and incomplete references to *Lamar Plain,* which was never again mentioned by name.

Major General Melvin Zais' Promotion and New Command. Though not a factor in deciding to keep *Lamar Plain* undisclosed, on a personal level another negative news story about 101st high casualties could have adversely affected Major General Melvin Zais. This outstanding, departing commanding general of the 101st Airborne

Division had already been unfairly criticized publicly for Hamburger Hill by opponents of the war. Zais had successfully led the Screaming Eagles since July 1968. He gave up command of the division on 28 May as planned, just after the Hamburger Hill battle ended. Already slated for promotion to lieutenant general, he had been selected to command the XXIV Corps in Vietnam, 1969–1970.

Though only speculation, had the high casualties of *Lamar Plain* been disclosed, Zais' promotion, which required approval of Congress, may have been unjustly delayed by Nixon's political opponents. Worse, Nixon may have been forced to withdraw his support for one of the US Army's top generals. Fortunately, General Zais was promoted and reassigned without protest and continued to serve the nation with distinction. At the end of every general officer command tour in Vietnam, they submitted a summary of their command called a Senior Officer Debriefing Report. A review of the report by MG Zais dated 28 May 1969 to Commanding General, US Army Vietnam shows that he listed and briefly described 19 different operations by name and date that had been started or completed during his command tenure. *Operation Lamar Plain*, which began two weeks before he completed his command, is not listed nor mentioned.[53] General Zais was later promoted to the rank of four-star general in 1973. He retired 31 May 1976 and died 5 May 1981 at Beaufort, South Carolina, after a long and distinguished career.

A check of the 11 May 1970 debriefing report by MG John M. Wright Jr., who succeeded MG Zais, found a brief mention of *Operation Lamar Plain* without details in his report. This entry is made under *Operation Kentucky Jumper.*

> The scope of the operation changed on 15 May, when the lst Brigade headquarters, two infantry battalions, and supporting units moved to Tam Ky and initiated Operation LAMAR PLAIN under the operational control of the Americal Division.[54]

Lamar Plain is Missing from Most Vietnam War Histories. After the war, formal official US military histories of the Vietnam War continued to omit mention of *Lamar Plain*. For example, *The Joint Chiefs of Staff and the War in Vietnam, 1969–1970*, says plainly, "Except for the Hamburger Hill and Ben Het battles, enemy activity dropped to a low level following the May high point." No mention of *Lamar Plain* is made in any of the US Army Center of Military History publications referenced in this appendix or my bibliography. The reason is clear. MACV did not disclose it, the media did not report it, and Nixon's political adversaries did not hear of it. Neither did the American people. It is as if the operation and fighting never happened. As a result, one of the last large-scale battles of the Vietnam War fought by the 101st Airborne Division in 1969 remains largely unknown.

Battle Records and Eyewitnesses Tell the Real Story. There are several extant battle records that detail *Operation Lamar Plain* results, including *The Americal Division Operational Report for Quarterly Period Ending 31 October 1969*

(RCS-CSFOR-6S) dated 10 November 1969. The report states under the title "Terminated Operation":

> *Operation Lamar Plain*, initiated on 16 May 1969 with 1-501 and 1-502 Infantry Battalions of the 1st Brigade, 101st Airborne Division (AM) and 1-46 Infantry Battalion of the 196th Infantry Brigade, terminated on 13 August 1969 having successfully relieved the pressure on the GVN population center of Tam Ky and New Hau Due by eliminating the forces of the 2nd NVA Division and their VC counterparts who had previously been operating in Base Area 117. In the first 13 days of the reporting period, three battalions concluded the third phase of Operation Lamer Plain, a large scale combat operation in the Song Tram Valley initiated with combat air assaults into the area after a series of Arc light strikes, and began redeploying from the area. In the last days of *Operation Lamar Plain* allied forces met little enemy resistance and were able to successfully conclude the operation with negative significant incidents.

- Results for *Operation Lamar Plain* during the reporting period are as follows: 1 July–13 August 1969: US: 6 KIA, 23 WIA. ENEMY: 19 NVA and 32 VC KIA, 17 Detained, 1 VC POW
- Total results for *Operation Lamar Plain* since its inception are as follows:15 May–13 August 1969: US: 105 KIA, 333 WIA. ENEMY: 346 NVA and 178 VC KIA, 422 Detained (includes POWs). [These casualties were later updated and revised, but establish that US casualties were indeed known to be significant in the first six weeks of the operation.]

1st Brigade 101st Airborne Battle Records. The official, detailed *Lamar Plain* battle records of the 1st Brigade and its three battalions were used extensively in writing *Courage Under Fire.* See the list in the bibliography. Fortunately, they are preserved and accessible in archives and online sites available to the public and I was able to obtain copies. The battle records along with eyewitness accounts of 101st soldiers who fought in *Lamar Plain* tell a far different story than was reported in MACV monthly summaries and the two short media articles. What follows is a brief extract of US casualties during the first 28 days (15 May to 13 June) of *Lamar Plain's* heaviest fighting taken from 1st Brigade's final after action report dated 15 September 1969.

Eighty-five percent of 1st Brigade casualties occurred in the first 28 days. An additional 15% of casualties occurred over the next 60 days until the operation's end on 13 August 1969. If the information in the 1st Brigade's after action report had been disclosed to the media, there is little doubt the news stories would have been unhappy, front-page news in the US.

Battle Action 15–31 May 1969. Total US Casualties 39 KIA and 93 WIA:

18 May "sharp clashes," 7 KIA including a company commander, 7 WIA; 20 May "enemy continued attacks," 2 KIA, 5 WIA; 21 May "heavy contact," 12 KIA, 46 WIA; 22 May "enemy activity continued," 3 KIA, 10 WIA (in addition a UH-1 medevac was shot down with a crew of three lost and 12 US MIA were recovered as US KIA from Operation Frederick Hill); 23 May "contact continued," 3 KIA, 8 WIA; 24–26 May "sporadic action continued" 4 KIA, 14 WIA; 31 May "action flared," 2 KIA, 3 WIA.

Battle Action 1–13 June 1969. Total US Casualties 38 KIA, 1 MIA, 109 WIA:

2–3 June "activity increased" and "extremely bitter fighting," 5 KIA, 7 WIA; 4 June, "action increased sharply" 2 KIA, 9 WIA (in addition a HU1H was hit and crashed killing all 5 on board); **5 June** "significant contact continued," 4 KIA, 1 MIA, and 1 WIA; **6 June** "activity increased throughout the area of operations," 2 WIA; **7 June** "bitter fighting continued, 7 KIA, 18 WIA; **8 June** "fighting continued into the fifth day," 1 KIA, 13 WIA; **9 June** "heavy fighting continued broke out in the area of Hill 376," 10 KIA, 19 WIA; **10 June** "activity slackened," 8 WIA; **13 June** "enemy resorted to attacks by fire" 4 KIA, 32 WIA.

A Final Word. This appendix and my book, *Courage Under Fire*, are only a small part of the untold story of the 101st Airborne Division's *Operation Lamar Plain* at Tam Ky. Over 50 years have passed since the Battle of Tam Ky was fought. Many of the young 101st soldiers are now in their seventies and older as of this writing. Of those who survived the fighting, large numbers were wounded. Many now suffer serious illnesses from Agent Orange. PTSD continues for some. Old age is taking its toll on all. A growing number have already died. Hopefully, before more of those who fought valiantly with the 101st Airborne at Tam Ky pass off the scene, their story will no longer be forgotten, but finally and fully told.

APPENDIX 2

The Enemy at Tam Ky

Extract from *1st Brigade, 101st Airborne Division, Operation Lamar Plain After Action Report,* dated 15 September 1969. Intelligence Enclosure 1, page 35.

"Description of Enemy Activities During the Operation: Initially, *Operation Lamar Plain* was characterized by heavy contact with the enemy conducting a sustained offensive operation against LZ Professional. The enemy was well trained, well supplied, and, as a result of previous successful operations in the area, highly motivated. The extent of his offensive capabilities was indicated by the large number of ground to air contact reported during the early stages of the operation. Ordnance encountered included .51 cal, 75 mm Recoilless Rifles, 82 mm and 60 mm mortars, .30 cal and numerous automatic small arms. *Following contact with the 1st Bn, 501st Inf. near Hill 376 (Ban Quan, BT2012) during the early part of June in which they (the enemy) took heavy casualties, the enemy began to conduct defensive operations.* [Italics added for emphasis.]

Confrontation with friendly forces was made only [should read "often"] from heavily fortified defensive positions normally consisting of mutually supporting concrete bunkers with 2–3 ft of overhead cover reinforced by numerous fighting positions and spider holes connected in a tunnel network. The enemy suffered heavy losses due to artillery, air strikes, aerial rocket artillery, causing him to disperse into small groups which avoided contact with friendly forces except when they could be assured success.

Throughout the operation, the enemy withdrew to the southeast, southwest, and west in order to reorganize, resupply and retrain. Confrontation with US forces, especially in large numbers, was avoided unless the enemy was numerically superior and relatively sure of victory. Accordingly, enemy operations changed to small size elements employing harassing and delaying tactics in order to cover their withdrawal. … At the termination of *Operation Lamar Plain* there were indications a new enemy offensive was being prepared, *although no significant incident occurred in the 1st Brigade area of operations."* [Italics added.]

Enemy Units Identified as Operating in or Near the 1st Brigade Area of Operations During *Operation Lamar Plain*: Primary Combat Elements of the 2nd NVA Division included approximately 7500 enemy soldiers. Units included: the 2nd NVA Regiment (likely reinforced by an anti-aircraft battalion armed with 12.7 mm or .51 cal heavy machine guns). The 3rd NVA Regiment (1st, 2nd, 3rd Battalions; 90th Main Force Battalion; 72nd Local Force Battalion; 74th Main Force Battalion); The 1st Main Force Regiment (40th, 60th, and 90th battalions); the 78th Rocket Battalion; 409th Sapper Battalion; and V-16 Sapper Battalion. Support units included: the GK 37 NVA Transportation Battalion and the GK 38 Medical Battalion. [All enemy units listed did not operate simultaneously in the 1st Brigade, 101st area of operations.]

Other after action reports indicate that elements of the 2nd NVA Regiment were likely located on Hill 376 during the time the 501st Infantry Battalion fought there from 3–12 June. By the end of the operation the strength of the regiment was estimated to be no greater than 520 soldiers and could have been much less. NVA regiments typically had a combat strength of 800–1200 soldiers. Elements of the regiment may have already begun withdrawal from Hill 376 before the 1-501st final engagement on 9 June. In September 1969, the 2nd NVA Division attempted a new offensive in Quant Tin Province, but the weakened division could not sustain combat operations.

Organization for Combat at Tam Ky

THE 101st AIRBORNE DIVISION (AIRMOBILE)

"The Screaming Eagles"

In 1969, the 101st Airborne is commanded by MG Melvin Zais until 28 May 1969 when MG John M. Wright assumes command for the remainder of *Operation Lamar Plain*. However, for *Lamar Plain*, the 101st's 1st Brigade fights under the operational control of the American Division from 15 May to 13 August 1969. The American also changes commanders at about the same time with MG Lloyd B. Ramsey assuming command from MG Charles G. Getty on 1 June 1969.

The 101st has three infantry brigades, a division artillery, aviation group, and support command. Each of these are commanded by a Colonel (O-6). The three infantry brigades are identified by a numerical designation (1st, 2nd, and 3rd Brigades). Colonel Richard Bresnahan is the 1st Brigade Commander from the beginning of *Lamar Plain* and during most of the operation. Frank L. Dietrich assumes command on 28 July 1969. The 1st Brigade deployed to Tam Ky with a "slice" of the division combat support and combat service support units.

THE 101ST HAS THREE INFANTRY BRIGADES

The "Always First" 1st Brigade at Tam Ky

Colonel Bresnahan is a decorated Korean War veteran. He and the 1st Brigade arrive at Tam Ky for *Operation Lamar Plain* with two infantry battalions, the 1-501st and 1-502nd. A third infantry battalion, the 1-46th, is attached to the brigade from the American's 196th Infantry Brigade for the duration of *Lamar Plain*. The Headquarters and Headquarters Company (HHC) and the brigade's combat support and service support units arriving at the start of the operation include: Alpha Battery, 4-77th Aerial Rocket Artillery Battalion; Bravo Troop, 2-17th Cavalry Squadron; Alpha Company, 101st Attack Helicopter Battalion; Charlie

Company, Assault Helicopter Battalion; Alpha Company, 326th Engineer Battalion; Alpha Company, 501st Signal Company; Alpha Company, 326th Medical Battalion; Bravo Company, 601st Maintenance Battalion; and other supply and special purpose units.

THE 101ST HAS TEN INFANTRY BATTALIONS

The 1-501st Infantry Battalion (Geronimo)

There are ten infantry battalions in the 101st. Each is assigned to an infantry brigade. However, infantry battalions may be temporarily attached or "task organized" to any of the three brigade headquarters for combat operations. For example, the 1-501st and 1-502nd are assigned to the 2nd Brigade, but at Tam Ky are attached to and under the operational control of the 1st Brigade.

Battalions in the 101st are commanded by a Lieutenant Colonel (O-5). In addition to ten infantry battalions, the 101st Division Artillery has six battalions of artillery and one separate artillery battery. The 101st Aviation Group has four aviation battalions and the Division Support Command has six battalions (transportation, engineer, medical, maintenance, signal, supply) and several companies and detachments with special functions.

LTC Raymond Singer is the battalion commander of 1st Battalion, 501st Infantry at Tam Ky. He served in WWII reaching the rank of staff sergeant, graduated from West Point in 1950, and served during the Korean War. He took command of the 1-501st on 29 March 1969 just before the battalion deployed to the southern end of the A Shau Valley. The 1-501st has six companies each normally commanded by a Captain (O-3) with a senior First Sergeant (enlisted grade E-8). The Headquarters and Headquarters Company (HHC) includes the battalion's command group, battalion staff, and administrative, medical, maintenance, transportation, and supply units.

Each 101st infantry battalion has four infantry (or rifle) companies each designated by a phonetic alphabet letter (Alpha, Bravo, Charlie, and Delta Company). Each infantry company has an artillery forward observer lieutenant attached to the company from one of the artillery battalions. In May 1969, according to the 1-501st after action report for *Lamar Plain*, the assigned strength of the battalion was 31 officers, 2 warrant officers, and 731 enlisted for a total of 764 personnel. (Due to R&R leaves, injuries, and casualties actual field strength at times could be far less. Most authorized positions in the platoons and squads were filled by soldiers who were much junior in rank to that authorized. At the end of heavy fighting in June, actual "field strength" of the battalion is almost half of the assigned strength. This is true of the infantry companies, platoons, and squads as well.)

THE 101ST HAS 50 INFANTRY COMPANIES

"Never Quit" Delta Company

Delta Company is commanded by CPT Bobby Begley from 1 January to 31May 1969. He commands the company at Tam Ky from 15 May for the initial two weeks (13–31 May). The company executive officer is 1st Lieutenant John Herschelman. Begley turns the company over to CPT Leland Roy on 1 June 1969. Roy leads the company during its ten-day fight on Hill 376 (3 June to 12 June) and afterwards until 11 September 1969. In May 1969, Delta Company's assigned strength was four officers and 106 enlisted for a total of 110.

Delta Company and every infantry company in the 101st has four platoons (three infantry platoons and one weapons platoon). Each is authorized a Lieutenant Platoon Leader (O-1 or O-2) and Sergeant First Class platoon sergeant (E-7). Each infantry platoon has three infantry squads authorized a squad leader, Staff Sergeant (E-6). Each infantry squad has two fireteams each authorized a fire team leader, Sergeant (E-5). The squad members are Specialists (E-4) and Privates First Class (E-3). In May 1969, each of the three infantry platoons had an assigned strength of approximately 30 soldiers. Infantry squads averaged an assigned strength of 8 to 10 soldiers.

The weapons platoon of 101st infantry companies is authorized a Lieutenant Platoon Leaders (01–02) and a Platoon Sergeant (E-7). The platoon has two sections each led by a Staff Sergeant (E-6). The mortar section has three 81 mm mortar crews and an anti-tank sections with three 90 mm recoilless rifle teams. The squads and teams are authorized a Sergeant (E-5) for each crew or team. Specialists (E-4) and Privates First Class (E-3) make up the crews and teams.

APPENDIX 4

Delta Company Soldiers

CPT Bobby Begley, D Co Commander, 1 Jan–31 May 1969

CPT Leland Roy, D Co Commander, 1 Jun–11 Sep 1969

2LT Paul Wharton, Artillery FO, 25 May–4 Aug 1969

1SG Paul Purcell, First Sergeant

SP4 Ed Medros, Company RTO, Command Net

SP4 Mark Moses, Company RTO, Logistics Net

Photo Not Available

"Doc," Company Medic

Trung, Kit Carson Scout

1LT Richard Boyd, 1st Platoon Leader, WIA 31 May 1969

1LT Ronald Black, 2nd Platoon Leader, WIA 21 May 1969

1LT Ed Sherwood, 3rd Platoon Leader, WIA 2 June 1969

Photo Not Available

Name Withhld, 2nd Platoon Leader, WIA 8 June 1969

Photo Not Available

1LT James Bryant, 3rd Platoon Leader, WIA 10 June 1969

SSG Ronald Sahrle, 1st Platoon Sergant (Acting Platoon Leader)

SFC Pedro Rios, 2nd
Platoon Sergeant, KIA 21
May 1969

SGT Mike Tomaszewski, 2nd
Platoon Squadron Leader,
Action 2nd Platoon Sergeant

SSG Gary Tepner, 3rd
Platoon Sergeant, Battalion
Operations NCO

SGT Jim Littleton, 3rd
Platoon Sergeant, Acting
Platoon Leader

SGT James Parvin, 3rd
Platoon, Squad Leader

SGT Larry Hoffa, 3rd
Platoon, Squad Leader

SP4 John Meade, 3rd
Platoon, Rifleman

PFC Rob Sitek, 3rd
Platoon, Rifleman

PFC Steven Strang, 3rd
Platoon, Machine Gunner

SGT Lyle Stoner, 3rd
Platoon, Rifleman

PFC George Dennis, 2nd
Platoon, RTO

PFC Bill Scott, 2nd
Platoon, RTO/Rifleman

PFC Phil Cravens, 1st
Platoon, Rifleman

PFC Jessie Harris, 2nd
Platoon, Rifleman

SP4 Gerald Winka, Medic 1st
Platoon, WIA 21 May 1969

SP4 Peter Rehbein, 2nd
Platoon, M-60 Gunner

SP4 Bill Stephens, 1st
Platoon, 1st Platoon
Squad Leader

Photo Not Available
SP4 Byron Bennet, 1st
Platoon, WIA RTO

Photo Not Available
PFC John Bishop, 3rd
Platoon, Rifleman

PFC Ken Hornbeck, 2nd
Platoon, Rifleman

Photo Not Availab[le]
PFC Vincent Earle,
1st Platoon, WIA
Rifleman

SGT Ed Flood, 2nd Platoon,
WIA Squad Leader

SP4 Forest Smith, 2nd
Platoon, WIA RTO

PFC Harvey Sullivan, 2nd
Platoon, Rifleman

Photo Not Available
PFC Paul Scouten, 3rd
Platoon, WIA Rifleman

Photo Not Available
SPF Ralph Franklin,
3rd Platoon, M-79
Gunner

Delta Soldiers Killed in Action, 1 March–13 August 1969

SGT John Clark, 1st Platoon, KIA 29 March 1969

SP4 Nickolas Garcia, 2nd Platoon, KIA 22 April 1969

SGT L. C. Carter, 2nd Platoon, KIA 21 May 1969

PFC Michael Hatzell, 1st Platoon, KIA 21 May 1969

PFC Charles Hawkins, 2nd Platoon, KIA 21 May 1969

PFC Edward Hogan, 2nd Platoon, KIA 21 May 1969

SFC Pedro Rios, 2nd Platoon Sergeant, KIA 21 May 1969

PFC James Sanford, 2nd Platoon, KIA 21 May 1969

PFC Philip Pratt, 1st
Platoon, KIA 31 May 1969

PFC Gary Silman, 1st
Platoon, KIA 4 June 1969

PFC Kevin Crowe, 1st
Platoon, KIA 5 June 1969

SP4 William Ayers, 1st
Platoon, KIA 5 June 1969

PFC Larry Mulvey, 1st
Platoon, KIA 5 June 1969

SP4 Robert Ruttle, 1st
Platoon, KIA 5 June 1969

SGT John Horan, 3rd
Platoon, KIA 6 June 1969

SP4 Terry Rada, 3rd
Platoon, KIA 9 June 1969

PFC Robert Sanford, ?
Platoon, KIA 20 July 1969

PFC Steve Larson, Recon
Platoon, KIA 7 June 1969

PFC John Lewis, Recon
Platoon, KIA 7 June 1969

1-501st Medics Killed In Action, 1 March–13 August 1969

SP5 Robert Lyons, Medic, HHC, KIA 4 April 1969

SP4 Paul Ganun, Medic, B Company, KIA 18 May 1969

SP5 Hans Mills, Medic, B Company, KIA 18 May 1969

SP4 Russel Jett, Medic, B Company, KIA 18 May 1969

SP4 Fletcher Nowlin, Medic, C Company, WIA 21 May, died 3 June 1969

SP4 Keith Starnes, Medic, D Company, KIA 21 May 1969

SP4 Roy Gargus, Medic, B Company, KIA 4 June 1969

PFC Christopher Bean, Medic, C Company, KIA 9 June 1969

SP4 Daniel Thurston, Recon Medic, KIA 9 June 1969

SP4 Gary Winkler, Recon Medic, KIA 9 June 1969

This photo was taken of the 1-501st medical platoon's aid station at LZ Sally. Pictured are four medics who survived the fighting at Tam Ky. They are standing behind an engraved stone plaque displaying the names of each of the nine medics killed in action at Tam Ky. Photo from lzsally.com.

Operation Lamar Plain Photos

These are official US Army photos. Larger images may be found in the National Archives at http://www.archives.gov/dc-metro/college-park/photographs-dc.html

2nd Platoon on the move (SP4 Pete Rehbein and SP4 Rob Sitek).

Loading up a Huey (HU-1) for a combat assault.

Resupply landing zones are often difficult.

A point man out front, expecting enemy contact.

A heavy load, extremely hot weather, and harsh terrain.

Finding the enemy means constant combat patrolling.

An M-60 gunner and his gun. He won't leave home without it.

When the enemy opens fire, get down and return fire.

Enemy bunker's back entry. Usually invisible from the front.

A destroyed enemy bunker is searched for enemy bodies.

Ruins of hooches like this often concealed enemy bunkers.

Exhaustion following a day-long firefight in sweltering heat.

Treating the wounded. A box of Cracker Jack from home makes things better.

With security out, soldiers in 1st Platoon take a needed break in a protected position.

Time for a quick meal after weapons cleaning.

Weapons cleaning never ends.

Repositioning and cleaning an 81 mm mortar.

A quick huddle on Hill 376.

SSG Sahrle (center) conferring with platoon members.

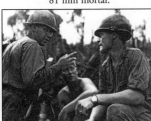

LT Wharton (left), artillery FO, had a key role on Hill 376.

Another critical supply of ammunition, water, and rations.

Unexploded US ordinance can be booby-trapped.

An unidentified soldier has a quiet, reflective moment.

PFC Bill "Scotty" Smith watches for enemy movement.

PTSD and Agent Orange

This appendix is not intended to provide medical advice of any kind. The US Department of Veteran Affairs is constantly updating its website and providing new information to veterans. The information listed here was current as of the time of writing Courage Under Fire. *Please check the appropriate US Department of Veteran Affairs for the latest information.* www.va.gov

Courage Under Fire gives careful and detailed attention to soldiers who were physically killed or wounded in action. This appendix concerns those who served in Vietnam and became war casualties of a different kind: 1) Veterans with Post-Traumatic Stress Disorder (PTSD) and its mental or emotional wounds from combat service; and 2) Veterans who were exposed to powerful herbicides like Agent Orange which later, often long after the war, resulted in a variety of physical infirmities and diseases.

The US Congress previously directed the Department of Veteran Affairs (VA) to conduct two studies concerning Vietnam veteran health issues. In 1983, the National Vietnam Veterans Readjustment Study (NVVRS) was the first study to evaluate the prevalence of PTSD among Vietnam veterans. It determined that as many as 15% of Vietnam veterans had PTSD.

In 2013, VA completed a follow-up study among the participants of the NVVRS, known as the National Vietnam Veterans Longitudinal Study. This study measured the long-term health and mental health of Vietnam veterans and included NVVLS the effect of herbicides on Vietnam veterans. The NVVLS concluded that though the majority of Vietnam theater veterans are both mentally and physically healthy, a significant number are still suffering from PTSD symptoms and other chronic health issues related to their service.[55]

Encountering PTSD in My Writing

In PTSD, the word "disorder" simply means that it can be a disruptive to those who suffer from it. For certain, the word "disorder" does not mean such veterans are dangerous or psychotic. More accurately, PTSD describes those who continue to have disturbing thoughts and feelings that last long after their combat experience. Some may relive the events through flashbacks and nightmares. In some cases, their memories may cause sadness, fear or anger.[56]

While writing *Courage Under Fire*, as I engaged many of the veterans of Delta Company in conversations about their personal combat experiences, it became clear to me that some were still dealing with troubling, unresolved memories over 50 years after the war. Others had no signs of PTSD. I was particularly concerned that as my fellow veterans revisited personal combat experiences, it could be difficult and even upsetting for some of them.

For the most part, my concerns were not realized. In fact, many of my fellow veterans whose shared personal accounts included in the book seemed to benefit from reading it. Some said reading my book helped put their personal memories in a broader, more understandable context. One veteran even said reading a draft of the book was "therapeutic." In other words, reading of his combat experiences so many years later helped him reorder his thoughts about what he had experienced. He began to understand having PTSD symptoms did not mean he was weak or in some way lacked courage in battle. On the contrary, he had performed bravely in combat despite the fears and anxiety he and all others had experienced.

That is the good news for veterans young or old who suffer from PTSD. It can be overcome. The US Department of Veteran Affairs has led the way in effective treatment of PTSD. Veterans who are suffering from PTSD should seek professional care. See the VA website at https://www.ptsd.va.gov/index.asp for further reading and assistance.

Encountering Agent Orange in My Writing

Agent Orange was sprayed extensively in all the areas in which we conducted combat operations. Many young soldiers came home having been exposed to the disease-causing herbicide. For the most part, the disabilities caused by the herbicide did not show up until later in life. A number of Vietnam veterans have died and will die prematurely because of Agent Orange, as the war continues to have its casualties long after it ended.

Practically every single member of Delta Company, 1st Battalion 501st Infantry whom I interviewed for my book and had been in the field for several months or more was believed to be experiencing one or more effects of exposure to Agent Orange. Not all had been validated by VA.

As of this writing, a growing number of diseases are presumptively considered to have been caused by Agent Orange. They include Type II Diabetes, ischemic heart disease, Parkinson's Disease, neuropathy, and a large list of cancers. (Check with VA for the latest information.) The following description of Agent Orange is provided by the US Department of Veteran Affairs:

Agent Orange was a tactical herbicide used by the US military from 1962 to 1975, named for the orange band around the storage barrel. The military sprayed millions of gallons of Agent Orange and other tactical herbicides on trees and vegetation during the Vietnam War. Veterans who may have been exposed to Agent Orange include Veterans who were in Vietnam, the Korean Demilitarized Zone, on Thai Air Force bases, and who flew on or worked on C-123 Aircraft. Several decades later, concerns about the health effects from these chemicals, including dioxin, a byproduct of Agent Orange production, continue. VA offers eligible Veterans a free Agent Orange Registry health exam for possible long-term health problems related to exposure. VA also offers health care, disability compensation, and other benefits to eligible Veterans for certain disease conditions, as well as benefits for children of Vietnam Veterans who have spina bifida. Dependents and survivors may also be eligible for other benefits.[57]

APPENDIX 9

Life After Vietnam

This appendix includes Delta Company soldiers mentioned in Courage Under Fire *who completed combat tours in Vietnam. Last names are in alphabetical order followed by the position they held in combat and a brief summary of their life after Vietnam. Asterisks indicate those now deceased. Not every Delta Company soldier mentioned in the book is included.*

*Bobby Begley. *Company Commander until 1 June 1969.* Retired as a Colonel in the US Army Reserve. Taught at Franklin Military Academy in Richmond Virginia. Died on 18 July 1991 at age 51 of a heart attack and is buried with honors in Arlington National Cemetery. Colonel Begley was married with one daughter.

Ronald Black. *Platoon Leader.* From Newhall, California. Father was a Navy veteran. Ron left active duty after a follow-on assignment with the Army in Germany. He has worked in agriculture for 45 years. With Grimmway Farms in Bakersfield, California, the last 30 years, he is the General Manager for Engineering and Construction. Married for 50 years, Ron has two children, four grandchildren, and two great-grandchildren. Ron has a VA disability and limited use of his left arm due his former wounds.

Richard Boyd. *Platoon Leader.* From Yakima, Washington. Boyd's father was a disabled US Army Air Corps WWII veteran. After Vietnam, Rich had a long career as an industrial designer and automotive journalist. Now semi-retired, he paints western heritage themes and portraits (see www.richboydart.com). Married for over 44 years with two children. Rich lives with his wife in Long Beach, California. He has a 60% VA disability and is a cancer survivor.

Phil Cravens. *Team Leader, Squad Leader.* From Anadarko, Oklahoma. After three months hospitalization from wounds, Phil attended college from 1970 to 1973, returned to the Army served at Fort Carson and Korea. After discharge, he worked as a driller and derrick hand in the oil fields of Oklahoma, then worked for the US Bureau of Reclamation until retirement in 1990. Married for over 53 years with two children. Phil lives in Boise, Idaho. He has a 100% VA disability.

George Dennis. *Rifleman, Platoon Radio-Telephone Operator.* Born in Landsberg Am Lech, Germany, his father was a US Army WWII veteran who continued living in Germany. George was a quality control inspector in electrical, welding, and structural engineering as a General Electric contractor. He attended the Kentucky National Guard Officer Candidate School and was commissioned in 1978 and served four years. Formerly married with one daughter, George retired in Bardstown, Kentucky, and has a 100% VA disability.

Vincent Earley. *Rifleman.* From Keysville, Virginia. Vincent is married with children and grandchildren and is enjoying life serving others. Other family members live close by and he remains active in his church and in good health. He continues to live in Keysville, Virginia.

Edwin Flood. *Team Leader, Squad Leader.* From Brookline, Massachusetts. Ed completed a 30-year Federal law enforcement career. Married for over 44 years with a son and daughter. Ed's son is a US Army Special Forces Captain. His daughter is an intensive care nurse. Ed is retired and lives in Live Oak, Florida. He has a 100% VA disability.

*Ralph C. Franklin. *M-79 Grenadier.* Died 26 November 2006 at age 58. Buried with military honors at Garrison Forest Veterans Cemetery at Ownings Mill, Maryland.

Roger Georgette. *Rifleman.* From Stoneham, Massachusetts. Roger worked for John Hancock in Information Technology for over 35 years. Roger's father was in the D-Day landing on Omaha beach in WWII. Married with two sons and five grandchildren, Roger is retired and lives 12 miles north of Boston.

Jessie Harris. *Rifleman.* From Tuscaloosa, Alabama. Jessie had a long period of hospitalization after returning from Vietnam. He is still employed with the US Post Office Service after 32 years of service. He was formerly married and has three daughters and two sons and five grandchildren. Jessie lives in Westchester, New York.

*John Herschelman. *Company Executive Officer.* After Vietnam, John lived in Port Angeles, Washington. He served in Delta Company as both 2nd Platoon Leader and Company Executive Officer in 1968 and early 1969. John was married for a long number of years and had children and grandchildren. He died peacefully at home on 9 July 2018 due to cancer related to his service in Vietnam.

Tom Higgins. *M-60 Machine Gunner.* From Brooklyn, New York. Worked initially in a technical and sales jobs at IBM and relocated to Atlanta in 1996. After retirement from IBM in 1999, Tom worked in sales with Pitney Bowles until retirement in 2018. Married with four children, four grandchildren. Living in Woodstock, Georgia.

Larry Hoffa. *Squad Leader.* From Stouchsburg, Pennsylvania. Larry received an accounting degree in 1973 and worked for the Internal Revenue Service for several years. In 1985, he became a Certified Public Accountant and established Larry E. Hoffa & Company in Boyertown, PA providing financial, estate, and tax planning. He has been married for over 40 years, has two children and three grandchildren. Larry currently lives in Fleetwood, Pennsylvania and has a 40% VA disability due to his wounds in Vietnam.

Ken Hornbeck. *Rifleman, Platoon Radio-Telephone Operator.* From Hyde Park, New York. Ken has been an active sportsman participating in sky diving, scuba diving, walking the Appalachian Trail, and receiving his private pilot license. His most rewarding life accomplishment is being a loving father to his son. He has a loving relationship with a woman who has brought him much happiness. Ken is retired living in Ironton, Ohio and has a 100% VA disability.

*Stephen Klubock. *Combat Photographer.* Steve's company, Klubock & Associates provided career coaching and resume services. Previously he had several positions in career development and human resources. Steve was married and living in Apopka, Florida, Steve's death in 2019 at age 71 was believed to be related to his exposure to Agent Orange. Steve had a 100% VA disability.

*James Littleton. *Squad Leader, Acting Platoon Leader.* From Wilhite, Louisiana. Father was airborne infantry WWII veteran. Retired after a career as a long-haul truck driver known by his handle "Duster." Jim lived in Horn Lake, Mississippi, where he spent the last years of his life serving his church. He was married with five children, many grandchildren, and great-grandchildren. Jim died 19 October 2018 at age 70 and was buried with military honors at West Tennessee State Veterans Cemetery, Memphis, Tennessee. He had a 100% VA disability and died of a military service-connected illness.

John Meade. *Rifleman. Team Leader.* From Butler, New Jersey. Retired after a career in the HVAC industry. Lives in Jacksonville, Florida with his wife of over 50 years. They have two children and four grandchildren. John has a 100% VA disability from his military service.

Ed Medros. *Company Radio-Telephone Operator.* From Boston, Massachusetts. Worked as a Supplier Engineer for various companies. Married over 50 years with two children and five grandchildren. Retired and living in Portsmouth, New Hampshire.

James Parvin. *Squad Leader.* From Caldwell, Idaho. After two years of college, he completed 26 years with Sherwin Williams Paint, and is married with three children, five grandchildren, and two great-grandchildren. Living in League City, Texas and has a 100% VA Disability.

*Paul C. Purcell. *Company First Sergeant.* From Alexandria, Louisiana. Having completed one tour during the Korean War and two tours in Vietnam, Paul retired from active duty and served for 21 years as a claims supervisor with the State of

Louisiana. Paul was married with five children and nine grandchildren. He died 12 July 2012 at age 77 and is buried with military honors in the Central Louisiana Veterans Cemetery, Leesville, Louisiana.

Peter Rehbein. *M-60 Machine Gunner.* From Chicago, Illinois. Pete worked at S&C Electric Co. (Chicago Il.) for 50 years and is now retired. He has been married for 38 years and has two daughters (both doctors). Pete now lives in Sevierville, Tennessee near the Smokey Mountains.

Leland Roy. *Company Commander from 1 June 1969.* From Evangeline, Louisiana. Leland devoted his entire working life to the military. After retiring from the Army, he taught JROTC two years in Texas' Houston Independent School District and over 18 years in Georgia's Fulton County School District. Retired in 2001, Leland lives with his wife near Orlando, Florida. He has a 100% VA disability.

Ron Sahrle. *Platoon Sergeant, Acting Platoon Leader.* From Wayland, New York. Completed Army service as a Master Sergeant, US Army Reserve. Retired after a management career in boiler manufacturing and instructor with the Army Reserves. Married to his wife of over 50 years with two sons and two daughters and many grandchildren. Living in western Finger Lakes, New York.

Bill (Scotty) Scott. *Rifleman, Platoon Radio-Telephone Operator.* From Coronado, California. Taught tennis in La Jolla, California, from 1978 to 1992. Moved to Montana and built a tennis club in Kalispell, returned to California worked as Athletic Director and Tennis Coach at several high schools in the Monterey Bay area. Married with two sons. Retired in Nellysford, Virginia, Scotty is 100% VA disabled.

Ed Sherwood. *Platoon Leader.* From Atlanta, Georgia. Step-father was WWII, Korea, and Vietnam infantry veteran. Ed left active duty in 1988 as a Lieutenant Colonel due to medical reasons. He taught college business courses, served as new church pastor, and defense contractor. He retired in 2017 due to his daughter's health and to write. Married for over 52 years, with three children, seven grandchildren, and ten great-grandchildren. Ed's son was a US Army combat veteran. Three grandsons are veterans, one still on active duty. Ed lives in Peachtree City, Georgia.

Robert Sitek. *Rifleman, Team Leader.* From Springfield, Massachusetts. Rob was in public service for 32 years and later served as a supervisor in a reform school for troubled youth. Married for over 40 years with three children, four grandchildren, and one great-grand child. Rob lives in Florida and has a 100% VA disability.

Forest (Smitty) Smith. *Platoon Radio-Telephone Operator.* From Peoria, Illinois. Employed by Caterpillar Tractor in Peoria, Illinois, for 39 years. Formerly married with two children and nine grandchildren. His son is an Army veteran. Four grandchildren serve in the military. Forest lives in Germantown, Illinois and has a 90% disability.

Bill Stephens. *Team Leader, Squad Leader.* From Princeton, Kentucky. Prior to Vietnam, Bill worked on a team building the heart-lung machine for the first attempted heart transplant at Stanford University in Palo Alto, California. After Vietnam, he worked in the chemistry and insurance industry, before changing careers and becoming one of the world's top greyhound racing handicappers for 27 years. Bill has been married for over 40 years and has six children and seven grandchildren. He lives in Tuscaloosa, Alabama and has a 100% VA disability.

Lyle Stoner. *Rifleman, Team Leader.* From Minnesota. Lyle is semi-retired after 35 years as a craftsman farrier taking care of horse hooves and shoes. He is formerly married, remarried and has three daughters and one granddaughter. Now living in southeast Wisconsin.

Steve Strand. *Rifleman.* From Sandpoint, Idaho. After some college work, Steve began work as an ironworker apprentice became an ironworker foreman for nearly 40 years. He retired with good health in 2012 and is married with two sons, five grandchildren and two great-grandsons.

Gil Taylor. *Rifleman.* From Taylor, Michigan. After 15 months hospitalization and multiple operations, Gil returned to Michigan and worked for Ford Motor Company. Leaving Ford, Gil attended nursing school on the GI Bill and became a Registered Nurse in 1984. Later he owned two Subway stores. He has three sons from a former marriage and is now retired and remarried living in Grosse Isle, Michigan.

Gary Tepner. *Platoon Sergeant, Battalion Operations NCO.* From San Diego, California. Gary returned to his hometown, pre-military job at Commercial Press, became a partner, and then purchased the company in 1978. He expanded to include customers throughout the US and sold the company in 1999. Married with three children and one grandchild, Gary is retired and lives with his wife of over 55 years in San Diego.

Michael "Big Mike" Tomaszewski. *Squad Leader, Acting Platoon Leader.* From Radom, Illinois. Mike worked as an agronomist for 35 years then retired, went back to work and tried retirement three more times. Finally in March 2020 retired, hopefully for the last time. He has been married for over 50 years with one daughter. Mike enjoys working on their hobby farm and collecting antique tractors. Mike and his wife continue to live in Radom in southern Illinois.

Paul Wharton. *Artillery Forward Observer.* From Kenmore, New York. Paul's father was a bombardier on a B-29 in WWII. Paul left Army active duty in 1991. For 20 years, he led his own financial planning business. Retiring in 1998 as Army Reserve Colonel, he served in executive positions with Occidental Petroleum, two other corporations, and on the Alabama governor's senior staff. From 2007–2012 as a US contractor and Program Manager, he was responsible for Afghan Army logistical training. He is married with three children. His son is a Squadron Commander in the 101st Airborne Division. Retired and living in Bass Lake, Wisconsin, Paul has a 90% VA disability.

*Gerald Winka. *Platoon Medic.* From Saint Louis, Missouri. Jerry became a pharmacist and owned the Duchesne Pharmacy in Florissant, MO from 1986–1993. Jerry was married and had two children and four grandchildren. He died 20 January 2006 at age 57 as a result of complications from his war wounds and contributing illnesses. Jerry was buried with military honors at Saint Charles Memorial Gardens in Saint Charles, Missouri.

Glossary of Terms and Abbreviations

This glossary is designed to assist readers who have limited knowledge about the US Army or combat operations in the Vietnam War. Many of the definitions are based on their use by the author and how the terms and abbreviations were applied in Vietnam during 1969 combat operations by the 101st Airborne Division. (Due to space limitations many key words and abbreviations were not included.)

Part 1: Abbreviations

1LT	First Lieutenant (Officer Grade O-2)
2LT	Second Lieutenant (Officer Grade O-1)
1SG	First Sergeant (Senior Enlisted Position in a Company, Enlisted Grade E-8)
AAR	After Action Review or After Action Report
AD	Americal Division
AD	Airborne Division (Would be after numeric numbers)
AH	Attack Helicopter
AIR CAV	Air Cavalry
AK	Avtomat Kalashnikov (AK-47 Rifle invented by Mikhail Kalashnikov)
AMBL	Airmobile
AN-PRC	Army Navy – Portable Radio Communications
AO	Area of Operations
AOR	Area of Operational Responsibility
ARA	Aerial Rocket Artillery
ARCOM	Army Commendation Medal
ARVN	Army of the Republic of Viet Nam (aka South Vietnamese Army or SVA)
BDE	Brigade
BN	Battalion
BBT	Booby Traps
BT	Bravo Tango (two-letter military map grid designation system reference)
CA	Combat Assault
CAV	Cavalry (usually refers to air cavalry in this book)

CH	Cargo Helicopter
CIB	Combat Infantryman's Badge
CMH	Center of Military History (for US Army)
CO	Company
COFRAM	Controlled Fragmentation
COL	Colonel (Officer Grade O-6)
CONEX	Container Express
CP	Command Post
CPT	Captain (Officer Grade O-3)
C-Ration	Type C Ration
CSM	Command Sergeant Major (Senior Enlisted Grade E-9)
DMZ	De-Militarized Zone
DIV	Division
DOC	Slang name for medic (doctor)
DSC	Distinguished Service Cross
FAC	Forward Air Controller
FO	Forward Observer
FRAGORD	Fragmentary (or partial) Order
FSB	Fire Support Base
GVN	Government of (South) Vietnam
H	Hour, when used with 24 hour military time
HHC	Headquarters and Headquarters Company
HQ	Headquarters
HU	Helicopter Utility
IN	Infantry
INF	Infantry
INTEL	Intelligence
JCS	Joint Chiefs of Staff
KCS	Kit Carson Scout
KHA	Killed by Hostile Action
KIA	Killed in Action
KM	Kilometer
LBE	Load Bearing Equipment
LRRP	Long Range Reconnaissance Patrol
LOH	Light Observation Helicopter
LT	Lieutenant (Officer Grade 0-1 or 0-2)
LTC	Lieutenant Colonel (Officer Grade O-5)
LZ	Landing Zone
M	Meter
MACV	Military Assistance Command - Vietnam
MAJ	Major (Officer Grade O-4)
MEDEVAC	Medical Evacuation

MI	Military Intelligence
MIA	Missing in Action
MM	Millimeter
MOH	Medal of Honor
MP	Military Police
MSG	Master Sergeant (Senior Enlisted Grade E-8)
NCO	Non-Commissioned Officer
NDP	Night Defensive Position
NHA	Non-Hostile Action
NLF	National Liberation Front
NVA	North Vietnamese Army
OH	Observation Helicopter
OBJ	Objective
OP	Observation Post
OPCON	Operational Control
OPORD	Operations Order
OPN	Operation
PFC	Private First Class (Enlisted Grade E-3)
PLT or PLAT	Platoon
PNCOC	Primary Non-Commissioned Officer Course
POW	Prisoner of War
PTSD	Post-Traumatic Stress Syndrome
PYSOPS	Psychological Operations
PZ	Pick-up Zone
RR	Recoilless Rifle
R&R	Rest and Recuperation
Recon Platoon	Reconnaissance Platoon
RIF	Reconnaissance in Force
RPD	Ruchnoy Pulemyot Degtyaryova (hand-held, machine gun developed by Vasily Degtyaryova)
RPG	Rocket Propelled Grenade
RPM	Rounds Per Minute (Rate of Fire)
RTO	Radio Telephone Operator
S-1	Administration/Personnel Staff Section (at Battalion or Brigade HQ)
S-2	Intelligence Staff Section (at Battalion or Brigade HQ)
S-3	Operations Staff Section (at Battalion or Brigade HQ)
S-4	Supply/Logistics Staff Section (at Battalion or Brigade HQ)
SFC	Sergeant First Class (Senior Enlisted Grade E-7)
SITREP	Situation Report
SGM	Sergeant Major (Senior Enlisted Grade E-9)
SGT	Sergeant (Enlisted Grade E-5)
SIGINT	Signal Intelligence

SP4	Specialist 4th Class (Enlisted Grade E-4)
SQD	Squad
SSG	Staff Sergeant (Enlisted Grade E-6)
SVA	South Vietnamese Army
TF	Task Force
TOC	Tactical Operations Center
TOT	Time on Target (Artillery Fire Mission) or Total (in casualty tables)
UH	Utility Helicopter
US	United States
USAF	US Air Force
USARV	United States Army Vietnam
USARPAC	United States Army Pacific
WIA	Wounded in Action
VA	US Department of Veteran Affairs
VC	Viet Cong
XO	Executive Officer
YC	Yankee Charlie (two-letter military map grid designation system reference)

Part 2: Definitions

After Action Review (AAR) – A review of a combat mission or operation after it is concluded to identify strengths and weaknesses and improve future operations.

After Action Report (AAR) – A summary report prepared by battalions and brigades following completion of a major combat operation. Both the 1-501st and 1st Brigade AARs prepared for *Operation Lamar Plain* are referenced in the bibliography and were used extensively in writing this book.

Agent Orange – A poisonous herbicide containing dioxin used throughout South Vietnam to defoliate enemy sanctuaries and destroy enemy crops. The herbicide has caused serious medical problems for Vietnamese civilians, enemy forces, and US military and allied forces. The name comes from the orange stripe that marked barrels containing the herbicide.

Air Cavalry (Air Cav) – Bravo Troop, 2-17th Cavalry was assigned to the 1st Brigade, 101st Airborne Division in 1969. It provided aerial and ground reconnaissance, fire support for troops in contact, and a ready reaction force for downed aircraft or other emergency type missions. Bravo Troop's Aero-Rifle Platoon was the first unit to be inserted on to Hill 376.

Airmobile – The 101st transitioned from an airborne division to an airmobile division in 1969. The airmobile designation meant the entire division was fully equipped with sufficient helicopters to conduct heliborne (or combat) assaults against enemy forces.

Army of South Vietnam (ARVN) – Formed in 1955, the ARVN surrendered in 1975 to the North Vietnamese Army. After the introduction of US military ground forces in 1965, the US did not give priority to training and equipping ARVN units until the early seventies after the withdrawal of US troops was underway.

A Shau Valley – A strategic valley 40 miles southwest of Hue which was a major base and supply route for both the NVA and VC. *See Chapter 3 for Delta Company's combat operations in the southern end of the valley.*

Area of Operations (AO) – During *Operation Lamar Plain* the 1st Brigade, 101st Airborne Division conducted combat operations in an area that was roughly oval shaped (25 km long and 13 km wide) from Tam Ky on the east, southwest to the village of Tien Phuoc. The 1-501st including Delta Company operated primarily in the eastern portion of the brigade's AO east and north of the Song Bong Mieu River. Hill 376 was the dominant terrain feature in the 1-501st AO.

Battalion (BN) – A 101st airborne or airmobile infantry battalion was made up of four infantry companies, one combat support company (with mortars and a reconnaissance platoon), and a headquarters company that provided staff, logistics, transportation, communications, and medical support to the companies.

Brigade (BDE) – Brigades were the major combat units of an airmobile division. There were three combat brigades in the 101st. The brigades normally had two to four infantry battalions assigned. During combat operations, battalions within a division could be put under the operational control (OPCON) of any of the three brigade headquarters.

Camp Eagle – This base camp located 7 km southeast of Hue was home of the headquarters for the 101st Airborne Division and 1st Brigade.

Camp Evans – This base camp was named after Marine Lance Corporal Paul Evans KIA in 1966 when the Marines occupied the base from 1966 to 1967. From 1969 to 1972, the base was the home of the 3rd Brigade Headquarters of the 101st Airborne Division. It was located 24 km northwest of Hue on Highway 1.

Close Air Support – Air attacks by fixed wing or rotary wing aircraft using bombs, rockets, cannon, and other weapons in close proximity to friendly forces. "Air strikes" is a term typically used to describe close air support by US Air Force, US Navy, or US Marines jet fighters. *See F4 Phantom and A4 Skyhawk under Weapons.*

Combat Infantryman Badge (CIB) – This coveted badge was and still is awarded to infantry soldiers who have served in an infantry unit in combat.

Colonel (COL) – In the 101st Airborne Division, colonels were commanders of brigades, the division artillery, and the support (logistics) command. Colonels also served in division-level staff positions. Today most division staff positions except the Chief of Staff are filled by Lieutenant Colonels. *See Lieutenant Colonel.*

Combat Assault (CA) – In the 101st Airborne Division, a "combat assault" or CA was the term used to describe an offensive action conducted by infantry units using helicopters. The UH-1 Iroquois helicopter affectionately named "Huey" was the primary helicopter which carried soldiers into battle. *Also see Landing Zone (LZ).*

Commander – The senior leader in an infantry company, battalion, and brigade. The division also has a commander referred to as the commanding general. The commander of companies are normally Captains (CPT), battalions are commanded by Lieutenant Colonels (LTC), and brigades are commanded by Colonels (COL).

Company (CO) – An airborne or airmobile infantry company typically has three infantry platoons and one weapons platoon with 81 mm mortars, 7.62 mm M60 machine guns, and 90 mm recoilless rifles. Infantry companies typically had a field strength of a hundred or so soldiers, which could be significant reduced by casualties. *See Platoon and Squad.*

Company Commander – No one was more important than the infantry company commander in combat operations in Vietnam during 1969. He had the capability through his personal leadership and expertise to employ available maneuver units (platoons and squads) and firepower to engage and defeat larger enemy forces. Through his Forward Observer and Radio-Telephone Operators, he had the capability to employ the significant combat power of the division's artillery, attack helicopters, and USAF or Marine close air support in battle. *See Commander.*

Courage – The willingness to persevere in combat by overcoming fear of one's personal safety no matter the danger from the enemy or the difficulty of battlefield conditions.

Captain (CPT) – Captains (pay grade 0-3) in airborne or airmobile infantry units served as company commanders or staff officers at battalion and brigade level.

Danger Close. This term is used in calling in mortar, artillery, and naval gun fire support or close air support by attack helicopters and fixed-wing aircraft to alert those providing the support that friendly troops are in close proximity to the intended enemy target (200 m for artillery, 600 m for jet fighter-bombers.)

Enemy Forces:

North Vietnamese Army (NVA) – The primary combat forces in the Vietnam War in 1969. The NVA infiltrated from and were under the control of North Vietnam. Generally, they were well-trained, well-equipped, and disciplined fighters in infantry operations. In *Operation Lamar Plain*, the 1st Brigade, 101st Airborne Division faced elements of the 2nd NVA Division.

Viet Cong (VC) – The VC were organized into Main Force Units and Irregular Forces. Main Force elements were well-trained and equipped and like the NVA fought major engagements. Irregular VC units were not as well equipped or trained and often provided support to the NVA and VC main force units and typically used harassing attacks, ambushes, and booby-traps.

Fire Support Base (FSB) – FSBs were typically located on mountain tops or other locations where the artillery can provide support to infantry operation within range of the guns. They were normally large enough for an artillery battery or two, a couple of helipads, and defensive fortifications for an infantry company.

Fire Support Base (FSB) Lash – The 1-502nd Infantry Battalion conducted combat operations from this FSB located astride Route 614 (the "Yellow Brick Road"), the main enemy supply route through the A Shau Valley.

Fire Base Support (FSB) Pike – The 1-501st tactical operations center (TOC) was located at FSB Pike during operations in the southern end of the A Shau Valley. Delta and Bravo Company alternated on providing security for FSB Pike or conducting combat operations around Pike. *See Chapter 3.*

Fire Support Base (FSB) Shield – This FSB was opened briefly to serve as a base for short-term combat operations by the 1-501st in the southern A Shau area.

Fire Base Support (FSB) Thor – This was the temporary location of the 1-501st TOC while FSB Pike construction was being completed. Alpha and Charlie Companies alternated providing security and conducting combat operations.

Fire Support Base (FSB) Whip – The temporary location of the 2nd Brigade TOC during *Operations Massachusetts Striker* in the southern A Shau. Bravo Troop, 2-17th Cavalry provided security and conducted combat operations near Whip.

First Sergeant (1SG) – The senior NCO (pay grade E-8) in an infantry company. In Delta Company the 1SG managed the company's rear area including all administrative matters relating to soldiers, supplies, and accountability of weapons and other equipment.

First-Termer – An enlisted or officer soldier on their first term of service with the US Army. Typically, as "first-termer" infantry soldiers in the field approached the end of their tour of duty in Vietnam, they had acquired considerable combat experience. Many first-termers became seasoned combat soldiers after six months in the field.

Forward Air Controller (FAC) – By 1969, a USAF pilot flying a small OV-10 Bronco above battlefields, usually accompanied by an artillery forward observer, played a vital role in directing close air support and integrating artillery fires. They were also able to provide reconnaissance and intelligence on enemy locations or movement.

Forward Observer (FO) – FOs, usually a Second or First Lieutenant. were attached to infantry companies from parent artillery units. Under the direction of the infantry company commander, they provided coordination and control of artillery fires, attack helicopter, and close air support. They were indispensable in providing valuable combat support to infantry.

Friendly Fire Accident or Incident – A regrettable event in which US or allied soldiers are killed or wounded while on a combat operation by US or allied weapons.

Grid Coordinates – Grid coordinates on military maps are typically six digits and are used to identify specific locations to the nearest 100 m. Readers may obtain digital copies of Vietnam maps to follow Delta Company's combat operations. *See Maps.*

Hamburger Hill – *See* Operation Apache Snow.

Hill 376 – A large, flat mountain, 376 m (1,240 ft high), 15 km southwest of Tam Ky. It was the site of a grueling ten-day battle where the 1st Battalion, 501st Infantry fought the decisive battle of *Operation Lamar Plain. See Chapter 16.*

Hue – Hue is the capital of Thua Tien Province and the largest city in the north of South Vietnam or Military Region 1 also known as 1 Corps. In 1968, Hue was the site of one of the largest battles in the Vietnam War. The area immediately east of Hue was called "Eight Click Ville" and was the main area of operations of Delta Company in early 1969. The name was based on the area being approximately 8 km of connected village. A "click" is slang for a kilometer. *See Chapter 2.*

I Corps (or Military Region 4) – South Vietnam was divided into four corps tactical zones. Each zone was occupied by a South Vietnamese Army corps. I Corps was the northernmost region of South Vietnam and was bounded by the Demilitarized Zone (DMZ) in the north marking the border between North and South Vietnam, Laos in the west, the China Sea in the east, and II Corps in the South. The latter generally included the area known as the central highlands. I Corps included the major towns of Hue, Quang Tri, Quang Ngai, Danang, Chu Lai, and Tam Ky. In 1969, all of the combat operations of Delta Company and the 1-501st occurred in I Corps. I Corps had more US battle casualties than any other corps or military region in the Vietnam War (and particularly in 1969).

Infantry Small Unit Tactics – Infantry small unit tactics included the combat operations of squads, platoons, and companies. The most common US small unit tactics were combat patrols, ambushes, ground attacks, combat assaults, and reconnaissance missions. The most common enemy small unit tactics included ambushes, hit-and-run attacks, booby traps, sapper attacks, and reconnaissance.

Junior-Enlisted Soldier – Soldiers in the first five enlisted pay grades (E-1 through E-5) which includes the enlisted ranks of PFC, SP4 (or SP5), and SGT. Privates (E-1) usually do not serve in combat zones.

Kill Radius – The distance defined by the probability of kill (or lethal) for an exploding round or device. A fully exposed soldier standing upright within the kill radius has a 100% probability of being killed by the explosive force, shrapnel (metal fragments), or debris caused by the round or device.

Killed in Action (KIA) – US military members killed as a direct result of hostile action by the enemy. *See WIA and MIA.*

Kilometer (KM) – Military distances are usually measured in kilometers and meters. Military maps are divided into 1 km grid squares. One kilometer is equal to .6 miles. To convert kilometers to miles, multiply the number of kilometers by 1.6 (km × 1.6 = miles). Each kilometer equals 1,000 m. A meter is roughly equal to 1.1 yards (number of meters × 1.1 = number of yards). *See Maps.*

Landing Zone (LZ) – Combat assaults (see definition) always had one or more LZ's designated as the point where combat units would be inserted on the battlefield. If the enemy was encountered on the LZ, it was called a "hot" or "red" LZ. A "cold" or "green" LZ meant there was no enemy contact on landing. *See Pick Up Zone (PZ).*

Lieutenant (LT) – Lieutenants may be a second or first lieutenant (pay grade O-1 or O-2). In infantry units, they typically serve as platoon leaders or company executive officers. They may also serve on battalion staffs.

Lieutenant Colonel (LTC) – Lieutenant Colonel (pay grade O-5) is the rank between Major and Colonel. LTCs were commanders of infantry and other types of battalions in the 101st Airborne Division. They also served in staff positions at brigade and division level.

Log Bird – A logistics helicopter (usually a UH-1 Huey) used to deliver supplies to units at fire support bases or in the field. They frequently doubled up to evacuate soldiers WIA or KIA when medevacs were not available or would not make pickups due to close by enemy forces.

LZ Professional – This Fire Support Base was initially established by and named for the 1-46th Infantry Battalion (The Professionals). 1-501st companies were rotated to pull security on the firebase. The 1-501st TOC and A Battery, 2-320th Artillery was located there during *Operation Lamar Plain*.

LZ Sally – The headquarters for 2nd Brigade 101st Airborne Division and the temporary home and rear area of 1-501st and its six companies in Vietnam during most of 1968 and 1969. Since the battalion was almost always in the field on combat operations, the battalion's companies seldom returned to LZ Sally. Soldiers typically in-processed and out-processed at Sally coming into and going out of Vietnam.

LZ Young – The location of C/2-320 Artillery and a battery from the 2nd ARVN Division during *Operation Lamar Plain*. LZ Young was secured by the 5th ARVN Regiment.

Maps – Military maps used in Vietnam for combat operations were typically 1:50,000 scale. This means 1 cm (.394") on the map equals 0.5 km on the ground. Map grid squares were 1,000 m or 1 km on each side. Digital copies of the maps used in Vietnam are available. See University of Texas under Web References in the Bibliography.

Medics – No position in an infantry unit was more important than the company or platoon medic. The medic's MOS was 91B. Medics were trained in advanced life-saving skills and carried basic medical supplies to treat soldiers WIA. Nine medics were KIA during *Operation Lamar Plain*. Many more were WIA.

Military Occupational Specialty (MOS) – Each officer and enlisted soldier has an MOS. An infantry company had the following for enlisted soldiers: 11B Infantryman (aka 11 Bravo or 11 Bush; 11C, Indirect Fire Infantryman (81 mm and 4.2" mortars); some infantry soldiers had the MOS 11H 90 mm Recoilless Rifle Gunner. MOS 91B Medical Corpsman (medic)were attached to infantry platoons and companies from the medical platoon in the battalion headquarters company. Infantry officers in infantry companies were either MOS 71542 (airborne qualified) or 1542. Officers with Special Forces qualifications were 31542. The Artillery Forward Observer MOS was 13A for officers and 13F for enlisted.

Military Region 4 – *See I Corps.*

Mission – Infantry unit operations were guided and controlled by a brief, but clear mission statement which was part of an operations order. The mission statement includes what the unit is to do or accomplish and its purpose in performing the mission. A complete mission statement includes who, what, when, where, why, and how. For example, "Delta Company conducts a combat assault on 030900JUN69 to grid coordinate BT179145 on Hill 376 to engage and destroy enemy forces by conducting direct ground attacks on enemy positions." *See Operations Order.*

Missing in Action (MIA) – US military members missing in combat with the enemy were designated as missing in action. This term applies when the whereabouts of a soldier on the battlefield cannot be determined. In some cases, soldiers MIA may be captured or later found alive or dead. *See KIA and WIA.*

Napalm – A jelly-like mixture made primarily of gasoline which burns at an extremely high temperature. It was dropped from fighter bombers in large bomb-like cannisters. It was a feared and destructive weapon whose psychological effects were often as strong as its destructive force. International law permits its use against military targets, but forbids its use against civilian populations.

National Liberation Front (NLF) – The Viet Cong senior headquarters in South Vietnam.

Non-Commissioned Officer (NCO) – Non-commissioned officers in an infantry company include the four ranks and pay grades: Sergeant (E-5), Staff Sergeant (E-6), Sergeant First Class (E-7), and First Sergeant (E-8). Typically, NCOs obtain their rank by promotion within the enlisted ranks for meritorious performance and/or time in grade.

Non-Hostile Action (NHA) – Death occurred due to accident while not in actual combat.

Night Defensive Position (NDP) – Typically infantry units in the field in Vietnam would assume a defensive position at dusk which was generally circular providing 360° security against enemy attack.

Objective (OBJ) – Units are assigned objectives in offensive combat operations to identify enemy terrain or positions that are to be captured or held. Often in reconnaissance in force (RIF) operations, objectives are assigned to control the movement of friendly forces seeking the enemy.

Operation – When capitalized, an operation is typically a large scale military action designed with a specific mission in mind (e.g. *Operation Lamar Plain*). When uncapitalized, "operation" or "operations" may refer generally to unnamed combat operations or the combat operations that occur within a named Operation. (Yes, that is confusing to civilian readers.)

Operation Apache Snow – Led by the 3rd Brigade, 101st Airborne Division, this operation began on 10 May 1969 and officially ended 7 June 1969. The area of operations was near the northern portion of the A Shau Valley centered around Hill 957. The heaviest fighting occurred during the first ten days of the operation. It was one of largest and most well-known 101st battles of the Vietnam War. Though a decisive military victory it received much criticism by opponents of the Vietnam War. Named by soldiers who fought there as "Hamburger Hill," the battle was featured in a 1987 movie by the same name and later portrayed negatively in Ken Burns' documentary series, *The Vietnam War.*

Operation Lamar Plain – Led by the 1st Brigade, 101st Airborne, the operation began on 15 May 1969 and officially ended on 13 August 1969. The 1st Brigade was under the operational control of the Americal Division and had an assigned area of operations near Tam Ky. The heaviest fighting occurred during the first 28 days of the operation. It was one of the largest and least known battles of the Vietnam War. Due to its high casualties, the Nixon administration withheld information on this operation from the media, war protestors, and the American public. Information concerning the operation was not declassified until well after the Vietnam War ended. Delta Company, and its parent unit, the 1-501st Infantry Battalion fought in this operation and on 9 June during fighting on Hill 376, had a lead role in the operation's decisive battle. *See Chapter 16.*

Operation Massachusetts Striker – Led by 2nd Brigade, the operation began on 1 March 1969 and officially ended on 8 May 1969. Four battalions, including the 1-501st Infantry Battalion (and Delta Company) participated in operations. The operational area was in and near the southern end of the A Shau Valley and east of the valley. Most of the major enemy forces had withdrawn prior to the arrival of the brigade, but the operation was a major success in that it found and destroyed significant amounts of enemy supplies which were being stockpiled for offensive operations. *See Chapter 3.*

Operational Area – The assigned area of a company, battalion, or brigade in which combat operations were conducted. Alternate term "Operations Area." *See also Area of Operations.*

Operational Control (OPCON) – Any one Army unit may be placed under the operational control of another unit. During *Lamar Plain*, the 1st Brigade of the 101st Airborne Division was OPCON to the Americal Division. The Americal's 1-46th Infantry Battalion was OPCON to the 1st Brigade of the 101st. This is typically done to efficiently use available combat units.

Operations Order (OPORD) – Typically OPORDs were used to give a new mission to an infantry unit. The order has a standard format that gives the Situation (friendly and enemy situation), the Mission (what the unit is to do), Execution (concept of operation including coordinating instructions), Service Support (supply, transportation, medical and other administrative matters), and Command and Signal (chain of command and communications). Written orders were usually given at the start of a major operation and then follow on orders were given orally or in a brief written form called a fragmentary (or frag) order. Warning orders were short orders giving advance notice to units to prepare for an upcoming new mission. *See Mission.*

Pick-up Zone (PZ) – When units were moved by helicopters or fixed wing aircraft, the pick-up point was known as the PZ. As in the case of landing zones, for anyone unit move there may be multiple PZs.

Platoon (PLT or PLAT) – During 1969, in the 101st Airborne Division there were three infantry platoons and a weapons platoon in an infantry company. The three infantry platoons each had three infantry squads. Each squad was authorized a Staff Sergeant squad leader and ten soldiers. Typically, they were led by Sergeants, one grade lower, and had about eight soldiers assigned and in the field (before casualties). Infantry squads were further divided into fire teams each led by another junior sergeant or more often a Specialist or experienced Private First Class. Platoons carried one M-60 machine gun and one M-79 grenadier. The infantry platoon was led by a lieutenant platoon leader with a platoon sergeant as second in the chain of command. Each had a radio-telephone operator (RTO) who carried a AN/PRC-25 radio. A medic was normally attached to each platoon if available. The weapons platoon was equipped with three 81 mm mortars and two 90 mm recoilless rifles. *See Company.*

Platoon Leader – Typically infantry platoon leaders are second or first lieutenants. They are the lowest level of officer combat leaders in an infantry company. They lead by personal example and are up front with their soldiers during engagement with the enemy. In the absence of officers due to casualties or other causes, NCOs in the platoon lead the platoon.

Platoon Sergeant – Platoon sergeants with the rank of Sergeant First Class (SFC) are typically the most experienced infantry soldier in the infantry platoon. They serve under the platoon leader and may act as platoon leader if the position is vacant. In 1969, infantry platoon sergeants in the 1-501st Infantry were often junior NCOs (Staff Sergeants and even Sergeants).

Point Man – An experienced soldier who walks out in front ("on point") of an infantry squad, platoon, or patrol. He has primary responsibility for providing frontal security by detecting the enemy's presence, booby traps, or other hazardous situations. Point men are usually skilled navigators and are closely followed by a "slack man" who provides additional security for the point man.

Post-Traumatic Stress Disorder (PTSD) – A mental and emotional condition of persistent, continuing stress incurred through severe psychological trauma. PTSD may occur as a result of battle or from the other near death experiences which induce significant and continuing anxiety or fear. *See Appendix 8.*

Primary Non-Commissioned Officer's Course (PNCOC) – This course at the US Army Infantry School was instrumental in producing junior NCOs to serve in infantry units in Vietnam due to the shortage of experienced NCOs. On the whole, they performed exceedingly well often serving in positions well above their rank of Sergeant or Staff Sergeant.

Private First Class (PFC) – PFCs (pay grade E-3) are normally riflemen or other members of an infantry squad.

Prisoner of War (POW) – An enemy of friendly soldier captured in battle. The Geneva Convention prescribes international laws for the treatment and behavior of prisoners of war. North Vietnam did not sign the Geneva Convention and did not consider they were bound by it.

Quang Tin Province – The province was the scene of heavy fighting in 1968 and 1969. It was merged into Quang Nam Province in 1976. Tam Ky, the former provincial capital of Quang Tin Province is now the capital of Quang Nam. *See Tam Ky.*

Radio-Telephone Operator (RTO) – RTOs had a vital role at the company and platoon level in an infantry company. They were usually experienced combat soldiers who had a basic understanding of infantry operations and could communicate clearly during enemy contact. Most carried the PRC-25, the most prevalent field radio in Vietnam. Typically, there were four RTOs at company level. One RTO was responsible for the company command radio net which included the company's platoons. A second RTO carried the radio for the battalion command net which communicated with the battalion tactical operations center (TOC). The RTO on the battalion net typically had a PRC-77 radio (an improvement on the PRC-25) and also had a KY-38 secure voice encryption device. The latter device was about the same weight and size as the PRC-77 or PRC-25 doubling the weight of the RTO's communication equipment. The KY-38 was difficult to use and was sometimes carried by a soldier other than the RTO. A third RTO operated on the battalion logistics radio net and was responsible for supplies, medevacs, and administrative radio traffic. The fourth RTO supported the artillery forward observer and operated on the battalion's fire direction net. In an infantry platoon, there were two RTOs, one for the platoon leader and one for the platoon sergeant. On occasion, squads may be assigned the PRC-25 when operating independently on a combat patrol or ambush.

Recon – The act of reconnaissance or shorthand for Reconnaissance Platoon.

Reconnaissance – Typically, a reconnaissance may be done by air or ground to scout out an area of operations. The intent of reconnaissance is to gain information on the enemy or terrain where the enemy or friendly units may be operating or plan to operate.

Reconnaissance in Force – A combat mission assigned to infantry units in which the intention is to locate and engage enemy forces. Previously such missions were called, "search and destroy" missions, but that term was dropped for political reasons.

Rest and Recuperation (R&R) – Each soldier serving a 12-month Vietnam tour was allowed a five or seven day R&R tour to various cities outside of Vietnam. Sydney Australia and Hawaii were the furthest away with Hawaii the most popular destination for married soldiers.

Sergeant First Class (SFC) – Platoon sergeants in infantry platoons are authorized the SFC rank (pay grade E-7). Most infantry companies in 1969 were short SFCs. When available, they were typically the most experienced combat leaders in a platoon. *See Platoon Sergeant.*

Sergeant (SGT) – The lowest non-commissioned officer rank (pay grade E-5) in an infantry company. They led an infantry fire team. Infantry squads usually had two fire teams. During *Operation Lamar Plain*, in the absence of more senior sergeants, they led squads, or served as acting platoon sergeants or even platoon leaders. *See Squad Leader.*

Situation Report (SITREP) – A report usually made on a periodic basis by subordinate units to their higher headquarters. SITREPs may also be called in as needed or required to report on combat actions or other battlefield events, activities, or circumstances.

Specialist Fourth Class (SP4) – A rank (paygrade E-4) between PFC and SGT, designating a soldier who has become proficient in his military occupational specialty (MOS).

Squad (SQD) – There are typically three infantry squads in an infantry platoon. An infantry squad typically is authorized ten soldiers assigned, but due to casualties, leaves, sickness, or other assigned duties most infantry squads in the field averaged six to eight infantry soldiers. Infantry squads are authorized a Staff Sergeant (E-6) squad leader, but often were led by Sergeants (E-5), the most junior NCO rank. *See Squad Leader and Platoon.*

Squad Leader – Squad leaders in infantry platoons are the leaders who have the closest relationship with squad members and have the most influence on the squad's effectiveness in combat. *See Squad.*

Staff Journal – Staff journals are typically prepared at the Battalion or Brigade TOC by operations sergeants. The journals are a record of times, events, situation reports, locations, orders, enemy contact, or any other significant matter pertinent to combat operations. A new journal is prepared for each 24-hour day. The 1-501st daily staff journals have been preserved in the National Archives and were used extensively in writing this book.

Staff Sergeant (SSG) – The rank (paygrade E-6) immediately above SGT. SSG's typically lead infantry squads. They may be called upon to fill platoon sergeant or even platoon leader positions temporarily.

Tactical Operations Center (TOC) – The TOC is the command post of a battalion or brigade. Officers and NCOs from the brigade or battalion staff operate the TOC. Typically, the TOC is managed by the S-3 Operations Officer, who at battalion level is usually a major. The Battalion TOC maintained communications with the battalion's companies and with the brigade TOC. Battle reports and situation reports from the companies came into the TOC and the TOC maintained an updated status of combat operations and kept the brigade TOC informed of all developments.

Tam Ky – The coastal capital of Quang Tin Province. The 2nd NVA Division attempted to capture Tam Ky, but failed due to the timely arrival of the 101st Airborne Division's 1st Brigade on 15 May 1969. *See Quang Tin Province.*

Terrain – Like weather, terrain has a major influence on combat and must always be considered in planning and conducting operations. Though soldiers are required to operate in all types of terrain (e.g. coastal areas, swamps, built up areas, and mountains), each one presents specific challenges. In Vietnam, familiarity with the terrain in battle often benefited the enemy more than friendly units.

Time-on-Target (TOT) – An artillery fire mission using massed fires of several artillery batteries in which the rounds arrive at or near the same time on the target.

Weapons, US and Enemy: includes US Weapons and Enemy Weapons

US WEAPONS:

A1 Skyraider – Single-seat, propeller-driven, all-services attack aircraft. Though it had a maximum speed of 320 mph, it could fly low and slow loitering over battlefields. Its heavily armored cockpit and heavy payload of armaments made the A1 an ideal close support asset. It was armed with four 20 mm wing-mounted cannons and a max bomb load of 8,000 lbs. mounted to 14 wing hard points. A total of 144 pilots and 266 planes were lost during the Vietnam War.

A4 Skyhawk – A single-seat, subsonic (670 mph), carrier-based attack aircraft. The delta-winged, single turbojet-powered, jet-carried sidewinder missiles for self-defense along with two 20 mm cannons and wing hard points for a max bomb load of 10,000 lbs.

AH-1G HueyCobra – The name was later shortened to "Cobra."The US Army's AH designation stands for "attack helicopter." It entered service in Vietnam in June 1967. Arming of the Cobra was flexible. Two chin or nose turrets held a 7.62 mini gun with 8,000 rounds in one, while the other held a 40 mm grenade launcher with 400 rounds. Four rocket pods with nineteen 70 mm Mark 40 rockets each could be mounted under the wings.

F4-Phantom – A US Air Force, Navy, or Marine two-seat, twin-engine, long-range, supersonic jet interceptor and fighter bomber. When used in close air support for ground forces, it was typically equipped with 500 lb. explosive bombs, napalm and the 20 mm M61 Vulcan cannon with a rate of fire of 6,000 rounds per minute

M2 60 mm Mortar – Smoothbore, muzzle-loading indirect fire weapon. Combined weight of 42 lbs. for tube, bi-pod, and base plate. Max range of 3,490 m (2.17 mi), blast radius of 20–25 m. H/E (high explosive) round weight: 3lbs.

M16A1 Rifle – The basic infantry rifle adapted from the Armalite AR-15 for the United States military. The M16A1 is a shoulder-fired, gas-operated, light-weight rifle that uses a 20-round box magazine. Muzzle velocity is 3150 FPS with a maximum effective range of 400 m. It could be fired on semi-automatic or automatic fire using a selector switch.

M18 Claymore Mine – A directional anti-personnel mine with an effective range of 50 m, containing 700 ball bearing-like, steel spheres backed with 1.5 lbs. of C-4 explosives. These mines were especially valuable in ambushes and night defensive positions. An infantry platoon carried 15 to 20 of the mines distributed among its soldiers.

M18 Colored Smoke Grenade – This 19 oz grenade is used as a ground-to-ground or ground-to-air signaling device, a target or landing zone marking device, or a screening device for unit movements. It came in four colors: red, green, yellow, and violet.

M21 Sniper Rifle – A match grade M-14 rifle fitted with a civilian 3 × 9 magnification telescopic sight using a 20-round box magazine with 7.62 × 51 mm ammunition. Most infantry platoons in the 1-501st had one sniper.

M26, M33 and M67 Fragmentation Hand Grenades – The M26 fragmentation hand grenade was an early version first used in the Korean War. The

M33 began to replace it during the latter years of the Vietnam War. It was used to supplement small arms fire against the enemy in close combat. Round in shape (referred to as a "baseball" grenade) and at 14 oz, it contained 6.5 oz of Composition B high explosive with a 4 to 5 second delay fuse. It had a kill radius of 5 m and casualty radius of 15 m. The M67 was a newer version of the M33 grenade with an additional safety clip.

M29 81 mm Mortar – A high-angle, smooth-bore, indirect fire weapon. Max range of 4,500 m. Can also fire night illumination rounds.

M-60 Machine Gun – The most important weapon in an infantry platoon. Typically, each platoon had one M-60. The gun fires a 7.62 mm round and is belt-fed, gas-operated, and air-cooled with an effective range of 1,100 m. Rate of fire is approximately 600 rounds per minute. Weight is 23 lbs. unloaded.

M72 Light Antitank Weapon (LAW) – An 8 lb., 24.8", one-shot, shoulder-fired 66 mm anti-tank rocket with an effective range of 200 m. Also used against enemy bunkers.

M79 Grenade Launcher – A single-shot, shoulder-fired, break-open to reload, capable of firing a 40 mm grenade to an effective range of 350 m. Nick-named "the Thumper" because of its distinctive sound, the M-79 could fire several types of rounds: high explosive (HE), night illumination, anti-personnel flechette (steel darts), and buckshot. The launcher was near 29" in length and weighed 6 lbs. empty. The 40 mm heavy explosive (HE) round weighed about .5 lbs. and was nearly 4" long.

M102 105 mm Howitzer – This howitzer was the artillery's most prevalent indirect fire weapon in Vietnam. Found at almost every firebase supporting infantry units in the field, it was easily moved by helicopter. Six M102s made up a 105 mm artillery battery. From muzzle to end of its carriage, the howitzer was 21.8 ft long, 5.2 ft high, and 6.4 ft wide weighing 3,298 lbs. Its maximum effective range is 7.1 miles or just over 11 km. The barrel is 7 ft, 7 in. A typical crew could fire ten rounds in a minute or fire a sustained rate of fire of three rounds a minute. A crew of eight was authorized, but the howitzer could be operated with fewer if required. A high explosive (HE) round was 4.2" in diameter had a kill radius of 30 m.

M107 175 mm Gun – A self-propelled, direct fire support weapon introduced in 1963. Weight 28 tons. Manned by a crew of 13 the M107 had a maximum rate of fire of 1 round per minute and a sustained rate of 1 round per two minutes. Weight of round: 66.6 kg (147 lbs.) with a kill radius of 80 m. Maximum effective range is 40 km (25 mi). Because of the high chamber pressure and heat to achieve maximum range, the barrels would wear out and be replaced after only 300 rounds. Later, improved barrels would last to 1,000 rounds.

M109 155 mm Howitzer – A turreted self-propelled, indirect fire support weapon introduced in 1963. Weight: 27.5 tons. Manned by a crew of four, the M109 had a maximum rate of fire of 4 rounds per minute and a sustained rate of 1 rpm. Weight of round: 43.2 kg (95 lbs.) with a kill radius of 50 m. Maximum effective range is 18 km (11 mi).

M110 203 mm (8") Howitzer – A self-propelled, indirect fire support weapon introduced in 1963. Weight: 28.3 tons. Manned by a crew of 13, the M110 had a maximum rate of fire of 3 rounds per two minutes and sustained rate of 1 round per two minutes. The high explosive (H/E) round weighed approximately 91 kg (200 lbs.) with a kill radius of 80 m. Maximum effective range is 23 km (14 mi). The M110 also fired a Controlled Fragmentation (COFRAM) round containing 108 bomblets that air burst over enemy positions. This devastating round was nick-named a "Firecracker" round because of the sound it made when all 108 bomblets rapidly exploded over the target. Similar versions were available for the 105 mm and 155 mm howitzers.

ENEMY WEAPONS

AK-47 Rifle – Designed in the Soviet Union, this assault rifle fires a 7.62 × 39 mm round either semi or full automatic. The rifle's weight fully loaded with a 30-round magazine is 8.5 lbs. Shoulder-fired and gas-operated with a muzzle velocity of 2350 FPS, the AK-47 went into limited production in July 1947, was improved over two years and was accepted by the Russian military and went into full production in 1949.

DShK 12.7 mm (.51 cal) Heavy Machine Gun – This 55 lb. gun was first encountered by Delta Company in *Operation Lamar Plain* at Tam Ky. It was extensively used in both a ground and anti-aircraft role with great effectiveness. It was capable of 600–700 rpm and had a maximum effective range of 1,500 m against air targets or 2,000 m for ground targets.

Katyusha 122 mm Rocket – The rocket had a range 11 km (6.5 mi). Its length was 6.2 ft, weight 102 lbs. with an explosive warhead that was 86% TNT. It was used as heavy artillery by the NVA along with 120 mm mortars. This weapon was not encountered by Delta Company in the field, however the 122 mm rocket was used against LZ Professional and US military facilities at Chu Lai.

RPD 7.62 mm Light Machine Gun – This light Russian machine gun was a standard and deadly weapon for both the NVA and VC. It fired 7.62 mm rounds 650–750 rounds/minute to an effective range of 1,000 m. It could be fired hand-held or on its bi-pod. Ammunition was fed via a 100-round cylindrical drum mounted on the underside of the gun or it could be continuously fed by belted ammunition. At 14.5 lbs., it was ten pounds lighter than the US M60 machine gun. The RPD is named for its Russian inventor, Ruchnoy Pulemyot Degtyaryova.

RPG-2/RPG-7 Rocket-Propelled Grenade Launcher – A man-portable, shoulder-fired, anti-tank weapon widely used against US forces. The launcher

298 • COURAGE UNDER FIRE

with its rocket weighed just over 10 lbs. and was 27.2" in length. The steel launcher barrel was 40 mm. An 82 mm rocket was inserted in the muzzle and protruded from the launcher. With an effective firing range of 150 m using an iron sight, 3–4 rounds per minute could be fired against US ground forces and low-flying or landing helicopters.

SKS 7.62 mm Rifle – Originally designed and manufactured between 1949–1956 by the Soviet Union. The rifle was manufactured as semi-automatic with a non-removable magazine fed by a 10-round stripper clip. Some rifles were later modified to fire full automatic and had removable magazines. Muzzle velocity was 2350 FPS. The Chinese also made a version called the "Type 56" from 1956 onward. Both types were used in Vietnam.

Type 31 60 mm Mortar – A Chinese made smooth bore indirect fire weapon. It was a copy of the American M2, which copied the French "Mortimer Modele 1935." The Type 31's weight assembled was 44 lbs. It fired a 3lb. round to a maximum range of 1,529 m, a shorter range than the American M2 (3,490 m) due to the Type 31's shorter firing tube. It had a blast radius of 20–25 m.

Type 67 82 mm Mortar – A Chinese indirect fire weapon developed in 1967. It is an updated version of the older type 53, which is a Chinese copy of the Soviet PM-41 82 mm mortar. It was widely used in Vietnam by the NVA. Its weight assembled was 123 lbs. It fired a 3.72 kg (8.2 lbs.) shell to a maximum range of 3,040 m with a kill radius of 30 m.

Weather – Like terrain, weather plays a major role in combat and must always be considered in planning and conduct of operations. Infantry and other soldiers are trained to operate under all types of weather. Hot, humid weather is hard on soldiers carrying heavy combat loads. Rain and thunderstorms also impede movement and visibility and may limit the combat effectiveness of soldiers and equipment. *See Terrain.*

Wounded in Action (WIA) – One of three categories of combat casualties that describes soldiers wounded by hostile enemy action. Most WIA soldiers required medical evacuation at some point due to the danger of infection. In some limited cases, a soldier may be first reported as WIA and is later changed to KIA if he dies. *See KIA and MIA.*

Bibliography

Websites referenced in this bibliography were active as of the time of writing Courage Under Fire. *Over time some URL links may have changed or been discontinued.*

Articles

Ables, Roger. "Bitter Fighting in Quang Tin: Operation Lamar Plain." *The Vietnam Veterans of America Magazine*, September/October 2009 issue.

Filardo, Lou. "Searching for Answers to Sharon Lane's Death in Vietnam." Posted 10 June 2015 at 5:11pm. https://www.cantonrep.com/article/20150610/OPINION/150619917.

Kilner, Pete (Lieutenant Colonel, US Army, Retired). "Know Thy Enemy: Better Understanding Foes Can Prevent Debilitating Hatred." Washington DC: Association of the United States Army, 2017. Available at https://www.ausa.org/articles/know-thy-enemy.

"Two New Offenses Underway." *New York Times*, 27 May 1969, p. 3.

Books

Allen, Michael J. *Until the Last Man Comes Home*. Chapel Hill, NC: University of North Carolina Press, 2010.

Bell, Jessie Grover. *Here's How by Who's Who*. Cleveland: Jesse Grover Bell Bonne Bell Inc., 1965.

Bowden, Mark. *Hue 1968; A Turning Point of the American War in Vietnam*. New York: Atlantic Monthly Press, 2017.

Clausewitz, Carl Von. *On War*. Princeton: Princeton University Press, 1976.

Garland, Albert N. *A Distant Challenge: The US Infantryman in Vietnam. 1967–1972*. Nashville, Tennessee: The Battery Press, 1983.

Halberstam, David. *The Best and the Brightest: Kennedy-Johnson Administrations*. New York: Modern Library (Penguin Random House), 2002.

Hackworth, David. *About Face: The Odyssey of An American Warrior*. New York: Simon and Schuster, 1989.

Hastings, Max. *Vietnam: An Epic Tragedy, 1945–1975*. New York: Harper Collins, 2018.

Karnow, Stanley. *Vietnam: A History*. New York: The Viking Press, 1983.

Kolb, Richard K. editor and contributing author. *Brutal Battles of Vietnam: America's Deadliest Days 1965–1972*. Kansas City: Veterans of Foreign Wars, 2017.

Kitfield, James. *Prodigal Soldiers: How the Generation of Officers Born of Vietnam Revolutionized the American Style of War*. Washington: Brassey's, 1995.

Lamb, David. *Vietnam Now: A Reporter Returns*. New York: Public Affairs, 2002

Lucas, Stephen. *The Quotable George Washington: The Wisdom of an American Patriot*. Lanham, Maryland: Rowman & Littlefield, 1999.

McMaster, H. R. *Dereliction of Duty: Johnson, McNamara, the Joint Chiefs of Staff and the Lies That Led to Vietnam.* New York: Harper Collins, 1997.
Nolan, Keith. *Ripcord: Screaming Eagles Under Siege.* New York: Ballantine Books, 2003.
Santoli, Al. *Leading the Way: How Vietnam Veterans Rebuilt the US Military—An Oral History.* New York: Ballantine Books, 1993.
Sawyer, Ralph D. *Sun-tzu, The Art of War. A New Translation.* New York: Fall River Press, 1994.
Scales, Robert H. (Brigadier General, US Army Retired). *Certain Victory: The US Army in the Gulf War.* The Desert Storm Study Project. Washington: Brassey's, 1997.
Schmitz, David F. *Richard Nixon and the Vietnam War.* Lanham, Maryland: Rowman & Littlefield, 2014.
Sorley, Lewis. *A Better War: The Unexamined Victories and Final Tragedy of America's Last Years in Vietnam.* Orlando, Florida; Harcourt Brace & Company, 1999.
Wright, James. *Enduring Vietnam: An American Generation and It's War.* New York: Thomas Dunne Books, Saint Martin's Press, 2017.
Yancey, Dianne. *The Vietnam War (Turning Points in World History Series).* San Diego: Greenhaven Press Inc, 2001.
Yarborough, Thomas R. *A Shau Valor: American Combat Operations in the Valley of Death 1963–1971.* Philadelphia: Casemate Publishers, 2016.

Combat Records and Documents

1st Battalion, 46th Infantry Regiment, Americal Division, *Operation Lamar Plain After Action Report,* dated 15 August 1969, signed by LTC Craig Coverdale. (This is a partial report.) https://www.vietnam.ttu.edu/reports/images.php?img=/images/1387/1387AAR46091969.pdf.
1st Battalion, 501st Infantry Regiment (Airmobile), *Combat After Action Report (AAR) for Operation Lamar Plain,* dated 15 August 1969.
1st Battalion, 501st Infantry Regiment (Airmobile), *Subject: Summary of Combat Operations Attack on a Fortified Position 21–22 May 1969, Operation Lamar Plain,* dated 17 June 1969.
1st Battalion, 501st Infantry Regiment (Airmobile), *Daily Staff Journals for S2/S3 Staff Sections,* 501st Tactical Operations Center (TOC), from 1 March through 15 August 1969.
1st Brigade, 101st Airborne Division (Airmobile), *Combat After Action Report (AAR), Operation Lamar Plain,* dated 15 September 1969.
1st Brigade Aviation Platoon, 101st Airborne Division. *A Mini History July 1965 January 1972,* as of 3 January 2016. http://www.vhpa.org/unit/HHC1BDE101ABN.pdf.
2nd Brigade, 101st Airborne Division (Airmobile), *Combat After Action Report (AAR), Operation Massachusetts Striker,* dated 25 May 1969.
101st Airborne Division *Fact Sheet, Summary of Actions and Results (Assault on Dong Ap Bia),* dated 24 May 1969.
101st Airborne Division, *Operational Report - Lessons Learned Period Ending 31 July 1969,* dated 9 December 1969.
101st Airborne Division Headquarter letter, Office of the Commanding General to Commanding General, US Army Vietnam, ATTN: AVHT-DST, *SUBJECT: Senior Officer's Debriefing Report,* dated 28 May 1969, signed by MG Melvin Zais.
Americal Division. *Operational Report for Quarterly Period Ending 31 October 1969,* dated 10 November 1969.
Aviation Platoon, HHC, 1st Brigade, 101st Airborne Division, *A Mini-History of,* July 1965 – January 1972 South Vietnam, 1 January 2019, https://www.vhpa.org/unit/HHC1BDE101ABN.pdf
B Troop, 2nd Squadron 17th Cavalry, *Lamar Plain After Action,* 16 August 1969.

Wright, John H. Jr. (Major General, US Army). *Senior Officer's Debriefing Report.* Letter to Commanding General, US Army Vietnam, ATTN: AVHT-DST. 11 May 1970.

Zais, Melvin (Major General, US Army). *Senior Officer's Debriefing Report.* Letter to Commanding General, US Army Vietnam, ATTN: AVHT-DST. 28 May 1969.

US Government, US Military, or Contractor Publications

Connable, Ben et al. *Will to Fight: Analyzing, Modelling, and Simulating the Will to Fight of Military Units.* Santa Monica, CA: Rand, 2018. https://www.rand.org/pubs/research_briefs/RB10040. html.

Cosmas, Graham A. *CMH Pub 91-7, MACV- The Joint Command in the Years of Withdrawal, 1968–1973.* Washington DC: US Army Center of Military History, 2007.

Department of Army, US Army Infantry School. *FM-7-20, The Infantry Battalion*, Fort Benning Georgia, 1962.

Dorland, Peter and James Nanney. *CMH Pub 90- 28- 1, Dust Off: Army Aeromedical Evacuation in Vietnam.* Washington DC: US Army Centerof Military History, 2008.

Hammond, William H. *CMH Pub 91-2B,Public Affairs: The Military and the Media, 1968-1973.* Washington DC: US Army Center of Military History, 1996.

Keefer, Edward. Editor, *Vietnam, January 1969-July 1970, Foreign Relations of the United States, 1969–1976 Volume IV.* Washington DC: United States Government Printing Office, 2006.

Larsen, Eric V. *The Historical Role of Casualties in Domestic Support of Operations.* Santa Monica, CA: Rand, 1996. https://www.rand.org/pubs/monograph_reports/MR726.html.

Mahon, John K., and Romana Danysh. *CMH 60-3-1, Infantry, Part 1 – Regular Army (Army Lineage Series).* Washington DC: US Army Center for Military History, 1972.

Military History Branch, Office of the Secretary, Joint Staff Headquarters, USMACV. *United States Military Assistance Command - Vietnam Command History, Volume 1-1969.* Alexandria, Virginia: Department of the Army, 1969.

National Archives.*Vietnam Conflict Extract Data File of the Defense Casualty Analysis Section (DCAS)* updated 11 January 2018, https://www.archives.gov/research/military/vietnam-war/casualty-statistics.

National Security Study Memorandum 1, *The Situation in Vietnam. Volume VI, Vietnam, January 1969–July 1970, Document 4.* Washington DC: US Department of State, 21 January 1969. https//history.state.gov.

Ott, David Ewing. *CMH Pub 90-12, Field Artillery, 1954–1973 (Vietnam Studies).* Washington DC: US Army Center of Military History, 1975 and 2007.

Pearson, Willard, Lieutenant General. *CMH Pub 94-20-1, The War in the Northern Provinces.* Washington DC: US Army Center of Military History, 1991.

Tolson, John J. *CMH Pub 90-4-B, Airmobility, 1961–1971 (Vietnam Studies).* Washington DC: US Army Center of Military History, 1999.

Traas, Adrian G. *CMH Pub 76, Transition—November 1968–December 1969: The US Army Campaigns of the Vietnam War.* Washington DC: US Army Center of Military History, 2018.

Villard, Erik. *CMH Study, The 1968 Tet Offensive Battles of Quang Tri and Hue.* Washington DC: US Army Center of Military History, 2008.

Webb, Willard J. *The Joint Chiefs of Staff and the War in Vietnam, 1969-1970,* from the series, *History of the Joint Chiefs of Staff.* Washington DC: Office of the Joint Chiefs of Staff, 2002.

Wilbanks, James H. *Vietnam: The Course of a Conflict.* Fort Leavenworth: Army University Press, 2018.

Web References

Bombardier, MilitaryImages.net, https://www.militaryimages.net/threads/ubique-by-rudyard-kipling.412/. 30 May 2004.

Burns, Ken and Lynn Novick, *The Vietnam War: A Film by Ken Burns and Lynn Novick*. http://www.pbds.org/kenburns/the-vietnam-war /home/.

CIA Fact Book, https://www.cia.gov/library/publications/the-world-factbook/geos/vm.html.

General Westmoreland's Speech, National Press Club in Washington DC, 21 November 1967. https://www.cfr.org/blog/twe-remembers-general-westmoreland-says-end-begins-come-view-vietnam.

Kennedy, Edward M. "The Hamburger Hill Speech" from *In His Own Words* series, Edward M. Kennedy Institute, 20 May 1969. http://www.tedkennedy.org/ownwords/event/vietnam.html.

Niebuhr, Ryan. 2nd Brigade, 101st AB, Vietnam War History. http://www.2ndbde.org/preface.php.

Nixon, Richard M. "Address to the Nation on Vietnam, May 14, 1969." Yorba Linda, CA: Richard Nixon Foundation. https://www.nixonfoundation.org.

Pyle, Ernie. Excerpt from Ernie Pyle's *Stars and Stripes* column written 2 May 1943 in North Africa, https://sites.mediaschool.indiana.edu/erniepyle/1943/05/02/the-god-damned-infantry/.

Summer, Harry (Colonel US Army, Retired). Book Review of *Dereliction of Duty* by H. R. McMaster, https://www.historynet.com/book-review-dereliction-of-duty-johnson-mcnamara-the-joint-chiefs-of-staff-and-the-lies-that-led-to-vietnam-hr-mcmaster-vn.htm.

Texas Tech University Vietnam Center and Archive, https://www.vietnam.ttu.edu/. Vietnam maps used in this book may be found via a search of the maps located in the Virtual Archive. See University of Texas reference for easier location of maps.

United States of America Vietnam War 50th Year Commemoration, "Week of February 23, 1969." https://www.vietnamwar50th.com/education/week_of_february_23/.

University of Texas at Austin, University of Texas Libraries. List of Vietnam Topographic Maps 1:50,000, http://legacy.lib.utexas.edu/maps/topo/vietnam/.

US Army Military Map Series L7014: Vietnam. A Shau Valley: Sheet 6441 IV, A Luoi (*Operation Apache Snow*); A Shau Valley: Sheet 6441 II, A Sap (*Operation Massachusetts Striker*); Hue: Sheet 6541 IV, Hue (Prior to *Operation Massachusetts Striker*); Tam Ky: Sheet 6639 I, Tien Phuoc (*Operation Lamar Plain*).

Veterans Administration. PTSD: National Center for PTSD. https://www.ptsd.va.gov/

Vietnam Helicopter Pilots Association (VHPA). "Helicopter Losses in Vietnam." https://www.vhpa.org/heliloss.pdf.

Endnotes

Websites referenced in this bibliography were active as of the time of writing Courage Under Fire. *Over time some URL links may have changed or been discontinued.*

1. Map adapted from *CIA Fact Book,* https://www.cia.gov/library/publications/the-world-factbook/geos/vm.html.
2. General Douglas MacArthur, US Army, as quoted in *Here's How by Who's Who* (Cleveland: Jesse Grover Bell Bonne Bell Inc., 1965).
3. US *Army, 1969 101st Airborne Hamburger Hill AAR - After Action Report, Battle of Dong Ap Bia (Hill 937), 10–21 May 1969,* Item Number: 168300010494, https://vva.vietnam.ttu.edu/.
4. Adrian G. Traas, *CMH Pub 76-6, Transition: The Vietnam War 1968–1969* (Washington DC: US Army, 2018), p. 39.
5. Graham A. Cosmas, *CMH Pub 91-7, MACV: The Joint Command in the Years of Withdrawal 1968–1973* (Washington DC: US Army, 2007), p. 149.
6. LTG Willard Pearson, *CMH Pub 94-20-1, The War in the Northern Provinces 1966–1968* (Washington DC: US Army, 1991), p. 5.
7. Ernie Pyle, https://www.quotetab.com/quotes/by-ernie-pyle.
8. Mark Bowden, *Hue 1968: A Turning Point of the American War in Vietnam* (New York: Atlantic Monthly Press, 2017).
9. Erik Villard, *The 1968 Tet Offensive Battles of Quang Tri and Hue* (Washington DC: Normanby Press, 2008), p. 10
10. Graham A. Cosmas, *CMH Pub 91-7, MACV: The Joint Command in the Years of Withdrawal, 1968–1973,* p. 17.
11. James H. Wilbanks, *Vietnam: The Course of a Conflict* (Fort Leavenworth: Army University Press, 2018), p. 115. (Wilbanks quotes David F. Schmitz's *The Tet Offensive: Politics, War, and Public Opinion* in which National Security Staff member, William Jorden, cables presidential advisor Walt Rostow.)
12. Adrian G. Traas, *Transition,* p. 29.
13. US Army, *FM 7-20, The Infantry Battalion* (Washington DC: Department of the Army, 1962), p. 143.
14. Thomas R. Yarborough, *A Shau Valor: American Combat Operations in the Valley of Death* (Havertown, PA: Casemate Publishers, 2016), from the preface.
15. Stephen Lucas, *The Quotable George Washington: The Wisdom of an American Patriot* (Landham, MD: Rowman & Littlefield, 1999), p. 24.
16. Richard Nixon, *Address to the Nation on Vietnam, May 14, 1969* (Yorba Linda, CA: Richard Nixon Foundation), https://www.nixonfoundation.org.
17. Excerpt from Ernie Pyle's *Stars and Stripes* column written 2 May 1943 in North Africa, https://sites.mediaschool.indiana.edu/erniepyle/1943/05/02/the-god-damned-infantry/.

18. EdwardM. Kennedy, "The Hamburger Hill Speech" from *In His Own Words* series, Edward M. Kennedy Institute, 20 May 1969. http://www.tedkennedy.org/ownwords/event/vietnam.html.

19. Carl Von Clausewitz, *On War* (Princeton: Princeton University Press, 1976), p. 86.

20. Bobby Begley (Captain, US Army), *Summary of Combat Operations Attack on a Fortified Position 21–22 May 1969* (College Park MD: National Archives and Records Administration). From the records of 1st Battalion, 501st Infantry (Airborne), 101st Airborne Infantry Division (Airmobile).

21. Headquarters 101st Airborne Division (Airmobile), *Operational Report—Lessons Learned, Period Ending 31 July 1969* dated 20 August 1969. Texas Tech University, The Vietnam Center and Sam Johnson Vietnam Archive, https://www.vietnam.ttu.edu/reports/images.php?img=/images/2624/26240224004.pdf.

22. Ken Burns and Lynn Novick, *The Vietnam War: A Film by Ken Burns and Lynn Novick,* http://www.pbs.org/kenburns/the-vietnam-war/home/

23. Lou Filardo, "Searching for Answers to Sharon Lane's Death in Vietnam," posted 10 June 2015 at 1711H, https://www.cantonrep.com/article/20150610/OPINION/150619917.

24. Michael J. Allen, *Until the Last Man Comes Hom,* (Chapel Hill NC: University of North Carolina Press, 2010), p. 43.

25. By Bombardier, posted 30 May 2004, https://www.militaryimages.net/threads/ubique-by-rudyard-kipling.412/.

26. Peter Kilner (Lieutenant Colonel, US Army, Retired), "Know Thy Enemy: Better Understanding Foes Can Prevent Debilitating Hatred," 26 June 2017; https://www.ausa.org/articles/know-thy-enemy.

27. Headquarters, US Military Assistance Command-Vietnam (MACV), *MACV Command History 1969—Volume 1* (Alexandria VA: Department of the Army Information Management Support Agency, 1969), p. III–6.

28. Headquarters, 1st Brigade, 101st Airborne Division (Airmobile), *Operation Lamar Plain After Action Report*, dated 15 September 1969, p. 35.

29. Headquarters, Americal Division, *Operational Report for Quarterly Period Ending 31 October 1969,* dated 10 November 1969, p. 9.

30. National Archives, *Vietnam Conflict Extract Data File of the Defense Casualty Analysis Section (DCAS) updated 11 January 2018,* https://www.archives.gov/research/military/vietnam-war/casualty-statistics.

31. Harry Summers (Colonel, US Army, Retired), Book Review of *Dereliction of Duty* by H. R. McMaster, https://www.historynet.com/book-review-dereliction-of-duty-johnson-mcnamara-the-joint-chiefs-of-staff-and-the-lies-that-led-to-vietnam-hr-mcmaster-vn.htm.

32. Robert H. Scales Jr., (Brigadier General, US Army), *Certain Victory: The US Army in the Gulf War* (Washington DC: Brassey's, 1994), p. 6.

33. Al Santoli, *Leading the Way: How Vietnam Veterans Rebuilt the US Military* (New York: Ballantine Books, 1993),

34. James Wright. *Enduring Vietnam: An American Generation and Its War* (New York: Thomas Donne Books, 2017), p. 308.

35. Edward Keefer (Editor), *Vietnam, January 1969–July 1970, Foreign Relations of the United States, 1969–1976 Volume IV* (Washington DC: United States Government Printing Office, 2006), p. 397.

36. Willard J. Webb, *The Joint Chiefs of Staff and the War in Vietnam, 1969–1970,* from the series, *History of the Joint Chiefs of Staff* (Washington DC: Office of the Joint Chiefs of Staff, 2002), pp. 49–50.

37. The US Army Center of Military History fully describes this year in its excellent 2018 publication from its *US Army in Vietnam series, CMH Pub 76-6, Transition: November 1968–December 1969.*

38. Graham A. Cosmas, *CMH Pub 91-7, The Joint Command in the Years of Withdrawal, 1968–1973,* pp. 147–148.

39. Webb, *The Joint Chiefs of Staff and the War in Vietnam, 1969–1970*, p. 49.
40. William H. Hammond, *CMH Pub 91-2B, Public Affairs: The Military and the Media, 1968–1973, The US Army in Vietnam Series* (Washington DC: US Army Center of Military History, 1996), p. 71.
41. Webb, *The Joint Chiefs of Staff and the War in Vietnam, 1969–1970*, p. 51.
42. Hammond, *CMH Pub 91-2B, Public Affairs: The Military and the Media, 1968–1973*, p. 82.
43. Eric V. Larsen. *The Historical Role of Casualties in Domestic Support of Operations* (Santa Monica, CA: Rand, 1996), p. 28–29.
44. Adrian G. Traas, *Transition*, p. 39.
45. *Ibid.*
46. Edward M. Kennedy, "The Hamburger Hill Speech."
47. Hammond, *Public Affairs: The Military and the Media: 1968–1973*, p. 87.
48. *Ibid*, p. 89.
49. *Ibid*, pp. 93–97.
50. *Ibid*, p. 103.
51. *Ibid*, pp. 97–98.
52. Associated Press Release, Saigon, "Two New Offenses Underway," *New York Times*, 27 May 1969, p. 3.
53. MG Melvin G Zais letter to Commanding General, US Army Vietnam, ATTN: AVHT-DST, SUBJECT: *Senior Officer's Debriefing Report*, dated 28 May 1969.
54. MG John H. Wright Jr, letter to Commanding General, US Army Vietnam, ATTN: AVHT-DST, SUBJECT: *Senior Officer's Debriefing Report*, dated 11 May 1970.
55. https://www.publichealth.va.gov/exposures/publications/agent-orange/agent-orange-summer-2015/nvvls.asp.

Index

In addition to many terms and abbreviations used in 1969 during the Vietnam War, this index is unique in that it contains the names of all the soldiers who are mentioned in this book. This includes soldiers mentioned in their own personal accounts, soldiers mentioned in the personal accounts of others, and soldiers listed as killed in action, wounded in action, or missing in action.